Cultural Expression in Arab Society Today

Modern Middle East Series, No. 3
Sponsored by the Center for Middle Eastern Studies
The University of Texas at Austin

Cultural Expression in Arab Society Today

(Langages arabes du présent)

by Jacques Berque

Translated by Robert W. Stookey
Poetry Translated by Basima Bezirgan & Elizabeth Fernea

University of Texas Press, Austin & London

Certain passages of the Introduction and of the second section of Chapter I have been reproduced from articles previously published, respectively, in *Le Monde*, March 15, 1973, and *Le Nouvel Observateur*, October 12, 1970. My thanks are due the directors of these periodicals for their permission to reproduce these texts.—J. B.

Originally published as *Langages arabes du présent*

Library of Congress Cataloging in Publication Data
Berque, Jacques.
Cultural expression in Arab society today = Langages arabes du présent.
(Modern Middle East series; no. 3)
1. Arab countries—Civilization. 2. Arabic literature—History and criticism. I. Title. II. Title: Langages arabes du présent. III. Series.
DS36.8.B4413 909'.09'74927 77-16099
ISBN 0-292-70330-9

Printed in the United States of America

Contents

Translators' Notes

This English-language version of *Langages arabes du présent*, based on the 1974 Gallimard edition, incorporates a number of refinements of style and substance provided by the author. I am furthermore indebted to Professor Berque for his patience in clarifying the meaning of some rare or technical terms.

The Library of Congress system of Romanization has been followed in transliterating Arabic words and names, except in cases where a Gallicized version has become current and is therefore employed in the French text.

As a possible help to the reader, footnote references have in a few instances been revised to refer to corresponding passages in English-language versions of the works, where these are readily accessible.

The graceful, sensitive renditions of the poetry selections were prepared by Basima Bezirgan and Elizabeth Fernea. I here record my appreciation of their contribution.—R.W.S.

•

Classical poetry, such as that of Imrūʾ al-Qays, has in the past been translated into somewhat archaic English to approximate the Arabic employed at the time the poems were created. However, in the translations here, we have followed the lead of the book's distinguished author, Jacques Berque. Professor Berque has chosen to translate the classical Arabic into modern French, and we have accordingly used modern English for our renditions. Sources for the Arabic texts that we used are cited in Appendix B. Professor Berque's French translation of Imrūʾ al-Qays is given in Appendix A.

When texts were unavailable in the original Arabic, such as Badawī al-Jabal's poem recited in 1950 at the coronation of King Faisal II and the Wādī al-Dawāsir poem (recited orally to M. Berque by the poet himself), the poems were translated from the French. Other short excerpts of poems scattered throughout the work were translated from the French in order to retain their contextual fidelity.—B.B. & E.F.

Cultural Expression in Arab Society Today

Why the Arabs?

Is the contribution of their contemporary history to the theory and practice of civilizations due to what it has in common with all the others, or instead to its distinctive features?

•

They provide continental depths, while concealing them behind a Mediterranean façade; and behind a classical tradition they hide much of what Africa and Asia have not yet revealed to others, nor even to themselves. Our era is one of internal explosions: within countries, society, the individual, and language. Will it not alter a situation linked to centuries-old relations with the West?

Altercation and affinity with the West have always characterized the Arabs. They carry this dual trait further than other oriental peoples. It is true that Ottoman history long practiced (and how energetically!) the same conflicting proximities. But behind it was no classicism of such ancient vintage. No Zoroaster, nor any Heraclitus or Panini. The Arabs, indeed, share these classical harmonies with the Indians and the Persians. But these two great peoples, thanks to a relative remoteness, escaped some of the more intimate aspects of aggression. And the Arabs alone, in our view, combine two relationships with the West which might be called contradictory were it not that our era, by bringing forth the modern nation from the colonial establishment, has bound these relationships—altercation and affinity—so closely together as to make them the ambiguous mainspring of many forms of conduct and awareness.

This first observation, however, needs correcting. The Arabs' historical entity can no more be restricted to its hostile kinship with Europe than the interior of a geographical unit could be reduced to the shape of its outer borders. Paradoxically, their historical being became aware of this at the height of its tension with the old empires. It began to free itself from an oppressive reciprocity at the moment when it became able to demand a dialog between true partners. It knows now that the world is plural. It knows it must conquer its place therein not so much against the former ruler as apart from him. Not only does it know this, but it also is beginning to put it into practice: a salutary enterprise in which our study will accompany it.

It is nonetheless true that, like continuity in certain languages, difference with respect to the West still largely dominates the Arabs' approach, as well as ours with respect to them; that, also, cannot be ignored. Our Middle Ages saw in their Averroës the great commentator on Aristotle: the chief harbinger, that is, of Hellenic reason which they acknowledge as one of their intellectual buttresses. Their peasantry is an integral part of those of the Mediterranean periphery. Emigration is producing, among hundreds of thousands of laborers, adaptations and demands destined to play a role, in both host country and country of origin, of which the importance has scarcely begun to be measured. Many of their intellectuals participate so fully in French, English, or Hispanic cultures as to share in creating them. These results of proximity and interchange are of course reinforced by the progress of information and communications media.

The altercation has nevertheless not abated. A dispute over petroleum, or the death of an immigrant worker, can reignite it at any moment. The use of Western languages, carried by some to the point of linguistic expatriation, interpenetration of ideas and customs in broad areas, must have contributed, to say the least, more to dispute than to agreement. Moreover, we ordinarily look at these peoples from the point of view of their national revival, their anticolonial virulence, their struggle, successful or abortive, against an underdevelopment for which we, furthermore, are in part accountable. We belittle many of their efforts. We find unsettling or disconcerting their moves toward socialism, with which we ought to sympathize. We are generally ignorant of their literature and modern arts when, indeed, we do not disdain them. Too often, our indifference or resentment propagates a climate disastrous for analysis and more so for friendship.

I shall not deny that these attitudes provoke a retort, and that the blame must be shared. Let us at least acknowledge that very few Westerners recognize among the Arabs that two-way debate between same and other, between act and dream, which today is arousing all the world's cultures precisely because they must sustain themselves by and in spite of technology, by and in spite of the world-wide extension of histories.

•

We are not wrong certainly, in seeing them as champions of identity. Whether in the Maghreb or in the East, indeed, they thrust aside the alleged laws of convergence which were to remake the world according to the outlook of the industrial societies. How could they accept the force that drives them from their land in the name of an idea valid only for the occupier? It is true that this resistance has scandalized some, and still does. In any repression there is some astonishment: How could anyone resist? How could anyone disagree? Disagreement and resistance are nevertheless there. Since these latter have been able to put old empires in a bad way, and since we have become accustomed to the idea that there are Arabs, the surprise and anger of non-Arabs have become centered on the Palestine problem.

In an era like ours, fertile in the uprooting of peoples and imposed partitions, the persistance of the Arabs in demanding a right to the land, transmuted into a right to misfortune, bothers diplomats and troubles broad sectors of opinion. But if the inherited analyses fail to account for such behavior, perhaps it is because they indicate not only injury and dispossession, which no longer shock anyone, but also an intervention of tragedy in history. What is tragedy? I would say that, as in *Antigone*, it is the quality in persons, things, and situations that puts unwritten laws into operation.

These laws do not necessarily come from heaven. In speaking of Arabs the sacred has been somewhat abused. The striking thing in their way of conceiving and living Islam is naturalism. It follows that the relationships between sacred and profane, between master and crowd, between dogma and daily life, are arranged among them otherwise than in Europe. Louis Massignon spoke of a "lay theocracy" in discussing them. Theocracy is rooted in the past, but it is quite true that explicit references to God are constantly on the Arabs' lips, and that the Koran, by which I mean not only the veneration and observance of a text but also a vocal stream, a linguistic enchantment, oriented the bulk of their social and moral life until certain changes took place which, however, did not occur everywhere or always penetrate deeply. Islam, I would say, is less the presence of the sacred in modes of conduct, in individuals, almost in things, than the surrounding of them by a totality of itself, one not merely "sweet" as Hegel said, but intense, combative: virile, in short. Arab Islam is ardent totality.

However, the Koran's ubiquity, so marked among them (but which should not make us forget the persistance of active Christian minorities), has never made them put off pre-Prophetic man completely. To the great scandal of jurists and preachers, there are broad social sectors, such as Bedouin life, from which he did not disappear, any more than from more general attitudes in customs and character. Although in poetry there is a religious and mystical genre, one may say that Arab poetry in general maintained, against the religious models, openings upon another sort of truth: that of adventure, pleasure, and formal beauty. When the Prophet, of two beverages offered him by the Archangel—wine and milk—chose the milk, he opted for the goodness of nature. A highly conciliatory gesture! For this nature was already present all around him in the person of those charming and detestable heroes, the poets, flower of the Bedouin world, of whom the greatest, Imrūʾ al-Qays, according to a *ḥadīth*,[1] was to bear their banner proudly into the depths of hell.

Our times make us particularly attentive to combinatives. Two deserve our attention here: one which, in Islam's second century, permitted the Arabs to assimilate numerous cultural materials of the time, including Hellenistic ones; and one which, under our very eyes, is striving to combine elements drawn, this time, from industrial societies. At that earlier time, by a symmetry that today one would call structural, the ethical and the poetic were ordered between single and multiple. The unitary principle of religion was to have its counterbalance in the profusion of schools and the kaleidoscopic diversity of legal systems, while an unbelievably rigorous prosodic norm was to be imposed upon the exuberance of poetic invention and language. It remained unchanged until the quite recent expansion of free compositions. If, in this ordered system, poetry occupies such a high rank and if its lawgiver, Khalīl, seems to give the cue—with a dogmatism so much more arrogant—to the founders of the great rites, it is because his contemporaries considered poetry a major dimension of their societies: that is, the agonistic dimension. Even today one would not have to look far to find in the Arab world persons, patterns of behavior, and, especially, cultural survivals to illustrate the great role of games, which the West shoved back into the shadows for so long, almost as prudishly as it did sexuality.

•

There is admittedly something strange in invoking, at the outset of a study concerned with the present and future, traits rooted more than a thousand years in the past. Does this not suggest a certain cult of the past on the part of the observer? Would he not do better to apply to Islam and the Arabs a lens which would reduce the former to an ideology and survivals, however persistent, and seek to subsume the latter under categories derived from the industrial world? I am not unaware of the arguments used to justify such a way of viewing. The trouble is that it has failed in practice almost everywhere. Perhaps it has made the people involved feel too strongly that they were being studied not to be understood but to be reduced. Such an approach, certainly, may succeed in explaining, and to some extent in inflecting, current trends. But these trends are not those of a cosmopolitan predicate. They concern a more and more demanding subject. If it evades our grasp should we accuse it of aberrancy or reaction?

Contrary to a too prevalent opinion, specificity does not mean that you are cast in the mold you inherit from your parents, nor should authenticity mean conservatism. When, at an Islamic congress held at Algiers in the summer of 1972, the poet Mufdī Zakaria, author of the FLN anthem, declares: "We have won the battle for liberation. Our revolution today concerns *authenticity*," let us welcome this fine word *aṣāla*, so active in the being and behavior of Arabs, while positing that they interpret it not as a falling back on tradition but as the impulse toward basic principles.

What basic principles? We have seen them looked for, serially or simultaneously, in the Prophetic message; in the people, who are its most faithful guardians; in nature, which that message came not to deny but to instruct; or in the inclinations, even the drives, which translate nature within us. These divergent possible relationships with the fundamental can result in differing choices, defy ideologies, and defeat classification. They do not modify that trait common to Arabs of insisting upon the immediate and genuine, questioning the order of things in the name of a pristine state still present, and searching in memory for future powers. Nor do they modify the idea that beings and things have a claim on our will, that life can and must burn and enjoy, at the expense of a ceaseless confrontation with its own foundations; nor the propensity for testing oneself over space and time, as if on a single battlefield, subject to endless repetition and to incurable disillusion. In the last analysis it is in the sense of wholeness and recapitulation that these attitudes contrast most sharply with those of a West so proud of its divisions of labor, which has become the realm of the relative and the compartmentalized.

•

This evidence of a distinct character, however, can henceforth merely indicate the approach to a collective personality and the contribution it promises to the history of all. The Arab identity is no longer distinct from that of others except insofar as all act within the perspectives of a growing world-wide unity, and are acted upon by it. In the final third of the twentieth century this is a universal fate. But several aspects of this redefinition, or recasting, to which all the world's cultures are subject, offer a significant vigor in this specific case. If one gain made by our era is the enrichment of the various paths of history and their mutual implications—so that it no longer suffices to offer European models, for example, to Afro-Asian countries, but these must enlighten and perfect themselves by Third World models which will become applicable to the West—there is no doubt that the Arabs' experience can add many things to this progress in practice and theory. This necessity, however, remains hidden to too many investigators and militants.

Although the contribution of an ethnography of those who used to be called primitives long influenced the analysis, even in Marxism, of so-called civilized societies, our long exchanges with Muslim, Ottoman, Persian, and, particularly, Arab cultures have produced no such effect. Why should they have been set aside from international explanation while one clan or other of American Indians, Eskimos, or Aruntas has been found necessary to the analyses of Spencer, of Durkheim, and yet more recently of Lévi-Strauss and provided, as it still does, a reference point for so many genetic or structural hypotheses bearing on our own societies? The reason for such a striking disparity is no doubt that the Arabs, in their relations with us, are distinguished, to repeat, by a dual character of altercation and affinity. The tensions issuing from a long combat, aggravated further by imperialism, were in their case too strong, and investigatory procedures were not yet strong enough, for anyone to think of sorting out resemblances, differences, and ambivalences and to draw the proper lessons.

That is why orientalism has shown itself so timid on everything connected with the modernization of peoples who are too close by and who had, indeed, to win their modernity from us. On the best hypothesis, orientalism thus cleaved to its classical attributes. It left interdisciplinary exchange and the mutual enrichment of practice and theory to other specialists. That is furthermore why at least a century and a half of coexistence between Arabs and Westerners, which should have produced scientific advantage, did just the opposite. Study and action were both ruined by it. To the melancholy effects on the ground corresponded the stagnation of a research which, as if ashamed of itself, isolated itself from the most active branches of knowledge: linguistics, social history, and ethnology, among others. Cut off from other researchers and from the Arabs themselves, the Arabist became an isolated man.

For this stage to be transcended it was no doubt necessary for relations between Arabs and the West to undergo the radical transformation which we are witnessing these days and which is obliging both partners, in spite of themselves, to go beyond their outmoded jousting and to learn to know each other on new bases. At the very least it is today no longer possible to address many existing problems without taking into account the lessons of a history which, because it was so long one-sided, demands reason and justice all the more urgently.

But if such a choice is so obviously inescapable, many of the above views, while compressed as dictated by the need for brevity in an introduction, sin as much by excess as by omission. If the purpose were a scientific summation, homage would have to be paid to certain studies that impose respect and sometimes admiration. If the purpose were to define the Arabs, distinctions would have to be made among many diverse societies, for the Arabs, morally one, are sociologically many. It would have to be explained how their traits, according to their respective groups, persist, disappear, or are compromised in adapting to the world, to the new, and to the external. Let us admit that those who share a collective identity—peoples, cultures, and so on—even if they make free use of "we" to refer to themselves have every right to take exception to the "they" on the lips of others. They alone, after all, have the right to single out the subject and his choices among a body of complex and sometimes divergent features.

Despite these risks, with these reservations, and assuming the burden of these complexities, we shall endeavor to explore the portrait and to draw up the balance sheet. This will be done under three major criteria:

- Is there a contemporary Arab culture? If so, how is it to be defined with respect to its own past and to the current changes in the world?
- What practical or theoretical perspectives emerge, for the Arabs and others, through such a placing in context?
- To what extent, finally, does their self-expression respond to their own problems and cause values for all to emerge?

PART ONE

History and Discourse

I
The City Speaks

When the Arabs, in the second third of the nineteenth century, sustained the first challenges of modernism, they had already abandoned use of the classical word *ʿimrān*[1] in speaking of "civilization" or "culture." On one hand, in the eyes of a Jirjī Zaydān,[2] civilization was all of a piece. Why should that of the Arabs in the golden age have differed in kind from that of the Hellenes of old, or the Europeans in our day? Thus he used, quite consistently, *tamaddun*, something like "urbanness," a generic term behind which disquieting compromises lurked and which current usage has abandoned. On the other hand, Ṭaha Ḥusain spoke of *thaqāfa* in a celebrated book.[3] But *thaqāfa*, with all due respect to certain contemporary writers, including some Marxists,[4] refers to "acculturation" rather than to "culture," and the word has taken on an elitist character. Too often, the *muthaqqaf* becomes separated from the masses in that he has mastered one or two foreign languages, or reached an intimacy amounting nearly to ritual initiation with the much-touted "heritage," *al-turāth*: in short, either expatriation or mythology. The connotation of *ḥaḍāra* is more promising. It posits a whole, in which aesthetic achievements are merely the apex. A whole that is no longer, if it ever was, unique on earth. For the Arabs, like many others, are involved in the becoming of a diversified world. Like many others they must, on pain of failure, arrive at a certain stage, that of industrial civilization, a programmatic notion they have borrowed on faith from the West without hailing it before the court of reason and predilection, any more than the West itself yet has.

Reading an Urban Landscape

In Cairo, beginning with Khedive Ismail, national urbanization had opened up streets, laid out gardens, and neatly delimited boroughs by the T square. The Nile remained, hidden along many segments of its banks, unseen by the riparians, interrupted over quite some distance by the walls of the British Agency. Not until the Nasserist revolution could a corniche be built, extending kilometer after kilometer from Ismail's canal to Maʿādī and even farther up and down stream, from Ḥalwān to the Barrage, to make the river fully accessible to its sons. At last they were going to benefit: *tamattaʿ*, "enjoy it," they were advised by many billboards when the Abdin Palace collections were nationalized. They responded to the invitation. A mob gesticulating as exuberantly, but restrained just as subtly, as in the streets of Fatimid Cairo erupted into the proudly named Liberation Square. There, where in 1953 I saw the rosy walls of English barracks blocking the view of the river, now rises the gigantic silhouette of the Mugammaʿ, a pandemonium of central bureaus where every summer a cobra is discovered curled up in the files. Then recourse is had to a snake charmer's piping.

Could this eternal, cold monster, the State, however revolutionary it is purported, be the sole culmination of so many struggles? In any event it ensures itself an escort of national identity supernaturals. The Arab League headquarters testifies to an ethnicity determined to revive. That of the Socialist Union appeals, though with many reservations, to a world ideology. An elegant little mosque pleads, duly if cautiously, for Islam. A Hilton violently plastered with Egyptries proclaims the earning of foreign exchange and the reduction of the foreigner to what he is wanted henceforth to be: a tourist richly caged or an aseptic technician. In short, the Square has provided itself with instruments for putting things in order.

At least the mob, which had meanwhile become the people, or the mass, or the base, flocks to the area ennobled by the project. The little casinos, the open-air coffee shops lining the opposite bank downstream from a colossal fountain inspired by the one in Geneva, swarm with men and women one would never have seen even fifteen years ago in these solemn precincts. History had expropriated them; the revolution has established them. The bridges, intended for their service and edification, are resplendent with flags. Everywhere, streamers and posters announce a conference of the world's nations as guests, even allies, but no longer masters. Others exhort the crowd to rejoice over the evacuation of the Canal, the shaky union with Syria or Libya, or the incessant Third World gatherings in which, there is a desire to believe, a new planet-wide order is being mapped out. Whatever the political vicissitudes, the successes or the setbacks, ruin or prosperity, nothing henceforth can prevent the recovery of Khedive Ismail's New City by its own. May it bring them more fortune than it brought him!

But the city, like the nation surrounding it, does not simply show itself off, arouse emotions, channel activity, and offer new symbols for labor or leisure. It speaks; it speaks to itself. From a thousand mouths the radio thunders forth political discourse, or else a song by ʿAbd al-Ḥalīm Ḥāfiẓ. The muezzin's arabesque call issues from the minarets at the specified times. He has long been using the loud-speaker's power. He too has thus become part of the mass media. Under the arm of many passers-by, or on the laps of colossal, placid *bawwābs*, transistors echo this vocal consciousness of the crowd, which means that your own is never left to itself. To breathe is to hear. To be is to be together: an insistent invitation to think in unison. Prayer, music, or harangue, the collective voice raised on all sides is animated by the very movement composing the urban landscapes that affirm the future ever more insistently. For this assertion, this action, perhaps tragic but certainly obsessive, arising from the distribution of space, the increase of volumes, and the immense swarming of human shapes, goes beyond a dull impulse. From these signs a discourse is fashioned; from these clamors a personality is constructed; from this stage setting arises a history, revised and corrected.

A Recollection of Gamal Abdul Nasser

Night falls very early in Cairo, because the official time is as little ahead of European time as possible. We pass several guard posts, many checkpoints. Haykal's lighted cigar leads us like a lantern. We are given seats in a small English-style sitting room where a wide mantelpiece holds the inscribed portraits of chiefs of state, among them Lyndon Johnson's. To the left of my armchair a French door looks out into darkness. We are being watched from out there, or at least I imagine we are. He is indeed threatened, the man who enters the room with a military stride, sits down, and looks intently at me as he listens, one ear cupped in his hand. At some remarks he breaks into a restrained laugh in a sardonic falsetto: the laugh of Suez.

The man is at once feline and massive. His square build speaks of a peasant ancestry, the long remembrance of stubborn, fleshy gestures, the recompense of a heavy, miserable diet over many generations. But this son of the Middle Valley also carries Arab descent in his blood: a Bedouin strain had pursued for several centuries in Banī Murr District the synthesis of Ishmael and Pharaoh. Perhaps this gives his physique that deliberate alertness, his face that sharp breadth, his eyes that brooding nostalgia behind their hard, almost green, gaze. The Arab has risen ponderously, one might say, from his long submergence in the soil of Egypt.

This postman's son was born in Alexandria. There he rubbed elbows with the cosmopolitanism then triumphant, which dominated the foreign city hunched over its warehouses, mortgaged to the sea. Later, by the chance of his father's transfer, he lived in a house in the Jewish quarter of Old Cairo's Gamāliya. He was educated in that interwar era when bourgeois Egypt, aspiring to bourgeois freedoms, was shillyshallying and making compromises. Today, if he has renounced Zaghlūl, the great parliamentarian, and Muḥammad ʿAlī, the great pasha, it is because he is continuing their work. The future will perform the task of measuring the differences and resemblances. In any case, the people place him at their own level. Feared like Muḥammad ʿAlī, voted for like Zaghlūl, he is nevertheless something other than they. A socialist? In any case, ancient land of Egypt, he has plowed you deeply, toppled your hierarchies, flung before you many governing phrases, restored to you many sources of pride.

This was not accomplished without damage. The well-founded resentment of yesterday's oppressors has done even more to eliminate their contribution than their threat. With regard to other Arab countries and ideologies, action has been more domineering than brotherly, as many came to realize before the end. At home, false elites collapsed but no genuine elite took their place. Profoundly acculturated, although uncultured, the country suffers deeply from this loss of its own advance guard. It needs a light-hearted culture, *dammuhu khafīf*, and so much the better for socialism if it were to provide it. But the intelligentsia, at first beguiled, then rejected, then recruited, then disillusioned once more, is seeking its way in exile, in silence, or in compromise. A magnificent trade union movement similarly seeks freedom, as against a uniformity imposed on the pretext that it works. The country's five thousand villages still know nothing of communalism. Fifteen years have gone by without progress on this fundamental point. Not desiring to be anything more than authoritarian pedagogy and mass manipulation, this socialism should at least have required itself to be productive. In that it has succeeded no better than other socialisms which have lost their utopias without achieving their realities.

Nevertheless, the people, denouncing excesses and mistakes, condemning them or laughing at them, remained loyal to Gamal Abdul Nasser. We saw this clearly after June 9, 1967, following the disastrous Sinai campaign. Disaster could become victory if it led to crucial reforms. That is what Nasser and Egypt undertook to do.

Through analysis and discussion the way was opened for the country to regain control of itself.

In any event Nasser's temptations and challenges, even his failures, were to make Egypt better able to question herself than when he discovered her. This avenger of countless humiliated people, unlucky like every Spartacus, in the final analysis left her more conscious of herself and of the world.[5]

From the City's "Text" to the Text Proper

What the news vendors distribute in Cairo, in ever-bulkier bundles, is a vision which makes a daily tour of the city and the world, while dropping enticing tangents from the tight curves of event, trend, and mood toward that recent kind of infinity: history.

The vision thereby competes, like a veritable modern-day *khuṭba*,[6] with the call to prayer and the chanting of the sacred texts. But the Absolute to which it refers, which it acts out or feigns, now reveals itself as secular. It is an unsatisfied and unsatisfying Word, even competitive (and lucrative), because its audience argues over it page by page. Old *Al-Ahrām* still cuts a classic figure. It has the widest circulation: not much under 700,000 readers for its Friday issue.[7] It has its own authorities, glories, traditions, innovations, and diversions. Its obituary page is always the most thoroughly researched: a veritable honors list of social success and a sociological balance sheet of the rise of families. But sometimes one sector of opinion or another prefers another title. There was a time shortly after the Suez nationalization when the hawkers of *Al-Masā*ʾ, then reputedly a radical sheet, raised their cheery cries early in the afternoon, and the intelligentsia showed a lively spirit of participation. The paper, of course, had its ups and, especially, its downs. It was, and is, the same with *Al-Akhbār* and *Al-Gumhūriya.* These flashes, momentary or not, unfortunately often cool off into disappointment or are suspected of subversive agitation; they leave to *Al-Ahrām* the task of embodying permanence quasi officially. Moreover, whether the quality and freedom of the press rise or decline, the role of the newspapers nevertheless expresses the ever-quickening growth of linkages between industrial technology and collective life, through the connecting information, and lays hold of collective life by this growth. . . .

Informing and communicating would yet be too little. Not only does the press act upon the city: at certain times it becomes the city itself. Do its pages not provide a space for interchange and passage to and fro among its various topologies: the city's façades, the faces in the crowd, the shape of events, the arrangement of text and sections? Now this space, far from inert, is oriented by a self-activating achievement, that of the word. It subordinates all its components to one linguistic dimension, which soon becomes literary. The newspaper is a "second articulation" of the city. Professors and writers share in its development and its end product. On the newsstands and on the sidewalks their works, issued in massive, cheap editions, enter into the continuum in which periodicals are classified as daily, weekly, and monthly, and which links them with the nameless languages of the urban landscape. That is one success of the regime, or rather of the present era. Even the classics, both the Arab and the foreign legacy, have leaped from the austere bookstore showcases and are now spread out at street level: an underpinning for a socialistic education if there ever was one!

A single issue of one of these sheets, a single face daily turned toward the public, and everything begins to take its proper place in the image the society intends to present of itself. Pure phenomenology or, instead, intellectual and aesthetic choice? Just as, on radio and television, audio-visual material begins by unfolding in haphazard series where only picture and sound count, then becomes organized in dialogs, fables, and songs by which the crowd interacts with its artists and ends up rising, in one or another broadcast, to the cultural preoccupations of the day, unless it relates itself to a timeless classicism—just so, from page to page of the newspaper the multifarious strata are ordered, the rise and fall of the text in the making. The *ijtimāʿiyāt* [8] skim the cream from the city's social gatherings, what is said there, the ideas disseminated, worry alternating with amusement, gravity with diversion, the advertisements speak for productivity and consumption; literary criticism and court reports reflect other domains, other motives. The front page clips out the world's problems and distributes them among its favored columns where position, length, and headline type, to say nothing of how often a certain word is used, all reflect choices and classifications. The editorial is the capstone of all. Whether it expresses independent or "inspired" views is a doubt which quite properly preoccupies the democrat; there is no such doubt for the sociologist who, by contrast, observes how the word has access to the mass, and the mass to the word, and the verbal transformations arising from this dual interplay. The manner of phrasing, punctuation, and type style all count in Ḥasanain Haykal's editorials.

From the news briefs and reports of dogs run over to the backgrounder, from the fawning on the rulers of the moment to the obligatory review of international friendships and enmities, from the most obscure news maker to the name-dropping on the literary page, the various phases of a way of shaping and thinking rub elbows. An exciting process indeed! Between the city and country, on one hand, and the newspaper, on the other, a reciprocal assimilation is at work. If the paper seeks to be the artful image of the city, it invites the city to incarnate the paper. Tirelessly, it exhorts the city to repeat these ready-made phrases, to resemble these many pictures on each page, to conform to these models of behavior, to remake its universe to these specifications. The exhortation re-echoes in successive readings and group discussions in coffee shops.[9] The junior official begins his day by going through the whole bundle, before even tasting his horsebean sandwich. On finishing his day he would not think of going back to his home neighborhood without a periodical, or preferably several, under his arm. Until quite late at night porters, artisans, the people of modest station will solemnly spell out these communications laden with modern power. The city has become information; information rebuilds the city.

In all these exchanges, naturally, expression and meaning are not simply verbal but more broadly semiotic as they embrace gestures, artifacts, and conduct, all against a monumental backdrop. But conduct, artifact, and gesture contribute to culture in the making only insofar as they look toward certain values, and are felt and interpreted accordingly. Just reading the paper is not enough for the simple people of Cairo to enhance their potential culture, of which information is of course only one level and one means. A culture demands dynamic participation, not passive reception. Even the ill-educated are not so easy to delude where meaning is concerned. The prestige of the printed word and the broadcast sound has in no way diminished the exacting judgment which comes to them from a great past. It would be wrong to think that nationalism excuses them from measuring themselves against what is achieved elsewhere: their pride is simply the more deeply wounded. In vain do rulers, publicists, and pedagogues bring their monopoly of the mass media into play on them; they let themselves be remodeled only in part. Their conformity and docility are tempered with suspicion and irony. To the culture thrust upon them, to which they appear to adhere, they oppose a sly hesitation, the *nukta*,[10] sometimes flat refusal: incipient elements of another culture, perhaps the true one. For information sets counterforces in motion, and the creativity of both elite and masses rises from these off-beat beginnings.

Mutation and Preservation

Although scandalously privileged by the power relationships of the contemporary world, economics, or rather technology, endows community life with only one of its many dimensions. Other dimensions—the aesthetic, the agonistic, the sacral, and so on—combine with technology in an operation of interchange and, we believe, reciprocal transformation.[11] Only the multivalence of a community's foundations makes this operation possible. Now there are societies cut off from their foundations, clinging tightly to one axis or other, clamped more and more firmly to their superficial levels. Such are the so-called consumer societies which the American example calls to mind and which William Blake stigmatized more than a century ago under the names of Beulap and Ulro. But there are others, such as the Afro-Asian societies, that feel and express extravagantly the ruggedness of the fundamental. The latter's presence takes on many forms. Where can it be recognized? In that fixation on origins glorified in Arabic usage by the term *aṣāla*, "authenticity"? In fulfilling the role which bourgeois democracy assigns to majorities? In the creativity of the masses put forward by socialism? From one to another of so many usages transfers are possible, not always metaphorical ones—how lucky for the politicians!

Moreover, this shifting complexity, this metamorphosis in train, breaks through and is experienced only in community life. For the Arabs, a tormented, lacerating, contradictory life. How is its positive side to be separated from the negative? How to strengthen its grandiose heartbeat, how cure its distressing weaknesses? And this gravest of questions: how is a people to appropriate the dynamisms of the world outside while remaining itself? But which self? The necessity stumbles against so many ambiguities, so many risks! A people can let its personality consist of its own continuities, that is, of a credulous loyalty to those forms by which it has arrived at its present self from yesterday and the day before: but thereby it will merely have founded a cult of the past. If, on the other hand, it aligns itself with an external, seemingly universal model, it will lose itself in cosmopolitanism. Difficult choices, bitter alternatives! How are community life, these ever-present foundations, this exchange with the other, and these transfers among interchangeable dimensions which shape personality to be made real, with their mutual relationships? And how are these relationships which ensure identity to be maintained notwithstanding the indispensable changes?

This problem is also the researcher's. How can any of these motivating factors be excluded from scrutiny? But then how is one to avoid sinking into banality and lack of focus? A culture, certainly, is defined by the overall movement of a social whole. But it is not, as such, that movement. Culture emerges only as the movement strives for expression and meaning: for *ʿibāra* and *dalāla*, to speak as the Arabs do. A cultural approach thus implies reference to concrete, overall history but cannot be confined to it. It must try to learn to what extent and how this history tends to become expressive and meaningful: for itself, but also for others. For one is no longer alone in our age, however alone one may have been in the past. Furthermore, a culture defines itself by setting itself apart from others, that is, implicitly, by postulating their existence as rivals. The boundaries it sets around itself bear witness to its specific contribution to our present-day world. A new problem! One which necessitates a correlative investigation into invention, styles, and forms. For whence can these distinguishing features, which are also those by which a culture tests and lives itself, becomes recognizable by others and by itself, derive their power otherwise than from the depths?

Another Urban Landscape

Old Rashīd Street, a thoroughfare parallel to the Tigris, its overhangs with their jig-saw embellishments rising above false arcades of a very British slenderness, is now but a memory of colonial times. The city has swarmed in all directions, blending imitation and invention with the unfinished. An unrestricted sprawl, thanks to the adoption of a referential type: the quiet, tidy little colonial cottage with its square of lawn in back. The proliferation is already being organized into life by distinct wards and has its occasional triumphs of modernistic architecture, of statuary at the street intersections, or the skillful restoration of mosques, like the one in which the Sūq al-Ghazl minaret is now mounted like a jewel. The immense esplanade at Bāb Sharqī, adorned on one side by a metal fresco in relief, now opens onto a Newtown, less than ten years old, which compares favorably with Cairo's best neighborhoods. The newspapers sold there are now nothing like the provincial sheets in which, only fifteen years ago, the editorial set forth day after day the Hashemite reply to Nasserist attacks. As everywhere in the Arab world, the development of the press in both technique and quality, which here coincided with that of the Republic, stimulates and comments upon the abrupt transition to new vistas.

Let us open one of these dailies, *Al-Thawra*, whose front pages give the lion's share, as they should, to government actions. Information/incantation. Many photos of politicians, properly, and lengthy expositions of activity begging for popular support. The space left for the rest of the world, and for the country's life, is diminished proportionately. Here, journalistic progress does not go so far as the invaluable social chronicles of *Al-Akhbār* or *Al-Ahrām*. This axis insists upon being ideological, or rather partisan, and without futile insipidity. There is a doctrine, committees to decide on it, books to discuss it, a Michel Aflaq to monitor it at a distance. The country is vast, the will adamant. Could a post-Nasserism be a-borning? In any event, conviction is not lacking. The undisguised primacy of politics is thus spread on the screen of the printed page. But other cultural functions are also present there: sports, needless to say; multiple references to educational effort, concern for the university, the same here as elsewhere—a fervor that summons the future and a prudence that seeks to keep it at bay.

As elsewhere, in any case, the newspaper, this piece of the city detached from its facades like a leaf falling from a tree and suddenly starting to speak, demonstrates a quest in which this ancient land commits itself by an expression, and this tormented people commits itself by a meaning. Keep turning the pages. The transportation question naturally takes up much space, evoking, as it does, physical and social mobility, even potential democracy. Less systematically than in Cairo, but in lively and often talented manner, news reports try to grasp the inflections of a life torn between old and new. Here is one on "survivals of the past": these displays of amulets and good luck charms so often seen on public sidewalks, these puppet shows, these fortune tellers and palm readers, this man showing off a magic rabbit which will foretell your future. . . . Here progressive man becomes indignant. Nevertheless, he does not neglect his folklore, which lately won a prize at a Bratislava competition. A watchful effort in this direction is made by the Ministry of Culture, which devotes a very well-produced magazine to these often-neglected subjects. Indeed, here is a photograph of a character in a long white gown, his head covered with the familiar red-checked scarf; the late sculptor Munʿim Barbūt, who has just died and whose talent brought forth out of humble materials graceful shapes in which something of the ancient still palpitates.

Archaeology, indeed, is never far away in Iraq. If need be, there are pictures to confirm that the undertakings of this people, now called upon to be revolutionary, must heed the constraint of its unfathomable past. This past which, after all, is classical not only for the remote descendants of Sumer and Akkad but also for all peoples of the earth converges with myriad references to international culture into a universal humanism. A literary page, with the broad coverage found everywhere in the Arab East, gives us a picture of Saint-John Perse and a defense of free verse. Yes, this poetry so often criticized for its obscurity and its narrow public is by no means responsible for the misunderstanding it suffers. It has its own *jamhūr*, its own "masses," not necessarily coinciding with those touched by more accessible arts. Let us be grateful to this critic for not indulging in the cheap satisfactions of that so-called social art that feeds such docile vulgarities. He would not be believed. Here, poetry flares up everywhere, whether traditional like the sermons of Najaf or modernist like Sayyāb's lament. It is the dream of these ancient alluvia.

Historicity: Variables and Invariables

Why was the press selected from among so many cultural instances? Would the same process not have been placed in relief and carried even further by distinguishing a literature, starting with the cheap editions scattered over the sidewalk[12] or, even better, starting with everyday modes of communication? Does not broadcasting, which makes antenna guy wires shaped like the Eiffel Tower sprout on the flat roofs, unfold a broader fan of audio-visual deployment and, after all, of mass exhortation? Among the gestures and images of the city, why not bring forth the theatricality that has spread there over the last few years and that, from the patriotic plays performed in the Izbekiya after the Suez coup to the avant-garde adaptations and original works staged at the Experimental Theater, reiterates the same process?

Why, moreover, choose the city among so many vehicles of culture? The factory, that reason in space, displays in its *mise-en-scène* a culture on the march and embodies it in its products: technological, labor minded, potentially socialist, taut with great collective projects, and fed by the power of the machines it sets in operation. Also, the village—resting on its millenary customs, a tremendous matrix of humanity, in perpetual dialog with the earth's verdant permanences, a conduit for a flood of rustic poetry, secretly committed to Islamic learning—maintains a culture and even fashions it. This is particularly noticeable in Egypt; one might observe it elsewhere under different forms. Why was the village not chosen?

If I have chosen the daily newspaper it is because it is a fragment of the city's time and space; because its temporal regularity, and its arrangement in rectangles covered with signs, brings the objective and subjective conveniently into conjunction; because, in its mechanization and communication techniques, it arises from the industrial age; because, among the Arabs, it has its titles of nobility, matched in detail with the stages of a historical progression. Even more, because the appearance of the newspaper demonstrates each day the links between a metaphorical text, that of the city, and a printed text, the newspaper's—utterances that will be still more truly texts in the sense given to that term today.[13]

This movement rises from landscape, objects, and situations toward human discourse, and from the latter toward the search for a meaning and a form. Culture is what arrives, by way of these successive levels, at the form and meaning that the group appropriates as its own. A meaning that, reciprocally, will extend even to the foundations. It is true that in that Cairo square where I wondered how a meaning and a physiognomy came to be constructed out of backdrops, gestures, and signs we did not grasp the outer limits of such a process, either at the foundation or by the results achieved. What we do nevertheless grasp is one part and one phase of the movement that prompts an oriental society, carried along by all its own internal stirrings as well as those of the universe, to clarify and to discover itself.

This cannot be done without standards and models. The timely article, the rousing speech, the poem or analysis that extends reality and gives it meaning, everything, in short, that is at the various peaks of this process, is determining at this level only by virtue of invariables: unwritten conditions, a social and moral system, aesthetic imperatives, a linguistic structure. Not far from here a foreign general had invoked the "forty centuries" which in Egypt "look down on you." They did not bat an eye. Their eye is that of an immemorial heritage and the enduring promptings derived from it: paradigms, the linguist would say.

Relative invariables, the historian will say, ones which are perhaps simply the regularities affecting the group in the long run, or the rules that make it possible for the group to find itself, in the guise it desires, under the random events of its daily life. Tawfīq al-

Ḥakīm, returning just now from *Al-Ahrām* to his Garden City apartment, is not free to place the correcting stamp of his eclecticism upon these reference points: they are bigger than he is, and he knows it. For if beauty, especially verbal beauty, is one achievement toward which the crowd is oriented, beauty is not alone in exercising such magnetism. Historical effort in all its forms, metaphysical hope as well as desire, irony, anger, bitterness, even the common sense that tests, deplores, or mocks shortcomings and lies—all these enter the equation to the extent that they participate in the operation of a culture in the sense of putting to work all possible contingencies, happenstances, and variations in man, as functions of the invariables that may perhaps transcend him statutorily, as the vast majority in these crowds believes, or instead flow from his own tireless transcendence, as Marxist optimism would have it.

Algeria "Ten Years After"

In 1972, the tenth anniversary of a dearly won independence, Algerian Culture Weeks organized in the four corners of the world undertook to speak of effort and hope. Never, seemingly, had a revival begun from so far back: from a foreign tongue and culture sinking its roots into this Muslim soil down to the levels of spontaneity; from an altercation so profound and so ancient that the dispute with the adversary had become as ambivalent as it was bloody; from a literary flowering in French prompted, perhaps, by an international propaganda with foreign objectives, but with enough talent to balance truly national names with that of Albert Camus, genuinely "The Foreigner" in his native land. But who was, and who was not, really foreign in this land where the colonist had for so long called himself Algerian, even pro-Algerian, where the Arabo-Berber elite had so long pleaded for identification with France? Worse still, the barriers suddenly collapsing: perhaps the last remaining rampart shielding the North Africans' honor and survival from depersonalization. Henceforth they will no longer have to reject values propagated inadvertently by colonialism or despite it, in order to survive and to preserve their honor. Perhaps even more embarrassing: those intemperate renewals of contact with the East, the waves of Arab teachers and experts breaking over the country and, beneath the fraternal joy felt in so many eloquent embraces, the fear of having to judge. . . .

Algeria has lived nearly all the themes of the Arab quest and still lives them at a high level of burning intensity and spirit. But they have not been culturally exemplified in any comprehensive statement, nor any masterwork. Yes, the Algerian University is being organized. It even has the virtue of doing so by the lights of its own personality, dismissing foreign models. But it is still at its very first stage in the field of human sciences, which alone can make all it learns truly its own. As for novelists, dramatists, film scenarists, and poets, they are still (understandably) inspired by the intense moments lived through more than ten years ago. Their art had been slow in speaking for the resistance; it is still slower in going beyond it. The debates of the time have not, to our knowledge, exerted their value as a literary stimulant: too close to things, perhaps, or too much respect? So, Malek, Kateb, and you younger ones, will you go on singing yesterday's dispossession instead of today's, or eternity's? The national publishing company's endeavors are meritorious and sometimes excellent. But it is a state agency; and the poverty of bookstore display windows, whether or not due to the economizing of foreign exchange, disturbs or bores the passer-by. The hand-to-hand encounter with a great Western culture was oppressive or, as they like to say, fatal. Ruptures have the property of firing enthusiasm. But beware, comrades! Liberty must bring much more than it destroys. At least, that is the meaning the democrat assigns to it, and what your people expect from it.

One can understand the anxiety of the basic choices to be made, the perplexities they raise, the vulnerability of an act that must accept so many risks. It is precisely the assumed risks that render today's Algeria pregnant with tomorrow's. Is community life anything other than assumed risk? But in that case we should like to see these risks set forth in the language of art and analysis. Is this so, as yet?

At least one may consult with interest the doctrinal signposts erected from time to time by an official responsible for this policy in the magazine *Al-Thaqāfa*. In one tenth-anniversary issue is published the full text of an address delivered February 18, 1972, under the suggestive title "The Algerian Experience in the Cultural Revolution."[14] Here one meets again that twin affirmation of the modern in the authentic, the universal in the specific, in which I see the capstone, so to speak, of any contemporary culture. Perhaps for the first time a role for the French tongue emerges in a realistic way, and the definition of Arabism as a cultural coat of arms seeking neither to deny nor to repress the Berber underpinnings it covers over in the Maghreb.

Turn another page. Here are precious documents on Algerian

poets who, between the two world wars or even earlier, were able to translate the sadnesses of alienation: for them history went forward with a pigeon-toed gait.[15] Here is a rather iconoclastic appraisal of the role of Frantz Fanon, that poignant analyst of depersonalization but one who, if we are to believe Mr. Mīlī, remained captive of a Western manner of seeing even though it reverted to negroism. And also an eloquent survey of the country's manuscript resources and the invitation to exploit them—an invitation, indeed, to which a few Algerian scholars have begun to respond. Always and everywhere, investigation into the two great themes of "authenticity," *aṣāla*, and "openness," *tafattuḥ*. The name *Aṣāla* has, moreover, been given to another Algerian magazine, more specifically Islamic. The term lends itself, in fact, to various interpretations, and one might regret that a theoretical approach to it is employed only rarely, except for a very lucid article by ʿAbd al-Majīd Meziane.[16] It would be only too convenient, even dangerous, to indict currents coming from outside as responsible for every deterioration. For, after all, where does "outside" begin? Such verdicts are fortunately becoming fewer. One may set against them those that condemn an entire aestheticizing tradition, however "oriental," and see salvation only in scientific apprenticeships. But the latter will remain cosmopolitan in the absence of regulators inherent in the national genius. Whether or not that genius gives weight to feeling, to the word, to the poem, one cannot make light of the choices the Algerians share with other Arabs.

The unspoken wish in all these pages, we repeat, is to resume Frenchness. But how, and to what extent, is this resumption to be brought into operation? More a question of levels and forms, doubtless, than of limits. The worst would be to treat things by pretermission. A formidable miscalculation would then open up between the explicit and the implied, between the ideal and the facts. The greatest lack is of definitions establishing the respective status and role of the two languages and the two cultures. Insofar as the necessary criticism of colonization's consequences becomes polarized into increasingly anachronistic attacks against yesterday's ruler, will it not neglect more recent wounds and thus more militant angers? Retrospective polemic should not divert attention from other operative themes. What, then, must be done? Always to "advance backward into the future," as Valéry said? We need not worry. By instinct and experience most Arabs know that the necessary liquidation of the past is only one way among others to build the future, which belongs to no one.

Imbalances of Progress

What, from now on, are societies in their entirety? We see them all carried along by a movement that might adumbrate their world-wide fusion. The Earth is becoming our only boundary. Arab societies are no exception to the rule. And both their access to world norms and their self-preservation even depend, in sometimes contradictory fashion, upon their being situated in this framework.

We see them all engaged in the same dispute between two equally attractive poles. This one: technical development, with the social and mental mutations it expresses and provokes. That one: the activation of other series we may call generally cultural. Here: material accomplishments. There: collective symbols, among them the most widely shared of all, language. Between the one and the other boils a discord favoring irreversible failures, illusory recoveries, and, above all, incoherence. It is true that this discord is apparent everywhere. It divides us as it divides the Arabs. But they compound it by heart-rending contrasts between the glories of their classical legacy and the mediocrities of the present; between the primacy of Islam as symbol and preserver of the whole and the implacable advance of secularism; between the self-willed (though imitative) nature of many of their technical performances and their compensating insistance on other dimensions, their foundations, their life experience. Let us explain ourselves on this last point.

All Third World societies are affected by technology, whether directly, by reason of their own industrial change, or indirectly, by the numerous effects this change induces, as an economist might say, in all the other sectors. Their own will to progress is not the least of these effects—progress understood as access to historical reason, in turn understood as linked to manufacturing capabilities. But the impulse that carries these societies along is much broader and richer. Nevertheless, their officials want to reduce it to a single dimension considered operative. What an ironic counterimage of the old era! The resistance had long drawn its strengths from sentiment alone. Since then, has adoption of Western causality made the Afro-Asians more efficient? Yes and no. Let us acknowledge, at any rate, that in order to modify the crushing disparity of power they had to engulf themselves in the very domain of those on top, get a grip on them through petroleum and natural gas; it was best to partake of the same industrial revolution, and participate in it if possible. But this progress in resisting the other implies eventual adherence to the other's system. It took time to realize this. The failure of many imitations, of the zeal of many students and initiates, was required before the decolonized peoples became frightened at the extent of the lesion suffered, and thus at how grave the problem was. For this lesion was not confined to the terms of production. It embraced also cultural wastage, personality disorders, the erasure of distinguishing features. But the struggle against those on top has generally remained so deferential that it still essentially accepts for itself their reduction of progress to industrial mechanization.

Now in order for the Arabs, for example, to remain themselves while joining the industrial world that surrounds them and beleaguers them from within they would have to impress the rhythm of their material advancement upon all their other modes. Al-Azhar's religious culture would have to project its doctrinal elucidations and its social ethic with the rhythm at which Egypt's industrialization goes forward. Shaikh ʿAbduh, after all, postulated this for his time, which was that of the first Aswan Dam. But what has happened? I would not ask whether the religious sciences have "adapted" (the absurd plea of a defunct positivism) to the development instituted by the High Dam; but have they been brought, in their own fashion, to the same degree of advancement?[17] It is quite true that their way of responding to the rhythms of the time, even when it is animated by industrial growth, must remain their own. We no longer believe that the totality of social dynamisms flows from technology, still less that they are its "reflection" or "superstructure." At the least, this totality receives from technology an invitation, or even a peremptory summons, that obliges it, if it is to remain global, to accelerate all its domains—aesthetic, normative, religious, and so on—at the same rate as the domain of production.

Even that would not be enough. Exchange and reciprocity must operate among all these modes. We may, indeed, observe that if there are failures it is not so much because one lags behind another. Such dislocations are of the order of things, and dislocations are legitimate provided only that they be propulsive. But the release of energy requires tension, and thus a relationship between each mode and the others. The thing to be feared is that some lose their correspondence with others and that all follow their respective paths under disparate signs. Only too often that is what occurs. If the society in question imitates the foreigner for the sake of technology and all it makes possible, and consents to be conditioned, if not by the foreigner at least by his models, it shelters its identity in those parts of itself in which it believes it can recognize and preserve itself. It will then speak two languages. The one that seeks to adapt to the industrial age is obviously compelling, in that it addresses evident ills and puts to work shattering innovations in the material, intellectual, and social realms. But the other, which seeks self-preservation and permanence, responds to secret commands. The two registers must be unified if genuine modernity is to be instituted. Otherwise the possibility of conversion, interchange, and co-creation between technology and all the rest disappears. Then the rupture appears, in society, personality, and landscape, that the economists deplore in their own field: modern sector/traditional sector. The future explodes.

What acceleration, really, should be impressed upon such categories as art, ethics, and religion? How is the interchange and reciprocity between them and economic acceleration to be restored? Not having found, nor sought, the answer, any more than we have, the East attributes symbolic power to these categories. It believes they can thereby be preserved as they are, that is, as it imagines they are or, worse still, as they once were. Islam, the Arab language and patrimony, a continuity of attitudes, will be glorified with a faithfulness all the less innovative because it proposes to act as a counterweight to what is being transformed elsewhere in the collective entity. The risky calculation will be made that intensities can be regulated by means of surrogates: inflating the merit of "revered ancestors" instead of a true return to sources; withdrawal into the self instead of individuality; exaggeration of distinguishing traits simply in exasperated reaction to the cosmopolitanism rising on all sides; assertion of the spiritual against the temporal, *rūḥ* against *mādda* [18] (a strange way, be it said in passing, to regain ground lost in the temporal domain); the quest for a false unanimity, unfortunately simply a nostalgic and distorted form of *ijmāʿ*.[19] Accentuation, finally, of everything in the interdimensional interplay of the society that transcends, offsets, or contradicts entry into the industrial age. Hence a glorification of the "authentic" and the "individual," real or assumed, proportional to the encroachments they have undergone, the compromises they must accept, and, finally and generally, their mutual deterioration.

But this is not the only perspective. This one results, true enough, from many observed facts, but there are other, more encouraging, ones. From the rupture between the foundations and life as it is experienced, from the disequilibrium among these categories and their very incommunicability, overall existence is intensified. Exposed to distortions, threatened by inertia, men's aspiration becomes more violent. Revolutionary hope and practice constitute its reply to the imbalances of progress. Opposed to the culture that offers to sublimate cleavage, discord, and privation stands the one that denounces and condemns them.[20] Through the latter, imbalance becomes a motivating force.

II
Trajectory of a Language

Free the Arabic language from the isolation to which so many specialists relegate it; examine it in the global context of the evolutions in language the world has experienced over the past century and a half: that is what a ground-breaking text of Roman Jakobson urges us to do. In his famous article "What Is Poetry?" he observed that "the second half of the nineteenth century was a period of sharp inflation in linguistic signs. . . . The most typical cultural expressions of the period are animated by the effort to conceal this verbal inflation at all costs, and to enhance by all possible means confidence in the word, this paper word. Positivism and naïve realism in philosophy, liberalism in politics, a grammatical orientation in linguistics, a lulling illusionism in literature and on the stage (whether a naturalistic illusion or a decadent, solipsistic illusion), atomizing methods in the science of literature (in fact in science generally): by these various means the repute of the word was purified and faith in its genuine value reinforced."[1]

A Hypothesis of Roman Jakobson

This synoptic approach subjects heterogeneous cultural orders to a single central perspective that, for a linguist, is of course that of language. Once the starting point is conceded Jakobson's finding can hardly be rejected. Since the mid-nineteenth century, many kinds of efforts have been made, out of what one might call a spirit of trusteeship, to reduce (or rather to disguise) the inflation of the word. But where did this inflation come from? Historical sociology might try to illuminate this facet of the dazzling hypothesis.

The verbal inflation pointed out here was not an isolated phenomenon. It could doubtless be called bourgeois. But one would have to lump together under that heading the harshness of Maupassant and *Les Déliquescences d'Adoré Floupette*, which would nonetheless be going a little too far. I prefer, true to the position asserted constantly throughout these pages, to proceed more radically and go to the root of all the accelerations of that period and our own: namely, the industrial revolution. If positivism, naturalism, and realism appear to be a series of subsidings of the romantic tide, what exactly had the latter been? Within the analytical scheme already used, let us risk the definition of romanticism as a growth in sentiment and expression in compensation for technological change. The latter has, since the end of the eighteenth century, produced an unlimited burgeoning of the material, economic, and technical content of Western societies. The expansion of the word was, we believe, among the things the Western societies then sought to regulate. These attempts at regulation assumed the most diverse forms. The bourgeois Revolution may have been one of them. Stylistic change, itself corresponding to change in imagination and taste, was most certainly another. But the counterpoise was also sought in the encyclopedic and ideological form, as with Saint-Simon, Owen, Fourier. And also in the expansion of education which, at the mass level, is in effect an attempt to render language able to cope with the enrichment of the referential context.

Western Europe did not, however, manage to free itself from its asymmetries. Its counterpoises generally failed to restore equilibrium. To use an expression of the time, a critical period had begun: the search for regulatory means, that is, went forward under the pressure of imbalances. On rare occasions a revolution mobilized all sectors of society in a single rhythm, thus producing one of those sublime coincidences that Fichte was able to discern in his time. More usually, discord between the individual's categories and those of society spread a dissatisfaction which described itself as romantic. It was to find its principal outlet in literature, painting, and music. But even here a creativity capable of bringing the material accomplishments of the time into balance was the possession only of elites isolated from the masses, without a real audience, and hemmed in by Philistines. The feeling that genius is solitary was thus recognized as romantic, and also the feeling that cultural values were in decline, that never again would there be a masterpiece or a meaningful adventure. The revolution had subsided, or reappeared only spasmodically to be stifled immediately by restoration and restitution. As morphological counterpart to the colossal transformations which continued to rock the material context there remained only the tidal wave of stock phrases.

Meaning, which thus moved feverishly about seeking supposed congruities with persons and things, was reduced to a waterskin bloated with words. In literature, romantic lyricism lost its sincerity and degenerated into phrase making. Teaching disseminated nomenclatures and recipes while abandoning its true aim of transmitting creative ability. More and more, the face value of the linguistic promissory note exceeded its real worth. Amid the dizzying progress of machines, the amassing of products, and human abundance, individual aspiration and the dynamism of societies suffered distortions which the unleashing of words aggravated by disguising them. Regulation could be made to work only at the price of such revolutions as technology has borne untiringly for more than 150 years. Let us recall that the middle of the nineteenth century, identified by R. Jakobson as the phenomenon's point of origin, was the moment of the Communist Manifesto, that *Tristesse d'Olympio* of industrial progress.

The Hypothesis Tested and Amended

This mid-nineteenth century represented a watershed in the history of Arab societies also. There was one who understood and said it: the *muʿallim* Buṭros Bustānī, whose *Essay on Arabic Literature* is in fact dated 1859.[2] This ground-breaking text glimpses the end of the old ages of decadence, if you will, but in any event of technical stagnation and political decline, to be followed by what was to be called, somewhat optimistically, the Eastern "Renaissance," or Nahḍa. Thenceforth objects, practices, sentiments, ideas, and also new forms of constraint came swarming in. Here we grasp a process characteristic of all contemporary history of the Arabs, in the extent to which it multiplies its own problems by those coming from abroad. Those distortions which became apparent in the European languages during the latter half of the nineteenth century because of the rupture between technical advance and the social or moral synchronisms which alone could humanize it: what would such distortions become in that oriental world where until quite recently a large proportion of "progress" was received in the form of expropriation of property, as in Khedive Ismail's Egypt or in Algeria after the Conquest!

Algeria, it is true, was to be long silent. But the East spoke, even chattered. The new rhetoric founded by Bustānī, Yāzijī, and their like responded to the same compensatory need as the romantic word, but with two complicating differences. On one hand, it came up against an ancient rhetoric consecrated by a peerless model; on the other, it had to borrow from others the bulk of its new content. The true significatum in Arabic languages was for a long time to reside less in what they referred to or connoted than in the effort of the speaker to adapt to the modern world by means of the word while still preserving his identity.

Linguistic virtuosity, moreover, had never been lacking. From his golden centuries the Arab had inherited, and never let slip from his grasp, a verbal archetype in the Koran, and a copious flora of anthology and lexicography. Versification, which relates to language as a system, still flowed in torrents among the educated as well as among the common people. Expansion remained operative in certain genres, linked to a tireless use of assonance. *Saj'*[3] in fact permits expansions of which the impact must have been powerful, judging by the effect it still produces today. It consists in deploying a virtually infinite series of analogous syntagms, all ending with the same phoneme. It mattered little to the listeners if this virtuosity destroyed precision and sincerity, or that this rhetoric almost entirely devoid of objective referents kept both listener and speakers in a narcissistic fixation on the past. At the turn of the nineteenth century it was still proudly displayed in Damascus, Cairo, Baghdad, Beirut, and Tunis so that, by contrast with our romanticism, the renewal of prose had to take place more in the direction of sobriety than of rhetoric. Only specialized studies in this field, going even as far as quantification, will be able to delineate the differences between the old style, that of the traditional men of letters and that of the innovators who at an early date embraced renewal in both content and form: a Shidyāq or a Ṭahṭāwī, for example, or those I have already quoted.[4]

In any event, Arabic proved able from the first to learn from others without forsaking itself. It was not necessary to renew or invent words, as French lexicography had to do at the time of the Pléiade. Arabic words were never lacking. On the contrary, they were there in swarms. Vocabulary innovation, which figured so prominently among the preoccupations of those concerned, under the curious name of "conventions," *iṣṭilāḥāt*, was thus, in our view, only a minor phenomenon, but one which could distort the problem. Certainly, a great effort, and the most sustained one put forth by the Arab academies to modernize the language, was concentrated on the translation of foreign technical terms. 'Abd al-Qādir al-Maghribī counted about 42,000 in medicine alone. Have they all now been Arabized? Further developments have doubtless occurred in the meantime in this discipline as in others, making the dogged effort of the institutes a Sisyphean one, however desperately they work to produce words rather than knowledge, practice, and attitudes. Let us note, however, the interest devoted by these official agencies to technology, for it is through and in technology that the Arab world and the industrial West showed themselves most obviously out of phase. A salutary reaction against the abuse of words could be hoped for to the extent that a style came into general use aimed at objectivity, based on concision, and free of ambiguity.

The abuse of words did not have only negative aspects. It represented a specific reaction to the flood of materials and powers from the West. This "romantic" feature (in the sense given above to the term) remains visible in our day. In recent times the use of language in speech, printed article, and broadcasting has endowed the formerly colonized peoples with a rather effective weapon. If today it has been turned against its own users, who have been too slow in emerging from that enchanted kingdom, it is more a question of a passing phase than of merit or blame. Phases, moreover, succeed one another. From the very beginning, almost, the need for more precision, more simplicity, and more information with fewer words was apparent (as it still is) in the Arab world and produced definite results. The humanists of the Nahḍa, animated by a very exact sense of their people's needs, worked less to develop vocabulary than to develop usage, turns of phrase, and, especially, the various roles of language. Here homage must be paid to magazines, encyclopedic and often scientific, such as *Al-Muqtaṭaf*, as well as to militant rationalisms like those of Shiblī Shumayyil and, nearer our time, Salāma Mūsā or some Marxists. They were, and are, right to react against the abuse of language, but wrong in failing to appreciate certain powers of language which are far from precluded. Yesterday, today, and far into the future one axis of Arab modernity passed, passes, and will pass through words.

Oratory: Wring Its Neck!

Words, in fact, can master things. Several generations of scholars devoted themselves to mobilizing words so as to grasp the new and to place them at the service of an inspiration which could put all those disparate elements back together. Their encyclopedic, pedagogic, and literary effort has unfolded without surcease into our own day. The language thus reacted to the massive borrowing of ideas and things, to reiterate, with compensatory processes. To those, in particular, who spoke it, it appeared capable not only of assimilating novelty itself, but also of assimilating it into the Arabs' very being by setting against that devastating forest fire (if I may be pardoned this sylvan metaphor) the backfire of word and sentiment. But it thereby assumed a value less cognitive or pragmatic than existential. That could, in time, disturb the relationships within the language between signifiers and the things signified, and thus eventually the relationships between society and its words and things. Today, that still remains one of its major problems.

Thus far Jakobson's theory, as adjusted to the sociological counterpoint we have given it, holds true except that the inflation here affects roles, styles, and literary forms rather than words, where it already reigned supreme but is now tending to regress. Another difference: the compensatory function of language with respect to the pressure of the industrial world asserts itself here much more strongly than in the West, renders more services, and wreaks more destruction. Many Arab educators are more sensitive to the destruction than to the services. How can one blame them? It must be admitted that a redundant phraseology, wrongly invoking classical authority, accompanies modernity. Until the recent, so-called revolutionary, period this dubious association overflowed the creation of history, long prevented and always deformed by action of the foreigner. Must we therefore conclude that there is a linguistic propensity, atavistic among the Arabs, which vitiates their ability to achieve genuine development? We all know what to think of national psychologies of that sort! Neither Arab specificity nor the Arabic language is responsible for the all too evident evils, but rather the morphological irregularities I endeavored to describe above. Let us go further. The *lugha*[5] is not to be feared for its aesthetic or agonistic qualities, which are very precious things, but for its possible impingement upon other categories of social activity. That is what many Arabs have denounced since World War II under the name of "verbalism," *lafẓiya*.

Lafẓiya is distinguished, in the first place, by a redundancy which, often even in the best writers, transposes a feature of oral communication into written style. It turns even a poetic text into an oration, although symmetries and repetitions play a very different role from those in the usual oration. I recall that a Syrian minister once showed me a poem in a magazine in which he had encircled many terms in pencil; these were "rare words," *gharīb*. "That's why I have given up poetry," he sighed. This taste for the *gharīb* presupposes a wealth of vocabulary, striking less because it is occasionally drawn upon than because it survives outside its proper function. Let us nevertheless not forget that resort to the ancient keyboards of synonyms may be one means of self-affirmation. Like redundancy, it reveals not only a taste for affective nuances but also, to talk like the linguists, the presence of paradigms in discourse. The well-justified struggle against verbalism must thus, while getting rid of these inflationary features, discover other means of repersonalizing Arabic style. Some are trying to do so, as some among us tried in the past, such as Mallarmé and Rimbaud.

Approaches to a New Creativity

The proving ground of all this evolution is the finished work. Hence a questioning all the more anxious because these societies justly feel that they were once creative, and they still devotedly recite to one another fragments of their heritage. How was it in that last third of the nineteenth century when they felt alienation rising on all sides? Was it not enough for them to be exploited, humiliated? They wondered whether they would ever again be creative. It was one thing to react eloquently to the other's message. More practically, it was necessary to counter it with achievements worthy of the past. But everything began in a kind of muteness. There was a time in the 1880s and 1890s when, despite the extraordinary wealth of the language, many Eastern scholars despaired of the possibility of a modern literature or even a modern mode of expression.[6] Ibrāhīm al-Yāzijī, in a short work of 1893, expressed his pessimism at the paralysis with which, he said, his contemporaries were stricken when they tried to give names to the circumstances and even the objects of their daily lives. But less than ten years later, in 1901, he attacked the language of the newspapers in another small work, *Lughat al-Jarā'id* ("Newspaper language"). Notwithstanding his puristic comments on the dialect then in the making, let us note that Arabic had by then begun to translate this intrusive modernity, whether or not it had truly assimilated it.

To some degree the challenge had thus met its response. The latter was to become more and more insistent during the next two decades, which witnessed, on a broadly sociological scale, the development of the Arabic press in Egypt. The pen of Shaikh ʿAlī Yūsuf in *Al-Mu'ayyad* achieved, his contemporaries said, a union between the al-Azhar style and the Syrian style. By the Syrian style was meant the one for which the Beirut *Al-Nahḍa* had won respect, and which Egyptian writers carried forward in the years 1900–1910 and thereafter. As for the Azhar style, it was the one preserved by Koranic exegesis and the religious sciences without apparent break from the Middle Ages to our own time.

In any event, in 1907 there appeared a decisive work, Muwayliḥī's *Ḥadīth ʿĪsā bin Hishām*. This was a "Menippiad," as students of the new rhetoric say, and it was not by accident that this innovative work claimed to be inspired by the *maqāma*, or "assembly," genre.[7] Indeed, like the *maqāma*, and doubtless by virtue of the same socio-historical conditions, the "Menippiad" is a baroque mode of expression that strings together apparently unrelated passages one after another, lumping adventures, essays, fantasies, and controversies of all sorts, sketching the most comical of profiles along the way, and bringing into play the most extraordinary verbal racket. That had been the case with the great assemblies, those of Ḥarīrī and of Hamadhānī. This was likewise the case with Muwayliḥī's *Ḥadīth*, which depicted in this appropriate form all the hurly-burly of the Cairene world at the beginning of the twentieth century.

Another phenomenon that must be dated from this time is the change in character, not yet of the public speech, *al-khiṭāb*, but of the *khuṭba*, the weekly Friday sermon. This is a socially important form involving a combination of three participants: the *jamāʿa*, or congregation of worshipers; a solemn discourse delivered from the elevated pulpit; and a transcendental ethic. Until the end of the nineteenth century the *khuṭba* had remained stereotyped. Most preachers simply read it out, with a few minor adaptations—hence an extremely arid elocution without value beyond acknowledging allegiance to the legitimacy of the caliphate. But now the *khuṭba* becomes a literary and political, as well as moral, form. Whence a new sort of expression, a new kind of stimulus, to which we must relate the modernism and critical rationalism that Shaikh ʿAbduh was at that very moment introducing into the language of *ḍād*.

As for the political speech, its appearance as a distinct form is evidently linked to the birth of collective self-awareness among the Arabs as Arabs. In this connection let us note the part played by King Ḥusain of Hijaz[8] in this resurrection of the old *khiṭāba*, and still more the Wafd orators, particularly Zaghlūl. Prospectively, in fact, all the great agitators of *qawmiya*[9] from its first glimmerings in the aftermath of World War I down to our own days, with names as different as they are prestigious, including ʿAllāl al-Fāsī, Bourguiba, and Abdul Nasser, the last two furthermore making a legitimate place in political elocution for the colloquial.

Thus even before the First World War public speaking, literary texts, and newspaper articles all exhibited a marked dynamism.

Were we to summarize in a few words our impression of *al-nahḍa*'s first decades from the language viewpoint, we would say that Arabic was then able to inventory its means of facing up to aggression from the external world, and moreover embarked on a few trial runs of which some resulted in masterpieces. Within a single generation it had certainly not created equivalents to its legacy from the past, nor attained the level of Western literatures, but it had at least demonstrated its capacity for renewal.[10]

Grandeur and Misery of Bourgeois Culture

The linguistic value of Arabic has long been, and is still, attached to a culture of elites, not to say of initiates. Not so much because its underpinning, its inventory, and its embodiment remain a sacred book. A generation or two ago the archetype offered itself to, even imposed itself upon, everyone. The Koranic school touched the masses, directly or indirectly. But this education, which a small elite was able to carry to the summits of *ʿilm* and *maʿrifa*,[11] proved to be more effective as a propaedeutic of the subconscious than as modern-type academic training. Today, now that its field has shrunk and it forms only one part (and how deeply transformed) of primary education, one may regret that the specific opportunities it opened up toward a true cultural democracy were not exploited.

The latter has been sought by other routes. Propagated on the basis of European models, it has not always found the paths toward integration with the popular substance. It still seems, in many circumstances, to come from others, while many internal potentials, neglected or repressed, seek their revenge elsewhere. It is true that what these potentials lose in their action in the modern sectors they make up in the sectors of conservation. The prestigious *lugha* still appears to be the certificate of authenticity. Thus far only rare attempts have been made to challenge it at the level of principle. In practice it forces itself even upon those who have not mastered it, and that is what has made possible the mass triumphs of the neoclassicism of a Shawqī.

Shawqī's literary career was well under way before the 1914 war. He was a man who worked in the thickness of the language,[12] and this explains the seemingly paradoxical result that such a poet, whose work is very difficult to translate satisfactorily into a European language, remains in the eyes of the great majority of Arab masses the major creative light of the time, and certainly the only modern writer from whom exemplary quotations, or *shawāhid*, are drawn. Along with Shawqī, let us salute two rival heralds of the interwar period, Muṣṭafā Ṣādiq al-Rāfiʿī and Ṭaha Ḥusain.[13] It is provocative to speak of these two adversaries in the same breath, but their duel is to a degree outdated. Rāfiʿī felt himself threatened, and with him the language and even Islam as a whole, when certain modernists preached a simplicity of expression which he himself condemned as *rakāka*.[14] An ardent partisan of *jazāla*,[15] which is to style what plumpness is to a woman, smitten with tradition, setting off thunderclaps like those of our Bossuet with an "ethical roar" that sweeps one along rather than persuading, alternately menacing, sardonic, and seductive, he uses the kind of diction that seems to be inspired and guided by a gaze from on high. At the same time, his adversary Ṭaha Ḥusain, who introduced the manner of such French moderns as Anatole France, for example, into the same classicizing Arabic discourse, was no less "paradigmatic." In his prose, one might say, that echo of the Absolute which Rāfiʿī obeyed became immanent and dispersed in redundancy. The style of a great vintage, in any event.[16]

Let us slip into this file also the work of the universities, just beginning to appear on the scene. Then add the work of remarkable educators and humanists, such as the Syrian Sālim al-Jundī, the Egyptian Aḥmad Amīn, or the Lebanese Fuʾād al-Bustānī. Mention the works that punctuated the period between the two world wars: those of ʿAqqād, Tawfīq al-Ḥakīm, or, leaving Egypt, of a Rīḥānī, author of that quest for a lost authenticity, tinged with autoexoticism, which is his book on the kings of the Arabs, *Mulūk al-ʿArab.* Of course Rīḥānī participated in a different current of this Arab dynamism: that of expatriation, an expatriation in two meanings of the word. It is no accident that it was from his pen, through contact with a rediscovered nature, that the first principles of what would later be called free verse flowed. The change to a new environment and new experiences is no doubt responsible for the innovation: that had lately been the case with Jubrān, although his masterwork was written in English, as it is with Mikhāʾīl Nuʿaymé and all that emigrant poetry still present among us.

But may the success of a school not consist in its having failed? To the extent that it establishes the credentials of a language, thereby rendering it banal, one literary generation contrasts with the next only in its negative aspects. The much-needed message of these emigrants, like the reforming rationalism of Shaikh ʿAbduh in dogma, has been so incorporated in contemporary Arab inspiration that today it seems simply to have filled a vacuum. Besides, what else could it do but oscillate between a really somewhat narrow cosmopolitanism and a lyricism running to catch up? The expression is not necessarily pejorative. The *al-mahjar* school, which one may compare on this point with that of Apollo, infused poetic speech with an anxiousness and an affectivity that we are accustomed to call romantic and that, there as among ourselves, serves as complement to technological pressure and social explosiveness.

Of course, the interesting thing about these poets is perhaps not their rather complacent subjectivism but the accents of revolt and errantry, of return to nature, which one may follow from *The Prophet* to those *Songs of Life* of the Tunisian Shabbī, that apostle of sincere renewals who died so early. The language had always been reflexive. Now it became endowed with a sort of redoubling, auspicious either for sentimental effusion or for the quest for art, both finding their echo in the rise of the parliamentary speech and the press article. This epochal style, now old-fashioned, nevertheless reflected worthily the birth in the Near East of the "second person," *al-kāʾin al-thānī* (Abū Shādī):[17] that is to say, progress in self-awareness.

Nevertheless, this phase, of which the fecundity in various fields must be acknowledged, was that of bourgeois classicism. It sinned by its oratorical quality and self-conceit and failed to master or even to distinguish its own acculturation. Whether submissive or not to those in power, it accommodated itself to a vassalage with respect to the West, under the name of universalism. It is disturbing that it enjoys, in retrospect, a certain immunity. The masses followed its lead, in short. Several of its writers, whether one likes it or not, are still popular classics and have been little affected by the ideological condemnations heaped upon them by later regimes. Through them the language achieved some undeniable accomplishments within a harmony of formal development and majority support which their successors do not yet enjoy.

New Adequacies

To assert oneself as "subject" one must grasp oneself as objects (plural). The individual is measured by his capacity to produce: at least that is the law imposed by the industrial West. As for the Arab East, it had to wait until the 1930s to begin its industrial odyssey. The efforts of the Miṣr group and its director, Ṭalʿat Ḥarb, have become the shining example. Let us note this curious sentence which connects economic and linguistic labor: "It used to be said that spinning was impossible in Egypt. They said also that the use of Arabic in the banking industry was impossible."[18] Ṭal'at Ḥarb, the author of the sentence, was to apply himself with some success to the refutation of this double denial. One might observe, however, that Arabic had not yet become a banking language and did not until the Nasserist revolution. At the very moment when the speech nationalizing the Suez Canal was being delivered, a meeting was in progress in Cairo of the Council of Banks, which at that time were mostly foreign and mixed, and the language of discussion was French! A witness who attended the meeting sensed the irony of the contrast. Had Egyptian capitalism failed to liberate the language, or was it instead settling for an attenuated liberation?

Much progress has been made since then toward Arabic technical expression. In this field of thought one should take inventory of other phenomena, no matter how heterogeneous they seem, which have appeared especially since World War II and notably after 1961, when the Nasser regime became radicalized. Let us mention, at random, the proliferation of scientific publishing and cheap books, the increasing vogue for translations transmitting a substantive culture, and the progress of exact and technical education, still a pious hope in too many instances but nevertheless more conspicuous day by day. All are deflationary processes, we might say, if we must follow up R. Jakobson's metaphor. From the same viewpoint something very different, but convergent, must be taken into account: the attention devoted to popular art in a much more systematic way than even a short time ago. The inaugural book in this field was that by Rushdī Ṣāliḥ, *Al-Adab al-Sha'bī*, which appeared as early as 1954. Recognition must also be accorded the thesis of 'Abd al-Majīd Yūnus on the popular epic of the Banī Hilāl, and the tapestries that Ramses Wissa Wassef had executed by village children. Efforts of this sort elsewhere than in Egypt could be cited. It is not a question here of investigating whether the interest focused on these matters was taken in hand by some regime or other as a propaganda device and perverted under the name of folklore. It nonetheless marked a return to fundamentals, a pricking of the bubble of artifice, and a potential revival of inspiration. It found a sometimes embarrassing ally in socialist realism and in the thunderous progress of the political address. When Nasser began his long, choleric improvisings, it was a great shock. Many men of letters brought their irony into play on this oratory which was to prove itself in spite of them, and against them. At the time of the separation between Egypt and Syria, the Damascus press parodied it maliciously. But the innovation had taken hold. In the Arab world people would never again speak as they did before Nasser.

Another facet to mention: the effort to reduce the gap between literary language and the language actually spoken. It is well known that this "diglossia," sometimes deliberately exaggerated (for, after all, these are two forms or rather two systems of a single language), constantly preoccupies rulers and pedagogues. Much effort is expended in analyzing the sociological, historical, and linguistic reasons for it, and also to find cures for it, for example by trying to simplify grammar, spread the use of a "middle" Arabic, *ʿarabiya wusṭā*; or even to consecrate it in the form of a "third language"[19] in a stage dialog which represents perhaps the greatest success of the 1960s.

This middle Arabic, disseminated today by the press and airwaves and constantly trained for new feats—since for the teacher, the participant in so many congresses, for all those who from one Arab country to another seek to communicate, the requirements of an expression responding to all the stimuli of the surrounding world must be met—seems to have won the contest. It reacts upon dialects, solicits even the illiterate through the voice of the radio, importunes the masses by the boom of the loudspeaker and the whisper of the transistor. In short, in the Arab countries it has made it possible for the word, linked originally to the Archetype, to leap over the phase, hardly begun, of written culture and become inflated with the world-wide powers of the audio-visual. Along the way it has had to absorb the various contents of the modern experience, make them transmissible, and even subject them to that never-ending reinvention which life demands. Should it therefore sing a victory song?

Anxieties and Quests

Just at the time when Arabic discourse appears to have triumphed, it is being gripped by dissatisfactions and fears. This third language which has thus been fashioned has proved itself by replacing French or English in some of their roles and by relegating the colloquial to certain levels of practical life. It has thus performed the most urgent task, that of resisting invasion by multilingualism or being bogged down in the vernacular. But is that all it has done? And what is it really? Does it constitute a return to square 1 of the classical word, so that the man of letters, or even the ordinary citizen, has only to raise his tone, as Buffon of old simply put on his cuffs in order to recapture the superb old idiom? Or, on the other hand, has this new language, disjunctive without thereby becoming analytical, redundant but not periodic, born of the need to adapt but nevertheless tangential with respect to the world, preserved only the words of Arabic while losing its personality? To what extent has it not cut itself off from its lofty sources without replanting itself accordingly in the compost of the masses?

When Ṭaha Ḥusain wrote his pastiches of al-Jāḥiẓ' epistles he was the equal of his model, not its serf. To rediscover the ancient genius and make it sprout again, so to speak, in fresh conceptual soil was the desire of our André Chénier; such is the desire, in no way chimerical, of many Arabs, and one can only be glad of that in view of the testimony of so many successful accomplishments.

In the opposite direction, there are the attempts to promote dialectical literature. Not only through the increasing attention paid to popular poetry (where poetry, period, may have taken refuge at an early date, as Ḥ. Ḥ. ʿAbd al-Wahhāb used to say impudently), but even more through the massive introduction of colloquial phrases and locutions into dialog on the stage and in fiction.

Other attempts, thus far experimental, go further. They are aimed at rooting Arabic instruction anew in its economic functionality,[20] which would eventually re-establish it on a solid base of pragmatism. Or, still more boldly, "renaturalizing" it by overturning the habits and norms which make it something which "descends" from on high. On the contrary, it would be made to "rise" from actual usage in one country or another, but without in any way abandoning its structural demands, much as the *koïnè* of the poets must have been constructed in pre-Islamic Arabia.[21] However, nothing says what would have been achieved upon completion of this "ascent," what distance would set the idiom thus derived off from the classical idiom and middle Arabic, or what unity could be restored among all the developments of this type which each country would pursue on its own.

Life, in the end, will be the arbiter, but we should not underestimate the role that linguistic developments pursued at other levels than that of daily life can play: in literature, for example, and particularly poetry. During the last few years pieces of research in

Arabic have been produced which are of extreme interest in making this language suitable not only to express but also to innovate in the field of both collective endeavor and ideas.

Aesthetic accomplishment, reversing the evolution which produced middle Arabic, endeavors to express the inexpressible: that is, not what is borrowed but what is created new.[22] In French, that was Rimbaud's problem. He resolved it by verbal alchemies. In prose a Rāmiz Sarkīs or an Antoine Ghaṭṭās Karam and in poetry the Shiʿr school have striven in the same path, at the price of cutting themselves off (temporarily) from the crowd. For this avant-garde it was a question of breaking with a linguistic *sunna*, with a "normal course of things," or again with a conformism tied to all the wrongs of dependence on others and a false emancipation: in short, continuing in canonical terms, to "reopen the door of *ijtihād*" and drive out *taqlīd*, or conformism, even in linguistics.

What if this conformism, to oneself as well as to others, had heretofore been the weapon by which all the appropriations had been made, an effective weapon after all? What if waging war on *tarkīb* and *siyar*, synonymy and redundancy, meant not only wringing banality's neck but also doing violence to a necessary continuity? Among these efforts of the avant-garde, which ones would the masses follow, not merely follow but assimilate and reflect? That is precisely the stake in any revolutionary movement, and some Arabs proceed openly to the most subversive of conclusions. Ill-satisfied with precedents and even with linguistic achievements, they seek to set up a counterdiscourse against the established discourse.

They dare to ask whether overvaluation of a linguistic convention, supposedly safeguarding the heritage and transmitting its original gratification, has not in fact compromised with alienation and decadence. Are all these locutions and clichés by which the language has made itself banal over the past century under pretext of modernization not the sign of guilty transactions? Does not creativity imply that these sediments of the bourgeois era, of false Nahḍa, must be broken up, that they must be systematically challenged? Some link this agonizing necessity to the "desirable tempests" of social upheaval. Since 1967 statements and attempts of this sort have proliferated. The Syrian Nizār Qabbānī has been heard to say, "My friends, I announce to you the death of the old language."[23] The Tunisian Bel Madanī, playing comically with the language's sonorities, parodies the speech of the ulama and pretends to be astonished when he is accused of blasphemy. For Adonis: "If revolution is the science of changing reality, revolutionary poetry is the linguistic counterpart of this revolutionary science. Poetry is what seeks to produce the breakdown of the old order. It is not just something that accompanies that breakdown."

•

This is all the easier to believe since, during a development which has now lasted more than a century, the effort of the language upon itself and upon the world has shown itself on the whole to be more effective than many other undertakings by these societies. Most of the facts we have described as denoting progress—that deflation of the language which makes it increasingly able to latch onto reality, even its own reality which is its own distinctive field; the undeniable finding that it has become possible to deal in the Arabic language with the subtlest of contemporary problems; the fact that the delineation of weaknesses existing among youth is expressed so lucidly—all these simply illustrate and even accentuate a dramatic maladjustment in the respective evolution of the Arabic language and Arab society, or rather societies. If the latter do not as yet have the history they deserve, the Arabic language is still far from having the societies it deserves.

III
Unitary and Plural

The Arab world insists that it is unitary by reason of a shared legacy and language, espousal of the same ideals, and assertion of identical solidarities. More than a sentiment or a rhetorical expression, this is a spell cast over a reality which never acknowledges defeat despite repeated disappointments. Now there may well be only one Arabism; but there are many Arab societies, and this results in the prejudicial fact that they approach their encounters with the world and history in misunderstanding. They feel deep anger and remorse at this misunderstanding. Nevertheless, they can but admit that there is no uniformity among the environments and junctures in which their claim to unity is brought into question. By the same token, analysis must constantly distinguish among specificities of nation, country, and even changing circumstances.

Of course these are family differences, or are generally considered such. Indeed, the Arab area is marked by a quite impressive community of fundamentals, whether these arise from ecology, archaeology, ethnography, or history. Toward the lands to the north of the Mediterranean, and the world at large, the same attitudes are found throughout, the same acquisitions, or also indifference toward the same things. Everywhere one is backed up against the desert, everywhere there is the same dispute between a semiarid continental system and encroachment by the sea, between a classicizing diction and potentialities largely unarticulated. Everywhere three phases have succeeded one another: the precolonial, almost entirely embraced in the Ottoman system; the colonial, divided between French and British influences; and emancipation, bifurcating in widely differing directions under disparate regimes. . . .

Recollection of Fez on the Morrow of Independence

Was I at ease? I gave that impression, at any rate. I was a partisan of the new Morocco, which was welcoming me as a friend from the evil days. A minister was on my right hand, as reassurance. He himself was the host, the rector of the Qarawiyīn University at Fez. We were in the vast library hall next to the sanctuary, and I was the first Westerner to speak publicly in this venerated spot. A few years before, this French professor had moreover administered the medina as a municipal official. The audience nevertheless appeared sympathetic.

My remarks, couched in a classical Arabic with a Maghrebi accent as yet unadulterated, seemed to be going over well. Was this simply courtesy toward a guest? Suddenly a tumult erupted at the door, from which a stairway led down to the noisy copperworkers' souk, an old hotbed of opposition and authenticity. I had noticed that the governor was not present: did he expect trouble? I knew by experience how readily the seething, thoroughbred city overwhelmed its rulers. But I had only a moment's apprehension. The shouts died down. Files of young men, having demolished the barrier of the door, invaded the hall and gravely sat down. I resumed my lecture, which was well received.

My renewal of acquaintance with Fez had occurred shortly after independence, under the auspices of the Istiqlāl, still united, of which ʿAllāl al-Fāsī was president, and the late Ben Barka with Bouabid the most active leaders. I was thus able to resume contact with the city from within. It had not as yet undergone the alterations which today have stripped it of most of its urban attributes. That sumptuous maze of alleys dating from ancient times still came down to you apparently unaffected by the passing of the Protectorate. One did not yet know that the restoration of national identity simply perpetuated the city's crisis, and that the winning of independence was to be merely one stage, and not the most radical one, in an infinite series of accelerations. The crowd was vibrant, having repressed its resentments. Its victory was restrained. Here one carefully avoided the claim of having crushed France or the West. The sole resentment was against a form of intervention and its negative aspects, which the leaders distinguished meticulously from a positive side which was still appreciated. At least that was the working hypothesis, which concealed certain solidarities between the former colonial power and the Moroccan ruling class which had, of course, been rejuvenated by its take-over from the Protectorate! But who knew or said this, or felt it then, amid the virtually universal gaiety on the Moroccan side?

I made one of my first return visits to Fez in the company of Louis

Massignon, as representatives of UNESCO at an Arab League cultural congress. The admirable old shaikh, a little piqued that the city was as familiar to me as the Baghdad of 1908 was to him, had me pilot him through its labyrinths. He wanted to pray at the tomb of Muḥammad V's mother, who had died in obscurity during her son's exile in Madagascar. Such a visit to a grave was resented as more Christian than Islamic. I had to insist a great deal before we were led into a small cemetery surrounded by houses in the Moulay 'Abdullah quarter, not far from the giant waterwheel. Our companions stayed with me in the street, chatting without the slightest compunction while the strange visitor performed his rites. Then, when he expressed his intention of meditating also over the burial place of the victims of 1944, interred clandestinely in certain bourgeois *riyāḍs*,[1] he encountered outright refusal. *Dāzet*, they told him: "That is over and done with." Yes, many things were over and done with, among them a part of ourselves.

On this visit, or another the same year, we went to dine at the home of a militant where I felt, for once, a cold, almost hostile, atmosphere. Afterward, we climbed back up the precipitous street through the night, our way ill lit by lanterns. There is something grossly ridiculous in these homecomings of notables (what else were we?) after a copious dinner. The oldest, or fattest, guests are hoisted onto the backs of donkeys. When the route leads upward, they lean forward, displaying enormous backsides, while a slender servant hangs onto the animal's tail and keeps it in motion by voice and stick. As for myself, I walked on the slippery ground, mulling over morose thoughts. Throughout these days we had been acclaimed in the medina under the escort of Arabism, as several of us had been a few years before under the Protectorate's escort. Who, then, is to be accused of inconstancy?

From 1936 to 1939 I had lived here a life in which action and desire were identical, but under an aegis which, in the end, I challenged and even fought in vain: I foresaw, but did not welcome, its defeat. The Moroccans might well say the opposite. It was not simply our imperialism (to hell with it!) which had lost, but also what had been incidental to it, everything it had exploited and falsified: all that labor, those lives of my own people squandered under that sinister aegis, the future of all those children and young women nullified by the ineptitude of our rulers and the avidity of our merchants! My youth, finally, but let us not speak of that. . . . One might even say that it was precisely the service rendered, the disinterested act, which had lost, whereas those notorious "French interests" remained faithfully on station; at the very moment our flag was lowered our banks were blithely opening branches at Larache and Tetouan!

I was thinking of all that in the muddy night when I felt someone's arm on my shoulder. It was ʿAllāl al-Fāsī.

At that time he presided almost singlehandedly over a national movement in which both forms of liberation were still combined:[2] affirmation of specific identity and the appeal of democracy. His picture was seen in homes and in the souks almost as often as Muḥammad V's. By a strange complexity this Muslim thinker, this Arab of ancient blood, this man whose words had been France's most unyielding adversary, would soon reject alignment with that Arab League we had come to celebrate. In retrospect, had the spontaneous enthusiasm of the Tangier speech of 1947 in which the sultan had shouted his adherence to Arabism provided the struggle with but one lever? In any event, from the moment of independence the East was kept at arm's length. Morocco's Islamic and Arab fervor in no way wiped out a quality which was something more and better than particularism.

This can be stated in scholastic terms: at what level of group classification—global society, sub- or superglobal—did Morocco really wish to place itself with respect to the Arab world? The question was to arise in Algeria and Tunisia, not to mention Egypt. A difficult problem which the citizen had not resolved, and one virtually incomprehensible to the foreigner, for whom it had been, and was yet to be, the source of many misunderstandings.

Unitary Ethic, Objective Multiplicity

Might this fragmentation be simply a makeshift? One would say that a single, extremely ductile sociological and cultural field, although shocked by its superficial divisions, in practice seeks to demarcate these divisions' borders. One would say that, from country to country, the Arabs' performance in the nation-building, social, artistic, and other such fields is competitive rather than complementary. One might nevertheless draw up an inventory which, overall, would represent a clear success, if only its localization and distribution were more concentrated. Suppose that the industrial energy deployed here neighbored upon the innovation in civic or labor matters observed elsewhere, with the cultural flowering in some other region, with the communication with the outside world or the ideological quest in yet another. It could then be claimed that the Arabs are on the way to solving the problems of modernity in a more decisive way than many other peoples: Greeks, Turks, or Persians, to name only their classical neighbors. They might well become again what they were in their golden centuries.

How far they are from such a condition! The fragmentation in which contemporary life finds them and bogs them down has not merely weakened them politically. The situation is both alleviated and aggravated by the sharp contrast with a unity of ideals and culture which makes the shortcomings and differences all the more glaring, while dissociating them (I almost said "delivering" them) from their true foundations. In 1958 one would have had to be a very hardened reactionary to contest the union under one flag of Egypt and Syria, shortly afterward Yemen, soon perhaps Iraq. I still recall the clamor of the crowds gathered in Abdin Square when Nasser proclaimed the union. Twelve years later Libyan policy, born of oil messianism, arouses the same metonymical enthusiasms, still as devoid of preparatory study. Why Libya and Syria, or even Tunisia, and not the Sudan? Mystery, accident, or rather maneuver! Will union among countries, and its dissolution, forever be the jurisdiction of enthusiasm or conspiracy, rather than of objectivity? Let us in any case note that the long-standing inability of the concert of Arab nations to settle the Palestine problem is always blamed upon defection by men or governments rather than on one simple fact: the gap between cultural and moral solidarity and a practical commitment located on the plane of diplomacy, politics, and war. Hence many defeats. The most dangerous thing would certainly be to ignore the cause of these defeats, which is the taking of one of the various levels and categories of praxis for another.

Nevertheless, although the Arab world has long been cut up into autonomous countries, and while a quarter-century of independence has further accentuated the division, we would not assert with its adversaries that "Arab world" boils down to a semantic choice of terms. Its utopia of unity may, can, and must be realized, but this will require an end to confusion among levels and categories. For the moment, the political and cultural fields overflow onto one another. Taken individually, the nations correspond to subcultures to a lesser degree than they group themselves; taken together, into a sociological whole. To the disharmonies resulting from the approach to modernity are thus added other discords: those stemming from the Arabs' failure to follow either their unity or their division through to the end. The principal source of their weaknesses may be their timidity!

What is unitary, and what is multiple, in the Arab world?[3] That is a problem which should engage, for example, the Directorate of Education and Culture recently established in the Arab League Secretariat. One of its recent colloquia explored the cleavages apparent among Arab countries not only in the field of social and political life, which was to be expected, but also in the heterogeneity or, one might say, the absence of a complementary quality in the cultural effort itself. Many examples were adduced and deplored: particularism in national broadcasting, frontiers obstructing the movement of cultural works and even the exchange of books, rivalry among governments forcing intellectuals into conflicting orientations, and so on. Setbacks for continuity; setbacks for the unity of that which is pre-eminently one and continuous. But what was the remedy? Would the very faith of the participants in the congress, who were, so to speak, professional unionists, not merely palliate the lack of a positive quest? That, at least, was what one of them was to ask: the publisher of the Tunisian magazine *Al-Fikr*. A sociologist, on the other hand, might have been surprised that, as the Arab unity movement had adopted the term *qawmiya* to refer to itself, it was a restrictive and even pejorative term, *maḥalliya*, or "localism," which was used to designate national personalities which were in fact the objective components of a differentiated Arab culture. Doubtless, the intermediate term for "country," *quṭr*, had been avoided because of its Ba'thist overtones. Nevertheless, with what jealous energy the countries themselves, modestly absent from the gathering, rose up in anger!

As long as the problem is approached in this way, efforts at education and cultural promotion expended in one or another of these countries, which are at once diverse and solidary, will not bring either diversity or solidarity into operation in concrete instances. The sociological contexts in which culture expresses itself in the manner, at once unanimous and differential, which I have stated will never be regarded as anything but a stage of decadence and injustice which the choices of renewal ought to abolish by decree. To the same degree the unity of heritage and hope, no matter how heavily laden with potentialities, will permit itself to be undermined by realities considered secondary but increasingly potent because they are avoided. To the historical misfortune (which is also a privilege) for the Arabs consisting in their being so near, and yet so far away, with respect to Europe must thus be added the further misfortune that they so resemble, and differ from, each other to such an extent, and that they can put their similarities and differences alternately to such a use. . . .

Multilingualism: Obstacle or Auxiliary?

But here is a new observation, embarrassing for the foreigner and scandalous for the citizen. Many Arab works these days use languages other than Arabic.

If it were primarily a question of works of an academic nature, that proving ground to which so many young Easterners afflicted with diploma fever are subjected, that would only be expected. As long as custom—and even more than custom: a utility felt by all—forces so many youths to attain a doctoral degree abroad, it is natural that a significant number of their theses should be written in foreign languages. If many Arabs make their careers abroad,[4] they will produce their works in those languages, as witnessed by Phillip Hitti's *History of the Arabs*, retranslated long afterward into Arabic. Even though university education in Egypt is more than fifty years old, and despite the expansion of schools and the Arabization policies which have kept pace with the radicalizing of independence movements, the use across the board of Arabic as the language of instruction in these countries themselves has by no means become the rule.[5]

But all this, which is simply a legacy of imperialism, could be converted into anticipations of a world-wide future. Depersonalization is not linked to the intimate use of foreign languages, but to the conditions in which it operates. It is fortunate for the Arabs that a Georges Henein, a René Habachi, a Samir Amin write, or wrote, their literary, philosophical, or economic essays in what we would call a highly competitive French. Others do the same in English, Portuguese, Spanish. Who among Westerners can boast of the converse?[6] But this mastery becomes pernicious as soon as it sets person and group apart according to differing ranges of expression. Algerian writers, especially Malek Ḥaddād, have made a literary theme of this alienation, which is one way of exorcizing it. Daily life is not so lucky. It hesitates, deteriorates, or shatters. This confronts Arab educators with a hard problem which involves the most dramatic of choices. For collusion among languages only demonstrates, while aggravating, the cleavage among environments, classes, and even psychic strata affected by it. Any national endeavor, and even the universal Arab endeavor, surely depends on how this fragmentation can be reduced.

A controversy among various educators arose recently in the Beirut press over the total Arabization of instruction.[7] Regrettably, it seems that this problem is always addressed at the level of political expediency or even propaganda, instead of that of culture and education. For Saʿīd Bustānī, what should be taught is not foreign languages as a tool, but foreign cultures. That view presupposes a certain reservation, at least tentative, with respect to contemporary Arab culture. Is it capable, in and by itself, of founding an up-to-date system of education? If so, let it suffice to study foreign languages as an ancillary means, as is already declared in the curricula. Otherwise, in addition to the national culture one must acquire a foreign culture, as profoundly as possible, which means beginning in the elementary grades. But will it remain simply an auxiliary if acquired in this way? As a matter of fact, there is in the Arab world a disjunction between a unitary culture (sometimes only a potential one, but one which is in process of formation), that is, Arab culture, and, on the other hand, a sociological reality to which the foreign still clings in many different ways.

It is only too true. For many Arabs, to be cultivated means to be cultivated in a European language. At least, this is the case in the field of the exact sciences, economics, and, paradoxically, Islamics. Let us furthermore point out another current: that of political thought, particularly of the avant-garde, influenced by broadly global disseminations, which often chooses a foreign language, if not to express itself, at least to inform itself and to think. In some respects these intrusions, which admittedly have some positive effect, are a part of the set of stimuli received by the Arabs from an external world which preceded them in the path of history. The parlance of the exact sciences, as well as that in which the social problems born of industrialization, imperialism, and decolonization are defined, naturally follows its planet-wide reality. That is by no means shocking, to the extent that a new alienation does not result. Who can deny, however, that this is still often the case? A polemical literature justly denounces evil. It would do so more convincingly if it used the national language more readily, rather than the languages that have usurped its place.

Depersonalization, certainly, is related more to the stirrings of reality than to the latter's linguistic vesture. Conversely, there can be no Arabization of speech without modernization of society, mores, and concepts. It is because this has not been understood and, worse, because Arabization has been treated as sentimental revolt or as a political process without being scientifically conditioned that so many ambitions are defeated. Here and there it has been thought that supposed reforms could restore the Arabness of expression while leaving aside the conquest (or reconquest?) of a civilization. But restoring the creativity of Arabs in Arabic is the real problem, and it arises in terms not of languages as "vehicles" but of true intimacy with the world's motion. If this condition came about, Arabization of the language would then accompany quite faithfully the modernization of Arab societies. Let us recognize, however, that this condition is an essential factor. It is not surprising that so many cultural actions are based on the assumption that language takes precedence over other social phenomena. The latter impose their dynamism in the direction of a cosmopolitan progress which it is thus necessary to balance and compensate for through insistence on language. Hence the role which devolves upon literature. If we further add the word's symbolic values, its links with political oratory, along with the training of the individual and the masses, we shall be less hasty in dismissing certain insistences on language as vain. But how can such delicate relationships be placed in equilibrium? The respective weights of thing and sign, of fact and value, can be measured only analytically, in each particular case. Ambition on the part of responsible officials should not permit them to rely on long-term interactions between the form and the content of their society. Both today demand, in a context of urgent reality, the least improvised of measures, prepared by mature study.[8]

Short of, or beyond, those particular fields where the pedagogue can operate on the distinction between form and content—where, that is, verbal material is in itself form/content, to wit, in everything touching letters and the arts—the problem becomes poignant. Without wishing to raise the matter too indiscreetly, let us say that it is not normal that an avant-garde in Arabic literature, including poetry, should express itself in someone else's language. When this happens, has not a sort of internal expatriation taken place? Only too true. One of the founders of contemporary Arabic poetry, Jubrān, wrote his most significant works in English. Only quite recently was *The Prophet* restored to Arabic.[9] Meanwhile, another great Lebanese poet, Georges Schéhadé, had written in French his *Monsieur Bobble*, a poem of exile which, unbeknownst to the author (as I verified in conversation with him), when placed beside the work of

Jubrān, formed a diptych. By dozens, from Nadia Tuéni to Salah Stétié, without mentioning the North Africans, who are the most heart-rending, there flames in the language of Rimbaud a poetry and a novelistic fiction which will long be without a counterpart in the language of their native land. Whatever the value of Najīb Maḥfūẓ' *Miramar*, the really great Alexandrine novels will long remain those of Durrell and Tsirkas. And what is to be said of Kavafys' poetry! . . . On the other hand, and no less paradoxically, it was only on the eve of North African independence that literature in French, by Algerian pens, burst out in a flowering of the novel, poetry, and theater. The success of Kateb Yasin and many others nevertheless confronted the rediscovered nation with a problem of conscience and a doubt as to the future. To different degrees, and *mutatis mutandis*, that is the case with *Soleil arachnide* and *Mémoire tatouée*, recent and remarkable Moroccan works.

But is this only a feature of dispossession and depersonalization as Jean Amrouche, that son of a double truth, said in unforgettable words? Or, on the contrary, a feature of appropriation and even reconquest, as Kateb Yāsīn implied? Should the North African intellectual, and the Arab intellectual in general, base his struggle so squarely on assimilating (which is also being assimilated by) the language of another? [10]

"—But what if, in any extended composition, *I were necessarily someone else*? What if, in such texts, the 'literary' quality or the poetry went so far as to break any ordinary communicating link? Perhaps, in their case, it is a question of a language not derived from everyday speech, nor borrowed, but coming from nowhere—I mean, coming from itself. . . ."

"But you are taking the exception for the rule! . . ."

"But suppose that the exception were essentially more meaningful than the general; if the exceptional and anomalous were, in some circumstances, the most truly laden with collective values? . . ."

The dialog could be extended. Let us not pursue it. Many arguments on both sides cross swords, and many are plausible. Some decision must be made, and that is what this book will do by studying, under the heading of contemporary Arab culture, only works in the Arabic language. This excludes many other works, some of great significance. But principle should and must be preserved. To repeat, unless very serious cleavages are to occur, which would prolong or even aggravate the conditions of colonial times, the language of

Arab creativity must again become that of the Arab peoples, that is, Arabic, even if the masses use it only in corrupted and fragmented forms. This re-establishment of the "authenticity," *aṣāla*, of utterances, of persons, of things, even of landscapes, is worth the most costly efforts.

Global Culture and Subcultures

The acknowledgment just made is radical. But it is a conditional acknowledgment. For, we shall say with the same brutality, restoration of Arabic involves as many duties incumbent upon it as rights restored.

In the name of that very authenticity which pleads for the national language and thus for a truly Arab culture, the subcultures within it must be respected.[11] I am speaking not only of those of minorities like the Berbers, Kurds, and others, but also the use of international languages, such as English, French, tomorrow perhaps Russian or—who knows?—Chinese. If the problem stirs up so much passion it is because it is treated as a function of the past, not the future. The national entity, recovered at great cost, fears divisions in which it sees merely the legacy of archaism (dialects) or of dependence (foreign languages). All becomes different when it is a question not of these old cleavages, which can be dealt with through national unity, but of differentiations through which unity will assert its primacy.

Any bilingual program in these countries arouses objections which are legitimate insofar as it is a question of the sort of linguistic collusions, the fruit of inequality and chance, which have made the speech of so many North Africans and Levantines so sadly picturesque. In several of these countries colonization might soon have led to the degradation of the national language into dialect, and the medium of practical communication into pidgin talk. The displacement of a few works of art into the French idiom would have been merely the specious recompense for a terrible loss. But the situation would change if a scientific education put into operation a bilingualism *at different levels* according to the stages of the child's development. That would combine, instead of contaminating or degrading the personality. It would reserve the deepest levels for Arabic: the nourishing return to fundamentals; the guarantees of identity; the dialectic, never complete, between nature and culture, between raw material and the finished product. Foreign languages would be lodged in precisely circumscribed functions. Thereby would be constructed, among the Arabs and on their own initiative, a linguistic pluralism which would soon, in our opinion, impose itself upon the West. This would have the additional advantage that the contrast between the two language systems, Semitic and Indo-European, would permit the richest of combinations of the sort that resulted, in the past, in the prose of Ibn Muqaffaʿ, or Bīrūnī's synthesis.[12]

Let us follow the hypothesis through to the end. A future national culture will be national only to the degree that it husbands its subcultures. The current rather general, and perfectly justified, condemnation of cultural centralism in a country like France surely provides us a model not to be copied. The Soviet example seems more positive in this respect, and one can only applaud the applications of it which have recently been sketched out in a country like Iraq with respect to Kurdish, Turkman, Syriac, and other such cultures. Will this be the case in the Sudan, the Maghreb, and Mauretania? One would like to think so. In any case, independence, with the perspectives it opens up for collective endeavor, is able, we feel, to resolve these two symmetrical problems raised for it in the Arab countries: the presence of popular cultures, Arab or non-Arab, and the pressure of acculturation to the West. For this it is necessary and sufficient that the primacy of the national culture be established, pedagogically and socially, and placed in operation. Then its unity would be reinforced by a differentiation of level and of situation which imperialism usurped and distorted until quite recently, to the point of making it a detonator for social explosions.

Things have budged a little between the two eras. The Arab world would do well to resume study of problems now on dead center, such as that of dialects, in the light of its new capabilities. It is all too evident that its study remains too often faithful to backward-looking arguments, which see in the vernacular languages only the raw material for reactionary plots. But what was once true may no longer be, and today analysis must take into consideration the links between these languages and the foundation, daily life, and democracy. This consideration is incumbent upon any policy attached to popular ideals, or to harmony with fundamentals. Of course, the interest taken over the past ten years in musical and poetic folklore does honor to several prominent practitioners in the field, such as Sarwat Okasha in Egypt. But one must also observe the dislocation between this high-minded realism and the stereotypes that still color discussion of the status of languages. In several of these countries there is indeed at least an apparent contradiction that contrasts the declared socialism of goals and the selective, inevitably minoritarian, aspect of linguistic choices, inasmuch as these latter support the practice of grammarians against the speech of the masses. The gap between the two may well be reduced through the influence of mass communications; but it would be illusory to expect from usage and habituation a genuine regulation, which presupposes prior analysis and strategic choice. One thing at any rate is certain: Arabization must not mean the degradation and impoverishment of models, or a limitation of potentialities at the foundation for the sake of conformity, censure, or austerity. Otherwise, the creative impulse would seek its outlets in rupture with the group, at least as the latter is interpreted by the men, parties, and trends in power.

Reigning Culture and the Culture to Come

But how is this right to create to be reconciled with its sociological links—its duties, as some would say? It has no long-term value except for and through the collectivity from which it arises and to which it will return in the end. But how soon, and at what level? That is the crucial thing. Here we encounter a very lively quarrel: that which is over the creative man's obligation, his *iltizām*. The problem has arisen in specific terms since Nasser's revolution. But who knows whether its chroniclers have phrased it correctly or whether, even in its passion and sincerity, it has not been a victim of what I shall call the devastations of linguistic analogy.

I agree that all art is language. All art must consequently, sooner or later, communicate: that is, produce collective effects and thus enter into the activating dynamisms of people and era. But communication of what, and how? The arts, including those of the word, literature as such and especially poetry, leave aside in whole or in part the denotative function of discourse. Their "meaning" rests not at all in a message offered to practical life, but rather in *sui generis* effects varying according to the genre in question. Language, in a work of art, serves not simply to communicate but to evoke. The work, precisely because it is a work, may gain in lasting potential what it loses in facility of communication. Almost always, in order to function truly, it presupposes a certain distance, an iteration, or a gap in time. Painting and sculpture can be appreciated only from a distance. A symphony, or even a melody, reveals its design only with repetition. A poem must be present in memory before it can arouse feelings. Much of culture is remembering. This break with the instantaneous implies different processes from those of informing. It places in relief the special nature of the artistic purpose, which is not to say something but to be "worth" something profound and lasting.

Now in Nasser's Egypt the thesis of socialist realism called upon the artist to make a specific contribution to the era's battles. To do this, the message had to touch the masses and support outspokenly some government program; otherwise it fell into the hell of art for art's sake or into bourgeois formalism. Alas! Today, with hindsight, one can pronounce a rather severe judgment on many products of *iltizām*. It is no disparagement of the importance of a work like that of Sharqāwī, who had the merit to publish one of the first real Arab novels (and what a powerful one, *Al-Arḍ*!), to admit that the great mass of supposedly realistic publications which flooded the East's bookstores over nearly a generation almost never attained the level of art. The apostles of obligation or socialist realism failed to understand that the artist has his own means of action and that, to serve history, he must use his own means rather than adopting those of the regime. Furthermore, the sphere in which creative activity takes place is not that of ideology, even less of propaganda. It is therefore improper to expect from artistic expression an impact on daily events. It is a long-term process because it operates at the deeper levels.

Traditional Muslim culture, in spite of all the obstacles impeding access to it—a language which must be learned before initiation, long apprenticeship given over to mnemonic techniques, obsessive reference to the distant past—remained popular, in the sense that the people professed it and identified with it. Is this true of the culture in search of itself today, even though it calls itself socialist? There are the same apprenticeship difficulties, or even more onerous ones because the factual content has increased and its manipulation has become more complicated; to these is added a further difficulty: it has constantly to prove itself legitimate. For, implying the use of foreign models in large part, it has an initial suspicion to overcome. Even aroused by unanimous enthusiasm and appropriately conditioned by the mass media, the masses do not recognize it as truly their own. One does not truly receive something without participating in it. Thus one should deplore a dangerous disparity in level between the peaks the Arabs thrust up, in one sector or another, and the surrounding flat terrain. What is true of technology is true, *mutatis mutandis,* of art and literature, notwithstanding the substantial changes that have rushed in during the past fifteen years or so.

By an ironical paradox, the literary and artistic avant-garde is thus prey to the same reservations as the political programs that seek public support. Whether one wishes it or not, the Arab masses, while sometimes illiterate or, more generally, undereducated, are, to repeat, profoundly cultivated. This subconscious heritage in which village civilization and desert civilization, Koranic heritage and poetic heritage, are intermingled is not unimportant. From there, one day, the real renewals will rise, questioningly.

It is not an inductive path that cultural effort has followed since the Nahḍa. One may ask whether even today, however insistently it professes democracy, it is not following the deductive path. Most often, models borrowed from Western societies, overcompensated by tradition and resentment, are imposed by virtue of a leadership which, though no longer generally that of religious law, remains equally dogmatic. By various processes, and with differing audiences, the political speech, academic course, press, and radio program all continue to lay down their criteria, all finally stemming from a studied compromise between classical and modern, native and imported, developed form and everyday speech: "third language," as Tawfīq al-Ḥakīm said only too well. And "language" here may designate not only the idiom but also the associations for which it serves as vehicle.

Now it is not certain that this "thirdness" gives all the answers. Resting on amalgam and interaction, it contradicts the aspiration toward the foundation which is one of the surest strengths of these societies. Operating on conventional assumptions that are not examined critically, whether inherited or imported, it is partly responsible for certain harmful misunderstandings: insufficient analysis of the dialog between unitary and multiple, confusion among different levels, reluctance to accept the minoritarian and marginal. That is why a fissure persists between the cultural activist and the crowd. That is why the necessary resort to fundamentals ends up so often in the vulgarities of populism.

Of course, now it is the masses that produce *muthaqqafīn* and *dakātira,*[13] and in large batches. Their recruitment is no longer fixed, as it was until recently, to a narrow social category. If not the lowest social strata, at least the members of the petite bourgeoisie and middle peasantry have for quite some time had access to all the academic degrees and all government offices. Many names come to mind to speak for the reality of democratization. That is incontrovertibly progress. Indeed, we do not criticize the origin of these representatives, but rather the cleavage between their message and what would be a release of fundamental potentials. What fundamentals?[14] In this particular case it is not a socioeconomic definition that will be proposed. In the cultural field we shall consider that the fundamentals include, along with these social depths, the unalloyed verity of the soil, the integrity of the linguistic system, the store of authentic resources in the national heritage, and the radical renewals involved in participating in the world's forward movement. Now these fundamentals are seldom drawn upon in cultural expression, and this relative disdain must be seen as related to the difficulties of forming a genuine elite. In short, two symmetrical deficiencies.

I admit that hardly a generation ago cultural activity recruited, all too jealously, among ethnic, confessional, even ideological minorities. That is so no longer, and so much the better! But the resulting vacuum is taking a long time to fill. Shortly after Nasser's revolution the cultural affairs counselor of the French Embassy noted sadly that, for the first time in Egypt's history, the minister of national education did not speak our language. This was Major Kamāl al-Dīn Ḥusain, whose English, moreover, was not above the Military Academy level. At the time, this vengeful ignorance was perhaps looked upon as a provocation. Some, at least, asserted that it was the revenge of a long-humiliated language over the languages of imperialism. But there is nothing to indicate that Major Kamāl was cultured in the classical, nor that he aspired to be the champion of a vernacular culture. After twenty years one may ask whether Egypt gained more than it lost by jettisoning the accumulated gains of three generations, and whether it has progressed thereby in Arabic and liberated its lost languages.[15]

The foregoing observations may seem pessimistic: decline of foreign languages and cultures, probably also of Arab classicism; spread of an intermediate culture; retreat of the *nukhba* or *khāṣṣa* categories,[16] to use words less compromised than "elite." Simultaneously, the pressure of bureaucracy, the pervasive banality, the temptation of mediocrity—all doubtless correspond to the rise of the petite bourgeoisie. A decay, certainly, which one hopes is transitory.

The largely inevitable contingencies of education and cultural policy in some of these countries obscure three considerations whose importance cannot be exaggerated: (*a*) democratization of education does not presuppose mediocre models; otherwise, standards would decline proportionally to the expansion; (*b*) the necessary homogenization in the cultural field need not require either uniformity or an abusive leveling; otherwise the inborn respect for culture among these peoples would be fixed upon false elites of diploma holders and bureaucrats, or else be transferred abroad; (*c*) any cultural renewal depends upon a criticism and a creativity which are equally radical; but radicalism is precisely what the so-called Nahḍa has lacked the most for nearly a century. Question: have the recent revolutions, despite appearances, shown themselves more radical? . . .

The Right to Differ

A contemporary Arab culture must define itself by reference to a modern-day world-wide culture. It must, therefore, in the first place demand from all its right to differ.[17] In many respects, what is currently called *qawmiya* merely expresses, under the often-extremist manifestations of nationalism, this demand which converges with numerous other premises of liberty common to all men of our time.

However, in order for such a claim to be admissible, any culture must consent internally to the same differential relationships it demands with respect to the outside. With regard to the Arabs, we have considered one after another the relationships between overall identity and national or regional identities; between the dominant system and subsystems; between elite and mass; between the reigning culture and its repressed potentialities; between the actualization of the language and its paradigm. Now these relationships, scrambled and distended by history, particularly its colonial phase, are hard to organize into a whole which they could articulate without fracturing. That is one, and not the least, of these societies' current problems. Although it confronts all others as well, in varying terms and degrees of gravity, the Arabs can neither minimize it nor expect it to be resolved by chance or by facile remedies.

The right to differ governs reciprocal relations not only among groups or collective phenomena, but also among individuals and groups, and theirs with society. A vain demand for liberalism? No! Liberalism, in the historical sense, proved itself only too well among the colonial peoples at the time when foreign and class domination triumphed to the point of sparing the ruler the outward signs of constraint: the Victorian age, the triumphs of the Third Republic! Then imperialism enforced itself less through tensions than through a general demobilization and enfeeblement. Upon the reconquest of independence, the requirements of reconstruction brought hardships sometimes unknown to the colonial classicism. People must accept them, in our opinion, or else conceal them by immobilism and deculturation, which is at times unfortunately the case: censorship of all free expression; restrictions imposed on any minority culture and on international interchange; commitment permitted only in the officially established direction; corruption, imprisonment, or exile of intellectuals—these too frequent vicissitudes do not reflect revolutionary violence. They deflect it. They usurp the energies of decolonization. In fact they conceal the exhaustion of social dynamism. This is neither the time nor the place to undertake, in this connection, a critical examination of individual situations. Such an examination is for the citizens themselves to undertake. We shall simply emphasize how closely it is related to the cultural act.

This relationship does not reside solely in a guarantee of that theoretical availability of choice upon which bourgeois democracy insists, but more concretely in that it destabilizes situations and thus permits that exchange and conversion among social categories which can be seen to be the precondition of all collective endeavor. The argument is thus not between liberty of expression on one side, in the sense the imperialist countries gave the word and applied to some extent even in their countries, and tyranny on the other side, but instead between inert discords and mobilizing tensions.

IV
Apprenticeships, but to What?

Let us return to that square in an Eastern city where I tried to glimpse the rise of a history and a word. It is the hour of youth. A crowd of rather thick-set adolescents in dark blue uniforms is making merry on the sidewalk. There are numerous educational establishments in the vicinity: the old Mubtadayān still laden with Khedivial memories, the French Lycée nationalized as the Ḥurriya Lycée, the American University, the Mère de Dieu Convent, and many others. In all of them the national language is regaining its rights, which is good, but at the expense of European languages, which is not so good. Never mind. Let us salute this magnificent enthusiasm. Let us be unreservedly glad of the insistence in all these countries on the task of education.

Here education does not consist simply of creating a transmission belt and passing on creativity or its preconditions, as should be the case in industrial societies. It is also the grafting of the world's changes onto the burgeoning stalk of life. Several government departments take this as their task. One, two, or even three of them have responsibility for the education of youth. Certain agencies are responsible for adult education and literacy campaigns. A Ministry of Culture tries to reach the entire diversified body of citizens of all ages through various approaches, including, notably, tours of the villages. Of course, mass communications, which here is the Ministry of Information's function, the spontaneous dynamism which National Orientation is trying to instill, and yet other efforts are all coalesced (or should be) in a single global effort which might be defined thus: to catch up with history, to create equal opportunity, and to organize collectively the encounter between modernity, even though it be borrowed from outside, and the most spontaneous element of a common becoming.

An enormous task at which few succeed, as might be expected. The definition I have given of it is obviously more comprehensive than the one the dozens of official agencies, individually, apply to themselves. Even so, I committed a sin of omission by leaving out that global educator which reforms while deforming: the industrial transformation of the world, its power to train these old-young peoples, and their determination to make it their own.

And all this, last but not least, among the perplexities of collective action, its forward leaps and setbacks, its vast stirrings and occasional heroic flashes, its endless gropings and publicly proclaimed certitudes—among the vicissitudes, in short, of politics.

Educators and Education

To repeat: to repair the deficiencies and solve the problems, the governments, responding to an explicit and nearly unanimous demand, are giving first priority to education as the solution.

Education is not simply the transmittal of what has been learned, and the methods by which it can be reacquired and rounded out. It is also the ratification of the acquired learning, in that it seeks to inscribe its partial dynamic upon the national dynamic, with the reciprocal effects which should ensue. It thus promises to reduce, over time, the disequilibria caused by the intrusion of foreign techniques, and the moral, social, and political problems which have resulted. Thirdly, education does not boil down to an exchange, at best, between youth and adults. Its mediating role goes further. In truth, it offers society one of its few opportunities to internalize collective mutation and, conversely, to project the individual's values onto the field of collective consciousness and action. It thus takes on increasing importance in this last third of the twentieth century throughout the world but especially in those countries which must, so to speak, reinvent themselves rather than simply collecting their own legacy.

The magnitude of the role and the privilege it should bring naturally encounter many obstacles. We may ignore those raised by conservatism; while still to be feared, they have long since been overrun. Today, the most dangerous obstacles stem from the feeble analysis made of these problems, and even more from the inadequate responsibility undertaken by the ruling groups to deal with them. Too often, that misunderstanding still rules whereby the *ne plus ultra* of education is to treat the children, or the adolescents, as small replicas of the adult, the ideal being to transform them into adults—which amounts to rejecting them as they are so as to make them conform to what their parents would like to be, or think they are. Events present in everyone's memory have exposed the absurdity of such a view. The child, the adolescent, and the youth as such participate in facts and values which cannot, without mutilation, be reduced to those of the adult. As society strives to reduce them, or "retrieve" them as is sometimes said, conflicts erupt between their anthropology, which is to say tomorrow's society, and today's "realities," which in fact are yesterday's. This sort of conflict can be observed in Arab countries as well as elsewhere. But here it is more virulent because between adults and the present youth who are tomorrow's society there is not simply a gap or a conflict but a qualitative leap.

If such is the role of education, how could it devolve only upon the teaching function? Everywhere, as a matter of fact, but especially in the developing countries, a diffuse education is the order of the day. It comes from many other sources, passing through many other channels, than the school and university. To speak only of the Arab lands, for example, how can we discount the millenary message of religious belief and practice? At least potentially, the culture of the mosque and the Koran still dominates the foundations of individual and collective psychology. Furthermore, and without any intention of introducing into this sort of enumeration the least-presumptuous judgment or even a classification, Arab societies are becoming urbanized like all the world's societies, to the point where modernization is becoming generally synonymous with urbanization. Perhaps the reader will have been convinced of this by the descriptions of crowds at the beginning of this book. We pointed out, in this connection, that the village or factory might also have furnished us examples of a culture in the making. It is unnecessary, also, to insist further on the mass media cultures, those of the press, broadcasting, the transistor: this is an international commonplace.

The school is thus responsible for only part of the tasks. Now for the time being it is the school which, at the Arab world level and that of the world generally, crystallizes the attention of militants and elicits the most-passionate judgments. But having defined its responsibilities by giving them limits, let us be careful not to neglect its symbolic values. One cannot write the history of the last century and a half in France without celebrating the values of the primary school. The same applies to the Arab world during the past fifty years, and God knows what values are imagined and derived by the modest artisan of compulsory, or *ilzāmī*, education. There is a whole ethic of the *ilzāmī*, that grade school teacher whom the peasants in Egypt call, colloquially, the *zāmī*.

Perhaps even more than the primary school symbol, at any rate at the upper social levels, the university symbol imposes itself. This stems from a historical tradition or turning point which has perhaps been a great misfortune and has in any case been the source of difficult problems: the fact that, in many respects, this Arab world began its modernization not at the base but at the top. Indeed, it was with teachers' colleges, military academies, and engineering schools that Muḥammad ʿAlī began the development of education in Egypt. It is on the university, or at least on its rudiments organized in Cairo before the First World War, and above all on the foreign university, that many members of the generation which still occupies, if not the center of the stage at least the upper ranks of Arab culture, have founded their glory. I am thinking, for example, of the overwhelming account by a man like Ṭaha Ḥusain of his first rediscovery (I was about to say "encounter") of the modern university. Rediscovery, because that was perhaps one way for the Arab world to find its place again in the advancing procession of civilization from which it had long since dropped out.

A Biographical Conducting Wire

Doubtless, indeed, the best way to grasp these problems in the human context is to examine how an Arab writer of central importance lived and reflected on almost all of them: Ṭaha Ḥusain,[1] who has just passed away. One cannot understand the Arab world without in some way referring to one who was beyond doubt its intellectual pioneer and remains its classic. In any event, the most pathetic representative of the battles fought to renew a civilization. Did the blind young Upper Egyptian disappointed with al-Azhar really feel, as he said he did, that unfailing enthusiasm and wholehearted commitment from the first lessons he heard at the National University sponsored by Prince Fuʾād? Was he already as he was later to be, and so many Arabs with him? Did he adopt without question the motivating factor in those courses in literary history: a rationality different both from that of the golden-age commentators and from that of the canonical reformers? He would be so much more convincing, and doubtless more truthful, if he told us of hesitations, of incipient strayings from the straight path, which must have occurred in his career just as they did in others'. . . . When we read his memoirs we thus receive, after the event, the future of a thought in process of formation, probably purged of the uncertainty it must have had in its early stages and thus of a part, precisely, of its historical significance. . . .

That is what I wonder when I look at that yellowed photo of 1906 taken on the front steps of the University.[2] Ṭaha Ḥusain, in al-Azhar robes, is standing in the second row. His face, at once reserved and ardent, is turned to one side of the camera lens. He is not yet concealing his blindness with dark glasses. His nose is prominent, his mouth uneasy, his hair abundant and ill-tamed, his forehead regular. There he is before us, the young man who retraced his apprenticeship in a sequel to *Al-Ayyām*.[3] He wrote the book in a style we know well, his own style, halfway between the most-impeccable classicism and modern-type expressivity. Such a reconciliation cannot be accomplished without effort, and if one must admire its musical success one notices also some rhetorical sins, notably that of redundancy.

"The young man's life in Paris was bittersweet, easy, and difficult. He found neither repose nor peace there, but felt a gladdening of the soul, a repose of the heart, a contentment, a pleasant awareness, which he had never before experienced, did not as yet know, and was never to forget. His material life was harsh, but be bore its harshness with courage, satisfaction, etc. . . ."—here follows a third paronym which French, less rich than Arabic, fails to translate. This two-way, even three-way, balancing recurs constantly and is not, in our opinion, only a matter of form. Any man of Ṭaha Ḥusain's generation, and educated as he was, lived as if in a hall of mirrors, with reflections of a tradition, an ethic, and a transcendence bouncing off him from all sides. The long sentence of Rāfiʿī carries, with a somber and magnificent archaism, that dialog with the unseen which many moderns already see as mere soliloquy. That of Ṭaha Ḥusain broke the giant mirror and reveals a new vision through the interstices of a fracture of which constant repetition, so to speak, puts the pieces back together. The prose of our Péguy did the same in a different way, but doubtless for the same reasons. . . .

The new *Memoirs* of Ṭaha Ḥusain provide a pathetic and intimate account of what the life of these young men before the First World War may have been. Of course, they did not utter the word *ḥirmān*—"frustration," "repression"—but they felt its pain. "The life of educated people at that time was a bizarre mixture of occasional hidden pleasures and of a moral suffering to which they subjected themselves as much as, or more than, life imposed it on them." Naturally hungry for happiness, but repressed by the environment, the student was a sufferer by definition. "He had chosen unhappiness for his companion, happiness for his dream."

The young man experienced a profound shock as soon as he began to attend the first Egyptian university. At the time it was located in a princely palace, the one, I am told, now occupied by the rectorate of ʿAin Shams University. Orientalists participated in establishing the earlier institution: Nallino, for example, and Littman. To Nallino is credited the first course in the history of Arab literature to be given in the East according to historical methods. Ṭaha Ḥusain, with all his fervor, attended, coming on foot (to save money) all the way from Gamāliya, where he lived with two others in one tiny room, living on provisions sent from his province: yes, even bread, the *qarāqish* his mother sent him and which he put in an earthen pot to dry. One may imagine the effect produced on this adolescent tenseness by the universe of scientific freedom adumbrated in the lectures of these foreign teachers.

After many efforts, the young man obtained a scholarship, for which he had to thank the Khedive. The latter was that unfortunate ʿAbbās Ḥilmī whom the British were soon to depose. The audience, described with bitter irony, placed two irreconcilable positions in confrontation. Upon learning that the student intended to go to France to study history and philosophy, the monarch said, "Not philosophy in any circumstances; that ruins people. . . ."

In France the scholarship student demonstrated the qualities for which he is known: a taste for general culture, an aptitude for learning anything at all, an appetite for reading which the present generation has not inherited. With a single hiatus he thus spent all the war years abroad, returning only after defending his thesis on Ibn Khaldūn. All went well, and better than well in that he found there his life-long companion. Here there are chapters of exquisite delicacy on the "sweet voice" thanks to which he came to know her who was to "become his eyes." Meanwhile, he was discovering Western, and particularly French, culture, which he did not distinguish from a Latinity or Mediterraneanism inherent, according to him, in the heart of the Arab message. Was this in fact Cartesianism? That is what he himself claimed. Had he joined the West, especially France? He has been accused of it, quite unjustly. He followed, over there, nothing but the deep necessities of his own being: the taste for life, the proselytization for reason to which his career bears witness and which the Arab world needed so badly.

Upon his return, clothed with a reputation on which he immediately capitalized (for this great intellectual was ambitious for power) in journalistic activity, he found Egypt in crisis. Here he is in conversation with Zaghlūl: "What are you studying?" "History." "Do you really believe in history?" Nevertheless, history was what

Zaghlūl was making at that very moment. Shall we allow Ṭaha Ḥusain to convince us that he gave Zaghlūl a lesson in optimism? We leave it to the chroniclers to follow our autobiographer's political meanderings, and to express to each other surprise that in the pre-Islamic poetry affair Zaghlūl did not place him under his protection. Whether Zaghlūl or Ṭaha Ḥusain, each applies his radicalism where he can and compromises elsewhere. Great men are great only at a distance, and we do not need Henri Guillemin's counternaïveties to teach us that.

The Above Continued and Challenged

Certain dates stick in everyone's memory. This man created a scandal in 1926 with a book in which he demythologized pre-Islamic poetry.[4] Not much survives of the book's subject matter, but the demythologizing spirit does survive, and that is a great deal. Three years later came *Al-Ayyām*. This biography of an Egyptian child won world-wide admiration through its French and English translations. In 1933 *ʿAlā Hāmish al-Sīra*, "On the margin of the Prophet's life," in which were combined a specialist's erudition, a genuine Islamic sensitivity, and a deep Western permeation, reached a wider local readership without exciting scandal. This is a book in which challenge to authority was made righteous. In 1949 a collection of tragic short stories, *Al-Muʿadhdhabūn fīl-Arḍ*, "The tormented on Earth," breathed the painful questioning of an Egypt disillusioned by independence, or rather by the use she was making of it: a foreshadow, though unrecognized, of the 1952 revolution.

It is true that in his introduction the author—ironically, in our opinion—branded himself a conservative. Certainly, he never played an active part in radical parties. He adhered to the Wafd—he was one of its ministers, and a great one—only as a government. It is nonetheless true that when he received some students just after World War II, at about the time a coalition was forming between students and labor—the magnificent preamble to a revolution yet to be carried out—he sharply reproached his guests for their lack of radicalism. Now among them was Maḥmūd Amīn al-ʿĀlim, who was soon to belabor him with the sort of attacks doctrinaires level at bourgeois liberals,[5] before being jailed by the military authorities. Nevertheless, on the seventy-fifth birthday of Ṭaha Ḥusain, by now the venerable dean, *ʿamīd*, of Arab letters, al-ʿĀlim devoted an article to him in which, passing blithely over many ambiguities, he no longer saw in him anything but a champion of practical reason, a determinist, a critic keenly interested in social conditionings.[6] Even in his style, he added, "the musical line and poetic vibrancy may be defined as the movement of reason and a summons to action. If we closely examine its rhythm, we find there now syllogistic deduction, now imitation, and in either case a creativity progressing toward the generalization of the scientific, literary, or historical phenomenon under study, so that it is mastered in all its aspects and is brought under that lens of practical reason which it trains not only on the phenomenon itself but also on the reader or listener." It could not be said better; but it would have been better to say it sooner.

One wonders whether the generation which has come to the front of the stage since World War II and is involved in the Nasserist revolution—whether conservatives, progressives, or liberals—has broadened the perspectives implicitly contained in the work and experience of its elders. I agree that it has found it more difficult to learn and to express itself, as Ghālī Shukrī has rather ingenuously confessed;[7] but that in itself, which it offers as excuse, changes nothing in the scale of values. Reading Zakī Najīb Maḥmūd today, one wonders whether the ideal of modernity in authenticity which, a third of a century ago, inspired Ṭaha Ḥusain, the dean of Arab letters, has not diminished, rather than increasing, its prospects of realization.

Balance Sheets and Perspectives in Education

We have drawn upon the biography of Ṭaha Ḥusain rather than those of ʿAqqād or Tawfīq al-Ḥakīm because its representative character led also to a warm and questioning work even before World War II: *Mustaqbal al-Thaqāfa fī Miṣr*, the "Future of culture in Egypt."[8] Three words forming a motto, each of which needs comment.

Mustaqbal, "future": this was in fact a projection into the future. *Thaqāfa*, and not *ḥaḍāra*: in Ṭara Ḥusain's mind it was still, it must be said, an elite culture, despite all the effort he expended as teacher, and later as minister, to disseminate it in his country. Finally, *fī Miṣr*: Egyptianism flows here at high tide; that is a characteristic of the author which he never lost. The book, written in 1938, was published in 1944. I will not repeat the principal points of his argument, which are well known: first a bitter attack against the dusty dogmatism of al-Azhar, whose failure to appreciate him Ṭaha Ḥusain never forgave. A no less harsh attack against verbalism. And against the diploma culture, responsible for all those mandarinates and bureaucracies which unfortunately ravage many of these societies. Finally, the profession of a Mediterranean faith. The author is one of those who do not dissociate Egyptianism from Western and, ultimately, Hellenic affinities. But is this not a retrospective utopia, the projecting into the past of a recent historical reality, namely, the role played by Mediterranean culture in the reawakening of modern Egypt? A role of which Ṭaha Ḥusain was one of the most-moving and, when all is said and done, most-effective interpreters. But there is some lack of proportion in speaking of Egypt's Mediterranean character while neglecting even to refer to what one might call its Asianism or Africanism. Dr. Jamāl Ḥamdān, in a much more recent work, considers Egypt multidimensional.[9] Quite right, since it bears within itself African, Asian, Mediterranean, and quite a few other legacies.

Besides, a collective personality consists less of its historical components than of the synthesis it is able to achieve among them, and even more of the always-unfinished relationship it adopts between its barest fundamentals and their most highly developed formulations. It is hardly debatable that, at least since Umayyad times, this relationship was felt and desired by the Arabs as an attachment to Hellenism; that many grandiose developments flowed from it in the fields of grammar, philosophy, and letters; and that since the Nahḍa the Arabs have continued, *volens nolens*, to press this relationship, in some cases to the point of identification. But our era knows that rationality is not exclusively classical, and that there are other classicisms than the Western. Our era, moreover, knows that the most dangerous bondages are those inherited, or accepted as the natural order of things. It is wary of the constraints which may be hidden behind a too-prestigious formal achievement. Such reconsiderations may one day turn upside down the Arabs' affinity horizons, as well as their own tradition.

These problems obviously did not arise at the time Ṭaha Ḥusain wrote his book. A generation later another book by an educator appeared which deserves to be compared with its predecessor: "The future of education in the Arab East,"[10] by Dean Jamīl Ṣalība. It is no accident that we meet the term *mustaqbal*, "future," again in the title. But it is henceforth less a question of culture, *thaqāfa*, than of pedagogy, *tarbiya*, and Egypt is urged to integrate with the Arab world as a whole. Ṣalība, it is true, wrote in a context of enthusiastic Arabism, in the years immediately following the nationalization of the Suez Canal. He is furthermore a Syrian, and his Arabism thus goes without saying. One of his virtues is precisely that he nevertheless does not give way to excessively facile enthusiasms.

Arab universities had certainly progressed in the meantime, propelled by a pleiad of militants: a Sāṭiʿ al-Ḥuṣrī, an Aḥmad Amīn, a Matta ʿAqrāwī, a Fuʾād Ṣarrūf, a Fuʾād Ephrem al-Bustānī. Ṣalība is perhaps only a great teacher like them, but he is surely that. His program reflects it: a very closely worked-out one which deals first with matters of principle, then of application, then branches out into problems of detail. Here, thus, is a chapter on primary education, then one on secondary, advanced, technical, and so on. Of most interest to us, naturally, are the principles he sets forth. One might say of this book, written at the apogee of Arab qawmiya *before it took a socializing direction in some of these countries, that its greatest concern was to establish a link—or, if you will, to resolve the antithesis—between Arabism and the rest of the world which was felt so poignantly at that time. But the term* qawmiya *is not all that aggressive! It is as "specificity," rather than as "nationalism," in fact, that we shall interpret it.*

Ṣalība has no trouble showing that no specificity in the world, whether that of the Athenians, the French of their great century, or the Elizabethan English, can be situated in isolation from the world at large, or make abstraction of features and ultimate concerns common to all humanity. Let us pause a moment—it is well worth our while—as he sketches a portrait of the Arabs. The things he finds most distinctive in describing the collective psychology are elements of the turāth, *that is, the classical legacy. Especially, these two extraordinary passages which I cannot resist the pleasure of quoting.*[11] *One is from Jāḥiẓ: "The Arabs have all gifts, but they content themselves with the off-hand and the improvised, as if that were sufficient inspiration. On the other hand, they are not diligent, or opinionated, caring little for propagating their thought or for seeking support for it." Yes, it is the theme of* fiṭra, *or innateness, we meet again here, with its good or bad consequences certainly applicable to today's scene. In the same vein, here is a passage from Shahrastānī on the nobility of empires. As a matter of fact, there was no ethnocentrism among the Arabs of the golden age, but rather an exceedingly lively taste in appreciating classical cultures other than their own. "There are four great nations: the Arab, the Persian, the Byzantine, and the Indian," four nations from the point of view of cultural proclivities, contrasting two against two. The*

Arabs and Indians are alike in one respect, that they tend to taqrīr khawāṣṣ al-ashyāʾ, *"determine the distinctive properties of things." The quest for these "natures," in the plural, led their alchemy to discoveries which impressed Marcelin Berthelot ten centuries later. But the sense of the* individuatio *among the Arabs is not limited to adopting one position or the other in the debate over universals; it impels them to search obstinately for their own essence. "Thus they are characterized by the impulse to base judgment on truths"—an essentialist, subjective, and predicative judgment rather than a relational, objective, and causal one—and also by their "reference to the sacred." Whereas the Byzantines and Persians resemble each other in the dominant inclination which leads them* ilā taqrīr ṭawābiʿ al-ashyāʾ, *"to determine the consequences of things," and to base thereon "qualitative and quantitative" judgments,* wa istiʿmāl al-umūr al-jismāniya, *"in putting material objects to use." In view of the precocity of such an analysis, how could one be surprised at the use a twentieth-century Arab thinker can contemplate for his cultural heritage?*

In short, Jamīl Ṣalība advocates a reconciliation between the specific and the global in the interest of restoring an *aṣāla*. *Aṣāla* here is the quest of personality in avenues excluding both imitation of the foreign and its xenophobic rejection. Writing in the early stages of decolonization, Ṣalība had the merit of not encouraging certain excesses and self-conceits. In his eyes, the Arabs' individuality assumed their membership in the world. More recently, in his estimable *Philosophic Dictionary,*[12] we encounter again that concern to appropriate the definition of concepts into Arab reality without the loss of their rigorous universalism.

Birth of an Institute of Social Sciences

It was at Beirut, around 1960. The UNESCO expert's job was to study the possibility of instruction in social sciences at the Lebanese University. The city then had, and has, three or four other universities. The American University had, in the field of political science and economics, won as many pedagogical laurels as that of the Jesuits in Islamics and literature. The former consequently felt the more directly threatened by the competition the project might generate. The expert naturally tried to avoid any pretext for rivalry. He even worked to persuade the Lebanese authorities to introduce a licentiate degree in sociology for which the equivalence of certain credits from the various other universities in the city would be recognized. Having made this concession to the cultural federalism he found reigning, as it still does, he concentrated his efforts on what was, for him, the essential thing: the creation at the Lebanese University of a center for teaching and research on Eastern societies. Sociology was then rather new in the East, and the novelty of the proposal was resented here and there more as a threat to established bailiwicks than as a stimulus to work.

In the meantime, the director of the department the expert served in arrived. Both went to pay a courtesy visit on the prime minister. The latter's first words expressed his full support for the UNESCO enterprise. In private conversation with him, the case for the project had already been appropriately presented. Thereupon, the director, who was English, took umbrage, stammered, and for a few minutes there was a piquant scene in which a high international official raised objections against the project he himself had come to support. The institute was nevertheless created. It is operating today with some success.

I shall not mention the names of those involved in this anecdote, which is recounted here only to illustrate two sorts of difficulties: (*a*) those which any development activity in these countries faces if it seeks to preserve autonomy and specificity; and (*b*) the internal difficulties an international agency has to deal with.

Balance Sheets and Perspectives in Education (continued)

A third balance sheet dates from 1966.[13] It comes from an author younger than Ṣalība, and although only a few years elapsed between the two books they are very different. The first expressed a generalist and humanist thought, that of a philosopher rather than an educator. Dr. ʿAbd al-Dāʾim, also a Syrian, who was even minister of education once or twice in Damascus, is above all a technician. The Arabs, indeed, have received the message of a technique, even a technocracy, which goes further than the older generation perceived, and the American model has come to complement (I was about to say "perfect," which would be inapt, or "replace," which would be exaggerated) French humanism and British empiricism which, allied in various often paradoxical ways with socialism, used to mold modernist Arab intellectuals but today no longer do so alone.

This 750-page manual seeks to be exhaustive and normative. When he wrote, the author was teaching at the Institute for Education Planning at Beirut sponsored by UNESCO. He endeavors to express himself in a clear, even didactic, manner, not without slipping into occasional oversimplification. The danger in an approach like his is that of specialization, which is to say deradicalization. By that, I do not mean that he falls behind his predecessors politically—far from it. But perhaps he is less inclined to base his work on the fundamental principles governing all social development, whereas they, faithful to their humanist training, insisted above all on broad perspectives. His book is supported by vast bibliographies in Arabic, French, and English. International publications and recent statistics are given a prominent place. It is a well-organized work, perhaps a little too rigidly divided into pigeonhole categories, but nonetheless substantial and convincing.

After stating the principles of planning, the author examines resources and means, which he calls "factors." We may comment here that this is a much-used term which leads to mechanistic analogies no longer very well regarded in the human sciences field. It is nevertheless interesting to see what contributing "factors" he assigns to education planning. First, the demographic factor: indeed one of the most-urgent realities of this world. Then the energy factor. Third, economic factors. Fourth, another factor, incommensurate with the others, that of pedagogical knowledge. This purely intellectual element is, perhaps wrongly, isolated from its sociological implications and its theoretical foundations. Finally, the sociological factors, which interest us the most. Some are structural or cultural, and others are related to social class. But their description takes only sixty pages, less than one-twelfth of the book.

If the previously ventured definition is correct—that education is that which effects the entry of partial social dynamisms into a society's development by means of interdimensional homologations —the problem remains unsolved. ʿAbd al-Dāʾim nevertheless is keenly aware that education, and especially education planning, involves a total social phenomenon, but one so social and so total that one is at a loss in coming to grips with it. And the educational and research schemas he had access to could not help him in this respect. Once again education which, in our view, essentially proposes to serve as collective creativity can do so only through its determination to be itself a perpetual creation.

What one finds in his, and in most Arab, research is a proper feeling of the responsibilities of teaching: teaching of youth, adults, at a more sophisticated stage "functional" education, and even popular education. There is insistence on the role of motivating ideologies, usually called socialism—or more directly still *thawriya*, "revolutionism"—and on the imperatives which should flow from "obligation," *iltizām*, or from mass dynamics, *jamāhīriya*. Finally, with an almost obsessive intensity, the discussion turns to the relationships between dominant and other cultures, and thus between "authenticity," *aṣāla*, and universalism, "opening up," *tafattuḥ*, or "renewal," *tajaddud*. In an account like Dr. ʿAbd al-Dāʾim's, purporting to be both descriptive and analytical, can the incontestable relevance of these themes make up for lacunae in the systemic framework? Perhaps because these programs all react against an integrated and integrative traditional model, the one which operated until recently in the education at the Great Mosque, he has exaggerated the distributive function, forgetting that no combination of factors can get the upper hand of a total social phenomenon which, moreover, changes in content as it modifies its mode of expression and discovers its own meaning.[14]

V
New Fields of Meaning

Whence will emerge that meaning without which action remains impotent and progress illusory if not from that social whole it proposes to mobilize? Only totality can act upon totality. Any genuine molding or stimulus must take account of all that which renews the semantic domain in a society.

Arab militants have registered noticeable progress from this point of view since the last world war. Revolutions have taught them that there are false elites, beautiful things that lie, truths that are compromises. That a sound program must appeal to all. That national dignity, the feeling that one can manufacture objects and machines, even alterations in the landscape, are all elements of culture. And, finally, this discovery which sums up all the foregoing: that progress is total or else there is no progress. This last idea, quite new in the Arab world, is today among the most widespread. It is strengthened by its disappointments, as well as by its successes. Official actions are expressly designed to respond to it. In order to get an idea of this, one need only read government programs and reports, or leaf through various publications, often quite well produced in Kuwait under the patronage of wealth, or those magazines with such promising names: *Al-Thaqāfa* and *Al-Aṣāla* (Algiers), *Al-Maʿrifa* (Damascus), *Al-Fikr* (Tunis), *Al-Aqlām* and *Al-Mawrid* (Baghdad), *Al-Ādāb* (Beirut), *Al-Hilāl* and until recently *Al-Majalla* (Cairo). One need only observe the cultural ferment reigning everywhere: tours, stage and film productions, Ramadan festivities, group trips, and progress in construction of stadiums, conference halls, auditoriums. Social service, aesthetics, holidays, democracy, pedagogy (but also, of course, government and party propaganda) all collaborate in these enterprises which mobilize the event and transform space, human faces, and daily life.

At the same time, to all these cultural agents must be added something beyond the reach of the officials: technical evolution and the consequences, reactions, and compensations it excites; conflicts and polarizations ensuing from the effort to integrate the complex and heterogeneous; the contribution of collective struggles and ideologies not only to awakening awareness but also to the creation of forms. It is true that such a quest will attain operative syntheses only when sufficiently precise parameters make it possible to calculate, and thus in some degree to manipulate, the interaction among these variables. Are there indices of cosignification, so to speak, which permit calculation of the effects of tension and convertibility in which we see the essence of all social dynamism, as well as study of the relationships between such effects and the evolution of styles? [1] All these are questions which have not been raised in connection with Arab data, as far as we are aware, and which can be fully clarified only by research conducted on the spot.

Access to the New Industrial World

The persistence with which millions of men pursue a linguistic debate, as is the case with the Arabs, may seem surprising to those of us who, forgetting so much *Défense et illustration* lavished over the centuries, reduce language and, more broadly, all expression in a society to a matter of form: that is, in their eyes, an ancillary matter.[2] Conditioned and remodeled by a science necessarily unitary, will the world not end up by rubbing out all such specious facets? Will cultures (in the plural), one after another, not dissolve under the concentrated fire of scientism? [3] Technology, proudly mastered by a handful of the world's peoples and resurgent in tyrannical relations with the rest of the world, certainly plays an increasingly arrogant role among the Arabs, as everywhere else. Is this not detrimental to other characteristics, allegedly invariable? The Western identity, one may say, has indeed stripped off a humanistic primacy to embrace ever more closely the traits of so-called consumer civilization. Some believe that it may be the same with the Arabs in time.

They attained industrial civilization during the nineteenth century through three major innovations, in all of which Egypt was both the protagonist and the stake. To list them: railway construction, undertaken there earlier than in many European countries; the substitution of perennial irrigation, by means of dams, canals, and pumps, for the seasonal Nile flood; and, finally, the digging and opening to traffic of the Suez Canal. If the Egyptians were the junior operators and sometimes the beneficiaries of these three facts, which transformed relationships between nature and culture, they were for a long time neither the entrepreneurs nor the managers. A long apprenticeship extending over a half-century and more and even a revolution—the nationalization of the Canal in 1956—were necessary before they could seize the initiative in the new era's forward movement. It can in fact be said that the rise of planning is a necessity almost anywhere.

How significant is it to single out this approach, seeing that the expertise belonged to foreigners, who furthermore reaped most of the profits? Is not the real series, which could be used as a parameter of all Oriental history, of an ethical and historical order instead of technical, properly speaking: first frustration, then a dramatic assumption of control coinciding in its decisive phase with the achievement of independence? In the final analysis is technology only a "bell buoy" or a "Plimsoll's line" of this modernized society, instead of one of its long-term operating factors?

Only twenty years ago, during the years after Nasser's revolution, the question everyone asked, including the Arabs themselves, was whether they were innately suited for technical modernization. The question could not be sidestepped even if one rejected many stereotypes of the time, such as a supposed fatalism or Islam's indifference toward technology. Heavy industry was just beginning, and in only a few of these countries. Today the focus of investigation has shifted. The problem for the Arabs is not their capability for technical achievement but their ability to practice it while preserving the essence of their personality. A universal problem, of course, but one which arises with special acuity in their case.

A brief historical review of this development, now well under way, will indicate the stages of a rather convincing progress. It was only in the 1930s that some Near Eastern countries were led to introduce or at least contemplate measures to protect their national economy. Until then they were captives of foreign production, whether as consumers, laborers, or sales agents. Already by 1925, however, the operations of the Miṣr group in Egypt had begun, through the initiative of the famous Ṭalʿat Ḥarb; and in 1930 the first textiles were produced at the Maḥallat al-Kubrā factory.

A second important stage: Toward the end of the 1950s Nasser's revolutionary regime created the Ḥalwān steel mills, long looked upon as a prestige project, as were many other factories built thereafter in the Arab world, including even Algeria's ʿAnnāba. Since its four-year plan Algeria, which is placing such emphasis on industrialization and regional decentralization, is taking the lead in these efforts, which have spilled over generally into collective life. A systematization already rich in multinational experience is thus taking shape which marks the general acceptance of a goal and even a method.

Finally, petroleum resources have provided the occasion for several of the producers, grouped in a consortium, to brandish thunderbolts calculated to recover their own. It is well known how the exploitation of this wealth began. The concession to a foreign promoter had as *quid pro quo* the placing of financial capabilities in the hands of the rulers. Black gold, as it was called at the time, filled only the black strong boxes of the monarchs and their vassals. This was logically followed by a new approach, consisting in diverting the windfall to development and modernization funds. Iraq was the first to do so, with the separate budget of its Development Board which, with some diligence and coherence, attempted to convert subsoil revenues into economic construction. But it was in the last phase that, in the case of Algeria, a more systematic effort was made to capitalize on these resources. This country sought to bend the provisions of international agreements to its own advantage. Relatively speaking, oil may become, for Algeria and others, what coal was for nineteenth-century England. Other aggressive moves by the producers have enabled the Arabs to force their customers to compensate for the decline of revenues due to devaluation of the dollar, and then to secure majority participation in production. On the financial level it is no longer rapacity or Malthusianism on the part of the exploiting companies but the very fact of foreign management, good or bad, that the new ambitions challenge. It would not be enough even if petroleum and its industrial applications served the Arabs: they now want to assume personal charge of responsibility for the process, and furthermore to use it as a political weapon. One more step, or rather leap, and the price rise decided upon by the producing countries' consortium upset the economic balance of the consuming countries and drained toward Arabia, the Gulf, and Iran a swelling flood of currency, making it possible for certain kings and amirs to manipulate the international economy. What is to be done with all this wealth? How is it to be "recycled"? It will be used for massive development programs, of course, but that is not enough. Beyond economic creation, self-creation or re-creation must be achieved. But so many problems are unresolved! The scandalous inequalities among Arab countries, and among classes within some of them. Some suitable technical, mental, and moral adaptation to these new assets and the responsibilities stemming from them. For, after all, will they not have escaped the clutches of foreign monopolies only to become monopolists themselves? Finally, to what extent will this wealth remain simply a windfall, something very different from a collective achievement? That is why the most clear-sighted Arabs are examining their consciences. Some day, perhaps, they will go still further and offer to transfer from people to people the gushing wealth of their deserts, bypassing the greedy brokerage both of the great companies and of national treasuries. It is true that the resolutions of the Non-Aligned Conference at Algiers in September 1973, while consecrating these premises, did not draw their ultimate conclusions.[4]

Factory Memories

The factory has become a part of Arab landscapes. It is not rare that one or another is boasted of as the largest on the continent. I heard that said of the Arzew plant, where Saharan gas is liquified, the textile mill at Fez, and still others. But, giantism aside, to what extent do these factories delivered on a turn-key basis contribute to a true evolution? They are important, certainly, for the services they provide, the value they add to the national product, and still more in that they introduce and strengthen a manufacturing-mindedness among the citizens. Above all, they are important in that they create the conditions for the growth of a laboring class and a trade union movement. Before us is being sketched the profile of a new kind of man.

I have often met this new man, his face lined by a new way of thinking. In Morocco, for example, deep in one of those coal mines over which Eirik Labonne was so enthusiastic. During a folklore festival at Tafilalt, I had heard the resident general exclaim, as he watched girls from Aït Hadiddou performing their traditional leapfrogging dance, "Tomorrow, all these people will be in overalls, won't they?" For this high bourgeois, of course, dancing conflicted with industrial production. But the miner of Bou Arfa who invited me to his two-room cottage, spread a little rug on the tile floor, and set the teapot singing was giving up nothing of himself. He was giving the party, which took place on his schedule.

And do the workers of Maḥallat al-Kubrā not revive and enlarge the twin heritage of artisanship and peasantry? Matured as men, certainly, and without split personality. . . .

I remember one who was recording, minute by minute, the operation of the electric turbines at Aswan, in Arabic, in a schoolboy's notebook. These laborers came by tens of thousands to this dam, and to the one at Ṭabaqa on the Euphrates. The landscape is mobilized with them. When the work is done and most of them disperse, who can say that their leaven will not play its part in the rising of their people's aspirations?

The date-packing plant at Basra, the ʿAnnāba steel mill, the urea extraction factory at Kuwait, the spinning and weaving mills almost everywhere, the little sugar plant at Mosul, the Shubra al-Khayma industrial complex with the gallery of workers' paintings: I congratulate all these men and places, this thought within space and enterprise within time, while recalling the moment (1946) when Moroccan and French trade union members decided to work overtime without pay to manufacture the first disc plow for the Department of Peasant Affairs.[5]

Progress of an Economic Culture

More exact analysis would require an investigation focused on strategic points: the lowering of cost prices and the state of ("undoctored") balance sheets; development of real expertise among supervisors, qualification and specialization among workers; hence the importance of scientific research, on one hand, and technical training, on the other. The acquisition and even the invention of technical skills, also and above all industrial invention, represent in this respect irrefutable tests on which we have as yet little information, unfortunately.[6]

Let us face the fact. So many brakes are limiting progress! Unreserved optimism regarding the relationships between the growth of industrial jobs and of the work force, the birth and development of articulation of labor demands and, especially, of new class attitudes is impossible because of the bureaucratic forms in which transformation is taking place. In retrospect, one may appreciate the role of the Sudan railway workers, that of a leader of Ferḥat Hashed's stature in Tunisia, the part played by the Algerian Centrale at the outset of the local management (*autogestion*) program. But even in the best cases Arab unionism has profited, and suffered, from mutual interference with the ruling party and government. We have yet to see Egypt's one million union members play an autonomous role, for example, nor the burgeoning working masses in North Africa. But there can be no doubt that this dynamism, still repressed and sometimes sidetracked, will one day have important consequences at the global level.

Awareness of the problems of production, trade, and labor is meanwhile spreading among the public. Let us look at one or two of the most recent of the economic publications which appear regularly, find subscribers, and contribute to informing the citizen. Leaf, for example, through *L'économie des pays arabes*, founded in 1958 in Damascus by Shafīq Akhras and now published in Beirut. You will find many features which reflect an informed, critical approach. It is true that the accuracy of basic data is always more or less problematical, and that the editor often works with faked documents. But he knows it, and so does the reader, and the requirements of exposition may themselves lead to useful cross checks.

The magazine estimated the petroleum revenues of all the Arab countries in 1971 at six billion dollars: an enormous inflow! In April 1973 the reserves of a mere four of these countries (Libya, Saudi Arabia, Iraq, and Kuwait) were above that figure, further inflated by the spectacular rise in exchange rates.[7] Other statistics, unfortunately, open up less-favorable perspectives. The economist is disturbed by uncontrolled population growth, low productivity, and the slow progress in the national producing sectors, particularly agriculture and industry. What, even industry? Yes, for even if one may point to progress in technology, one cannot ignore the factors which limit it. The cause of industrialization has by no means been won everywhere. Many Arab societies still emphasize commerce, and even speculation—a characteristic linked to a mercantilist past, as one might suppose, and not a very progressive one! Moreover, it is all very well to tot up revenues and figure the percentage devoted to development; but the more basic question of savings and reserves must not be overlooked. Estimating these is a chancy thing, in view of long-standing habits of hoarding and buying precious metals and, among some groups and individuals, of placing assets abroad. Of course, these external deposits provide certain means of action upon the countries where they are made, such as Switzerland and Great Britain; but this can lead also to sometimes picturesque vicissitudes, like that of the Intra Bank in Beirut a few years ago.

The very fact that the Arab economy gives rise to this sort of observations, however saddening or incomplete, signals a progress in information. The tone of the *Economic Ahrām*, which has appeared for the past fifteen years or so as a supplement to the well-known daily paper, oscillates quite felicitously between the technical and the popular. Here, for example, are significant articles from a single issue.[8] The periodical asks various officials the question, "What major difficulties do you have to overcome?" These officials, of course, are bureaucrats: none, naturally, blames the regime. Criticism of governments in most of these countries, whether ruled by a single party or not, is expressed only intermittently and irregularly, in the form of coups d'état. This obviously goes beyond the editor's intention; one is grateful, on the other hand, for the details he furnishes on certain points. In the same number, selected at random, one finds a good article on the progress made in labor legislation during the year 1971. Industrialization, indeed, does not simply involve material progress but also raises questions of more broadly human realities: the autonomy of the working masses, the role of intellectuals in research and management, and so on. In short, involvement of the totality. Despite all reservations respecting the literature on the subject, published under the circumstances one is well aware of, the fact emerges that not all the counterparts in social justice, prosperity, and cultural quickening are being drawn from the progress of enterprises. There are two reasons for this: many of these achievements are nothing more than achievements, accomplished in virtual isolation and registered in a so-called modern sector which seems too often to be an island in the ocean of a still-traditional society. There is thus a lack of correspondence, of homology if you will, between technical progress, on one hand, and progress in other social dimensions, on the other. In any event, progress in disseminating economic information is evident from the attention the papers and magazines give to topics whose relative technicality no longer removes them from everyday concern. Thus another issue of the same magazine lists a score of supplements, such as "Fiscal Guide," "What to Do about Social Security Insurance," "Labor Rights in the Public Sector," "Agricultural Cooperatives," "Banking Guide," and so on.[9]

If we add to these information channels those which result from the virtually immediate connection the consumer can perceive between planning and foreign policy, on one hand, and daily life, on the other, we realize the educational value of many of these facts. If meat is rationed in Egypt, or rice cannot be found at all, and if, by contrast and contrary to all expectations, food products mostly imported from the East flood the shops after the Six-Day War, these are data for the citizen on the country's economic policy and on politics in general. If it is easier to find parts for Soviet-made taxis in Kuwait's free market than in Baghdad, which imports the vehicles, that is food for thought. Of course, one cannot place confidence in a government according to the supply of shaving cream, transistors, or even Bulgarian cheese in the shops. Should the obvious and dismaying inequality in the so-called liberal democratic countries make us forget the austerity in the so-called socialist ones? For whom is life better in Beirut than in Damascus, and conversely? These are questions hard to evade. They are the subject of innumerable emotional but instructive debates.

The historian and sociologist will ask other questions. While engaging in these projects and instituting these activities, most often ordered from abroad or taken over from foreigners, what real responsibilities is the society as such going to assume? The oil producers' offensive has begun to reverse the tendency, which operated over a half-century, to cheapen raw materials to the profit of manufactured products, thus aggravating exploitation of the world. That is fine. It is fine that petroleum, formerly a black strong box but now black gold, is emerging as the *deus ex machina* of planetwide justice. But what is to be done with these successes? Will the Arab community simply behave as an unruly vassal of the mechanized nations, even though it now has the ability to buy their machine tools instead of merely buying their products? The problem does not go unnoticed; leaders are uneasy over it. The only basic answer leads to apprenticeships. Accordingly, the importance of developing local statistical and economic research institutions, and fostering professional training, cannot be overestimated. This is beginning to bear fruit, notably in the agriculture and hydrocarbons fields. We are beginning to find in the East individuals, in the rank of engineer or, particularly, the executive, capable of performing as well as their opposite numbers in comparable fields abroad. This was demonstrated recently in the discussions between Algerian and French petroleum experts or, still more recently, in a more broadly international gathering at Geneva.

These arguments have so far neglected the most important thing, which is discovery. Now integration does not operate until the machine is reinvented by the society using it, or at the very least until the society invents enough machines of its own to be no longer simply the foreigner's customer in its effort at renewal. To what extent is this true of these countries? The alarming thing is not, of course, that they buy so many foreign patents—or, more simply, use them without buying them, as reportedly in the case of one automobile plant in Egypt—but that the need is not yet acknowledged, and that once more the preconditions of creativity are passed over in silence. Now—must we repeat it?—the Arabs do not lack information, nor the right aptitudes and personalities. The press mentions with pride scientists like Dr. Musharrafa in Egypt and many others. But how many more could be named whose careers of discovery and innovation in academic and even industrial life are pursued in and for foreign lands, thus rounding the cape of expatriation from which there is no return! . . .

Parenthesis in Dialog Form

"It's your fault, after all!"

"I expected you would say that."

"Your training made them potential expatriates. Their degrees cut them off from their own countries . . ."

". . . or else it made them ambassadors and ministers instead of researchers and colonial doctors."

"That's an ugly term."

"But a fine enterprise. In the North African boondocks today the French doctor's place has been taken by Bulgarians or Chinese, while the native doctor opens a luxurious clinic . . ."

"You're exaggerating."

"Yes, I'm exaggerating. But let's continue the search for who is responsible for the ravages of the brain drain."

"They were potential expatriates. You demoralized them. It's only natural that you are grabbing them on your famous world market, and thus taking back much more than you paid out in scholarships, teachers, aid, technical institutes, and so on. However, the good citizens stay loyally on the job."

"Would you say, then, that your country is making room for them, giving them opportunity to live, act, and speak?"

"I wouldn't go so far. But it's their fault, after all."

"I expected you to say that, too."

"They are intellectuals cut off from the masses."

"While you yourselves are the people. Is that it?"

"You and I will agree on one thing, at least . . ."

"Yes, on the necessity to repatriate culture and training."

"And what else?"

"On the necessity to renounce that form of education that consists merely of debauchery and corruption."

"And what else?"

"The rest is up to you."

"What's that?"

"Freedom of speech for your intellectuals. Not to mention others."

"Ha, ha! Bourgeois freedoms!"

"Socialist freedom should go beyond them, not stop short of them. Otherwise, the exodus will go on."

"We have begun requiring exit visas."

"Whom do you mean by 'we'?"

Progress of a Political Culture

At the end of World War II, when one country after another was gaining its independence, the defeat of the Arabs in the United Nations over the Palestine question plunged them from enthusiasm into the depths of bitterness. Far to the West, the terrible repression at Sétif, in Algeria (1945), had already begun the vicious circle of all or nothing. During these years, also, the aspirations of these peoples toward the future took on new colorations. They became radicalized in North Africa and in Iraq. In Egypt, the alliance between students and labor (1946) seemed to foretell the future, while at the same time the free officers were putting together their clandestine plans. The Baʿth was born then (1946), and Jumblāṭ's Progressive party (1949): two formulations of unequal scope, but both distinguished by deep theoretical study and specific programs. The situation in the Maghreb was becoming radical. Everywhere, Marxist agitation strove to infiltrate the course of events and control it. It had going for it, in addition to courage, a method suited to analyzing class conflicts, but against it the unsuitability of this method, understood in deductive fashion, to deal with more general problems.

For the Arabs' unease goes far beyond the resentment of the disadvantaged classes. From that time on it has stemmed in large part from successive setbacks in the first stage of independence or socialism; from a depersonalization of which the first analysts were to be Memmi and Fanon; from an existential disquiet which ʿAbd al-Raḥmān Badawī portrayed as early as 1949 in his *Malady of Youth*[10] before deriving from it the bases for an extended discussion much closer to Husserl and Heidegger than to Marx; from the sentiment, already asserted in literature, that "God is dead"; from the moralities of refusal established as a priori in poetry by the 1950 generation; from an effervescent romanticism judiciously analyzed by Muṭāʿ al-Ṣafadī even before leftist movements or China provided it with models and programs. This miscellaneous list of aspects and tendencies is intended simply to give an idea of the impetuous seething among youth and the challenges they are flinging at mature or orthodox revolutionaries as well as at moderates and traditionalists.

For many Arabs, extremism, even if merely verbal, seemed a necessary first condition at a time when, in the field of actual events, failure followed failure—in 1948, 1956, 1967—in the struggle for Palestine, which had become the symbol for all the usurpations.

Visit to Karāme (1968)

As we descended toward the Jordan, the bucolic landscape, sered by an unusually early April heat but charming in its natural and man-made features, became tragic.

The vineyards, the orange and olive orchards in the valleys, the fields until recently irrigated and flourishing, now spoke dispossession and death. A sort of primordial silence weighed upon us—an anticipation, of which none of us spoke. A sense of menace, buzzing like a swarm of flies, made one's body alert even more than one's face. Suddenly, signs of destruction came into view. Here and there, a truck overturned with its load of vegetables, a burned-out automobile, a pump leveled by air attack, abandoned agricultural plots, all the destruction, all the persons and things headed in the wrong direction: war.

We followed the Jordan's west bank to the town of Karāme. A checkerboard of white, deserted streets, bearing traces of fire. In a devastated schoolhouse, among other debris, was a pile of pupils' notebooks. I picked one up, a little girl's notebook. The careful writing, with wise comments by the teacher in red pencil in the margin, was a dictation on the theme of patriotism.

Where had the little Palestinian girl gone? Probably to one of those camps where I found, mingled with peasants still stupefied by their recent misfortune, people like those of Karāme who were refugees for the second or even the third time, since after 1948 they had had to leave their land, then once or even twice their place of refuge. Exile can be multiple. Anger also.

Progress of a Political Culture (continued)

The 1948 disaster had rung the death knell for the old bourgeois and monarchical leaders.[11] At least one revolution ensued: Egypt's, in 1952, which for ten years or so seemed to provide the Arab countries a model and a hope. But its attempts at expansion failed in the lands of the Fertile Crescent and also in Yemen. Other experiments were taken in hand. A fresh disaster (1967) aroused increased opposition to them. Meanwhile, liberation of the Maghreb had shifted the front along which the Arab world, backed up against the wall of its collective identity, was launching its attack and quest toward an uncertain future. There was the trump of petroleum wealth; but the countries were very unequally endowed with it. There was the trump of geographic situation; yes, but it aroused dangerous competition between the world power blocs. The trump of an insatiable unrest, impatient at any delay, bringing a furious insistence upon absolutes to play upon history, but likely to lead to confusion, fragmentation, and lame excuses.

Independence had come; it was soon evident that it would remain hollow unless fleshed out with economic construction. But what would the latter be worth without social justice? Socialism alone, consequently, could liquidate a maleficent past. But the militant was suddenly seized by doubt. The movement to which he felt drawn was of international scope and promise—hence its strength. But would it not also liquidate faith, the national heritage, personality, in fact everything he had fought for? Whom to believe? The disappointments had been too bitter, the setbacks too heavy. Of course, some vestiges of the past will obviously fall of themselves: ritualism, conservatism, feudalism, sectarianism. But embracing the new "isms" has not produced convincing results thus far, despite an orgy of experiments, words, and figureheads.[12]

Hence this disillusioned observation by an exiled Syrian general: "The Arab mind has not freed itself from its time-worn, backward, mystical mentality, and cleaves to hollow concepts, adolescent attitudes, and ideological frameworks that are sunk in a new nebula of ambiguity, obscurity, and ignorance of the right way to proceed. . . . Parties and political factions are partly responsible for the prevailing distortion between the vicissitude of politics and the moral, economic, scientific, and ideological evolutions related to it. Youth always lets itself be seduced by the purely verbal externals of progressive propaganda which legitimize its liberation from the past without replacing the past with a true revolutionary commitment."[13]

This was a dissident speaking. He was later assassinated. Was he right? The Arabs' long march toward political innovation has been accompanied by falsification and violence which—far beyond the categories of slogans, conflicts among interests and blocs, and competition among individuals and classes—arise in the broadest sense from the problems inhering in education in these countries, by which we mean the integration of a truly modern culture with the pressure of people and things, with the fervor of youth, and with the energy of activism. But how are the progress and retreat, the truths and appearances, of this integration to be measured? Is there not some sociological criterion which can do so with some certainty? We believe there is. One purpose of this study is precisely to ask whether, at the Arab world level and at least potentially, interchange and permutation of the various modes of collective dynamics are taking place. That would be the criterion.

For the time being let us confine ourselves to two contradictory observations, precisely those which polarize the citizen's quest. The past two decades, nationalism of the 1950s and socialism in the 1960s, have seen Arab energies activated in all domains. Political liberations and economic transformations have resulted. It is too soon to say whether, after the 1967 disaster and the black autumn of 1970, recovery has begun to appear. In Algeria without doubt, in Iraq perhaps. Better than that: the first glimmerings of political imagination are appearing almost everywhere.

But let us note, too, that disillusion and defeat have plunged this world once again into doubt as to choices. The fact is that it finds most of these problems still pending: the debate between unity and plurality, between revolution and stability, between cosmopolitanism and specificity, between efficiency and freedom, and, finally, the debate over peace or war in Palestine which may be the most important because it reflects all the others and seems to condition them as a whole. The semisuccess of October 1973 and the subsequent progress in approaching the problem have not altered anything essential on this point.[14]

It is only too true. The magnificent uprising of the Arab masses, their zest for progress, their growing self-assertion before the world, their equally intense defiance and tenderness toward themselves—all that was generally falsified and ruined. No more than elsewhere, you think? On the contrary, much worse than elsewhere. Why so? Let us blame neither groups nor individual men, but a semantic disorder. Yes, a defect of configuration, a certain failure to place in their proper realtionship the ideal and the possible, the calculable and the dream, the symbolic and the effective, and, more generally, fact and value. Certainly, both terms of each of these pairings are necessary. The vitality of political programs comes by virtue of their common interplay. But the terms must not be confused with one another. The way they fit together cannot be left to chance or to *baraka*.[15] Too often, correction of the disorder in their configuration, when indeed it is corrected, is accomplished only through the fire of a sure instinct—as in struggles for independence—or through the fortuitous action of a single man. Hence the precarious results, and the relapses. Hence, conversely, the hope; for the accumulated experience and the analysis of successes and failures will in the end cure the Arabs of a history too faithful to ill fortune.

The disillusioned putschist whose words I quoted above was only partly right. His idea of politics was only an extrapolation of what he thought was "proper" politics, that is, that of the West, otherwise known as well-controlled anger, the masses' expression put into words, their misfortune exploited as fuel for history's new locomotives, a feigned attachment to the concrete, the "scientific" conduct of operations. Where had you seen that, General, if not in the textbooks? Please, do not cling to stereotypes which merely reproduce, with some distortion, foreign experiences. At the same time, that should not discourage you from seeking and putting into action the world's becoming and a logic of history. But this logic is complex and, as is said, dialectical. The face-to-face encounter of man with nature—that nature which is both within and outside him—of the idea with things, of signs and values with material processes, the debate, finally, between collective identity and its metamorphoses—you lived it and died of it—all this should have taught you the vanity of ready-made formulae and the necessity to begin analyses over again from the fundamentals. A problem of radicalism, thus, in the literal sense, and of creativity.

Silhouettes of Statesmen

I have known many of them, some over a long period of time, others intermittently. Some are dead, others in power or hoping to be, still others in retirement or prison.

Mehdi Ben Barka, a few weeks before he was assassinated, on one of those strange Cairo evenings when, in a luxurious home furnished with Louis XV moldings and Italian glass, a ravishing Marxist lady was entertaining her extraordinarily mixed coterie of acquaintances. The fall of Ben Bella, of which we had just learned, did not appear to surprise the UNFP leader. As he left us, I invited him to visit Paris. "You know I cannot go there," he said with a sadness in which, in retrospect, I read the portent of his fate.

Not far from the Tigris, in the solemn precincts of the Mustanṣiriya, still under reconstruction, we were received by ʿAbd al-Karīm Qāsim. He had closely followed the meetings held on al-Kindī's thousandth anniversary, always keeping his pistol holster open. Flaming eyes, in an intense, sincere face. When he spoke, the words of I know not what subconscious, what *sarādīb*,[16] seemed to rise within him. But capable, they say, of the most sanguine Machiavellianisms. He thanked R. Blachère and me warmly: "On your behalf, *li-ajlikum*, I am re-establishing cultural relations with France," he said with a smile. He had only a month or two to live before he was gunned down.

I was standing off to one side in that hyperbolical great hall of the Carthage Palace, where enormous crystal chandeliers cascade from the ceiling. Robert Buron and I wished to intercede for a Communist professor who had just been arrested. Aḥmad ben Ṣalāḥ was busily performing the honors of the reception. Bourguiba noticed me, called me over, and put on his Roman tribune's mask for the photographers' benefit. Once again I noticed that his human warmth was irresistible. He nevertheless turned down our request. But a few days later our colleague was released! For Ben Ṣalāḥ, then all-powerful, things were to go farther. Too far.

"What beautiful palaces you have in your country," said the foreign ambassador. But Shaikh Zakī Yamānī interrupted him in a biting tone: "All that is of the past. Arabian Nights, harems! We have better things to do now in Arabia: work, produce, organize!" The diplomat flushed with anger. As for myself, I wondered how far such strange Jacobinism might go. . . .

Shortly after the melancholy Suez affair, I disembarked at the Cairo airport, and when the official saw my French passport he could not repress a start of surprise. The document bore no visa, only a hand-written note by Sarwat Okasha, then ambassador at Rome. That was the first time I had met this sad-eyed man, his face the color of the Nile, who had not yet begun his career as a great minister of culture. Later we had many conversations, the last at the Collège de France where he had us listen to two musical phrases of a stunning parallelism, one from Mozart and the other from an ancient oriental *maqāma*. I thought, as I listened, that it may be thus with civilizations.

Michel Aflaq does not recognize, or recognizes very little, in the Ba'th factions presently in power what he has been working for for forty years. His wrinkled, oriental Christian's face betokens the exhaustion born of disappointment, but also the energy to continue the quest. That he has been disavowed by his own fatherland, that soldiers acting in the name of his principles have imprisoned him, and banished him, is as nothing for this reed which may bend but will never break.

Yāsir 'Arafāt is just a short man with irregular features, but his eyes are fine, his handshake firm and sincere. When he rose to cut up the excellent fish, called *shabbūṭ*, waiting on the table for us, I noticed how much the *quffiya* flopping on his shoulders resembled a horse's mane. Arabs of all times! . . . "We won't rest, and we won't let anyone else rest," he said as we parted.

If he did not wear on his face a whole Orient of secret truths he would remind one of a Tolstoy hero. A prince, of course, but a socialist, esoteric but a man of the people, wedded to Arabism if not to humanity in general, Jumblāṭ mingles in his strange conversation dream and sly calculation, the immemorial and the utopian. At this level the two ends meet and display the alchemy of their identity.

And others who have been, or will be, evoked in these pages: Muḥammad V; Nasser; ʿAllāl al-Fāsī; Dr. Aḥmad Ṭālib, that worthy son of Shaikh Ibrāhīmī; Ben Bella, whom the merits of present-day Algeria will not make me forget. Shaikh al-ʿAtīqī, Kuwaiti minister of petroleum, with his manners of a great lord. Khālid Muḥyī al-Dīn, Egyptian soldier with a progressive heart, carrying devotion to authenticity to the point of incompatible loyalties. Amar Ouzegane, the former Posts, Telephone, and Telegraph messenger, veteran trade unionist and Communist: he received me just when he was using abandoned tractors to plow independent Algeria's first fields. Labīb Shuqair, great economist and true democrat, speaker of the assembly of Nasser's people. Luṭfī Ḥaffār, who earned his stripes as a Syrian patriot and recovered for his city the management of the Fijè well but whose finest work is his lovely daughter Selma, the novelist. Shaikh Pierre Jamayyil, whose views you need not share in order to admire his courage, his tall Latin physique, and his integrity. Sulaimān al-Khashsh, rough and taciturn, who shared with me at Damascus some disrespectful research on religion and on Marx. Bouabid, parading first his face, melancholy like that of a Spanish grandee, and then his disillusion in Morocco's first postindependence cabinet. Others also, equally diverse and meaningful in my eyes for reasons as diverse as those mentioned; I shall speak of them some day.

The Era of Decolonization

In colonial times everything in these countries was insolently oriented in a single direction: that of the Other. Movements impressed upon society arose mainly as a function of the Other, but also of the resistances he aroused. Inherited influences, wounds sustained, uprisings and the safeguard of one's own, everything was falsified. Life lost its focus, even more than becoming alienated. Hence the striking limitation in types of conduct, even of facial expression, and the schizophrenic tension which eventually permeated modes of behavior. All this reached the point of paroxysm in the last days of the Egyptian monarchy, or of the colonial regime in Algeria. The ultimate destruction wrought by colonialism, and the cruelest, consisted perhaps in that maniacal impoverishment of faces and ways of action, save only that of combat, which then became necessary as the last recourse.

But if colonial society was unfocused, it was not therefore reduced, in the various meanings of this word, for the good reason that it remained largely unknown. The interests and security of the Other were so compelling that he contemplated only a single range of things, by processes more or less harsh or insidious, and let the rest drift as it might. The sinister tension of the final phase perhaps obscures the fact that the apogee of imperialism had also been that of liberalism in economy and customs. If we consider Egypt in Cromer's time, or Lyautey's Morocco, we observe that the British or French ruler imposed goals which were costly, certainly, and distortive for the national economy and personality but which touched only the outer shell. All the inside and the rest remained as if there were no colonization. That is an idea which may appear astonishing or paradoxical after the polemics which have demonstrated, justly but tardily, the final convulsions of foreign domination. Let us at least recognize that a great part of the geographical, social, and moral realities remained unknown to the intruder or beyond his reach. Otherwise, where would the forces of renewal have come from?

During the war this high official of the Algerian FLN commanded a frontier zone so murderous that the average life expectancy of the combatants was three months. I asked him where these men came from, what class, what social circumstances, what ideology. He replied that they came from the *jabals*, and that most were not as yet politicized. Courage, faith, and honor were what motivated them.[17] When I went to Algiers just after independence, an old woman of well over a hundred years died at Laghouat. She had never met a Frenchman. That was more than a casual news item. It was a symbol. If our analysis were capable of it, we might perhaps define entire areas of the country, the society, and the individual which, as in the case of that humble biography, had remained inaccessible to the colonizers, bypassed or unknown to them. Foreign rule had its vacuums as well as its filled spaces. Many more vacuums than occupied spaces! The forces of revival accumulated in these vacuums, where the anterior being lived on. Thus it was perhaps not from deterioration, or from a dialectic of altercation or resentment, as everyone believed, that the forces of resistance welled up, but from relatively undamaged internals.

By comparison, what happens in the postcolonial phase? At the very first, it exhibits its most creative features: an existential luxuriance, a passionate unfolding. Identity, recovered, is reoriented in the right direction. Its amplitude is similarly restored. Its differentiation is, or should be, rehabilitated. Differences of class, of age level, of stages of enterprise. Even faces lost that sort of uniformity subjection had induced. Expression diversifies, abounding in fresh nuances. A new person is everywhere, groping in all directions. He has regained the full spectrum of the differential, the pervasive complexity, access to a broad range of attitudes from militancy to refusal, passing through gratuitousness and detachment. Decolonized man recovers his unfinished quality, which is to say his potential for accomplishment.

Many of these attitudes are, alas, considered perversely oppositional. Before, in colonial times, they would have been impossible. Now they are called seditious. They are censured as if they did not offer the best prospects for the mutation under way. Of course society, in reorienting itself, must weave together all the fibers of its new growth. It justly professes the ideal of organization, justice, and rationality: that is one good side of managed economy. Colonial exploitation was beyond doubt oppressive, but above all it left much to chance. Postcolonial society cannot come to terms with contingency, which is simply the fickle reverse side of fatalism. It is thus right to wish to assert its will and project itself. But this projection and self-assertion should not be equivalent to diminishing itself. Independence restores sight to possibilities that were blind. Colonization was the Other's venture, at the price of an apparent penning-in of the colonized. What irony, and what a deception, if decolonization, on pretext of up-to-dateness, rejected potentiality!

Even that is the best hypothesis. There are also purportedly liberal, or rather mercantile, regimes whose guiding spirit is in fact the enrichment of the rulers. It is not evident that they succeed better than authoritarian regimes in guaranteeing the citizens' liberty. But what do I mean by "liberty"? Certainly not that conjectural category of public law manuals. No, what I call by that name is something far more serious. The liberty we must have is leaving the door open to latencies, preserving freedom of play, so that society shall be guaranteed the right to operate multidimensionally. That is not a theme for political controversy or idealistic hope: it is the irreplaceable criterion of collective creativity.

Let us take a still closer look. Whether authoritarian or liberal, the new regimes concentrate in the hands of one man or group the venture which the colonialist arrogated to himself in that same country. Admittedly, their instability acts to some extent to mitigate this takeover. The coup becomes the spasmodic substitute for the gamble. Effervescence of behavior, superabundance of public speeches, and the mishmash of the real and the imaginary sanction in their way repression of the game impulse and the reign of false authority.

This also should be said: It is not in decolonized countries alone but also in ours that global society amputates many of its own dimensions. Here as there, official action circumscribes collective life and devitalizes it under pretext of due process. There being an intimate link among the multidimensional profusion of life, its creativity, and its semantics, the signals by which I ought to recognize myself as a people, an individual, or an event become lost and all is engulfed in meaninglessness, which is the great malady of today's societies.

So that is not peculiar to countries which were once colonies. But there it is the more disappointing and grave. Loss of meaning is nowhere so destructive as where it affects societies which experience, in all their violence, a contrast between rising potentialities and what established institutions would make of them: the battle between newly liberated creative power and those who would shunt it aside, or deride it.

PART TWO

Culture and Memory

VI
In Search of Imrūʾ al-Qays

Petroleum and theology: anachronistically, mineral wealth has come to sustain the Wahhābī system. For how long? Everywhere else these radical gushers call forth a social transformation as violent, and coming from as great depths, as they. For the time being, in Saudi Arabia, the thing that stands out at the official level is a great conviction of the well-bridled virtues of developing the infrastructure. The 1970–1975 Plan, which bears the enormous price tag of 41 billion riyals, devoted only 2.7 percent to industry, 3.6 percent to agriculture, and 0.3 percent to "commerce and services." It is a safe bet that the 17.8 percent allocated to education is not intended to encourage the growth of an intelligentsia. A high official there recently reacted to the accusation of conservatism: "If progressivism means renewal, construction, justice, raising the standard of living, then we are progressives. But we will never renounce our belief and our faith." Who is asking you to, O Arabs? I see again, in this remark, the antithesis so often adduced between renewal and authenticity. It is alleged that they are mutually contradictory. You have to choose one or the other. If that were so, the whole world would be schizophrenic. Fortunately, disequilibria are not always locked in! Here in Saudi Arabia, how long will the typical reply of rulers to ruled be accepted: *al-shuyūkh abkhaṣ*, "the shaikhs see farther"?

Visit to Madāʾin Ṣāliḥ

The single-engined plane bumped wildly over the columns of heated air rising from the blackish hills over which it was flying at low altitude. As we flew north, leaving Jidda farther and farther behind, the plains from which these basaltic rocks thrust themselves up were dotted with dams to store water from flash floods, giving birth to cultivated patches, such as those of Umm al-Malḥ and Khalīṣ. Occasionally the plane passed over veritable avenues of vegetation descending from elevated ground, on both sides of a stream bed usually dry but suggesting the ever-present possibility of a freshet and the wide distribution of the floods. In Wādī Sattāra I noticed seven villages spaced along the slope like the rungs of a ladder. Rectangles of cultivation near the houses gave evidence of organized life and prosperity. Was this new reclamation? Or was it one of those Brotherhood colonies the old King ʿAbd al-ʿAzīz had begun to establish throughout the length and breadth of the land, even while loyally extolling its Bedouin values?

On the right, increasingly, black rocks were piled up in a chain roughly parallel with the coast. This "barrier," or Hijaz, obstructs the sea breezes and endows the coastal plain with a relative fertility. Elsewhere, the terrain extended over fields of volcanic lava, punctuated here and there with sharp peaks like Jabal Ṣabā. At nine o'clock we crossed the magnificently asphalted road that, at the latitude of Yanbuʿ and Rābugh, leaves the sea at right angles and leads inland to Medina and on to Taymāʾ.

At that moment we took an oblique course toward the north-northeast, leaving the coastal range on our left. In such country, erosion by the wind and temperature variations cleave boulders and may in time wear away mountains. Meanwhile, the land surface over which we were flying was gradually becoming sandy. This was the classical desert, though dotted here and there with what geologists call "cat's heads." Organized cultivation had long since disappeared from the terrain. Now one saw only the traces of unobstructed drainage forming mazes of curved lines, sprinkled with widely spaced spots where Bedouins had barely scratched the soil. Suddenly we passed the route of the ruined Hijaz Railway. The archaeological site I was to visit is near one of the stations on the lengthy stretch Madāʾin Ṣāliḥ–Tabūk–Maʿān, before the line rises toward Amman. The railroad, the target of T. E. Lawrence's sabotage during the First World War, has never recovered. Today they are discussing its reconstruction. Even so, one could still see a few locomotives, and some cars reduced to scrap iron. Finally, at Madāʾin Ṣāliḥ, appeared a station built of dressed stone, an enormous edifice in central European style. It was still standing there, laden with memories of the Hashemite adventure and the last convulsions of the Ottoman caliphate. But what is more striking at Madāʾin Ṣāliḥ is a group of black rocky hills, as if they were a conclave of giants. Muḥammad, who passed through these parts on his travels toward Syria, transmitted the terrible legend of the people of Thamūd. These stubborn people refused to believe in a prophet who had arisen among them; they were swept away by a hurricane of stones and perished en masse, "their eyes wide open."[1]

The above-mentioned spot, where I found myself beneath the sparse foliage of date palms and fruit trees, is called al-Ḥijr. This name, which I learned from the lips of one of those I was conversing with—he was of the Bili tribe—is not without significance: it was the traditional name given to the city of the Thamūdites, which Ptolemy distorted into "Hegra." Let us single out also some names of plants. The lemon tree shading me is of the variety called *benzbir*; two citrus trees have grown together and become grafted onto each other—that is called a *kubbādh*. Around us are palms of both sexes, of the *barzī*, *sāʾir*, *mutawwag*, *kassel*, and *ṭayba* varieties. Plants of the steppe: the *rtem*, a broom known by that name all the way to North Africa; *ramath*; and a thornbush I was to see again in the outskirts of Baghdad, the *ʿushshāz*. As a cross check, I asked them to point out to me certain plants mentioned in the old poetry: they knew them all, the *arṭā* and *ʿushar*, for example. I did not have to search far to find the melancholy foliage of the gum tree, *ṭalḥa*, and tamarisk, *ithl*.

In the afternoon we reached the town of al-ʿUlā,[2] of which Charles Doughty, the first European traveler to discover Madāʾin Ṣāliḥ, spoke at length. He was greatly impressed by this *madīna* made up of little cubes and square open spaces, cut by a sort of bony crest. A group of people lived there who had been able to maintain their autonomy with respect to rival factions of Saudis, Ibn Rashīd, and the Sharīf of Mecca. As for the Turks, they were represented here only by a small garrison from the Maghreb: an indirect effect of our conquest of Algeria. It was moreover a Maghrebi pilgrim who was said to have founded al-ʿUlā, making a miraculous spring gush forth with his staff. When Doughty passed by here, the city still followed the Malikite rite. Strong in its individualism, it paid no dues except to the mosque at Medina. Its inhabitants were "pious, good-humored, dreamers, more politic than fanatic," as Muḥammad himself must have been. Whereas the people of Nejd are much more crabbed and rough in their fanaticism. This was a Victorian Englishman speaking. He was able to continue his journey only through the goodwill of an Algerian *shāwish*. I myself dreamed of those group intimacies that the traveler in time and space is sometimes permitted to enjoy.

Al-ʿUlā still consists of small houses with interior courtyards, all huddled together; but on government initiative two palm plantations, to the north and south, have grown up—the trademark, so to speak, of the Saudi era. This era itself is being attracted by a quicker tempo of life, a broader horizon: a new stratum, already very different from the one Doughty discovered. Its counterpoint is all of Islamic history and, beyond (or short of) it, the immemorial cultures recalled by the Koran and to which the basalt conclave of Madāʾin Ṣāliḥ bears witness.

These hewn rocks reminded me of what I had seen at Petra, although less refined and more tragic. Into them are sunk deep caves that we are told were once tombs. One, called *bayt al-majlis* or *dīwān*, may have served as a public meeting place. Their lintels are decorated with solar motifs with a crudely Hellenistic look. As at Petra, there is an amalgam of intrusions from Mediterranean cultures and of the natives' propensity for burrowing and excavating. At Petra this is well organized and produces a style: all those planes of rock are incised with parallel lines, slanting at about 45 degrees from the vertical. The watershed thus traced seems to have conjured away the spaces created by the giant chisel which, by making use of the hollows and bulges, has accomplished a sculpture of a negative sort, in that the reliefs—pediments, capitals, and pilasters—are made to stand out, not by construction with assembled fragments, but by cutting away the surrounding rock. The artist was well served by his medium: a sandstone of an infinite range of oxydation and which exhibits all the colors of the rainbow on the walls of the largest of the caves. Three centuries of flowering are attributed to this city of Petra, capital of a Nabatean kingdom with a prosperous economy. At different periods, and with unequal degrees of splendor, Madāʾin Ṣāliḥ, Petra and Palmyra commanded, to their profit, the routes between the Roman north and "perfumed" Arabia, the latter itself a way station toward far-off Africa and Asia. But I have said enough about that visit to Petra of which my visit to Madāʾin Ṣāliḥ reminded me. What I recall of most importance is a solidarity with the Mediterranean world, but at the same time a contrast with it.

The rock people excavate rather than build, hollow out rather than joining things together.[3] In this they depart as far from Greek form as from the Koranic *bayān*. They furthermore contrast not only with the successes achieved by assembling parts into a whole but also with the Bedouin system, made up of tangents and slippages. They embrace a way of life consisting in total adherence to the rock—to the point where they end up petrified themselves, which displays the acme of integration! The exact opposite of such a type, the Bedouins, far from piercing stone, do not even turn over the soil. They lead a life that purely and simply skims over its surface: grazing, food gathering, hunting. The lives of their flocks, and their own, vanish as if they had never been. Nevertheless, they remain more a part of the Arabian scene than the people of Madāʾin, or Petra, or Sheba. Modeling nothingness, they draw from it indestructible symbols.

Honor and Revenge

The story was related to us as we passed in front of the judicial administration at Riyad, which bears the significant name Dār al-Qiṣāṣ. A few months ago an assault occurred against a taxi driver whom I shall call Fawāz. His passenger, Karīm, a young man of the Shammar, fired a pistol shot at him from behind, putting out one of his eyes. As punishment for his crime, Karīm was sentenced to lose an eye himself.

On the day the sentence was to be executed, in the very square where we were parked, he was led up, his hands tied behind his back, his eyes blindfolded; he knelt down and awaited the blow. A rather large crowd had gathered despite the early morning hour. A mournful silence was broken by an animated discussion. The condemned man thrilled with hope upon hearing the gutteral accent of his tribe. Several members of his clan were there, one of whom offered five thousand riyals to redeem him, another ten thousand, another still more. But the victim, masked with sinister dark glasses, obstinately spurned these offers. Karīm's relatives were not rich, and when they exhausted all their resources and fell silent, the condemned man lost all hope. Then he recognized the Hijaz accent in a new bid, raised to fifty thousand. It was Ḥājj ʿUmar al-Ṭāʾifī, a big electrical equipment importer, who had made this pious offer. But Fawāz said, "Brothers, this man has done wrong. He has mutilated me. He must be punished on earth before he is punished in hell. Look!" He uncovered the horrible wound made by the weapon used in the attack, a Beretta 45, imported from Hong Kong.

Muslim pity had seized those present, even though most were not Shammar people. The offers continued to rise. The chauffeur still refused. How could one blame him? He preferred to see his assailant suffer justly, to any compensation. That was furthermore what tradition called for. "One hundred thousand!" the Ḥājj called out, fingering his prayer beads. Then Fawāz, drawing a dagger from his belt, seized the condemned man by the nape of the neck and cut off a lock of his hair. "Go, you are free," he said, "May God pardon you." Disdainfully refusing the sum offered, he returned to his taxi in a nearby street.

In Wādī al-Dawāsir

Muḥammad ʿAlī was a doughty fellow. How could his generals possibly have dragged canons across Arabia all the way to Darʿiya, the cradle of Wahhābism (1813 and 1818)? In any case, the House of Saud's fortress has never been rebuilt. Gloomily, it thrusts up vast stumps of walls above the ruined town, connected with Riyad by a watercourse, now drying up. A little farther on, the town of Wādī Ḥanīf (population 10,000) boasts a large training center at which I admired a museum of the local handicrafts. Its director, a young Palestinian, showed us around amiably.

Then back to the road. We traveled southwest, passing enormous truckloads of tomatoes. They came from the market gardens of Ḥawṭā Banī Tamīm, near the city of Layla, where we stopped. Everyone connects this name with that of the romantic heroine who drove al-Majnūn mad with love. But the "virginal," *ʿudhrite*, poets, as nearly as they can be situated, lived far to the northeast of here, at the beginning of the Umayyad era. Never mind! Isn't the important thing what the name recalls to mind? It is precisely such remembrances I have come here to seek, on the advice of Shaikh Bulayhad,[4] a learned Arab who traversed the Peninsula on camelback for a full twenty years to pinpoint on the ground the place names mentioned in pre-Islamic poetry: specifically those assembled, for their euphony and imagery, in Imrūʾ al-Qays' *Muʿallaqa*. He found a whole cluster of them in Wādī al-Dawāsir, far from here toward Nejran; that, furthermore, is where the blacktop road ends. From Wādī al-Dawāsir one can continue by unsurfaced track either toward Mecca or toward Yemen.

At the moment, we are drinking tea at Layla, on the benches of a coffeehouse in the central square. It is time for the noon prayers. The shutters of the shops are being lowered. An old man armed with a staff is making the rounds uttering energetic cries of *ṣallū*, "pray." "It's the *nāʾib*," some small boys whisper to us, dismayed that we are continuing to chat peacefully. "We have already said the travelers' prayer," says one of my companions in a loud voice. We set off again, lucky to find the gasoline pump open for a few more minutes.

Space opens up immense and yellowish around our Toyota. It is broken at long intervals by plots dotted with vegetation. Here and there sand accumulates in small dunes. Outcroppings of black rock, or *khashm*, extend into the distance or are heaped up in strange shapes. Between Sulayyil and Wādī al-Dawāsir the road must detour around a peak in the form of a sphinx. Once or twice we passed files of women mounted on asses or mules. Even in these solitary surroundings they kept on their black veils, as if the desert itself were masculine. In fact, Arabic uses the same word, *ba'l*, to designate this searing earth and the male, as if reserving femininity for the oases.

For the needs of its herds, the great Dawāsir tribe swings back and forth over a distance of five or six hundred kilometers, north and south of a fixed habitat: seventeen villages disposed within a tract of vegetable gardens and palm groves. The emir is distinguished looking and good-natured. He comes from far to the north. He belongs to a family of Ruwala chiefs who, he tells us, enjoyed independence before the Saudis began their expansion. His house, distinguished by a dignified porch, crenelated walls, and painted doors, contrasts sharply with the ramshackle ocher surroundings.

We sit cross-legged in the *dīwān*, which is lit by flourescent tubes and filled with silent Bedouins. The latter follow our conversation with growing interest. An old Dawāsir shaikh stands out among them. He has lost all his power because of the royal policy of setting tribe against tribe and appointing outsiders to rule them. His manner nevertheless remains imposing. Here, such things are not lost as readily as elsewhere. Is poetry one of the things that do not change? I had not brought along the text of the *Mu'allaqa*. Not having full confidence in my memory, I asked for a textbook edition. They brought me a volume of selected readings from the local high school, which was all they could find. There was very little Imrū' al-Qays in it, and the *Mu'allaqa* was terribly expurgated. No matter: several persons present knew it by heart. As always happens on such occasions, those who fancied themselves choristers seized the stage. Unfortunately, one of them, the most voluble, knew nothing at all about the country. An expert accountant at Riyad, he had come on some Treasury business. He outrageously interrupted the nomads I was interrogating. With a few circumlocutions to avoid wounding his self-esteem, I nevertheless managed to carry on a dialog with one of my neighbors, a man with a sharply etched profile. As I had guessed, he knew the terrain well. "You, Maḥmūd, you old brigand," said the emir with a hearty laugh, "show off your knowledge to the professor."

Shaikh Bulayhad had not lied. I verified nearly all his identifications. The highway robber recognized al-Dakhkhūl and Ḥawmal without hesitation; Maʾsal had become Mwaysal; he cited a Bakra, which might possibly be the poet's Miqrāt. It now remained to locate the toponyms on the ground so as to determine whether they were chosen arbitrarily, or whether they reflected a logical configuration. If so, the hypercriticism that would deny that Imrūʾ al-Qays ever lived, or that his *Muʿallaqa* had the slightest authenticity, would be demolished. Should it not already have surrendered to poetic evidence? That evidence is indeed what counts, as the translation will attempt to demonstrate.[5]

The "Muʿallaqa"

"Stop! To weep over the memory of a beloved
And the ruin of the house of the beloved
In the soft sand that ripples
Between al-Dakhūl and Ḥawmal
As far as Tūḍīḥ and al-Miqrāt.
Here, in the sand, traces are still visible
Between the well-worn paths.
What sand the north wind pours over the ruins
The south wind scatters when it blows.
And in the empty, ruined courtyard
The spoor of the white gazelle
Lies like peppercorns.

On the morning of departure,
While they loaded the caravan in the acacia grove,
I wept uncontrollably;
My anguish and longing for my loved one
Were as sharp as the tears shed
By those who grind the bitter apple seed.
My companions reined their camels and called:
"Courage! Do not let grief overwhelm you!"
"Why do I weep over vestiges and ruins?
My sorrow has become mechanical, ordinary
Like the tears shed for old loves, Umm al-Ḥuwayrith
And her neighbor Umm al-Rabbāb, at Maʾsal."
Yet till tears gushed, from the depths of my anguish,
Coursed down my cheeks, my neck,
To the edge of my sword's scabbard.

Will good fortune ever visit me again
Like that memorable day at Juljul?
The day I slaughtered my camel for the virgins
And they, in turn, carried its load?

Oh, the lovelies, the young virgins,
The joyful, the playful,
Tossing the meat, its fat soft as white damask . . .

And the day I entered ʿUnayzah's litter
And she cried, "Beware! I shall make you walk!"
For the litter rocked with our weight.
"Get off, Imrūʾ al-Qays, you'll kill my camel!"
"Forget the camel," I said. "Don't let me go!
Don't deprive me of your passionate self!"

And many women have I approached,
Even those pregnant or nursing,
Who left their amuleted babies
For me. When the child cried,
The mother offered her breast
But gave the rest of her body to me.

Another day, on the hills of the dunes,
Fāṭimah turned away, and said she would leave me.
"Oh, my love," I begged, "don't tease me.
If you wish to part, let us do it cleanly.

If my actions grieve you,
Let us separate your clothes from mine.
Why have you become so proud and cold
When my heart bursts with love for you?
Your tears are not shed in sorrow,
But to wound my heart, already broken."

I enjoyed also great pleasure and ease
With a fair-skinned virgin who scorned others.
I braved danger to find her,
Passed guards sworn to slay me.
That evening, the Pleiades were waning
In the evening sky;
The stars winking like necklaces
Of pearls and gems.

When I reached her chamber, she was naked
Except for her last garment.
"My God," she cried, "you must be mad!
How did you come? Guards
Surround me everywhere."

We walked out into the desert,
She dragging her shawl
To erase our footprints.
From the camp we walked to the dunes,
Toward a bank where the sands
Knotted like ropes.
When she faced me, a fragrance
Washed over me like the morning breeze
Bearing the scent of cloves.

When I pleaded my desire,
She arched her elegant body,
Slender, narrow-waisted, fuller near the feet
Where her anklets ring.
She was taut and white
As a young gazelle,
Her breasts smooth as mirrors,
Her skin pale like the first egg of the ostrich,
Delicate as the new pearl
Fed by the waters of the sea.
When she turned, she brushed me with a smooth cheek
And the warm glance of a cow with her new calf.
Arching her neck like a wild gazelle,
Her jewelry adorning its bareness.
Hair dark as night, thick, black,
And tangled in its richness.
The tendrils curling of themselves,
Escaping the restraint of combs.
Her fingers in their delicacy
Are all soft and white
Like the bark of the walnut tree.
Willowy and sweet is her waist.
Her legs slender as the reeds of the palm.
Her beauty glows in the darkness of night
Like the fires on the hills
Pious monks light for travelers.
Ah, my lady rises late; she is not belted like a slave,

And her scent, the scent of musk,
Lingers in the bedclothes.
Yes, a wise man would love
A woman of her beauty
For she is in the prime of life.

Men forget their childish love games
As their youth passes,
But I still love with the joy
And the passion of youth.
Oh, my friends have offered much advice
And I have rejected all
Their suggestions;

Night, like the waves of the great sea
Has stretched its darkness over me,
Brought many sorrows to test me.
That long night I have wept,
While the night lifted its chest,
Stretched its body, and
Dragged its long tail behind.
"Oh, sorrowful, long night," I cried,
"Be finished, so morning may dawn,
A morning that cannot be as
Black as this moment.
Oh, unending night," I cried,
"Your stars are unmoving,
Tied to the mountain side
With braided, twisted ropes,
As though the Pleiades were tethered
On linen cables
To the solid granite
Of unmoving stone."

While birds are still in their nests, I rise and mount my horse—
My horse, massive as the temple, who leaves fleet animals behind . . .
He charges, turns, retreats, racing, his hoofs landing sure
As stones thrown by the force of a waterfall.
His back, this steed, is smooth as glass;
An ordinary rider slides off that great escarpment.
He attacks like a storm, a tempest, a torrent,
His legs stretch like a swimmer breasting the tide.
His hooves a cloud of dust when they touch the ground.

Racing, he is like a pot on the fire, bubbling higher and higher,
He runs as though fires burned at his heels.
He tosses the young untried riders, and clothes
Fly off the inept rider who dares to mount him.
Tireless as a child's spinning toy, he runs,
A toy used, broken, and retied for greater strength.
He has the flanks of a gazelle, ostrich's legs,
The stride of the wolf, the speed of the fox;
His neck shines like the smooth yellow stone
On which the bride's perfume is ground, the bitter apple crushed.
And he sleeps standing beside me,
Saddled and bridled for mounting at dawn.

Once we came upon a herd of black cattle, wild, white-tailed,
circling like the virgins of Dawar in their white trains;
they approached us, a string of black beads, punctuated
with pearls, like the necklaces worn by the noble boys of the
tribe; we rounded them up into a single herd, gently, carefully,
swiftly; my horse passing between a bull, then a cow, then a bull,
moving calmly, without the beads of sweat that might have
washed him. When we rode into camp that evening,
the cooks of the clan grilled the meat quickly.

My noble horse!
Who saw him then saw perfection,
Noted it with surprise
And looked away to avoid evil,
The wild cows' blood spattering his chest,
A stain of henna on whiteness,
His tail not long enough to brush the ground,
Yet not too short for beauty.

Now the lightning comes like two glittering hands
Moving to split the wreaths of clouds,
Shining and flaming like the monks' lampwicks,
Drenched with oil, and flaring brightly.
I have sat with friends to watch the storm
Moving toward us from between Ḥamir and Ikām,
The rain rushing down like milk from the she-camel,
Uprooting the broad-branched thorn trees before us;
Sparing no houses except those of stone,
Leaving no palm tree standing in Taymāʾ.
Water encircling Mount Abān
Like a great thread of mist twisting round a spindle.

After the storm, all lay green and blooming
From the hills of Qaṭān to al-Satār and Yadhbul.
Grass sprouted until the slope
Appeared like a great chief of the tribe in a striped cloak.
The mountain of Busyān was swelled by the flood
So its stone necklaces
Were everywhere loosened.
The rains came like a merchant from Yemen
Unfolding his goods on the desert of Ghabīṭ;
And in the morning we saw, scattered on the desert,
Like the bulbs of wild onions,
The drowned lions.

The Wādī al-Dawāsir Poem

The session continued nearly all night, interrupted by the passing around of bitter coffee and by a meal of mutton, milk, and dates. Compressed dates serve here as a staple food. There are numerous varieties, and many ways of serving them. I enquired about the names of the various kinds, of which the wealth is a sure social criterion. Right off, they cited a baker's dozen, which I transcribe here very roughly: *srī, maqfūzī, ʿanab, sofrī, khlas, khesh-khāsh, qlaykhī, hḍayk, dgel* (yes, the echo of the famous Algerian variety), *khḍīrī, nabet s-sīf, khashram, sellaj*.

But the hospitality would not have been complete had it been confined to ancient poetry. So, the next day a mulatto of imposing presence appeared: ʿUbayd al-Ḥamdān, headman of al-Nawʿaym Oasis and a poet in the Nabatean, *nabaṭī*, genre.[6] The man was affable, bubbling over with anecdotes and witticisms. At the insistent request of the audience, he recited several selections from a poetry of war and honor, praising "high-mindedness," *nāmūs*, and excoriating cowards, *al-lāshsh*. Erotic inspiration also, we may be sure, is not lacking, but is apparently reserved for less official circles.

I wrote down one of these *qaṣīdas*:

O God, to Whom we pray, Who forgives our sins, Who moves the planets,
Grant the wishes of your slave;
This I beg from You Who know all intentions and all secrets,
What lies deep in my heart, what I contemplate.

Yesterday, while I stood on the summit of the hill, I was suffused with sadness

As though I nestled in embers, in brooding flames.
I gazed about me.
Was there a being to whom I could confide my dreams,
Who could achieve what I could not achieve?
No, there is no one in this age when deception and indifference have destroyed all hope of gain
Except for the coward and the son of a coward, who abandons his children!

Now, what leads me to create a poem
Is a friend, who writes to me and reproaches me.
No, my companion, give me the best she-camel,
Lofty of shoulder, plump and pleasing of hump,
Undulating like the young girl in the host's courtyard
Who unloosens her tresses until her hair envelops her.
Ah, if she could only come when shadows fall
Along an empty road, where jackals howl,
To join Mashārī, who has received a feast of camels;
He is rich in *kayf*,[7] he lets *kayf* flow;
He empties the cups of al-Iḥsāʾ for the guests arriving.
At this great gathering the baseborn do not dare approach;
Greet him quickly and give him the news;
I think he will approve his friend's proposal.
Tell him and see how quickly you rise to the peak of his esteem.

Blessings on him who buys and offers *kayf*;
Dishonor on him who accepts humiliation;
But bravo to him who endures the injustice of banishment;
You see the messenger, bringing you the pages of letters,
You see the messenger; wherever he turns, my friends rise for him;
You are reviving an art, long lost, forgotten,
But my heart is troubled for you,
And hopes you pass quickly through that bad time
When camels are so thin their girths swing.
I swear to you, the baseborn man is the son of a sheep.

All my life I will practice my art, and it will be with me.
O men of passion, for passion, O men of character,
Makes great demands upon the generous;
You see their whole soul in their passion, O men of character,
And each acts according to the dictates of his heart.
As for me, I still hope for a lover with white teeth,
With breasts like apples no child has sucked.
Speak to me of the one I love in the desert,

A gazelle who plumbs my heart and disturbs its watering places.
And the name of my beloved? You see, Mashārī, the time has come
to tell it,
For where she blooms in the desert, only the moon knows.

It is a difficult text. I took it to Kuwait where, for its interpretation, I had to send for a commentary by the poet himself. Even so, it is not certain that the translation gives the meaning in all details. In any case it brings out amazingly how truly it belongs to a genre a thousand years old, in the typical alternation of conventional features and dazzling word combinations.

Birth of an Oasis

We passed again through Sulayyil.

"I have fourteen children," replied the driver. He was driving the Ford over the sands in full confidence. Two locks of black hair, the *swālif*, hung down to his shoulders. His face was of a grave and ancient beauty.

We were in central Arabia, on the edge of the Rubʿ al-Khālī, the immense desert extending over the southeast of the Peninsula. The government agency Petromin, that feather in the cap of Shaikh Zakī Yamānī, the energetic minister of petroleum, had only recently given up its prospecting licenses in the Rubʿ al-Khālī. Thus it is Agip and Phillips Petroleum, or Arkas (in which a French geophysics company participates), which some day will make the wells gush forth from these solitudes or, it is whispered, uncover their gold, iron, copper, or sulphur.

So much for the subsoil. As for the scenery, for one who knows something about it, monotony is giving way to variety in the lay of the land, to grasses or their vestiges, to places with names. The Dawāsir, just now in their summer pastures several hundred kilometers to the north, will return here in the winter. Where will they find drinking water? "Two weeks ago," said the emir of Sulayyil, forbidding looking with his trachoma-marred eyes and pock-marked face, "a woman died of thirst, her camel having injured itself." And yet, there is nothing more certain than the trustworthiness of these beasts. But the distances are even more powerful. A specially equipped Jeep will take a week to cross the Rubʿ al-Khālī. On the other hand, one steers as if at sea, by dead reckoning, without taking time to look for trails. At night, one is guided by the positions of the stars, and some old camel drivers are excellent at it, as in the case of our chauffeur.

We had passed the Sulayyil airport, where the weekly Riyad-Nejran mail plane lands. This is the spot called Farsha, or Barsha, a sort of underground reservoir, it seems, where water from the rainstorms collects. In fact one can see a few scattered shrubs, those thornbushes or *sumar* beside which fifteen centuries ago the poet, "working the bitter apple seed," wept over his beloved's absence. This other shrub, the *ghadā*, provides a much-sought-after wood for boiling coffee. Life clings in all its dimensions to this scarcity that endows its struggle with nothingness with a symbolic density.

Quite some way into the desert, we were led to a borehole from which fossil water from a great depth emerges almost boiling, and cools as it spreads over the surface of the ground. A population of bulrushes and other plants has grown up around this pond, which camels already visit regularly. Although a little brackish, the water has quickened life. Tomorrow the oasis will spread. On the banks we see footprints of animals and of men. A hunter must have crawled behind these tufts to get a better aim at his game, a fat bustard, perhaps, or a gazelle, although it is illegal to hunt the latter. Certainly not the onager of the poems, nor the wild ox, nor the ostrich. The chauffeur, who calls the ostrich by its old classical name, *al-ẓalīm*, tells me that a few specimens still exist in the inner mountains of Oman. The ruler of Qaṭar's brother had collected one or two for his oryx farm.[8]

Suddenly the emir threw himself to the ground. His robe bared a nomad's elegant thighs. "It really was a bustard," he said. He had identified the spoor. He was overjoyed. Hunting, sister of war and food-gathering, exerted upon him the same forces as on his ancestors. As a matter of fact, however much the landscape has changed in the direction of increasing aridity, one feels very close here to the poetry of pre-Islam. This is the very encounter I had sought in the birthplace of the great *Muʿallaqa*. The emir, who instinctively shared my impressions, embarked on a topical eulogy of Bedouin life. He proclaimed proudly that no woman of theirs would resign herself to a home in town. Umm al-Ḥuwayrith, Umm al-Rabbāb, "when they arose, the perfume of musk wafted from them . . ."

No more horses, the emir admitted. No more chivalry, as I see only too clearly. Here and there, imported pyramidal tents of canvas stand beside the ancient house of hair, or take its place. The American auto is the symbol of all wealth; much of the seasonal migration is made by truck. Then there are the deep wells, witnesses to industrial might. There are a dozen in Wādī al-Dawāsir alone. Government offices in these remote posts are lavishly furnished with mechanical equipment. In the very center of Arabia one observes that the country is entering the stage of infrastructure, with its basic virtues, while rigorously maintaining society as is. How long will the fragile companionship of machine and conservatism last? There is something naïvely tragic in this effort to modernize equipment and services—such as the many schools and the Wādī al-Dawāsir hospital with its sophisticated operating theater—while seeking to preserve not only fundamentals, which would be only legitimate, but also the derivations from primitive Islam, or rather the archaisms carted along with them.

A few days later we visited the Petroleum Institute at Dhahran. Its architects have succeeded in harmonizing its volumes and colors with the surrounding rock, as the people of Thamūd must have taken such pleasure in doing. But in this superb setting the obvious advance in scientific and technical apprenticeship is unaccompanied by preoccupation with the social sciences; not the slightest mention of them or of the very existence of societies, as if technique could exist without men, or vice versa. The fact that at this very moment a million Yemeni immigrants are in Saudi Arabia, substituting for the country's own sons not only in the factories but also in cultivating the oases and herding the flocks, does nothing to dispel the question

VII
Grandeur and Weaknesses of Agonistic Man

My only qualification to speak of ancient Arab poetry is that I like ancient Arab poetry. That may well be a serious handicap as far as competence goes. But as this same taste obviously exists among Arabs, forming one of the continuities of their psychological and social lives and perhaps their only enduring harmony, the study of their contemporary history and where their societies are headed must attach substantial importance to their old poetry; it constitutes beyond doubt one of their "living pillars."

History and Imagination

At the Mirbad Poetry Congress at Basra (spring 1971) many pieces heard dealt, as might have been expected, with current vicissitudes, and above all with the eviction of the Palestinians. This new kind of *ḥamāsa* carried the audience to a pitch of enthusiasm hard to imagine. Some strains of patriotic exaltation created such an illusion that, listening, one had to make an effort of will to keep from believing the problem was settled, or about to be. On the other hand, press campaigns opposed the very holding of the congress, questioning the propriety of this poetic display at a time when so many other more practical matters demanded the citizens' attention. A young Palestinian poet whispered to me, "Their *ḥamāsa* makes me laugh."

Basra itself contributed somewhat spuriously to this mythical or imaginary atmosphere.[1] Several sessions were held on Sindbad's Island—that Sindbad who was himself a fictitious character and whose Basra was furthermore twenty miles or so away from today's. Worse still, the Arabian Nights vaunted in Iraqi tourist brochures talk of Baghdad but this Baghdad may be a pseudonym for Cairo if, according to a recent theory,[2] it was actually in the Mamelukes' Cairo that this immense book was collated. Imagination, phantasmagoria if you will. Genuine historicity nevertheless, as we shall see.

The colloquium opened some distance from the present Basra, in the village of Zubayr, which partially occupies the city's ancient site, and more precisely on the Mirbad. What is this Mirbad, or Marbid? According to the etymology we are given, it was the esplanade where shackled camels were offered for sale, or else an area where dates were spread out to dry. In any case it was Islam's ʿUkāẓ, that is, its permanent fairground for economic, poetic, and political purposes. Imagine an enormous, milling crowd of bodies and cries so dense, tradition says, that if one threw a pebble from the adjacent hill he would inevitably hit someone's head. Innumerable customers thronged about the stalls of merchants of all sorts, restaurant keepers, and meat roasters, including some roasting those lizards prized by Bedouin gourmets. Animated conversations. Public orations. Conspiracies. From there arose some of the most violent seditious movements: rebellion against the Umayyads, rebellion against the Abbasids in the name of ʿAlī's descendants, revolt of the blacks against the Arab rulers. In short, Mirbad was both the focus of infection and its exutory. One ʿAlid pretender was killed on this feverish spot.

Above all, for our interest, it was a fairground for poetry frequented, according to tradition, by singers like Jarīr, Farazdaq, or Dhū al-Rumma. They recited their poems before a very critical audience. No love was lost between the first two, and both were arrogant toward the third. This latter found tormentors even among tradesmen: a tailor, for example, taunted him so severely for faults in composition that he reduced him to silence. Such was the literary exigency of this crowd, which appraised the great *fuḥūl* passionately, but without docility or human respect. Would that we had gathered here with the same integrity, fourteen centuries later, to talk poetry in this raging, tormented East! In the era of travel to the planets, at a time when, much nearer us, Palestine was suffering unatonable conflicts, when most of the Arab countries, among them Iraq, in more peaceful but equally tense fashion, were engaged in petroleum negotiations of decisive importance, was it not rather frivolous to talk poetry where one ought not simply to talk history, but to make it?

But that is a typically Western antithesis. Why forbid the Arabs to make of poetry, provisionally, their strong point? Why urge them to make the frightful cleavage all Europe has made between the real and the imaginary? In this field, Freud simply resumed the dualist tradition of Platonism or Platonized Christianity. For this Viennese, it was no longer the spirit or grace which should be released and take flight from the body and nature, but the libido. In symmetry with this flight, he contrived the excavation of the subconscious, well adapted to house subterranean realities repressed not only by heaven, as had theretofore been said, but also by society, the conscience, and civilization. Thus triply locked in, desire could free itself only by breaking out violently, or through therapy. But do therapy and even such effraction not simply solidify, after all, the layered structure into which they merely open peepholes?

Islam, on the other hand, digs no caves into nature. God Himself, an honest observer, granted sexuality to the Arabs. If He revealed Himself more stern toward their poetry, they have stood up to Him stoutly and preserved until our day that parallel reality with which the incandescence of verbal rhythm endows them. The danger for them lies not in remaining faithful to this parallelism but in denying it: that is, in confusing poetry with action. The danger is that the poem, not content with creating its own object, which is to arouse the individual or collective being to a certain mood, may be deceived by its presumed information content and offer itself as a surrogate for praxis.

Three Problems

The Koran, already, had reproached poets for preaching things they did not practice.[3] It thus denounced that referential illusion that is one characteristic of all poetry, although in unequal degree from one society to another. Now in the case of the Arabs it is paired with what I shall call textual illusion. Without endorsing the hypercriticism of those who ascribe a major part of pre-Islamic poems to subsequent writing, we must acknowledge that interpolation has been the constant rule, even if it is not so of the essential elements. This, of itself, constitutes a social reality. Accusations of plagiarism and repetition are coextensive with the history of Arab poetry. In our day we can hear the same sort of quarrels as erupted as early as Umayyad times. The misadventure of Elie Abū Māḍī is there to prove it.[4]

We are thus led to one of the most serious problems attending study of these materials: that of authenticity. The ultimate irony is that the most corrosive doubts raised concern Imrū᾿ al-Qays.[5] The second problem is that, even if there is no repetition or plagiarism properly speaking, even if one author or another does not see fit to take over, as his own, phrases, whole hemistichs, or entire passages from his predecessors, at least he does rehash age-old themes. Thus, one may trace the abandoned campsite feature in all Arab poetry from the beginning to the present day. Third, a feature often pointed out by detractors of these bards: the real or alleged incoherence they display in organization, when they pass from description of the campsite to that of a woman, then the she-camel, the morning hunt, the storm, and so on, without concern for logic or unity, the poem ending on an incident, without the slightest apparent logic of sentiment or narrative.

Two Answers

An academic tradition, firmly rooted among us since Taine and Lanson, consists in studying a work by beginning with its externals. What interests us here in the poem is neither its context nor even its genesis, but only its poetic quality. Let us nevertheless begin by establishing a historical perspective. A single field connects all Arabic poems, throughout successive generations and various milieus, and this field is sufficiently homogeneous that the same effects reverberate over its entire duration and its entire spatial extent. Yet today some of the greatest publication successes are of ancient poems. The *Rawāʾiʿ* collection is one of the most successful commercial ventures in the Arab world. The same, needless to say, does not happen among us when a Byzantinist prepares an edition of Romanos the Melodist, who was roughly Imrūʾ al-Qays' contemporary.

This unitary resonance, which of course has its sociological reasons, explains the role that repetition plays in such a poetry. A part of the poetic value is due to the recurrence of the same sonorities, the same figures of speech, the same themes, and, at the extreme, the same verses. This can be confirmed within a single poem and from century to century. It is probable that the beauty felt in our times by Arab readers of the *Muʿallaqa* owes much to the fact that it has lived in so many memories between Justinian's day and our own. If all poetry is echo poetry, since the poet, as Blanchot has said, is the "master of the memorable," this is further confirmed in this poetry. No Arab poet, I think, has considered that the main thing was to say something for the first time, although the best ones have considered that things should be said again in new ways. An invariability, thus, which slight metrical, lexical, and other variations clothed, in the best instances, with an individuality of composition, moment, and man. As to repeat is to remember, the theme of remembering, *dhikrā*, was the pre-eminent theme, since it coincides with the purpose and, to a point, with the mnemotechnical nature of the work.

In short, from the first of these poets onward, any creative act was considered an exercise in beginning over again. Thus the first line of the *Muʿallaqa* by that ʿAntar known to Western publics through comic opera: *hal ghādara al-shuʿarāʾ min mutaraddami am hal ʿariftu al-dāra baʿd tawahhumī?* ("Have the poets left off their patchwork / or do I recognize a site I had previously imagined?"). *Mutaraddam* is, for example, the theme of *aṭlāl*, or "vestiges of the abandoned camp," a virtually obligatory theme which will be attuned with others by "patchwork," that is, in rhapsodical form—were the *Iliad* and *Odyssey* not rhapsodies? However, the powers of the imaginary are such that this operation may lead the poet to the real site of an actual adventure. The referential illusion is thus preserved in the interrogative mood, and the violence of the sentiment is in no way affected by the repetition.

It is the same with Zuhayr: *Mā arānā naqūlu illa muʿāran aw muʿādan min lafẓinā makrūran* ("I see how we intone only borrowed or repeated songs, but retold in our own language"). It could not be said more clearly. This repetition avowed by the great bards reigns supreme over the collective subconscious. In the popular poetry of the Shāmiya, overlapping Saudi Arabia, Iraq, and Syria, as in that of southern Tunisia, one finds illiterate poets inserting even entire hemistichs from pre-Islamic poems in their compositions.[6] In this process, collective memory follows the path of ʿAntar and Zuhayr.

If this is so, it explains another peculiarity of many ancient pieces. Critics distinguish between those that result from long, studied composition and those that spring forth spontaneously. Both obey sophisticated meters, as well as a complex prosody which seems to defy improvisation. But tradition speaks of very lengthy works that are said to have been improvised all of a piece. The ode of Ḥarth bin Ḥilliza is one example, but not the only one. Must we assume the presence of a "geno-text,"[7] on-going throughout the Arab world, that now and again breaks through the surface in individual poets, while its generative character is imbedded in the Arab collectivity across space and time? Let us leave the question open, while urging the specialists to reflect on the explanatory possibilities that might be opened up by thus treating as a unitary propagation a poetry that spread for so many centuries from the Atlantic to the Indian Ocean.

The Preparatory Void

Where is sincerity in all this? This elegiac poetry deals only with conventional loves. Often the woman bears a name that recurs from author to author. Are we even sure that the poet was ever in love? These weepy nostalgias come too often to express, and thus to communicate, a deep perturbation. Let it be understood that we do not demand of the poet that sincerity of conduct that allegedly gives romantic-style poetry its strength. "O, beat thy breast . . ." But we have a right to expect from him truthfulness in sensation, sound, and image without which there is no meaningful expression.

But what if this vacancy of subject were laid down by rule: if, precisely, much of this poetry depended upon a sort of initial emptiness, the poet preparing a void as his first step, so as to draw his own creation from this very void? One would then understand why the evocation of the desert and of the vestiges that stand out from its emptiness occupies such a prominent place in most of these works. For the desert, surely, is one sort of void. And the poet, or his utterance, in the desert is truly a being endeavoring to situate himself in a negativity no longer endured but voluntary.

This bringing about of a poetic void is nevertheless sometimes accompanied by the most poignant realism. Some of the beauty of these texts comes from man's pathetic effort to transcend the void and transform it into linguistic reality. The role thus assigned to negativity is expressed grammatically by that of negation or of images evoking exclusion, effacement. One might say that every affirmation or evocation in the poem is accomplished by the device of one negation refuting another negation. Listen, for example, to the first poem of Dhū al-Rumma,[8] the camel driver and poet who wandered as a nomad between Mirbad and the desert and who died at the time of the Battle of Poitiers.

> The east wind unveiled,
> like unfolding a page of writing,
> the dark marks of a dwelling
> from the flow which had covered its traces;
> the breeze, after having hidden them,

swept the crest from the dune
and scattered the sand.

Such a poem follows an asymptote, so to speak, toward nothing, but a nothing that soon turns into resuscitation. That was precisely the stake in the game. The effacement of the dune reveals something permanent. The sentiment rests in the antithesis between the unvarying and the ephemeral. One day's adventure reveals by its very evanescence the sort of eternity that lies hidden in landscapes and their denizens, the wild beasts. To designate the latter, Arabic has the rather remarkable word *awābid*, which might be translated "perdurable creatures." They are so in the sense that they always stay the same, without event or history, whereas man trembles amid his vicissitudes. Even in man, by analogy with the general order of things, the *waḥshī*, "bestial," is opposed to the *anīs*, "human." The opposition is demonstrated in diction. The rough or rugged contrasts with the smooth and flowing: Farazdaq face to face with Jarīr. But all this stands in relation to the void, a void from which (*a*) material and immaterial invariables, (*b*) man's pathetic adventure, and (*c*) the poet's art itself stem (I was about to say "result dialectically").

More-searching study would reveal correspondences from level to level among these three categories. For the time being, let us simply hear the opening lines of a few *aṭlāl*. This is how that of Nābigha's *Dāliya* begins:

> Oh, the dwelling place of Mayya, on the summit and slopes of the mountain, is deserted. Long years have passed it by.
>
> Toward day's end, I paused for an instant to question it. But it had no power to respond. In all that place, there was not a single soul.

Or the opening of Ṭarafa's *Muʿallaqa*:

> On the stony ground of Thahmad, the remains of the house of Khaulah shine like the trace of a tattoo on the hand's surface.
>
> And there my companions, reining their mounts, said to me, "Do not expire of grief! Take heart!" . . .
>
> . . . and the tribe possessed a dark beauty, a gazelle of an age to enjoy the fruits of *arāk*, its neck adorned with two necklaces of pearls and chrysolite . . .

Let us yield here to the temptation to pursue this highly sensual page:

> In the camp there is a black-lipped woman
> who gathers fruit for *arāk*,
> a gazelle who displays two strings of pearls and onyx;
> she has abandoned her young, she grazes with the herd, in the shade;
> she stretches her body up to the branches of the *barīr*, to cover herself.
> Her smile is like a flower unfolding
> on the dark sand, disturbing the purity of the damp dune.
> Sunbeams radiate from her
> except from those kohl-tinted gums
> she does not hide while chewing;
> O luminous face, clear, unblemished,
> as though clothed in sunlight.

Listen, finally, to the first lines of Labīd's *Muʿallaqa*:

> They have left the places where they had established their camp, the traces of their nomadic dwelling; at Mina, which was for a long time their home, a frightening solitude reigns today, and on Ghūl, on Rijām, and on the cliffs of the mountain of Rayyān.
>
> There, like letters carved in rock, the traces of their dwelling have reappeared, discovered by the floods which have unveiled what before was hidden from sight.[9]

Labīd is beyond doubt the most Bedouin of them all, the crudest and most rugged. He is truly a tribesman; and what a tribe! The Banū ʿĀmir, the wildest, the most obstinately resistant to the new times. The dangerous cousins of those Banū Hilāl we know so well in the Maghreb. Now Labīd displays magnificently, and of course in a much harsher manner than the Old Regime French of Silvestre de Sacy can render, the alternation between man's emotion and nature's immutability, a theme which, long after him, Vigny was to utilize. Re-read this fragment in another language: ". . . I stood there questioning them. What use! Ask questions of permanencies whose language is indistinct?" This indistinct quality is the opposite of *bayān* and of *tafṣīl*, the "articulation" that does honor to human language. Nature's is a powerful but inert language, and the poet achieves an effect by this quasi-linguistic opposition between the inarticulate and the articulated.

Then this other verse: *fa madāfiʿ al-Rayyān ʿurriya rasmuhā khalaqan* ("The planes of Rayyān, their lineaments laid bare against its mass, like an inscription a rock might conceal"). *Khalaqan*—the word serves several purposes. It evokes creation: the rocks have been there through all eternity. But also the image of a smooth compactness. In Labīd one finds a number of instances where the same root is used to mean dense clouds laden with rain, or rocks worn away by abrasion. Let us agree that in both cases what is involved is a return to that primordial inarticulation from which, before the Prophet, only the poet could draw forth a word.

A Turnstile between Artificial and Original

Among these poets this fundamentalism at the origin ends up in contradiction. The images aroused in their mind by these rediscoveries evoke inscriptions, tattoos, embellishment: all flowing from artifice, not from the origin. In an admirable article, still often quoted, on artistic expression in Islam, Massignon remarked that most of the Arab poets' metaphors or images were descending metaphors, in the sense that they traverse from top to bottom the scale of creation in genera and species.[10] For example, they compare a bird to a precious stone, a plant to a mineral, and so on. What we are observing here is the exact contrary: an ascending comparison that projects the metaphor from such brutal and rough bases upward toward the acme of *tafṣīl*, the articulated. Besides, it is not by accident that we see the combinatorial so often recurring in Imrūʾ al-Qays' *Muʿallaqa*. Everywhere there are intricate pendants, composite jewels, Damascus textiles with their fringes: refined things, in short. This is not the only case where we find reference to the finished, the ornamented, and the perfected among these earliest poets. So with Dhū al-Rumma, in his *bāʾiya* already cited when, having cast up an affirmation of the desert's double negation, he proceeds immediately to a work of artifice:

. . . . No,
This is nostalgia for a place
Revealed now by a moving cloud, now by a violent storm;
Although the ruins are ancient, the eye still can see

The protective trenches, an old hearth, a slaughtering place;
At last the marks of the camp are revealed
Like the carving of a new scabbard
On the slope of Zurq;
Neither the dusty calms nor the winds nor the passage of
  seasons
Have demolished its traces.

Another striking thing about these pullulating images is, in spite of any poet's propensity to range the eternal feminine with the elemental, the equally great propensity to compare the beloved to a hand-fashioned thing: to a statue, for example, and even a Roman statue. That is the case of Nābigha al-Dhubyānī who, speaking of the woman he is describing with such warmth (and the warmth of his description, as is well known, was to get him into trouble), compares her to a marble[11] statue on a pedestal of brick. In the same spirit Akhṭal, praising the legs of his she-camel, compares them to the pilasters of a Roman fort. For if most of these poets are desert poets, many of them often visited Palmyra, the upper Euphrates, and the Damascene—that is, regions of Romano-Byzantine influence. This aspect of their imagery constitutes an Arab tribute to Mediterranean culture, and one wonders whether this is not the case with all their references to manufactures.

This is nothing to be astonished at. But how far we have come from a true nature poetry! The desert's emptiness melts into artifice. The murmur of the collective subconscious ends up as subtle prosody. Should we say that these achievements in turn call for a fertile nullification of the desert? In any case a revolution had to occur, that of the Koran, before man's "innateness," *fiṭra*, and Nature's truth could break out of this circle and be summoned together to the cosmic perspective and to the inimitable discourse.

Modal Deployment

Let us proceed to another point, which has aroused many controversies: the incoherence of composition from which the majority of these pieces is said to suffer.

To return to the great *Muʿallaqa*: It begins, as is proper, with the elegy on the traces of the encampment. Then it develops a series of recollections interspersed with descriptive passages and lyrical flights, producing juxtapositions so unexpected that some believe they were interpolated subsequently. But the criteria of choice are weak. Why discard lines where the poet compares himself to a wandering wolf, rather than one maxim or another intercalated in the account? And why not the apostrophe to the night? Admittedly, that would be a pity. But must one resign oneself to the arbitrary, or is the poem's composition arbitrary by definition? "Sorrowful, long night, . . . your stars . . . tethered on linen cables to the solid granite of unmoving stone." Have we passed from the circumstantial and cultural on to the cosmic? No, the account of a morning departure on horseback and then the story of a hunt bring us back to the life of men, mingled with that of beasts both tame and wild. Then suddenly the storm, a universal deluge in which seemingly all will be swept away, including the lions, whose carcasses will be tossed up by the flood like wild onion bulbs, except that they are immediately compared to the merchandise unpacked by a Yemeni trader, that is, brought back to the extremely artificial.

Beyond doubt one may assume a progression at the back of this apparent incoherence. Its culminating point would be the closing evocation of the cataclysm which, allegorically destroying the poet himself (poet = lion), washes him clean of all anecdote so as to leave us face to face with the grand motifs of man's existence in society and nature. Is this not a far-fetched explanation? Would it not be better to resign ourselves to these accumulations: here of motifs, there of apostrophes or parataxes simply connected one with another by *wa, wa, wa*? The poet roams the world with "the eye of the seer, *mutawassim*, seeking signs" (Zuhayr). Coherence is not his strong point. His role is to bear witness of the world, which is multiple. But from one mention to another, one comparison to the next, we lose sight of the principles on which his choices are made, and of where he will end up.

See, for example, Dhū al-Rumma: he begins with the expected description of the woman he loves. The evocation came to his mind as he slept in the desert. "The vision of Mayya visits his sleep, become the plaything of the deserts and the noble racing camels." The words *racing camel* ring a bell. So now here is a portrait of the camel. This particular camel is an unusually good goer, and one has only to touch her with one's heel to make her leap. Another bell rings: what is there that leaps? Onagers, for example. Hence a long passage telling the story of the dominant male onager leading a herd of females toward a problematic waterhole. Are we satisfied with this picture? Better retouch it: "Was it truly thus, or instead as if

. . ." The poet indeed shifts the comparison. He goes on to evoke the wild bull wandering over the dunes and eluding a hunter's attack. "Was it really thus, or instead as if . . ." But what is *really thus*? The leap of the camel? The camel was only an incident in the ode's development. It appeared there only as a "carrying" theme, vehicular in all meanings of the word but ultimately without link to love, the central theme. After this we find ostriches, hurrying through the desert storm to find their estrayed young. There it is, that incoherence that Ṭaha Ḥusain said made him blush for his compatriots!

But was his interpretation not rather typically occidental? What if it were not a question of a succession of themes dependent, of course, on an expository logic, but of unfolding the same thing, told successively according to several registers?[12] Those of elegy, sexuality, nature description, adventure, and so forth. Some of these codes ramify into subcodes. Thus, for the desert, the animal code that Dhū al-Rumma expands into three subcodes: onager/bull/ostrich. Who knows if, for him and his colleagues, composing a poem consisted in modulating the poem's idea, which itself was simply the idea of "poem"? This modulation, in which we can no longer see anything but the arbitrary juxtaposition of descriptive bits, consists of a synchronism of modes and codes that makes the *qaṣīda* as a whole one gigantic metaphor.[13]

If that is so, one would hope that a genuine criticism, at once historical and textual, of these works will some day inventory the density of their modulations, that is, find out how many codes are brought into play. A second evaluation would follow, which would scrutinize the details of the tropes within these codifications: their number, their sequence, the manner in which they are distributed, the gap dividing the elements they bring together. Such a criticism has never been undertaken, to the best of my knowledge. Nothing else could account for the aesthetic pleasure experienced by the Arab listener. Almost everywhere, for example, we find a camel description; nevertheless, it is never the same. As a matter of fact, what was expected of the bard, and what the tradition-minded public still expects, is not the taking up of new themes but variations on the invariable.[14] That might explain why so many pieces, even if they begin in the obligatory way—for example by evoking the *aṭlāl*, that is, the void from which the poem is to emerge, or the *nasīb*, the "description of the woman"—end in nothing; they are literally infinite. For neither a logical culmination, which goes without saying, nor a rhythmic clausula marks a *finale* properly speaking. Not only does the poem lack "organic unity," which is the complaint of so many contemporaries, but it also is never finished. It is one instant in a continuing flow.[15]

The Sociolinguistic Effect

But it is a privileged instant. Through it the poet, starting literally from nothing, attains to a particularly suggestive register of collective life.

"Noble, I slake with life my soul's thirst. If we died tomorrow, who among you would not die athirst?" (Ṭarafa). This liberty, this power, would be inconceivable if one attributed them only to an aesthetic endeavor, or to an informative social role. The poet is marginal. "Errant man, wandering the open spaces, the deserts pass him back and forth hirsute, dusty" (ʿUmar bin Abī Rabīʿa). But this asocial, effervescent man is capable of acting upon group structure, upon the collective morphology. The latter, as is well known, rests on genealogies, real or supposed. Now he is able to produce modifications in the landmarks of *nasab*.[16] Jarīr, in some of his poems, had so persistently castigated the Banū Numayr, who lived not far from Basra, that when they came to town they were obliged to identify themselves by passing over their eponym and claiming descent from a more remote ancestor. Jarīr's poetry had been so potent as to have destroyed socially one link in their lineage.

One of the few poets converted to Islam, Ḥasan bin Thābit, brought to the Prophet a devotion as intense as, and more sincere than, the one he had previously exhibited toward the potentates of Ghassān. But his malevolence became that of a bigot. The Prophet himself was surprised at it; he told him, "Your verses are like an arrow in the night, and more bitter than the waters of the sea." This raised a delicate problem. In attacking the unconverted, how were they to be dissociated from their proud lineage? The poet had to make clear that the one he was attacking was "not like his cousin, but a hybrid from whom the brand does not catch fire . . ."

The poets thus came to enjoy formidable political power. Simply by changing premises they could regain the favor of a ruler they had theretofore insulted. No one took exception to such a reversal, any more than anyone was bothered by Farazdaq's vindictive character, Ḥasan bin Thābit's cowardice, or ʿUmar bin Abī Rabīʿa's narcissistic debauchery. In legendary typology, furthermore, the poet was the king's counterpart. At the very least, he was king of the word. We even know of several kings, real or fictitious, among these poets. Imrū᾽ al-Qays was, properly speaking, a "vagabond king," *al-malik al-ḍillīl*. Another was afflicted with leprosy. Another, ʿAntar, royal in bravery, was a mulatto despised by his own father. One, Ṭarafa, ended up as a victim of assassination, while another himself assassinated a king. Listen to Akhṭal al-Taghlibī's apostrophe to the Banū Kulayb: "My two uncles have slain kings and shattered chains!" But if the poet was, so to speak, a parallel king, it was because he had full command of a verbal and agonistic genre in which the collectivity found its affirmation. Hence the astonishing dignity the Prophet conferred upon it by his very attacks: was the poetic not becoming a sort of rival of the sacred?

Now, during the gigantic taxonomical effort Islam undertook in its second century, prosody found a legislator, Khalīl bin Aḥmad, who built it into a system far more rigorous than that of the orthodox rites. The latter, in fact, were able to let the different jurisprudences drift by balancing their pluralism against the unity of the faith. Thenceforth, by contrast, all poetry, present and future, had to conform to a very small number of meters which were imposed upon it unchanged throughout Arab history until its expansion by free verse after the Second World War. Although the feet composing these meters were subject to many tolerances and irregularities, the constrictive model called forth a compensatory recourse in wealth of vocabulary.[17] Only an extensive set of synonyms, in fact, permitted the poet to pursue his idea while respecting metrical invariability. And if it is true that all poetry puts into operation the language's system, *splendor linguae ordinis*, this is further confirmed in the case of that Arabic poetry thus bidden from the beginning to combine rhythmical invariance with diverse kinds of variation governed by rule.

Shall we say that this poetry, by itself, equilibrated the organization of theology, morals, and law? At least it preserved until our day a certain dimension of Arab man.

A Hypothesis

Khalīl's system, a grandiose discovery that we today would call structural, accounted for the rhythm of the pre-Islamic and Umayyad poems and transformed this accounting into a norm. Its unit was the "foot," or *tafʿīla*, a group of phonemes alternating less by long and short, in the Greco-Latin manner, than by "movements" and "pauses," *taḥrīk* and *sukūn*. There were eight, which were grouped variously in fifteen (later sixteen) meters. However, some of these meters overlapped with respect to their middle part, which exhibited the same sequences. Khalīl diagrammed this peculiarity, representing the meters by concentric circles, themselves grouped in sets of three or four, within each of which this partial analogy was found. But the sets could not be reduced one to another. It is true also that innumerable exceptions or licenses disturbed these incomplete symmetries. The colossal effort at abstraction represented by Khalīlian prosody therefore remained largely inoperative and left too much room for empiricism. One could even wonder whether its pretended rigor was not on the scale of its derelictions.[18]

Recently someone had the idea of transcribing the constituent phonemes, according to whether they were *taḥrīk* or *sukūn*, as the figures one and zero, respectively. These series of figures, read continuously without regard for the original division into feet, gave binary numbers which one could transcribe in turn as decimal numbers. It was then perceived that the crazy multiplicity of exceptions and licenses in no way modified the sequences of values attributed to the various meters and which on either side of a central segment, identical for all, distinguished each one from the others. This rhythmic norm is only apparently subject to exception or license. Once converted to numbers, its irregularities disappear. It is absolute to the point that the classifier can identify any meter upon hearing its first syllables.

This discovery by an Iraqi engineer, Ṭāriq al-Kātib,[19] opens up many perspectives which he himself did not derive from it. It is of great importance that the sixteen Arabic meters coincide in mathematical value for an entire median zone that one might call the central matrix of prosody and thus, in many respects, the matrix of the Arabic language itself. Future research may show relationships between this structure and that of society—relationships of which Khalīl, furthermore, had an inkling, since he gave the "verse" the name "tent," *bayt*.

But perhaps the most important thing is that a mathematical reading of a line of poetry can neglect its prosodic division and render it largely superfluous.[20] There is thus now no need to reduce the text to feet before identifying the meter. The meters consist less in mechanical sequences of feet than in modulating sound sequences in a distinctive way. Each of them is defined by a particular combination of phonic values to which corresponds a specific emotion or evocation, as is also the case, in music, with the *maqāms*. It is the continuity, the flow, that counts here. Just as we suspected! While the old poetry has come down to us only in the form of fragments, arbitrary and usually short, various signs show that it was inscribed in an on-going social continuum.[21] The indefinite succession of monorhymed series that have a beginning but never an end, the fact that they involve unlimited variation on a small number of themes, always the same (a little like the *taqsīm* on the lute)—all this tends to support the idea that the *qaṣīda*, to repeat, is not yet quite a poem, but one moment of a certain type of verbal flow linked to certain collective emotions.

A Second Hypothesis

We have yet to determine at just what period the phonic continuum broke into pieces of which some tended toward an autonomous existence. Tradition reports hardly any poems earlier than those of Shanfarā and Muhalhal.[22] Much later Farazdaq, who died about 732, claimed a link with this very first formulation: "The poems have been given me by the Nābighas, who have passed away, and by Abū Zayd and the Ulcerous One (Imrū᾿ al-Qays) and Jarwal (al-Ḥaṭī᾿a) and the Brother of Banū Qays, whom they killed, and Muhalhal, of all poets the first . . ."

Was there, then, no one before *dhāk al-awwal*, "of all the poets the first"? This tender and flowing one and the one set up in contrast with him, the harsh, rugged Shanfarā, seem to be treated as symbols of rival styles:[23] an antithesis as elaborate as the terms it brings into play. But earlier still? Although allusions are occasionally made to earlier poets, their poetry is given only as an implicit precondition. None of it had come down to Muḥammad's contemporaries.[24] Could there then have been a pre-*jāhilite* phase in which what we call poetry, and the Arabs call *shiʿr*, differed so profoundly from what has come down to us that its very substance, even its memory, was so soon and so completely obliterated in this society of such tireless transmissions?

A poetry without texts, whose place was taken by that textual poetry of which the first anthology is said to have been compiled at the court of Ḥīra at the dawn of the seventh century,[25] thus shortly before the "descent" of the Koran. But before poetry became frozen in texts, the work of professionals, and liable to judgment according to an aesthetic and a metalanguage, what was that prepoetry postulated and conjured with by tradition? Doubtless, it represented an on-going activity, on the same basis as trade and war. Doubtless, also, like war and trade, it arose from the joust and the game, in short from the agonistic dimension of this society.[26]

Perhaps the first Arabic poems, which are also among the most beautiful, illustrate the rupturing of a seamless whole rather than the completion of a process. In the course of the sixth century, out of a collective poeticalness lived and sung, *shiʿr* may have become an art of language, with the reductions which that involves: the voluntary stemming of a verbal flow, the deformation of moods into themes, the collapse of a collective role into an individual art and of a continuum into chronological fragments. It was upon this first shattering of the Arab entity that the Koran came to lavish its threat and its consolation.

VIII
Dirge for Pre-Islam

The Banū ʿĀmir bin Ṣaʿṣaʿa had always wandered along the immense arc the plateau describes between the frontiers of Yemen and those of Syria at the border of Nejd. Now during the first half of the sixth century, there took place in the Arabian Peninsula what we should call a change of front. The ruler of Abyssinia occupied Yemen (533), allegiance to which the Banū ʿĀmir then shook off and turned toward the kings of Ḥīra, to the northeast. There they found themselves in conflict with Tamīm, Kinda, Ḥajr, and other warlike groups. One day in 554 (others say in 576) their warriors were beseiged on a mountain, and succeeded only by stratagem in extricating themselves. It appears that Labīd,[1] then a child or young man, took part in this sharp engagement. He must therefore have been born toward the middle of the sixth century, and of one of the noblest families. Interfactional struggle having erupted within the tribe, his clan had to retreat southward, and sojourned for a time on the Yemen border. To the north the Banū ʿĀmir now had to defend themselves against the Dhubyān, who were intriguing against them with the king of Ḥīra. It was even a panegyric pronounced by Labīd,[2] it is said, that ensured his fellow tribesmen's return to the king's favor.

The intervention of poetry in war and politics represented an interdimensional process safeguarding group life and even constituting an integral element of it. The famous war of Fijar had ended in 596, to the extent that such an ancestral mode of behavior could be interrupted. After 612 the Arabian Peninsula began to hear of an extraordinary nobleman of Quraysh who was announcing something quite new. Muḥammad's preaching rendered the agonistic prehistory of the Arabs a dead letter and invited it to become integrated in a more-universal history dominated by spiritual principles. The transition from one order to the other was not accomplished without shock. The terrible Banū ʿĀmir race, cousins of the Hawāzin and the Banū Hilāl, inveterate adversaries of the young Islamic state, was not converted without tribulations, in which Labīd was involved. At the very beginning of the seventh century, when the king of Ḥīra, al-Nuʿmān bin al-Mundhir, was killed in battle by his

Persian suzerains,[3] the tribe returned to its familiar home ground and was sojourning on the eastern border of Hijaz. At length, it apparently embraced Islam and sent a delegation to Medina.

Medina Then and Now[4]

"Cinch your saddles," the Prophet had said, "only to ride to three mosques: mine, that of Mecca, and Jerusalem's." "Mine" was the mosque of Medina. "And even," he continued, "if it were transported all the way to Sanaa, it would still be my sanctuary." For him, Medina was the center of the universe.

Before Islam, the region of the present Medina comprised an incoherent aggregation of small forts occupied by peoples of diverse origin: descendants of the giants, a clan of Banū Hīf, relatives of the still-extant Bili tribe, sections of Aws and Khazraj originally from the south, and Jews, finally, distributed among a score of groups. Medina at that time was not a city, nor even a town. It was an archipelago of habitats, each isolated within its palm groves and vegetable gardens. This plurality, this heterogeneity, connoted perhaps by the Aramaic name *medinata*, "district," was the countertype of Mecca, the bourgeois metropolis which formed a continuous urban unit. From these scattered elements, into which his own company of emigrants was integrated, the Prophet was to make a city which served as a model for all Islam's urban creations until the recent expansion of the new industrial cities.

To leap over the centuries: the founder of Wahhābism was born at the turn of the eighteenth century. While still quite young he was scandalized by the deformations religion had undergone. He was horrified by the mechanical performance of the rites, by supererogatory prayers, the worship of tombs and even sacred trees. He began to destroy these idols with his own hands, which aroused protests and hostility. Hounded out of Basra and nearly dead of thirst, he was succored on his way by a donkey driver.[5]

Welcomed in the town of Darʿiya, not far from present Riyad, by a local shaikh, the ancestor of the Saudi dynasty, he was able to conduct from there his proselytizing and reforming activity. Thenceforth a family of Bedouins thoroughly won over supported his cause. He died in 1791/2, having founded an expanding movement which, after seizing control of Medina, blunted its teeth against Egypt's rival expansion. Righteousness against acculturation! Muḥammad ʿAlī's army, proud of its cannons, twice seized Medina. Wahhābism returned to the desert, from which it emerged only after World War

I, to crush all its opponents. Then petroleum was to gush forth.

Let us return for a moment to events at Medina early in the twentieth century. The city was then governed casually by the Porte. In 1906 an Ottoman prefect, a little too inefficient and corrupt, provoked a revolt by his excesses. This had to be suppressed, and a Medinan prefect appointed in his place. The city had rebelled at the incitement of a sort of popular leader, Anwar al-ʿAshrī. Of course, as always happened in the histories of that period, the Turks regained the upper hand and ended by imprisoning a few dozen notables, whom they exiled to Ṭāʾif.[6] When World War I broke out and when in 1916 King Ḥusain of Mecca proclaimed his alliance with the British, he besieged Medina. But then he faced a Turk of the military species, Fakhrī Bey, who held out against the efforts of the Grand Sharīf and his British ally until the close of the war. In the end, this courageous man was surrendered by his own officers as he slept.[7] Thus ended the Ottoman history of Medina. Meanwhile, the governor, in order to sustain the siege, had expelled most of the civilians, retaining only the garrison, which could thus be more easily fed. The population was thus dispersed, and when it returned to the city it was reduced in size from 80,000 to 15,000.

This Medina which the Wahhābis were to reoccupy in 1924 had always been reputed a place of *faḍāʾil*, "divine grace." One may certainly say that it is still a place where attributes of a singular variety of categories are concentrated. Let's see. According to tradition the city bears ninety-five names, almost as many as God's epithets. Some are extremely curious, such as al-Wajh al-Awwal, "the first face," or Ākilat al-Buldān, "devourer of countries," perhaps an allusion to the fact that it was always regarded as a breeding ground of expansion, and even the center around which the earth rotated. This onomastic wealth is exhibited in the minutest detail. One scholar devotes two hundred pages to the listing and analysis of place names.[8] It is not by chance that the outpouring of a sanctified human intensity is expressed sociologically by the proliferation of its linguistic facets.

Correlatively, innumerable mosques, of which fourteen are very ancient. Innumerable archaeological sites also, many relics and hallowed spots. All of this is venerable, even liturgical, bristling with memories, illustrated by *ḥadīth* references. Anyone sojourning at Medina, one may say, experiences at each step the integration of the Prophetic *sīra* with the city's warp and woof. That is why many believers settle there to end their days, like my old Moroccan friend Ḥājj Faṭmī ben Slīmān.

The pilgrim usually arrives from Jidda, where there are now large hotels and where the first steel mill has just been built. Before the airplane was in general use, he made a taxing land journey of 425 kilometers. At a distance of 22 kilometers from the city, from Jabal Mafraḥa, he had the joy of glimpsing the city's cupolas and, especially, the minarets of the Prophet's mosque. Soon he was in Medina, the object of his pious desires, set like a jewel in a mountainous rectangle: to the east and west, two plateaus of black volcanic rock, the Lābas; to the north, Jabal Thūr, shaped like an enormous petrified tent, as if it had suffered the same curse as Thamūd. Behind it, as a backdrop of sinister mien, Mount Uḥud, where infant Islam suffered a cruel defeat. On the south, an elongated crest curved like a scimitar, Jabal ʿAyg, visible from every square and every window in the city. There are some 8 kilometers between the city and these confines. The area over which the city spreads is thus a quadrilateral of about 15 kilometers on a side.

Alternatively, one may approach by way of a more-august site, the one by which the Prophet descended, still sanctified by the first mosque founded there, the Qubāʾ or Taqwa.[9] This verdant terrain, irrigated by the clearest of water, contrasts with the lugubrious aridity of the surrounding cliffs. After this anteroom of freshness one is greeted by the modern quarter, Bāb al-ʿAnbariya. The offices of all the ministries are grouped in one administrative complex, the Majmaʿ, which has replaced the Turkish barracks where the notables involved in the 1906 revolt were incarcerated. The *baladiya*, the city hall, is also located there. From here you may either proceed to the right, into the center of the city toward the holy mosque and the Prophet's tomb, or continue straight ahead to the north toward the tomb of Sayyidnā Ḥamza, who fought at Uḥud, following al-Manākha Street, a boulevard with the two roadways separated by a broad lawn. Bāb al-ʿAnbariya has become a center of urban vitality. Mosques have been built there, but the one which has received the most attention is naturally that of the Prophet, in the old city. In 1946 the newspaper *Al-Madīna* urged the citizens to contribute to its pious "restoration," *tajdīd*. The work was completed in 1953.

Development of the city has nevertheless not neglected the agricultural horizons which were those of Medina in its most ancient days. It is well known that the typical Islamic city always reconciles the extremely urban with the extremely rural: Damascus with its Ghawṭāʾ, Fez and its marvelous gardens, Granada and the Vega. Symmetrically, the desert appeals for the luscious oasis with its ingenious, industrious agricultural population. In Arabia I have had the opportunity, around Burayda, ʿUnayza, and Majmaʿa, to admire the strange aptitude of these peasants to modernize without ill effects and, so to speak, without surprise, as if by a resurgence of immemorial *fiṭra*.[10] Nor am I surprised that modern Medina has developed agricultural suburbs. The unit for irrigation is the *ḥuḍ*, or "plank," a quite small measure of area. Plants grow in profusion. Mint is cultivated, even the North African variety. The tomato was introduced only recently, as indicated by its metaphorical name, "red eggplant." But that is only one level of cultivation, close to the ground. At the upper level the palm reigns. There are 750,000 of them, of 123 species: here again is found that quality of density, that sociological, kaleidoscopic intensification which here furnishes local erudites with material for special treatises, just as we have observed in Iraq. Among the best-known species we may mention the *chelebī*, the name of which refers to the Turks; the *ṣafawī*; the *ḥilwa*; the *rabīʿa*; and the *barzī*, which I had already listed at Madāʾin Ṣāliḥ. But these dates do not equal Iraqi dates in quality. They are eaten on the spot, and production is said to be declining. Fruit trees constitute an intermediate level: fig, guava, citrus, and mango blend Mediterranean and tropical flora. This is true to some extent of all these oasis microclimates. There are superb grapes which ripen twice a year. They produce the *sharīfī*, eaten immediately, and the *ḥijāzī*, which is left on the vine to be preserved by drying.

Cultivation of food grains apparently once flourished but has now nearly disappeared. Disappeared because, we are told, of high wages for labor. That is a fact which must be related to the steady inflation in oil profits. It must further be said that improvement in transportation makes it possible to import wheat at lower cost than it can be raised. Note, moreover, a rather disturbing phenomenon. Many consider Medina's agriculture doomed, or in any case gravely imperiled. The peaches, famous under the Turks, have been afflicted with all sorts of disease, and other species of trees are in jeopardy. All this, in spite of the regime's solicitude and the advantages that new technology can offer, may usher in the decadence of an ancestral order.[11] The decadence is restrained and masked by power, but it represents the reverse side of a conception of progress as leading in a single direction.

Desert and Words

The Banū ʿĀmir thus gave the impression of joining forces with the Prophet. But the delegation they had sent to Medina remained under suspicion. It was accused of conspiring to assassinate the Prophet.

Arbad, Labīd's brother, was struck by lightning on the way home and died. Was this in fulfillment of a curse by Muḥammad? Or had Arabia's supernatural powers, in which his clan had always believed, avenged themselves on him because he was leaning toward Islam? In any case it was a typical Bedouin death, brutal and ambiguous. Nonetheless, Labīd, rather courageously, celebrated it in verse.[12]

In this old poetry, to repeat, the poem is achieved as it recounts its birth out of a nothingness, which is the desert's emptiness. However conventional the genre had already become, it displayed basic images arising from series of equivalent words of which some are most likely dialectal doublets, although each evokes something distinctive. *Kharq* for "desert" suggests the idea of penetration; *qafr* speaks of widowhood; *daymūma*, of everlasting things; *falat, fayāfī, sabsab, dakdāk* call up still other ideas. A coupling of words, such as *mulajjaja azūm*, the "biting undulance"[13] or "undulant mordancy," goes beyond simple wealth of vocabulary to a literary quality in which Labīd takes evident pleasure. The Bedouin's wandering was perhaps never sung with greater love than his. "Son of the desert, his aspiration goes where it listeth. He migrates wherever he will." To sleep he simply spreads out his saddle blanket. Dawn will draw him from a "final puddle of sleep."[14] The image of the desert calls up dialectically that of the storm, just as that of dead space summons that of revitalization. In this poetry of aridity, water abounds, such as those flash floods which rush forth after the storm and joust one with another for championship.[15] The earth is thereby transfigured, and the nomad attributes its changes to the influence of the stars. What would nature be without the constellations? Hence also the idea of its cyclical eternity, contrasting with man's transitory life.[16]

"We perish, but the rising stars perish not";[17] thus begins the threnody for the lightning-struck brother, the poet's ill-fated surrogate in his combat with the dangerous powers which the Prophet of a new age was challenging.

By contrast with the Koran, it is not spiritual meanings that are ascribed here to words from the most-lively sources, but instead material evocations, profoundly physical, and as if laden with rough etymologies. Take for example the word *yaddāʿī*,[18] which has lost much of its colorful quality in later Arabic. Here it denotes, according to the commentators, the milk remaining in the teats of an animal one has not milked dry. Thence the idea of remaining, applied to an old man, tired of the endless Bedouin wandering, who huddles down miserably at each new encampment. Similarly, the term *ʿafiyāt*[19] does not have the moral meaning it has in contemporary

Arabic but means "gorged with meats." *Wahm*[20] is not yet an "illusory conjecture," but a trail winding in all directions on which one may easily lose his way. *Qalaq*[21] is not yet anxiety but the clattering which results from maladjustment between a thing and its container, such as a badly rigged pulley. Rain revives the *raṣad*; the reference, in the concrete, is to plant seeds beneath the soil's surface which the rain will cause to sprout.[22] "O distances gratified to their ultimate depths by the compact pourer-out until they are adorned with a swaying glory like a carpet, many colored and thickly tufted."[23]

"Compact pourer-out" *khalqāʾ ʿāmila*,[24] refers to a certain kind of cloud. The second term is considered to be a dialectal expression. Very well. But the first term is worth our attention. We have already met it, as will be recalled, at the beginning of the *Muʿallaqa*, where it is said that on the watersheds of Mount Rayyān the drainage channels *tajarrada khalaqan*, "lay bare the mass itself" (or "down to the primordial"). Thus, time's erosion, far from destroying, points up a message. Behind this there is a whole philosophy of nature.

Bedouin Chivalry

The primary characteristic of the Bedouin poet is the sociological origin of his utterance. He is his people's spokesman, who by his word exalts his own group against all others. Thus Labīd: *ulayka qawmī*,[25] "These are my people. If you seek to learn of their virtue, *bi-khīmihim*,[26] you will find it without trouble; every man is aware of their worth." This poetry of pride is also one of nomenclature, and the *Dīwān*'s index lists a very great number of proper names and place names. Incidentally, in this density of group and place names often attributed by both Eastern and Western commentators to a lexical or stylistic affectation, I think there is much more. A patient study seeking to determine the frequency and quality of the toponymy and anthroponymy of each Jāhiliya poet would, I believe, lead to different conclusions of considerable interest.

If knowledge of subgroups and of alliances is essential for a tribesman, it is because it governs the structure in which life is framed, together with the opportunities that exist to transcend it by war, love, and game. Labīd would not be reputed a wise man if he did not take the side of conformity. We hear him define himself as a "fortress of right." Nevertheless, he is a wanderer. "If, far from me, there is empty space, I explore it; and if absence, *al-ghayb*, . . . [should I say, 'mystery'?][27] . . . passes within reach, I seize the reins and leap into the saddle." He protects the supplicant, entertains his guests generously. But he is also a man of wiles who, like old Ulysses, boasts of battles from which he has managed to emerge honorably without fighting. For the nomad is economical of his blood, and the slenderness of the forces he can muster makes this economy obligatory. "How many stringencies and anxieties," as the old Frenchman said, "have I eluded *bi-maqāmī wa lisānī wa jadal*,[28] by my prestige, my eloquent tongue, and my art of debate!" Among the pieces of statutory inspiration there is one which ends with a description of the tribe's glories: "We have a customary law that we obey, also nourishment, renown, and honor." An infinitely concrete humanity pressured by the penury of surrounding nature and, therefore, feeling all the more passionately the moment's intensity. Its poetry will thus be that of invariance and variation.

She saw me,[29] drawn and pale,
Ravaged by sorrows and distant voyages;
Since we parted, how many troubles have I encountered,
How many difficulties faced and conquered—
But I endured.
She knows how my passions
Lead me into dangers and adventures.
Yet I have settled all conflicts without battle,
Without bitterness, without blood.
I have fought injustice among my own cousins,
And have in turn been treated unjustly.

How many empty lands have I crossed,
Riding camels, weary-footed, weary-fleshed,
Traveling at midday, burning with heat,
The legs of the camels dripping sweat,
Startling the peaceful partridges
From their quiet resting places,
Moving, moving through the fire of the sun
Across the sand, against the hot wind of the *simum*,
Pushing on five days and five nights
Through the deadly land of mirages,
Passing familiar bands, wretched people,
Thirsty and thin, riding weary camels,
Traversing unused tracks,
Searching for water beneath the earth.

By God, in the name of your father
This is no country for hospitality,

No country for the guest who comes
Like a cool breeze
Ruffling the dry limbs of the acacias.

The she-camels went dry
Hurrying to find shelter before sunset,
Before the coming of the fearsome cold;
But the males ran on faster, chasing the wind,
Outrunning the male ostrich.

There was no milk to offer our guests,
But we had at least the fat of camel meat,
For my people do not slaughter old, thin beasts;
We offer guests the best that we own;
We strike them down with a sword, the well endowed,
the best of the herd, and strip their bones of meat.

How often, when the country is barren and dry,
The people are more generous than nature,
Not scorning, coldly, their fellow man,
But giving as naturally as the wind blows.
Among our lineage, our ancestors, we see
How hospitable were the old ones of the tribe—

We come from a tradition of generosity,
Of riches, nobility, and greatness

The Binary Ode and Other Form/Meanings

Lexical and thematic commentary does not by any means exhaust all there is to say of this poetry. The verbal flow and the horizons to which it refers—the syntagm and paradigm, if you will—may help us to understand more clearly the opening of that *Muʿallaqa* of which I have already given an old version and which I shall now endeavor to grasp more closely.

Gone is the house of my beloved at Mina;
On the mountains of Ghūl and Rijām
The houses and camps, too, have disappeared,
Their traces erased by floods /
As water erodes inscriptions on stone. /
Years have passed since people abandoned these ruins,
Sacred months, profane months, years of travel. /
The constellations have turned in the heavens,

In spring bringing showers, turning the land green. /
Clouds covering the sky with a dark coverlet,
Answering each other in thunder and rain; /
The wild watercress now sprouts in the valley
Where the ostrich lays eggs, the gazelle gives birth, /
And the cattle, their dark eyes wide, suckle their newborn calves,
Calves soon to roam the desert, wild after tenderness. /
The mountain streams rush over the hidden ruins,
Retracing their outlines as scribes recopy a book, /
Or like tattooers applying pigment and colors
To retrace designs on skin. /
I pause to question the ruins,
But dumb stone cannot respond. /

These houses were abandoned early one morning,
Emptied of all but waterways and bushes; /
I remember the elegant women climbing into the litters,
Tents folded with them, on the backs of the camels, /
Covered by fine cotton, linked to canopies of cotton
Against the dust and the heat of the sun. /
Like the gazelles of Wajra with their loving fawns,
The women watched their little ones
With eyes luminous as the calves of Tūḍīḥ. /

The caravan moved, through the mirage,
Along the valley of Bīsha;[30]
The distant camels seemed like tamarisk bushes or stones
With the shimmering mirage behind them.

In the symmetry of these first lines two stanzas may be distinguished, one evoking the campsite restored by nature to its pristine state, the other the working of human memory. The "erased" of the first line corresponds to the interrogation of line 10. The "erodes" of line 2 corresponds to the "emptied" of 11, as the former's *khalaqan* is echoed by *ṣumman*. The rhyme in *hā*, sometimes repeated at the hemistich, with which each of the eighty-eight verses ends, is the feminine possessive, insisting on the appropriation, in the literal sense, of things one to another. A magnificent example of the "grammar" poetry so dear to Jakobson! And when the poem reverts to the "ruins" (10: "I pause to question" them, and they are now "emptied"), this simply accentuates this reciprocal relationship, constituting "familiarity" or "intimacy," *uns, anīs*. This last word, as it happens, is the object of a superb epitome. The whole selection, in fact, abounds in blocks of terms carried to the point of a quasi-epigraphic density. Labīd's style thus seems to emerge from stony shocks, in the way in which he himself describes the rough abrasion of a rock in the desert as the emergence of a hidden inscription. The repeated use of this sort of relative predicate, so striking in the old poetry and which seems a typical feature of the dialect, contributes to this monumental harshness. It is a nominal sentence, of which the predicate is juxtaposed with the last noun of the preceding syntagm, borrows its case, and assumes a verbal function, even if it is an adjective, while the following noun is parsed as subject. For example, line 5: *ʿashiyyatin mutajāwibin irzāmuhā,* "clouds . . . answering each other in thunder and rain," or the verse *ẓabāʿa Wajrata ʿuṭṭafan ārāmuhā,* "gazelles of Wajra with their loving fawns." This sort of construction, so favorable for oxymoron, brings out powerfully suggestive figures of speech. At this level the poem ascends to admirable heights, in the final line, when the silhouettes of the women perched on their camels eventually merge with those of the stones and tamarisks beside the stream, as if returning to nature.

But the most notable feature of the ode's opening lines, in which the whole *Muʿallaqa*'s beauty, in our opinion, is crystallized, is the deliberate doubling of nouns, images, and adjectives. "Houses" can thus be for a sojourn or simply for overnight. Within the year, "profane" and "sacred" seasons alternate. Clouds are of two kinds, as are the litter's cloths. In connection with this latter, the enigmatic word in line 13, *zawjan,* has intrigued commentators, who have glossed it laboriously. I have translated it as "linking," as I think it simply refers back to that dualism or alternation that imparts a pendulum motion to the ode's entire first section.

By virtue of all these features the prosodic rhythm is enlivened with a binary movement in which substantives and images are joined with sonorities in what has been called a *form/meaning.* The ode's sequence, whose syntactic aspect is intensified by all these repetitions or alternations, reflects a double paradigm: that of the language and that of Bedouin imagination. The same conclusions could be derived from the rest of the *Dīwān.* Here are some examples:

"I am not a precipice of al-Abān, nor yet a hill, nor permanence of the peaks and mountains,"[31] in which we meet again the antithesis between the duration of human life and of nature. Or, "It endures, but its inhabitants have not endured. It has changed into a scattered herd"[32] (flocks of ostriches probably, according to the commentators): all is metamorphosis. Besides, the wild creatures, *awābid*, as we have seen, represent by their very name a permanence, since they are exempt from human individuality and mobility. "Permanences do not presage variation."[33]

Labīd and Woman

The Koran accused the poets of preaching what they did not practice, that is, of not respecting imagination's charter, which is to operate without encroaching on real life. Their falsehood, to repeat, lies not in their inventiveness but in the trompe l'oeil they legitimize. Thus, they go bellowing through the valleys (as I translate *yahīmūna*), acting like fools without feeling genuine love. Is their love mere convention?

With Labīd, in any case, convention is acknowledged. He owes it to himself, of course, to chase after his tribe's pretty women. That is among the rules of the game. The principal truth in this belongs to the word when it leaps forth powerful and unexpected. That is how it is when the poet compares himself with "a camel whose hump is being eaten away by an ulcer and takes fright at the least raptor soaring overhead which might alight on its back to finish devouring its vertebrae."[34] The strong image, inspired from the desert, renews a stereotype. In short, Labīd could not be a man of his time and race without claiming to be in love. Furthermore, you have a prior right to marry your uncle's daughter upon payment of a lesser dowry than a stranger. This is a great advantage, but in some respects a servitude as well. For you must pay court to the daughters of your tribe. Thus, he assures us, "When Kubaysha goes away, she leaves Labīd as if out of his mind." How can she be brought back? She is like an animal that has broken its tether and runs away as you approach. However, that lasts only a few lines, and very soon desire turns to sorrow. A sorrow so precocious is outstandingly moderate.[35] Labīd resigns himself too easily, or makes it too clear that grief is no more than a stylistic device. For him, tribal love seems to owe more to the genre's requirements than to passion's disorders. In his poetry we can find many facile despairs or, rather, casual renunciations.

Meanwhile his lady fair has changed her name, which is also a rule of the genre. Besides, what else has she to offer, beyond her name? A musical emotion, of course: "Usayma prowls through my travelings. Her image inspires a *ṭarab* within me."[36] Is that not the main thing? Once again, poetry will be content with its own reality, which has little to do with any objective referent.

But Labīd makes up in nuances of love for his lack of intensity. We do not find in him the sensual images of Imrū᾽ al-Qays, ῾Umar bin Abī Rabī῾a, or Dhū al-Rumma. But there is more than one sort of love. Labīd also loves his brother, and his daughters, to whom he wrote a delicate epistle. He even feels the love that others are experiencing. This realistic Bedouin gives us a dialog between two lovers on the point of breaking up. The girl's recriminations so estrange the swain that he declares without ado that if she continues to reproach him it would be better to separate, as a length of cloth is cut in two.[37]

The poet, it would appear, derives a sly pleasure from separation; or, better, he is a man whose slyness as a "sage," *ḥakīm*, leads him to take literally the theme of the abandoned camp's vestiges. The woman has departed and is pursuing her desert wanderings far away. That's understood. Let's console ourselves. We shall seek other loves, or at least the serenity the desert brings. In a man who knows so well how to extricate himself from heartbreak, we can well imagine an independence that goes so far as to threaten the fair sex: "Do not forget that, as I know full well how to tie knots in the rope, I can sever them as well."[38] Watch out, we hear him say, you cannot take unlimited advantage of me. I am quite able to free myself of this love, which after all is perhaps only literary convention!

It is best to take this convention as such. All poetry is poetry at one remove, since it operates on pre-established themes. But should we accept these themes as themes, that is, play their game, or as an illusory referent, that is, beat them at their own game? Both, doubtless. And Labīd takes the same liberty with regard to *aṭlāl* as he does with respect to his elegiac heroine. "Shall a man like you be stirred by nostalgia for abodes / destroyed between Tukhtīm and al-Khilāl?"[39]

The Sage

Labīd's profound integration with his group, his manner of sharing its vicissitudes and rising above them all, his moderation respecting women, his extraordinary longevity, and even the gnomic turn of many of his lines had all won him a reputation as a wise man even before Islam. Nevertheless, he was neither an "authority on custom," *῾arrāf*,[40] nor a "mediator," *ḥakam*, nor a *ḥanīf*, a "repository of the ancient revelations." He escapes unqualified categorization within the framework of tribal institutions, or that of the patriarchal tradition of Abraham. On the other hand, his virtue crossed without shock the threshold of conversion to Islam, and he continued to be respected throughout his interminable old age.

For him, wisdom, in its secular form as in its religious form, is in the final analysis a matter of inborn character. He tells us: "Truth is known to men of heart," who also are men of authenticity, *aṣāla*. "I protest injustice, and lodge truth within me," *ba ʾūtu bi-haqqihā ʿindī*.[41] But nature's truth may no longer suffice for this sage. Vain grandeurs, excessive appetites, and the pettiness of Bedouin hierarchies have already aroused his doubt. "How we are is well known: bewitched by drink and food."[42] "When we prostrate ourselves at the door of a veiled man *nashīnu ṣiḥāḥ al-bayd*,[43] we corrupt the desert's integrity." Labīd perceives the ignominy in the manner, so prevalent, of the sycophant and the courtesan and that it does violence to nature's truth. There is, in the social expression of his time, something that seems to him to indicate a separation from straightforward nature. Who knows whether, in the mind of this contemplative Bedouin, criticism had not begun to germinate, and the feeling that a whole world was slipping into desuetude?

Hence his melancholy, his anxieties representing death. "Is the soul but *mutʿa mustaʿāra*,[44] borrowed pleasure, that returns to its master in a few brief months?" And when he cries, in his threnody for Arbad, "We perish, but the rising stars perish not,"[45] what is he referring to? Is it not the new constellations rising in Medina's sky? Iram, ʿĀd, and Thamūd have vanished. May we have better luck! "Ask of man what avail so many strivings. Has he any wish that can be fulfilled? Or simply wandering and vanity? Snares bestrew his path, and if they suffer him to pass, he arrives merely at decrepitude." This is said to the glory of al-Nuʿmān bin al-Mundhir, ruler of Ḥīra, that vassal of the Persian Empire who reigned in a poetic cycle as, much later, did King Arthur in a cycle of romance. By a strange coincidence, this potentate died (ca. 602) just as Muḥammad's preaching began to make itself heard.

The threnody continues on other nostalgias. As day follows day, and year follows year, what will remain if not hope, if not faith in the new promise? But this promise is not entirely new, since it purports to restore ancient messages, the remembrance of their old scriptures that Labīd regarded with such great respect. *Waḥy*, which has taken on the meaning of "revelation," is also "inscription." In another piece he speaks of a text written in gold on wooden tablets, safeguarding the "saying as manifest or as a seal."[46]

But is this pagan, questioning himself thus, not already quite near to Allah? "Every man of heart *ilā Allahi wāṣil*,[47] finds his way to God."

The Convert

Contrary to a rather general opinion, Labīd did not give up poetry after his conversion. Witness the series of poems inspired by the Koran cited rather disdainfully by R. Blachère. Conversely, there is said to be a *ḥadīth* of the Prophet quoting a hemistich of Labīd. Truth or invention, who knows? "Is not everything, God alone excepted, vain?"[48] In any case, it is a pure Muslim expression. Whenever his inspiration turns in this direction this difficult, rocky bard, heavy with dialectical terms, becomes simple and clear. As soon as his inspiration becomes monotheistic its tone changes. Not, however, without carrying along some of the old habits: whence some stylistic contaminations of great interest.

One of these poems begins with the *ḥamdallah.*[49] It is cited in *Lisān al-ʿArab* as representing an intuitive premonition of Islam. Was it written before, or after, the conversion? We have no way of knowing. The noteworthy thing for us is that everything that follows is a tasteful mixture of profession of divine unity and pre-Islamic description. It is just as if the Koranic formulae had replaced the opening passage on *aṭlāl*, after which the ode reverts to its usual themes.

Elsewhere we find Koranic expressions borrowed, purely and simply. Does not the line "If you find your head bared, a whiteness has taken possession of it and catches fire from it" remind one of the head in the Koran that "catches fire with whiteness"?[50] Is *khilfatan*,[51] "alternating," not typically Koranic? And when it is said that the *mudāris*[52] shall not enter paradise without first being exonerated, the word's ambivalence probably marks a drift from one semantic field toward another.

That is perhaps only a curiosity. But there is more than the simple borrowing of meanings, whether of term or phrase. Sometimes we have a true transcription of Koranic themes into Labīd's language. Thirty-odd have been noted, of which the following are the most remarkable.

This naturalistic culture, as we have said, had a predilection for human handiwork. But when the poet praises David as the artful blacksmith "shaping the iron into preserving mail,"[53] we have beyond doubt a reminiscence of verse 11 of the Saba sura.

Better still: "To Allah the booty due the worthiest and best. His the great height and the density of the deeply rooted" (*athīthu kulli mu'aththalin*).[54] This last word, evoking the root of a tree, is probably a dialectal term for *aṣl*. But note this sudden spurt of Bedouin nature into full monotheistic fervor. Also the dualism, the balance between the highly elevated and the deeply buried, in sum between transcendence and nature. Why not? In truth, the latter has less to defend itself against the new preaching than to fulfill itself therein.

> None can erase His Book;
> How can we, for His law is immutable;
> He has ordered, then enclosed beneath the splendor of His
>   throne
> Seven lines, seven levels within the bonds of the citadel;
> And deep in the earth itself, supported its masses
> By fixing them to the mute strength of the rock.[55]

Again,

> Water and fire are his signs,
> Signs which bear warning to those who are not mad,
> That all is vain, save piety;
> All things pass, as though they had never existed;
> If anything were eternal,
> What would survive would be
> The well-loved, tame gazelle of the regions of Ma'sal.[56]

Ma'sal and its gazelles have thus lost the sort of eternity evoked by the ancient name for wild animals, *awābid*, while the primordial masses, nature's buttresses, *khawāliq*, have now shed all collusion with the meaning, henceforth related to "creation," of the root *kh-l-q*. This disarming of nature extends to its most terrible champions, such as the lion (beginning at line 9). The "one with the augments" (the beast whose claws extend and retract), the redoubtable lion whose interlocking fangs, curved like daggers—well, his fangs now fall like the tip of a spear of which the shaft has rotted away.

There are other examples of this universal decline: among the great heroes, the great kings, not one will survive. Not Abraha, the Christian monarch who invaded Yemen at the beginning of the sixth century of our era, nor the Tubʿas, those legendary kings, nor (hold your hat!) Hercules (verse 58).[57] In this holy liquidation are involved also the "speaking poets" (verse 23): they have followed in the footsteps of Muraqqish and Muhalhal . . .

Thus ends this funeral chant for pre-Islam in which nature and the transcendental are curiously intermingled, the revelation that one has now embraced and the memories now raised to the status of *aṭlāl* of oneself as if, in the interplay of life and word, nothing can ever annihilate you! . . .

IX
Paradigm and Arab Rhetoric

Arabia of the revelation was by no means a primitive country, but a country in decline. It still had the vestiges and the influence of several foreign and indigenous civilizations. Its religion was probably no more than a decaying animism. It would be difficult to define precisely the social or moral strata it involved: ritual or conviction? folklore or global morphology? What exactly were those divinities whose names we are given? Were they not, as in other pantheons, simply debased versions of the Single Deity? The Arabs had indeed received, from within their own country, several monotheistic revelations which they had ignored or flouted, drawing God's vengeance upon themselves and their habitations. But this decline, which at the spiritual level made them poor relations of Judeo-Christianity, and at the level of secular history made them marginal to the Roman world, was compensated by their geographical situation, which held a kind of promise.

"We have made you a people in the middle, so that you may bear witness of men."[1] Would this be mere ethnocentrism? History and geography might prove the truth of this verse. A self-conscious Arab expression connects our era in a straight line with Muḥammad's. A collective identity and even a collective subjectivity are, as it happens, so commonly attested that one may well ask what witness they have borne, and may still bear, of their neighbors. The latter are numerous. Classical Arabia was surrounded on all sides by well-differentiated, rival systems: that of Rome and Byzantium to the north and northwest; the Persian to the northeast; toward the southeast, the Indian; on the south and southwest the ancient Abyssinian cultures; not to mention the Yemeni fringe and the outposts which Christianity and Judaism had thrust quite deeply into the Peninsula. Doubtless, the most recent phase of history, in which the Arabs have been annexed to Western initiatives or placed in confrontation with a Zionism which also arose from the West, has obscured this notion of a "people in the middle," although we are now seeing it opportunely reborn at the United Nations and elsewhere in the form of Afro-Asian solidarity. An outpost of Asia, Africa Minor, Mediterranean ports of call, a continental steppe, and an inner desert—the Arabs are all these things at one and the same time. And perhaps their history will recover its creativity only when they themselves have re-equilibriated within themselves the implications, in the form of conflicting or complementary demands, of a curious situation assured by a no less curious ambiguity.

The Impact of a Message

With respect to the Koran, do we have a right to speak of text, and particularly of a literary text?[2] Its message, at any rate, purports to be comparable to no other. *Mā huwa bi-qawli shā'irin wa lā bi-qawli kāhinin,* "it is the word neither of a prophet nor of a soothsayer."[3] On the other hand, it is expressed in freely assonated rhythms in a mode we assimilate today to poetry, but which the Arabs of that time could not recognize as such. Now this assonated, rhythmic discourse, *saj'*, of which the Koran is the prime example, was then to retreat for two centuries. Not until the ninth century did it reappear, timidly.[4] Far from being legitimized by the Prophetic message, on the contrary and probably because writers feared to model their style on the Book's and even more to imitate it, *saj'* dropped back for a long time into the shadows, or rather reverted to popular expression of which we know nothing.

Thus, early in the seventh century, appeared a discourse of a type which upset the stylistic norms of the time. Its verbal material was so integrated with its content and meaning, with its kerygma (to borrow a term from Christian theology), that listeners were stupefied by it. The Prophet, well aware of this effect, analyzed it several times in terms we today would call metalinguistic. For in the Koran there are not only several intersecting Words: that of God, that of His Messenger, that of their listeners. There is also discourse on the foregoing Word, notably that which describes the effect which would later be called *i'jāz*. This term, which may be translated, very badly, as "inimitability" or "unsurpassability," has long been entrenched. Its root appears in the Koran, which furthermore uses the fourth form of the verb, with the sense of "reducing someone to impotence." All those who heard Muḥammad's words were as if thunderstruck. He himself used this quality to fling a challenge at his listeners. "Produce such a Koran," he told them. "You will never succeed. Though men and genies joined together to produce such a preaching they would not produce it, even allied with each other."[5]

Various exegeses have been made on the subject: the Muslim one, which of course attributes to this quality of Koranic speech a metaphysical origin and an absolute character: and the European, which seeks to introduce relativity into this phenomenon and into its description. For R. Blachère, the concept of *iʿjāz* was not systematized until the end of the eighth century, that is, more than a century and a half after the revelation. Gustav von Grunebaum goes still further, asserting that it came into general use only toward the end of the ninth. The quality, moreover, did not go so far as to deter some audacious writers from taking up the Koranic "challenge." Reference was made above to Ibn Muqaffaʿ, al-Maʿarrī, and al-Mutanabbī, of whom R. Blachère even translated a passage. Today things go further, and the anti-Koran crops up in some texts by rebellious writers. The least we can say is that God did not carry so much weight, so to speak, in Islam's first centuries, that there were no artists who sought to rival the Koran by purely rhetorical or poetic effort. These attempts, or temptations, nevertheless remained sporadic and were deliberately subversive. It is one thing to note a certain usage by theologians and the infractions it provokes; it is another to distinguish a collective effect. The two eminent orientalists I mentioned above did not, perhaps, give sufficient attention to one observation: the effect produced by this discourse on Arabs at the beginning of the seventh century and ever since. This effect must have been shattering, and has generally remained so if contemporary testimony is to be believed.

This is a sociological reality beyond dispute. One can readily conceive how decisively such a discourse could win out over the poetic utterance of the time. The poets' odes, at least in the form they had by then assumed, had no more logical unity than the suras. But their unfolding, constricted by prosodic rule, was far from exhibiting the same liberty of composition as the *āyas* did among themselves. Free of any convention of meter or rhyme, even though assonance often governs long passages, the Koranic verse constitutes an infinitely more subtle unity than the poet's line, and one better adapted to the breath of inspiration. The meaning might, or might not, extend from one unit to the next, and similarly with the recurrence of sounds. From the time of the first compilations, however partial they were as yet, the text offered large masses which were at once divisible and unitary. This was not at all the case with the pieces of poetry which were then being assembled in collections without any criteria of classification except rhyme. Arabic poetry was doubtless already mature by the middle of the sixth century. It had ceased to be merely a tribal assertion and had attained literary status. One may even suppose that this constituted a revolution in Arab culture and society early in the sixth century. But the Koran's revolution was far more decisive still, since it broke with all the old norms and was established as God's word addressed to all humanity, while at the same time bringing a new word, a new rhythm, and a new classification.

The Koranic Combinatory

This classification has always been disconcerting. In the latter half of the nineteenth century, when the higher criticism of the Old and New Testaments evolved, dogmatists reacted to any historicizing relativism by asserting the absolute character of the message even in its form, which could not be touched without doing violence to the faith, to established institutions, and to patriotism. There is something of this in the reaction of traditional Islam (or, rather, its exponents) to various modern endeavors, even (or especially, it would seem) when they involve only the letter of the Book.

The latter, to repeat, consists of a multitude of fragments disparate as to tone and meaning but nevertheless grouped in suras. The groupings, of widely varying length, are arranged in an order which is neither logical nor chronological, but must be accepted by the believer as divinely instituted. Or else, indeed, it is thought, as by Western critics, either that incoherence reigns over most of the text, the same alleged incoherence as pre-Islamic poetry is accused of, or that a transcendental order reigns. But this may be only apparently a dilemma. What counts in fact, not only for faith but also for analysis, is that the Koran as a whole be felt as a fact and a unitary value; and also that each of its constituent units, the suras, is clothed with a very distinctive individuality, as for example in the case of Yāsīn, Ahl al-Kahf, or al-Raḥmān. A more insistent phenomenology would perhaps even pursue the same differentiation to the level of fragmentary sequences of verses. Certainly, in the eyes of Muslims, anything pertaining to the Koran, words and content, bears the accent of unity, unitarianism, uniquity: one could never overemphasize all the applications of the prestigious root *w-ḥ-d*, whose connotations cover equally the verbal form, the content, and the effects of the message. But as a corollary of this unity the same tradition places emphasis on *bayān* and *tafṣīl*, that is, on the compensatory variation which affects this unity through "elucidation" and "articulation." The error of Western exegesis is perhaps to have underestimated this complementarity.

The latter strives ingeniously to reconstruct an intrinsic chronology of the Koran, as has been done for the Old Testament and the Gospels. But it cannot rely upon the anecdotal and sapiential data accumulated by tradition under the name of *ḥadīth*, which has reached us in conditions of very uneven credibility even in the eyes of Islamic science,[6] as a commentary on the revelation. Only philology remains, therefore, with which to reconstruct the text's history. Thus, a multiplicity of styles is distinguished, alternating between two extremes: an apocalyptic violence, all in brief sentences; and declarations, narratives, or codifications in a more-moderate tone and expressed in more-ample periods. Here the analysis generally intersects with the traditional interpretation, which distinguishes between the tumultuous accent of the revelation's first stages and that of the legislator at Medina, who no longer needs to make God's indignation known to men but must organize a community. One thus moves from the metaphysical cry to teaching, codification, and civic policy.

But the convergence between the two exegeses does not extend to the details. Western criticism breaks violently with Muslim tradition when it judges that evolution occurred not only in the Koran's style but also in its concepts, including that of divine unity. Muḥammad's thought, like all human thought, is alleged to have varied on this topic. Muslim exegesis can only reject this in horror! It rejects as well the idea that the composition of the text which has come down to us reflects the efforts—not always coherent—of a generation of compilers working with more or less fragmentary or extensive recensions.

In both cases there remains the problem of a collection which makes no claim to chronology or human logic among its many-leveled elements, but whose unity is nevertheless as manifest as its differentiation is extreme. The key to the problem perhaps consists precisely in that relationship between the single and the diverse upon which anthropology and linguistics insist today.

The problem did not present itself in these terms to researchers dominated by diachronical perspectives, and who believed they had no recourse except to chronological sequence to account for any diversity. Now the "descent" of the Koran took place over a period of only some twenty years. Who can be so bold as to claim that he can detect, with the requisite plausibility, chronological stages and logical phases, fifteen centuries later and over such a brief span of time? It is far more likely that the Koran, contemporary with its revelation, having reverberated countless times up to our day while preserving the vocal unity and holding fast to its living link with the effects it arouses, offers a de facto synchronism whose differential aspects appear to stem more from variation than from succession in time. Is it not natural for the Prophet to have adopted now the mode of eschatological threat or promise, now that of recalling the ancient mythologies, or the stories of the condemned cities, or legislation, or polemic, when it was not that of naturalistic description or lyrical flight? The polymodal quality of the whole is furthermore observable within the longest suras, al-Baqara, for example. And the fact that they are arranged generally in order of decreasing length may not be as irrational as has been suggested. Indeed, this unitary differentiation, as we have recognized, also characterizes the Koran's effect, which can be dissociated neither from the text nor from a concrete continuity of reciters and believers.

Medina Then and Now (continued)

It has been estimated that the site of the Prophet's mosque, as he himself helped to build it, reportedly carrying stone, sand, and lime on his own shoulders, covered an area of 2,475 square meters.[7] Local scholars describe in minute detail the location of the first walls, which can still be discerned within the present sanctuary. The latter extends far beyond the original mosque. It covers 12,327 square meters: more than a hectare!

This typically Saudi giantism is found in all sorts of more or less successful urbanization projects. The city is obviously the object of constant attention by those in power, and I shall now investigate a few other features of the rejuvenation planned for it.

The field of agriculture, first, which here partakes of the oldest authenticity, since Medina's founding was the occasion for one of the first developments in Islamic law, with the institution of *musāqāt* and *mughārasa* contracts.[8] Today one may admire a fine experimental farm whose pilot plots and orchards attract visits by diplomats and prominent pilgrims. Also, something I had noticed at Basra, a date-processing center located on the north side, near the tomb of Sayyidnā Ḥamza, one of the martyrs of the ill-fated day of Uḥud. It is not rare to find in the city such unexpected conjunctions between the most-fervent archaeology and modernizing achievements.

Electricity had made its appearance at Medina before World War I, in the time of the Turks, simultaneously with the arrival of the railroad. Since then great efforts have been made not only to light the streets but also to distribute electricity to private customers. Today current is carried on pylons from an enormous generating plant, and the cables are laid underground after they enter the city at Bāb al-ʿAnbariya. A joint stock company, meeting Islamic standards, was founded for this purpose a few years ago. The number of subscribers, initially 2,735, now exceeds 10,000.

One of the points this modernization rightly emphasizes most strongly is irrigation,[9] particularly since the problems presented by agriculture and also, to repeat, the deterioration of the environment remain worrying. Today the city is supplied with drinking water from the spring of ʿAyn al-Zarqā, through canals constructed to modern hydrological specifications. Gardens were irrigated until about thirty years ago by means of springs and wells. These springs, locally called *khīf* (pl. *khuyūf*), bore names which could present some very interesting problems. The southeast section of the city was rich in sweet water, the northwest in water which, though somewhat brackish, could be used for some types of cultivation. It will be recalled that the town of Qubāʾ, with its marvelous vegetation, lies to the southwest.

Irrigation tools long remained primitive. We may mention water wheels turned by draft animals, and a contrivance comparable to the Egyptian *shādūf*: a pole mounted on a fulcrum, with a seat and a counterweight at one end permitting the laborer to lower the bucket at the other end and raise it full. The local term is *ghargházz*. Now the subsurface water table has been falling for twenty-some years. Whereas water used to be found at 7 or 8 meters, wells must now be drilled to depths of 20, 30, 35 meters or even more before it is found. This is a consequence of the density of social characteristics to which I have referred. Besides, the population has grown, exploitation activity has intensified, and modern technology is of course modifying the natural environment. Mechanical pumps had already appeared in Turkish times. The rise of this kind of progress was the work of certain clans, which moreover still take pride in it. One family installed power pumps in a certain quarter, another in another quarter. There were thus innovators who were also exploiters. After this avant-garde, the government itself entered the picture with the great resources it commands in this country. It imported hundreds of power pumps and distributed them at extremely advantageous prices.

Today there are 450. The result: an alarming drop in the water table in the wells and the drying up of several springs. A solution had to be found by aggravating the technique, so to speak, and installing deep wells. The chronicles tell of a Turkish diviner who performed marvels during the past few years. He was a devout man who had come from his country on pilgrimage. He demonstrated a special talent for finding water and eventually settled at Medina as a very energetic agent of modernization. He was credited with gifts not only of water divining but almost of sorcery. It seems that he predicted, in the presence of some Medinan farmers, that they would find at a certain depth not only water but also a petrified scorpion. They dug, not so much to find water as to verify the prediction, and in fact uncovered the fossil! The sinking of artesian wells has also begun. The innovator in this case was an Algerian: a ricochet of colonialism! In the final analysis, there will be the fossil water such as I saw flowing in the Rubʿ al-Khālī. It is from this deep table that Riyad, contrary to all expectations, has been drinking the last few years.[10] Medina may have to resort to that one day.

The Koran in Old Arabic Rhetoric

The Koran is thus a unitary object whose differential features can be singled out by successive decipherings or for purposes of analysis: it is the ensemble, however, of which the universal company of believers posits the quality of "unsurpassability," *iʿjāz*.

Over the ages, many studies have been devoted to this quality.[11] A work of Jāḥiẓ, which has come down to us only in fragments quoted by the author himself in the *Book of Animals*, emphasized various characteristics of this style: concision, frequency of ellipsis, wealth of metaphor. *Dalāʾil al-Iʿjāz*, "proofs" or "indications" of unsurpassability, is the title of a work by the philologist ʿAbd al-Qāhir al-Jurjānī (d. 1078). Treatises of this sort proliferated and became part of a science, or rather the sciences, of the Koran which reached encyclopedic proportions. A scholar of Seville, Ibn ʿArabī al-Rāfiʿī, who died in 1150, counted no less than 77,450! Another erudite, nearer our own time, Sūyūṭī (d. 1505), the famous and versatile Egyptian writer, recorded these sciences in a still-useful manual, *Al-Itqān fī ʿUlūm al-Qurʾān*. But let us take a closer look at the actual traits upon which most of these scholars concentrate their analysis.

Jāḥiẓ, for instance, cites as a wonderful example this expression applied to fruit-laden boughs in paradise: *lā maqṭūʿa wa lā mam-*

nū'a, "neither cut down nor forbidden." According to him, this is an inimitable model of concision. Certainly, much is contained, both literal and figurative, in this short syntagm. The two participles are asymmetrical in that their respective meanings are concrete, even visual, and abstract, even legal. Their conjunction conceals an observation and a norm, with a metaphysics in the background! The heavenly fruits, indeed, will not be left passively for the just man to do as he pleases with them. He will have access to them, but at the cost of an initiative, an effort. Many things in very few words.

Jurjānī greatly admires the words of that prophet of ancient times who spoke of his old age saying, *ishta'ala al-ra'su shayban*, "my head caught fire with whiteness," as Jean Grosjean translates it. Even in French this coupling of words is percussive. For the Arab commentators this constituted a rhetorical marvel (by the trope) and a grammatical one (by the use of the descriptive *ḥāl*). Another example cited by Jurjānī: *fa fajjarnā al-arḍa 'uyūnan*, "we made the earth erupt in springs of water." For the Arab taste, the expression executes extraordinary semantical shifts, since normally it is wells, not the earth, that flow with water. Naturally, in our twentieth-century French, accustomed to all sorts of metaphor, to the breaking of old associations and the devising of new ones, this seems less extraordinary than it could have to a man of the eleventh century. But this admiration gives us an idea of what we may dare to call the miraculous character attributed to such language.

Miraculous, of course, is not the right word. The Prophet stoutly denied that he was a miracle worker, as if he had foreseen Renan's famous comment, "It would have been a real miracle if he had worked none." Well, he did not work any; the sole *mu'jiza*, "miraculous challenge," he bequeathed was the Koran, of which he was no more than the inspired transmitter. Later, rhetorical commentaries reached a higher level of refinement, but also of scholastic complexity. To enter the domain of rhetoric is to enter that of *partitio*: subdivisions in orders and species. It has lately been said of rhetoric, back in fashion among certain avant-garde writers, that it was the only ancient science which really deserved the name of science,[12] as demonstrated by Quintilian. But for him it was still mostly a science of nomenclature and evaluation. Similarly, Sūyūṭī, for example, analyzing the *badī'*, "linguistic novelty and innovation," distinguishes a hundred kinds. Bāqillānī (d. 1013) devoted a lengthy treatise to comparing the Koran and the greatest writers of the Arab heritage, Imrū' al-Qays for example, from the rhetorical standpoint of employment of tropes.[13] Tropes are one sort of figure of speech.

Dumarsais' treatise, recently republished, defines them as "particular modifications of language which render expression more lively, more noble, or more pleasing." This is a man of a past era speaking, of course. For our part, we would say that tropes are a movement in language by which a semantical displacement is produced. Modern rhetoric knows tropes not only of the signified but also of the signifier, which it pedantically calls metabases.[14] As we have referred to Bāqillānī, if we examine his work in detail we find the Koran's formulations properly tagged according to grammatical, or rather rhetorical, species consisting of metaphor, allegory, catachresis, synecdoche, antonomasis, and so on and on!

The most-striking thing in these painstaking treatises is surely their profound relevance to everything Arab. Such masters, needless to say, are more intimately linked with the authenticity of the message than any Arabist, or any native speaker of Arabic, today. But in general they see only the detail. They were trained in a linguistic aesthetic which knows only words or, at most, word combinations.

First Impression of a Style

But a style does not consist solely of its words. Suyūṭī reports that some 77,000 have been found in the Koran.[15] But he probably means "occurrences." *Ikhtilāf* thus counts here for 36, whereas as a lexeme it should count as only one. But let us define the question precisely. How broad is the Koran's lexical range? The Cairo Academy has compiled a fine dictionary of this vocabulary in four volumes, and other alphabetical compilations exist where each occurrence is noted. Even the number of letters in the Book has been counted: one million, according to Ṭabarānī. But as far as we know, these speculations, obviously oriented toward the search for numerical rhythms to which symbolic value may be attached, have never raised the question of a vocabulary range which might be compared, for example, with that exhibited in the *Dīwān* of an accredited contemporary like Labīd. An extraordinary omission, if only too easily explained!

As a matter of fact, both learned and popular feeling agree on one obvious thing: the relative "simplicity" of Koranic language by comparison with that of the poets. There are, of course, treatises on the Koran's *gharīb*. In the Book one finds a whole class of strange words, which are commonly attributed to borrowing from Aramaic, Hebrew, Greek, and so on. Finally, there are several dozen dialectal terms. Thirty-three Arabic dialects are said to have been drawn upon for one or more of their words. Nevertheless, the conclusion everyone arrives at is that, if there is literary power in the Koran—evocative scope, that is, and explosive disproportion between signified and signifier—it is not at all due to lexical wealth or studied refinement in word choice, as is to some extent true of Imrū᾿ al-Qays' poems or the *Dīwān* of Dhū al-Rumma, which alone is said to contain one-third of the language. By contrast, in the Koran, save for those cases I have mentioned, understanding is immediate, and deliberately so. This, furthermore, was one of the things which so impressed contemporaries and set it off, in their eyes, from the earlier literature.

In New Arabic Rhetoric

Over the past fifty years some new commentaries have endeavored to renew the genre. We shall refer briefly to *Al-Manār*'s modernist commentary,[16] which has been the subject of a somewhat over-meticulous study by P. Jomier, and others, among which I might mention one by the Damascus Shaikh al-Qāsimī,[17] early in the century; one by the Egyptian Shaikh al-Marāghī,[18] of the interwar generation; and especially that by the Tunisian Shaikh Ṭāhir bin ʿĀshūr,[19] who died quite recently. All these works contain valuable comments on the Koranic *bayān*. But we must doubtless turn to a work of literary history which has nothing to do with *tafṣīr* to find the first concerted stylistic essay: that of Muṣṭafā Ṣādiq al-Rāfiʿī. The author belonged to that Rāfiʿī family which produced the Waṭanī party's great journalist, Amīn al-Rāfiʿī, and his historian brother, ʿAbd al-Raḥmān al-Rāfiʿī, who died in Egypt a few years ago. Originally from Tripoli, Lebanon, the family had long since put down roots in the Delta. Muṣṭafā Ṣādiq was endowed with formidable eloquence. He was perhaps the last to handle Arabic with that thunderous splendor of which Ṭaha Ḥusain was the unlucky butt at the time of their quarrel over pre-Islamic poetry. Rāfiʿī did not attack only the author of *Al-Shiʿr al-Jāhilī*; he handled just as roughly people of the "enlightenment" generation: Aḥmad Amīn, Ḥusain Haykal, al-ʿAqqād, and so on. Certain critics credit him with bringing them more or less back to the faith, after they had strayed from it in their youth.[20]

He devoted an entire volume to the Koran's *iʿjāz*, considered particularly from the point of view of style. Thus, he singled out one aspect among others composing the global approach to the text followed by Muslim scholars. He himself insisted upon the text's musical construction, on the astonishing harmony one finds in it between sounds and content. He had a penetrating feeling for a language which, "when it is angered becomes a resounding ocean; when it becomes calm suspires a breeze of paradise; when it speaks of this world structures and organizes it; when it describes the Beyond makes you see both Eden and the fiery pit; when it promises God's benefactions brings a smile to the face of mystery; and when it threatens divine torment stills the tongue by the heart's burning."[21] That is very well said, in the Eastern style, and although the book is old it is still useful for the way it emphasizes an integration, which we may properly call literary and even poetic, between the Koran's effects and its vocal consistency.

Rāfiʿī was considered a champion of orthodoxy. But other approaches, even when cautiously limited to stylistics, aroused suspicion. That is easy to understand. To study the Koran's style is to shatter a totality. It is to treat only one of many aspects of a unitary truth. Finally, and in spite of all the circumlocutions one might employ, it is more or less to put the Book's style on the same level as that of profane writers and thus to lump the Koran, *horribile dictu*, with *adab*. When one is not sustained by the combative prestige of a Rāfiʿī, recognized in his own time as a defender of Islam, when one is simply an academician and furthermore Westernized, it is very risky to raise such subjects. Amīn al-Khūlī, Muḥammad Khalafallah, and many others learned this by experience, in varying degrees and for various reasons. Similarly, transmission of the text over the airwaves and its translation into foreign languages had often aroused objection and sometimes polemic. How could one hope that stylistic analysis, inevitably critical no matter how carefully handled, could escape suspicion?

All religious faiths are tempted to regard their substance as indivisible, because it is intangible. Religious faiths only? "Revolution is all of a piece," some radical historian or other has said. To attack, in relativist fashion, one among the many facts of that totality was, according to him, to attack the whole thing. Of course the al-Azhar shaikhs go still further. They purport to be guardians of a tradition. Any pundit is suspicious of anything which seems to him to imply an attack, the least *masās*, upon the majesty of the legacy he administers. Until quite recently we have seen some ulama take exception to any proposal in the slightest degree liberal or innovative, even, for example, institution of a series of "recitations," or *tartīl*, of the Koran over the Egyptian radio.[22] Naturally, other shaikhs are more liberal-minded, and I could take note here of more-modernist thought, such as that of Shaikh Muḥammad al-Mubārak of Damascus, who may be grouped with Shaikh Drāz of Cairo and the Moroccan ʿAllāl al-Fāsī among the best interpreters of an Islam adapted to the struggle of the new times.

Thus the Arabs' exegetic tradition has continued into our day, not without making some progress along the way. Let us look, for example, at a recent *tafsīr*, the very latest Koranic commentary now being published by the Tunisian Shaikh Ṭāhir bin ʿĀshūr. In his monumental first volume he has thrown together a series of dissertations, one of which, as it happens, concerns *iʿjāz*.[23] Printed on large pages, written in the old-time condensed, even gnomic, style, it constitutes a veritable treatise. We probably cannot consider this the swan song of the old rhetoric, which will still find doughty practitioners. Notwithstanding, this sort of approach and (we may as well say it) this sort of scholar stem from a generation which is fast disappearing. Shaikh Ṭāhir bin ʿĀshūr, despite his surprising youthfulness, his strength of memory, and his powerful voice as an orator, died at nearly a hundred years of age. We must therefore hasten to lay hold of this type of science, compile it, and pass on whatever useful elements it contains to younger researchers, both Muslim and non-Muslim Islamologists, whose access to more-modern methods does not entirely compensate for their neglect in pursuing the prestigious continuity of the *ʿulūm al-dīn*.

Shaikh Ṭāhir, a little maliciously, begins by asserting that in the field of *tafṣīr* many are called but few are chosen. As a matter of fact, between the medieval commentators and himself there had intervened the people of the modernist school, ʿAbduh and others, whom he may have fought in his youth but from whom he could not help learning some lessons. *Iʿjāz*, in his view, must be studied, first, from the standpoint of its distinctive effects upon listeners in the past, and now. Second, from the standpoint of creativity and innovation: in what way did the Koran innovate? Not, obviously, by comparison with an already-existing Arabic prose, since there are hardly any examples earlier than the Koran or contemporaneous with it, but rather, so to speak, by comparison with the later Arabic style. Third, from the standpoint of the excellence of content, through deriving the knowledge embedded, explicitly or by indirection, in the unsurpassable text. A fourth aspect: the opening upon the unknowable the Koran provides. To tell the truth, is that not where one ought to have begun? Insofar as the Koran is a transcendental book, its very axis is mystery.

Erudite analyses follow, in which all categories of Arab criticism are passed in review, somewhat as Bāqillānī had done, but in more-reasoned fashion, more synthetic, in some respects more modern. Special mention should be made of the short chapter entitled "The Koran's Discoveries in the Language Field." For example, the straightforward clarity of the sentences, the sharp limning of narrative which of course is not that of the great Jāhiliya odes, the eurythmy and euphony of the verbal flow. For the Arab listener, in fact, such a text is flowing, not jarring or rocky as the old poetry too often is, notably because of the *gharīb*. Noteworthy are its parables, its constant return to *iltifāt*, that is, the introduction of dialog among several persons, proverbial turns of phrase, hyperbole, the ambivalence of certain terms which semantically open up apparently contradictory vistas, but of which reflection reveals the profound convergence. Finally, there is a more-technical passage, and one of the most remarkable, on the Koran's *ʿādāt*, its verbal "customs" if you will: that is, its associations among concepts. If mention is made of *jawʿ*, "hunger," then *khawf*, "fear," immediately crops up. If *jinna*, "paradise," is spoken of, *nār*, "hell," at once appears. If *jinn*, "demons" or genies, are mentioned, men follow immediately. Polarities, in short, and, more precisely still, verbal pairings of which detailed study would, I believe, guide a searching approach to this style.

If various efforts by academicians suspected of *tafarnug* have raised tempests in Egypt, by a strange irony it was a latter-day, ill-fated theoretician of the Muslim Brotherhood movement, at the antipodes with respect to Western liberalism and rationalism, who distinguished himself by an essay, *Al-Taṣwīr al-Fannī fīl-Qurʾān*, "Artistic portrayal in the Koran." The book is valuable less for its analysis than for its testimony. "I had studied the Koran since early childhood. My intelligence, of course, could not yet grasp its conceptual horizons, nor could my understanding encompass the majesty of its objectives. My soul nevertheless perceived something of this, and my childish imagination gave concrete interpretations to certain figures of speech, deflecting their meaning. However naïve they were, they moved my spirit while delighting my sensitivity. I meditated over them at length. At the end I was filled with joy and animation."[24] The book goes on to study successively the concrete power of figures of speech in the Koran, their coherence, the personalization of the account, and its existential logic.

But even if Arab rhetoric goes beyond mere observation of words and tropes to the study of other aspects—musical integration for

Rāfiʿī, imaginative power for Sayyid Quṭb—it has great trouble in putting sufficient distance between itself and its object of study. It suffers, one might say, from a shortcoming opposite to that of so many Western studies marred by an indifference, even a malevolent hypercriticism, toward Islam. Between a view too closely involved (of which the most constructive result would be to provide a phenomenology of itself) and the West's deceptive objectivity there has rarely been room for true understanding. Some recent endeavors permit us some hope in this regard.

A Tunisian critic, Bashīr bin Salāma,[25] notes the difficult features of Arabic writing and attributes them to a sort of divorce between the creative powers of the literary imagination in Arabic and the shortcomings of the script. The latter, even today,[26] presupposes that, in order to decipher it, you have already grasped the meaning by a process of intuition, for only such a grasp makes it possible for you to determine the spoken pronunciation which itself is necessary in order to grasp the meaning: thus a vicious circle is closed. In rather bold fashion, the author goes back to the first centuries of the Hegira, when an enormous poetic literature flourished, based entirely on memory. According to him, the uniqueness of the Koran as a genre, for it is neither poetry nor prose, consists in the fact that it broke with this tradition and reoriented it toward writing. References to writing as such, writing organized in lines and texts, are in fact frequent in the Koran, and it is no accident that the term Book *par excellence, kitāb*, has been applied to it. The Koran would thus have represented a revolution in writing, even if it was not written down, at least entirely, at the time it was handed down.[27]

From Rhetoric to "Re-Readings"

In many contemporary works we would encounter that preoccupation of deducing modern values from the venerable text: science, historic reason, and even socialism. Most of these efforts, often tinged with the assumption that all things are contained in the Koran, do not concern us here, but only those which propose to read the Koran anew, without dogmatic or ideological preconceptions and solely to derive whatever its word can offer to revitalize the soul in our time. As this is a process not of exploiting the text but of apprehending it directly, that is, in the literal sense of *dhikr* and *dhikrā*, the following observations are within the legitimate purview of the present chapter.

It is within this genre, called *tadabbur*, or "meditation" over the sacred texts, that the very widely read book of Dr. Muṣṭafā Maḥmūd stands out.[28] As a matter of fact, such a handling of the text, not by laymen (since this is not a very applicable term in Islam) but by men of letters untrained in the sacred sciences, had illustrious precedents. At an early date Ḥusain Haykal's *Muḥammad* renewed the prophetic *sīra*, as Ṭaha Ḥusain's *ʿAlā Hāmish* did the *ḥadīth*. Aḥmad Amīn and ʿAqqād also have their place in that gallery of elders who could be claimed as precursors by today's authors—such as Dr. Kāmil Ḥusain, Shawqī Ḍayf, Muṣṭafā Āl Shakʿa, Bint al-Shāṭiʾ, and others, more and more numerous, it would appear—who are taking up where the classical *tafṣīr* left off and are reading the Koran not so much as exegetes as to seek answers to contemporary anxieties.

The most renowned of these works, *The Koran: An Essay in Contemporary Comprehension*, comes from a physician who was for a long time irreligious. It appeared—quite significantly—in serial form in the very secular magazine *Ṣabāḥ al-Khayr*; these installments, collected in one volume, became the best seller of the year 1970. One sees the reason for this success as soon as one opens the book. "I remain speechless when I try to describe the feeling that overcame me the first time I heard a Koranic quotation. There are no words in which to discuss such a dim encounter, *istiqbāl ghāmiḍ*, of the soul. The Book's words returned spontaneously and beseechingly to my ear and memory. I was alone, and repeated silently to myself, "*wa al-layl idhā sajā* . . ."[29] Of course Dr. Maḥmūd does not always escape the trap of the universal "concordance": the subconscious, atomic structure, and so on seem to him to be foretold by one verse or another. Also regrettable are his frequent references to Ghandi's spiritualism which, however legitimate, lead the reader a little too far away from the Arab revelation. The importance of this manner of reading lies not in that direction, but in the lively stirrings it continues to arouse in the modern mind. The religion the Koran proclaimed consisted precisely in this intercommunication—hence the interest in understanding it anew in that manner. This could be a fertile orientation in Muslim theology, and the same tendency is spreading today in Christianity. Let us hope that such a re-reading will symmetrically "unfreeze" the *ḥadīth* which recorded this same dialog, for the first third of the seventh century, in descriptive and narrative terms of an extraordinarily dense realism.

In his commentary on Sura II, al-Baqara, Dr. Kāmil Ḥusain also proposes to reply to the modern era's questionings, including those of the nonbeliever, whose role, as he rightly observes, is growing and can no longer be treated by summary condemnation or preterition.[30] His interpretation, of a great and vital nobility, teaches us for example not to construe simply as alms the *yunfiqūna* in *mimmā razzaqnāhum yunfiqūna*: "who, out of what We have bestowed on them, disburse." The human will and the breadth of life thus contemplated by this exegete unquestionably lend a creative morality to twentieth-century man, besieged on all sides by artificiality and the second-hand. This amounts to restating, on the basis of the Koran, the principal problem of Arab societies, and of all others: creativity.

X
Reading the Koran

Just what is the Koran? But first I shall ask a leading question: What is it, if I may put it thus, in its own eyes? To learn the answer, let us listen to this curious passage from the fifty-fifth sura, al-Raḥmān, "The Benefactor."

God's beneficence is presented as consisting of a certain number of things, and the order in which they are listed has a certain significance: the Koran, first of all; then man; then *al-bayān*, which we might translate as "elucidation"; then *al-ḥusban*, and so forth. This latter term, coming from the root *ḥ-s-b*, evokes the scale of the cosmos. We see that it comes after elucidation, which follows the creation of man, which in turn follows the teaching of the Book. This is an inverted order if one is following strictly naturalistic views, but it is justified if one considers the Koran as an archetype in which "to be" and "being," the "real" and the "existing," are conjoined, as in *al-ḥaqīqa*. The late R. Blachère was right in translating thus the term *al-imām*, in which I see also "paradigm." The Koran, *imam mubīn*,[1] would thus be the "paradigm which elucidates itself" and, better still, "which unfolds itself." And its style would be *splendor ordinis*, the corruscating quality of this unfolding.

A style's power, indeed, does not proceed from its verbal constituents, nor from the manner in which they are combined in primary groups, but emerges from broader and more-ramified aggregates. If this is true of any literary work it is particularly so of the Koran, which is a system composed of parts each of which shares in a unitary meaning and draws its effect mainly through its relationship to the whole. What whole? The Koran itself, of course, of which the phonic duration—by which I mean the time required to recite it, *tilāwa*, although representing a certain lapse of physical time—can be concentrated into synchrony if many participate in the recitation. Synchronic, or at least unitary: that, furthermore, is how it is impressed on innumerable memories. The fact that each sura, each verse, even each fragment of a verse can be given a distinctive character in recitation or by suggestion is only a corollary of its participation in the whole, and of the presence of this whole. Whereas, to repeat Saussure's distinction, language is nowhere,[2] and speech actualizes only limited and transitory elements of it; the linguistic aggregate covered by the Koran, encompassing only a part of the Arabic language but endowing it with enormous value content,[3] is rendered no longer simply latent but continuously operative by virtue of an indefinitely repeated psalmody.

On the other hand, as we have said, the Koranic totality is not limited to its language. It is coextensive with the community in the latter's space and history, since it inspires so much of its behavior and since it is considered a universal point of reference. It is thus not merely that vocal column rising from the depths of the ages up to the Muslims of today. It is not simply a system of things signified. Nor is it only the synthesis of the former and the latter. It is also a continuity of attitudes and situations. Today, when Muslim proselytization, reacting against the compartmentalization of modern life, insists that in Islam no domain of life is excluded from religion, it begins with a correct view but ends with false consequences instead of the right ones which could be deduced from it. For the attempt to prevent a separation among the different modes of the collective process is an indefensible position, and a socially ruinous one. But to defend the relationship of immediacy among them, and their joint reference to the fundamental, is to take account of Arab specificity and to fortify it opportunely against the new age's dispersion.

To return to the Koran, let us also take note that its signifiers, the things it signifies, and its effect on individual consciousness and collective conduct cannot be dissociated from it. All these modes react upon each other. Like waves originating from many different directions, they intersect in patterns which lend to each parcel of the text its own strange power. That is what believers call *iʿjāz* and what doctrine attributes to inspiration and even supernatural composition. With all the respect due to a thousand-year-old conviction, we shall be content here with the sociological, one might even say the sociostylistic, explanation of that same fact.

Medina Then and Now (conclusion)

But let us renew our enthusiasm from Arabia at first hand. At Medina one of the most important administrative offices is that of the Pilgrimage. One may well imagine the immense possibility of conflict or difficulties attending a large crowd of pilgrims coming from fifty-odd of the world's nations. The Saudi government watches over it untiringly. Let us mention also the recent founding of an "agency," *hay'at al-amr bil-ma'rūf*, referring to the old Muslim adage on "commanding the good and rooting out evil." Its office is located on the mosque square, north of the sanctuary. Another sign of the times is the proliferation of social services, including *dār al-tarbiya*, the "house of education," a child care center. Finally, a Labor Office, opened in 1958 or 1959. The beginnings of trade unionism are already appearing and already loom large on the shores of the Gulf, in the vicinity of the great oilfields. I don't suppose it is particularly active at Medina, but at least the administration intends to be ready to deal with it. And that is a sign of the times.

Another sign: the organization of cultural institutions. Until a short time ago higher education was dispensed in the Great Mosque. No fewer than three hundred ulama of the generation that grew up between the two world wars were teaching simultaneously in the city. Here, too, the sociologist notes an indication of social concentration. But it goes without saying that this concentration operates under the sign of the faith, of religious practice, and even of continuity. Later, the teaching function was removed from the mosque and installed in more functional premises, better suited to university activity, as has happened almost everywhere in the Arab world except, so far, Najaf, Karbala, and a few minor centers. The Islamic University has thus been in operation at Medina since the 1960s. It has nevertheless retained a proselytizing objective, although it has adopted the al-Azhar model of division into colleges. One for the *sharī'a*, of course, but also a college of *da'wa*, or "missionary work," whereas at al-Azhar this is merely a suboffice. *Uṣūl* and Arabic language comprise a third college, while in the programs particular attention is devoted to "subversive sects," *al-madhāhib al-haddāma*. Thirty-four schools are also operating, including twenty-four primary schools, with 11,394 pupils distributed among 332 classes. These quantitative data have their utility, and I shall mention also that there exists an unusual "Sahara School," a few dozen kilometers from the city, built in the open desert to educate youths from Bedouin camps.[4] This school has succeeded so well, it is pridefully claimed, that it is diffusing a taste for modern education among Bedouin tribes throughout the Peninsula. I myself saw such schools functioning in Wādī al-Dawāsir, Qaṣīm, and Sudayr.

Like every Muslim city, Medina had always had an organization of notables, however formal or informal: the very ones who revolted against the Turkish government in 1906. Today the municipal council meets in a building called, by a curious allusion to the *ḥisba*, the *muḥtasib*'s "shack," *ʿishsha*. It engaged in "cooperation with the city authorities." A cooperation which, obviously, does not yet extend to identification. But that is a general lacuna in the East.

Meanwhile, the works undertaken by the regime in laudable profusion—this orgy of construction, the opening up of new streets and squares, with copious quantities of machines and scaffolding—are stimulating an extremely lucrative activity. Outstanding among the businessmen engaged in these projects is the "Muʿallim" Bin Lādin,[5] who carried out the work on the Great Mosque, among other projects. Already a modern entrepreneur? Here, as elsewhere, one opportunity for the future lies in the transition to industrial enterprise from subcontracting, however prosperous. It may yet take the direction either of liberalism or of state management if, that is, it manages to survive other "desirable storms" in the Arab world.

The Combinatory and the Articulated

More than reading material in the intellectual sense of the term, the Koran is the underpinning of a vocal flow that has reverberated from generation to generation since the Prophet, and that arouses in the individual and the community effects intimately linked with itself. This speech bearing on the immediate, the global, the invisible, and first things is articulated in large or small units. They may extend to the verse, or even a part of a verse. There is no reason not to believe, and this is moreover again confirmed by observation in many instances, that to this articulation of the phonic chain there correspond articulations not only semantic but also of the psychosociological "effect" in which we, in accord with Muslim tradition, see the intentionality of the message at work. These interacting rhythms escape us in large part. No one, for example, has studied with desirable precision the way in which Koranic invariance comes to terms with the variations of individual and collective life. It is perhaps too late to do so.[6] At any rate, what can still be observed in this order of things so late in the twentieth century gives some idea of the richness and complexity of this object of sociological meaning and the relevance of the teachings it brings to bear on the text itself, as in a recurrent mathematical series.

This valuable approach has been neglected by Western exegesis, which in this field has not yet taken advantage of recent progress in the social and human sciences. One of the most-useful contributions the latter might make would be to draw our attention to

Koranic articulation, particularly as the text itself makes incontestable allusions to it.

"And the unbelievers say: If at least the Koran had come down to him in a single unit, *jumlatan wāḥidatan*! Thus it is! Strengthen thy heart in that respect. And We have made it psalmody. They could produce nothing similar for you, were it not We who have brought you such a beautiful truth to unfold" (XXV, 32–33). The phonic signifier is thus important, and the fragmentation has a systematic character. Furthermore: "We have fragmented it that you may preach it to men *ʿalā mukthin*, discontinuously, and have sent it down a repeated descent" (XVII, 106). Also: "A book whose verses are articulated as an Arabic Koran, for a knowing people" (XLI, 3).

The respective autonomy of the fragments and their unitary solidarity are combined according to rules that largely escape us. It can happen that psalmody breaks a word in two; the old Islamic science knows a dozen examples of this sort. In Koranic encyclopedias, Sūyūṭī's for example, there is a chapter bearing the promising title "Munāsabāt al-ayāt wal-surāt,"[7] "On the correspondence between verses and suras." That is indeed the heart of the problem. It will be recalled that this correspondence is neither chronological, since a sura may combine elements sent down at different times, nor logical, since it often encompasses a series of apparently unconnected themes. Muslim investigators have addressed this problem, among them the great Ibn ʿArabī, but circumspectly as might be expected, since for them the order of arrangement as consecrated by the vulgate was inspired by God.

Would it be too risky to say that the only correspondence lies in the articulation itself, and that the latter is merely the reverse side of the combinatory character of the text: all in all, of its unitary violence?

Now this articulation can in no way be reduced to a formal principle but is based upon the cosmic order and bears witness of Nature. The root *kh-l-f*, *khilfa*, "alternation," *ikhtilāf*, "difference," also speaks of diversity. "Hast thou not seen how God has caused water to descend from heaven with which He has brought forth fruits of divers kinds, and on the mountains are white and red bands of various kinds, and strange black things?" (XXXV, 27). The preamble of the Torrent sura reveals one of these panoramas, opens up one of those imaged vistas in which the Book, taking up the same themes as profane poetry, seems to challenge it. But the description is at the same time a metalinguistic treatment of the one and the plural. "It is He who has spread out the earth, disposing therein the towering mountains and the rivers, and of all fruits has disposed therein two couples, He who has hidden from the night the day; so many signs for a heedful people. / And furthermore on the earth, neighboring fields, gardens of vines, grains, palms both tufted and tuftless, all irrigated by a single water, and in nourishment we give preference to one thing over another . . ." (XIII, 3–4). The hierarchical diversity of nature means only one thing, which is to invite man to observe the divine order by which merits and failings are described differently, and retribution articulated, *kullu shay*ʾ *faṣṣalnā tafṣīlan*, "all things have We articulated by articulation." *Mufaṣṣal* has been translated "intelligible." I agree that articulateness is a condition of intelligibility: that is one basic principle of linguistics. But here it is a question above all of insistence on the differential, at one and the same time, of language, of nature, and, so to speak, of Salvation. For, "Men: various is your behaving."[8] One must include under the same perspective the text's composition, moral injunction, diversity of conduct, and the cosmic order.

An Interlacing Structure

Far from ignoring this diversity or using it as an argument against Koranic unity, it must be considered as an extremely ramified combination of discrete parts. The suras, for example, are composed of fragments which themselves are divisible. In the opinion of the anecdotal exegesis provided by tradition to accompany the text, many of these fragments are of different dates. As it has come down to us, the Koran thus does not purport to be a temporal progression but instead a synchronous whole whose unity is paired with articulatory diversity. The latter, however, is recombined into sections (*ajzā*ʾ, *aḥzāb*, etc.) for the use of reciters. This purely practical segmentation does not conflict either with the unity of the whole Koran or with the relative autonomy of complete suras, parts of suras, or groups of words. Thus we have to deal with a two-way process from the whole to the parts, and from the parts to the whole, in which the level of division into suras affords an obvious stability.

It will be recalled that the suras do not appear in the traditional version in the order of their "descent," but roughly in the order of decreasing length, so that the longest, al-Baqara, appears at the beginning while the last two, the Muʿawwidhatān, or "preservers," are each no more than two lines in length. This division, which was fixed at the time the text was first written down, comes, in the eyes of believers, from the Prophet himself and through him from the divine paradigm. As it rests on no human principle of segmentation, it is "arbitrary" in the sense Saussure gives the word and thus cannot be dissociated from its "literariness," nor from the individualization of its effects. Among the personalistic effects of this division is the fact that the titles of certain suras are borne by men, such as ṬāHā and YāSīn.

Thus a sura like XVI, The Bees, presents an individuality itself composite, since it comprises a series of fragments combined without apparent coherence. Its major theme is that of divine beneficence. It recurs several times in the text, as well as the theme of omnipotence. But the backdrop of nature comes into play as proof or reminder of the Messenger's mission and as reference point for the transcendental. Within this framework other themes, or rather modes, appear: eschatological, polemical, or legislative. The sura thus rests on a rhythmic combinatory among diverse elements. It nevertheless offers, even for one who hears it without a preconceived idea, a unique accent, and this accent, in our opinion, bears upon the fearful ambiguity of the celestial gift. God endows you with your garden's prosperity, but He can deprive you of it from one day to the next. He can make you a master, which is much better than being a slave, but He can abolish your mastership at His discretion. Koranic discourse thus hangs its edification upon the ambivalence of the images and the circumstances of life. One commentator refers in this connection to the famous *aḍdād*, those "homophonic antonyms" in Arabic, where it is possible for a single word to mean both black and white. For linguistic ambivalence is also that of natural life, within which only appeal to, or remembrance of, the divinity can distinguish the true good. God thus represents, so to speak, the enigma's univocity.

If that is so, if on the one hand this sura has a single meaning or axis, and if on the other hand it is made up of bits and pieces lumped together, is this not simply to say that it rests on an interlacing structure?[9] This apparatus of interacting modes and levels therefore seems to me to characterize the "Koranic phenomenon" in all its aspects.

Symphonic Effects

The power of the injunction with which Sura LIII, The Star, closes was such, according to tradition, that all those present, believers and unbelievers alike, fell prostrate. The rumor of a general conversion of the Meccans spread as far as Abyssinia. An old man among those present, too feeble to bow down, picked up a little earth in his fingers and lifted it to his forehead.

This sura's sixty-two verses are distributed among three movements. Its date, or rather that of its constituent parts, is a matter of lively debate. The safest thing is to note, with Sayyid Quṭb, two flights of breathless musicality, framing a pause on a polemical accent (19–32). This, however, remains simply an impression which will in any case remain subjective until the text's three sequences are made the object of that phonological study which has apparently not yet been undertaken.

Because of a regrettable lag behind the analyses made possible by recent progress in phonology, rhetoric, and stylistics, study of the Koran seems to be generally stuck in nineteenth-century philology. Of course, lexical and syntactical analyses have been accomplished in which the admirable science of Nöldeke, for exampke, won its spurs. Concepts have been neatly classified and transferred to punchcards. But this recourse to a fashionable scientism, in its most arid form,[10] has not been complemented, so far as I know, by a textual analysis such as is applied these days to poetry in European languages, and even Hebrew and Sanskrit. And yet, such analysis has become possible. We have available to us today frequency tables for the phonemes recorded in the *Ṣiḥāḥ*.[11] There is nothing to prevent application of the same research techniques to the Koran itself. One could then construct a differential phonology of each sura or section of a sura. Complementing this initial approach, study of the regularities or asymmetries among syntagms would produce exact data on the individuality of the sections considered.[12]

In any event, although for the time being we must make do with impressions, note that the ternary or tripartite character of Sura LIII arises likewise from its content. First (*a*) confirmation of the prophetic discourse by means of the vision granted the Prophet (1–8), (*b*) dialectic of conjecture and truth (19–32), (*c*) an outburst directed toward the Rewarder; and, last, a brusque shift of assonances and a final imperative, "Prostrate thyself" (57–62).

This concave structure, so to speak, emerges additionally in the recurrence of certain themes or words between the first and third sections. Examples: "That which conceals," *yaghsha* (16) and *ghashsha* (54)—the "star" (1) and "Sirius" (49)—the vision vouchsafed the Prophet (11, 12, 17) and God's observation of our acts (40). The entire sura, as a matter of fact, is concerned with knowledge of various sorts: divine and providential in God's case, illuminative in that of the Prophet. Whence the essential term and concept "making manifest," which appears powerfully in verse 58: *laysa lahā min dūni Allāhi kāshifatun*, "there is none save God who manifests it." That is why man's "conjecture," *ẓann*, cannot attain to "knowledge," *ʿilm*, nor provide exemption from *ḥaqq*, that is, Truth, Being, and Reality. This pugnacious reference to false beliefs and opinionated, erroneous knowledge produces a noticeable break with the lyrical exaltation of the first and third movements. But this is not the only abrupt shift in tone. The affirmative testimony based on the vision (1–18) is followed by an ironical challenge of the false gods (19–27), then an epistemological discussion (28–30), a threat of punishment (31–32), a backward glance (33–35), a proclamation in the name of *dhikrā* (36–54), and finally the closing warning and command.

To the diversification resulting from the ternary structure and multiplicity of tones might be added one based on reading the text at different levels. This might proceed from simply lexical gloss to moral meditation and mystical speculation. This last, stimulated by the sura's invocation of the inequality among genera and among degrees of knowledge, is motivated to evoke the successively higher rungs, *marātib*, of the ladder leading to truth, that "hidden treasure." The ultimate ecstasy will flood the elect with both joy and pain, "for to the beloved in the divine presence, even though he is among those admitted to the presence, trial and suffering must be meted out, because if he did not experience pain to a degree proportionate to his objectives, his aspiration to divine love would be insincere." Naturally, orthodox exegesis does not enter into affective excesses which might spill over into theosophy or even theurgy. It nevertheless engages in excursuses in connection with virtually every word and its various "faces," *wujūh*. This, again, underscores the text's density and its power of suggestion at numerous levels. Thus, the three verbs of verses 2 and 3—*ḍalla*, *ghawā*, *hawā*—evoke for Shaikh Tījānī "what the soul commits to satisfy its appetites," but to Shaikh al-Marāghī they seem to contain precise allusions, respectively, to soothsayers, fools, and poets. How far should verse 4 be construed to extend: ". . . it is but revelation revealing itself"? Does the formula apply only to the Koran, or to all the Prophet's acts? Shaikh al-Qāsimī leans toward the narrow construction: otherwise, where would be the Prophet's freedom of will? And in his rationalistic commentary one may find judicious discussions pinpointing the vision: did it take place at the Archangel Gabriel's first apparition? This may give an idea of what commentary, exegesis, and hermeneutics can work out from a text equally vertical and synchronous, since it orchestrates effects in several modes at several levels.

Conjunctions beyond Measure

How could it be otherwise? The "psalmody," or *tilāwa*, of the Koran, that festival of the memory, produces an ever-renewed encounter between God and the community of believers. However, though of high spiritual value, this encounter has its limits in the fact that the divine entity remains beyond human grasp. Hence the reservations with which orthodoxy opposes both that ritualism which imputes to the text a sort of operative quality, and that intellectualism which seeks to reach the Creator's forever-hidden essence by way of presumed transparencies.

The second point should be emphasized. The Koranic "signifier" no more gives access to God's essence than a casual conversation gives me access to the soul of someone I am talking to, nor even to the "idea" inhering in the objects expressed. Of course, in that quite extraordinary passage by a Maghrebi shaikh of the late eighteenth century,[13] the fundamental inadequacy of language is applied to the Koran only by virtue of a double distinction which separates, on one hand, the dignity of the text itself from the feeble grasp of my own speech and, on the other, divine infiniteness from the debility of my approach. Although this statement by the founder of a sect was intended simply to justify the necessity of an esoteric and graded "path," and to discredit belief in effects derived *ex opere operato* from reading the text, we must admire the effort and modesty of thought upon which any proper exegesis is based. The Koranic meditations in the *Jawāhir* of Shaikh Tījānī, from which I have taken this remarkable passage, represent an abrupt departure from the virtually total aridity and sterility that had overtaken the science of *tafṣīr* in the Maghreb. It is true that in the East reservation was never carried to this extreme, and that in Tunisia the monumental *Commentary* by Shaikh Ṭāhir bin ʿĀshūr has recently given the lie to that excess of reverent fear to which the scarcity of *tafṣīrs* in the Maghreb is attributable.

This scarcity, however, was due not only to a justifiable fear but also to an intense feeling of *iʿjāz*. Indeed, independently of all other explanations of a metaphysical, psychological, or social order, this feeling results from a trait of this style, namely the contrast between the apparent simplicity of its signifiers and its transcendence through the evocative power of the things signified. This plus-value, so to speak, stems from very diverse procedures. Koranic elocution furthermore brings into play the properties of the terms it places in conjunction—at times their richness of imagery, at others even their disarrangements. Generally speaking, the result is a semantics opening upon a sort of infinity of content. We may ignore what modernistic Muslim readers seek to derive in the way of prediction of present or future scientific truths. It is unnecessary to discover in LXXXVI, 11–12, a premonition of atmospheric elasticity or of oil gushers[14] in order to admire the unspeakable grandeur of these two short verses: "By heaven, which reverberates, by the earth which bursts open." Many such examples could be cited.

Let us reread the famous Cave sura, a favorite of the late Louis Massignon. This sura, traditionally re-enacted every Friday in the mosques, overflows with vistas into the imaginary. First of all, the central theme, that of the Seven Sleepers, who may be only three, four, or five; and should we count their dog, watching over them as they sleep? Many exegeses have played this numbers game, which itself contributes to the poetic effect. The strangeness of the presentation invites the listener into a mysterious timelessness. Who are these young men removed from earthly time in a cavern which the sun visits allusively, "passing now to the left, now to the right"? Another figure of mysterious beauty . . .

In the same sura, consider the story of Alexander, Dhū al-Qurnayn, the "Two-Horned." Whereas in the *Isrāʾīliyāt* the Koran is based on scriptural traditions, or oral traditions with biblical overtones, here it seems to embark on pure romantic invention. By contrast with the *Ishrāqiyīn*, the hero does not set out toward the sunrise but, as later in Hölderlin's famous *Ode to a Journey*, travels toward an occidental Hesperides. Therein resides a terrible menace, for that is where two frightful monsters, Magog and Gog, are lurking to fall upon mankind. Entreated by the inhabitants, the Two-Horned builds a wall of iron and brass in a mountain gorge, which will pen up the monsters until the end of time. The text's suggestive power is wonderful. Without explicating it at length, we shall point out that it brings into play much besides tropes, metaphors, or word combinations, but rests on a constant irregularity between verbal material of apparent simplicity and its projection into the imaginary. Here everything seems to proceed in a direction contrary to that of *jāhilī* poetry, which is not always rescued from a certain mediocrity of lyric flight by its luxury of vocabulary and prosodic virtuosity.[15]

By these kinds of asymmetry, of course, the Koran summons up not only an imaginary domain of tale or dream but the *ghayb* itself, that "incommunicable" which by definition escapes any human grasp. Thus Sura X, Yūnis, verse 24: "Proximate life is like unto the water which I have made to descend from heaven, and the earth's vegetation imbibes it, of which man and beast eat, until the earth takes up its jewels and adorns itself therewith, while its inhabitants believe they have power over it, then comes Our decree by night or by day and We make thereof level, empty ground as if yesterday it had not been. This is how We articulate Our signs for him who would reflect." The restrained quality of the expression, which we have tried to preserve in the translation, seems to fade off here into infinity. If we applied the methods of a Jurjānī or a Bāqillānī to such a passage we could only gloss isolated words or word pairs, whereas the stylistic effect proceeds from a broader sequence cut in two by "then": the fertile field, the vegetation, its luxuriant growth, the naïve confidence of men, and "then" the divine decree which sweeps all away. The passage culminates in the sentence, "This is how We *nufaṣṣil*, articulate," which is of a metalinguistic order. The style, one might say, folds back upon itself and, in order to interpret its own efficacy, emphasizes its coincidence with a cosmic structure: a coincidence which opens up new vistas. *Nufaṣṣil* serves here, perhaps, the function of what English-speaking linguists call a "trigger," or a "shifter." The level of nature is thereby transmuted into that of the Providential order. Hence the ascending correspondences such images evoke.

The Arab listener feels deeply these verbal morphologies and follows their ascending flight. This would be impossible without the implicit culture that he absorbs through the millenary cohabitation between the text and the community. The characteristic applies both to the text as a whole and to its details, in such a way that the Koran is itself its own explication, each of the parts finding in the totality an "explicit paradigm," *al-imām al-mubīn*.

Universal Counterpoint: Two Examples

That a text's form and content are inseparably joined in its effect is only a banal observation which modern stylistics rejects, since it rightly questions this scholastic dualism, but at the same time perpetuates by introducing elements of a more-sophisticated diversity into a bipartite analysis. Thus, the succession and symmetry of sounds; the differential sequences that result; the segmentation by suras, fragments, and verses; the conjunctions and disjunctions of mode and register in the preceding pages—all may have seemed capable of accounting for the power of the text. These aspects would, of course, have to be studied through specialized approaches. This has not yet been done, as far as I know, and the present chapter does not, and could not, purport to be more than a rather conjectural effort in that direction. It is nevertheless safe to say that study of these convergences would permit resolution of the problem, not of *iʿjāz*, which in the eyes of believers always involves a metaphysical assumption, but of its procedures, which are nothing other than those of a style. At the very least, the systematic comprehension of the text's various planes, and its simultaneity, would clear up certain of its perplexing features. We shall endeavor to illustrate this by two examples.

First, Sura LV, al-Raḥmān, or the "Benefactor." This epithet inscribed in the Islamic credo has become so familiar that we must be grateful to Shawqī Ḍayf for having pointed out its uniqueness.[16] The sura strings together seventy-eight verses in brief stanzas punctuated thirty-one times by a refrain, "What benefactions of your Lord will you both deny?" After the glorification of these benefactions (1–24), an apocalyptic menace thunders, then the promise of paradise is sung, but with the bizarre feature that it is repeated twice in succession. All—the short stanzas and their tireless refrain—evokes the idea of response: a reciter and a chorus, perhaps. The description of the delights in the Beyond is perhaps not simply encored but told, alternately or simultaneously, by two sections of the chorus or two moods of a single character. This theatrical evocation remains conjectural, however. One is on surer ground in stressing the constancy of the rhyme in *ān*, interrupted now and then by other final syllables—*ām*, *ār*, and even *ūn*—with, naturally, a connection between the sound changes and some meaningful intention.

The sura has been felt to be so entrancing by many believers that some have nicknamed it *ʿarūs al-Qurʾān*, "the Koran's bride." As happened several times during the revelation, it inspired conversions of itself. Upon hearing it, a Bedouin of the Tamīm, a tribe of conquerors which would probably have extended its domination over all Arabia if the revelation had not intervened, asked the Prophet to repeat it to him. Then he exclaimed, in a voice one may imagine as rough and deep, "There is brilliance in it, and beauty. . . . Its foundation is *mukhziq*, and its capital *muthmir*," that is, water flows at its base and its peak is laden with fruits. Thereupon he became a Muslim.

It was a convention in the old poetry that direct address took the dual mode. It is thus not surprising that this mode governs the thirty-one repetitions of the refrain. But it has been less frequently noticed that the same doubling governs all the images from one end of the sura to the other. At the very beginning these intersecting alternations resound: the Benefactor (1) and man (3); the Koran (2) and the *bayān* (4). Immediately after come these pairings: the sun and the moon (5), the star and the tree (6). Later on: man of clay (14) and the demon of bright fire (15).

It is to both these classes of creatures, men and demons, that the sublime challenge is addressed: "I shall concern Myself with you, one liable to judgment and the other! . . . O company of demons, O that of men, could you but burst forth from the domain of heavens and earth, then do you so!" (31–33). The dual apostrophe thus cannot be boiled down to a cliché, nor to a rhyming device as Nöldeke believed. It proceeds from the very thickness of the inspiration. Indeed, it is sustained through the third movement, in which the idea "two" recurs no less than twenty-one times in twenty-two verses, if we trust R. Blachère's translation! Two gardens stand in opposition to the accursed pair, Gehenna and the Boiling Water (62); two springs will flow therein (51), and "of each fruit there shall be two species," *zawjān* (52). Shawqī Ḍayf considers, rather penetratingly, that this term evokes the idea of mating, related to the idea of egalitarian justice already present in the *mīzān*, or "balance," of verse 7. Sexuality, indeed, is rooted in cosmic polarity.

But if there are two descriptions, not just one, of this paradise with its dual delights, is it because there are two juxtaposed, of which one is simply encored or even added by interpolators? Is it not more economical to assume that the dual number, reaffirmed in the sura with tireless energy, reaches its paroxysm in this third movement? If so, the grammatical form is so integrated with the inspiration that the sura ends with the evocation of a binary paradise. Dare I go further? Might the passage on the houris, itself double (56–58 and 70–74), not simply illustrate, in the sexual mode, the same duality? . . .

Sura XXVII, The Ants, includes the marvelous account of the Queen of Sheba in verses 15–44. Solomon, the conqueror, advances at the head of a sort of Foreign Legion he has formed with contingents of demons, mortals, and birds. His personality is not devoid of self-conceit, of cruelty, nor of irony. He smiles, as he understands the ants' language and can thus surprise them. But the hoopoe's independent activity challenges his omniscience. It is she who, defying his orders, has left the procession and returns like an explorer to tell of the kingdom of Sheba. The King sends this strange people an ultimatum demanding that they embrace Islam. The Queen assembles a council which, amusingly, boasts of its own courage so as to avoid pronouncing an opinion.

Here also, phonological study of the text would contribute to understanding it. The shifts of assonance, in particular, are of interest. But what I should stress is the extent to which the text's symmetries can help us understand it. The ants fear that their homes will be crushed by the King (18). The council fears the same thing (34). The conquerors render the defeated "vile," *adhilla* (34). The same word reappears in verse 37. But this is where only the configurations of the signifier, I believe, can make it possible to interpret the account and point its lesson.

The Queen's famous throne is brought to Solomon as booty (38 ff.). We should construe this as a symbol of pre-Scriptural royalty. What does the King do with this prestigious object? Already happy to have it in his possession, he hastens to make of it a test for the Queen, *nakkiru lahā ʿarshahā* . . . (41). What does this mean? To send the throne back unrecognizable, as one translation has it, or to send her a counterfeit? Like everything stemming from the root *n-k-r*, *nakkara* has pejorative overtones. *Tanakkara*, according to the *Lisān*, said of things, is the act of changing into something different and unknown. The former interpretation would conform to this usage. But in this case the Queen, far from being deceived, has outsmarted the test and, on balance, seized the initiative over Solomon, since she says, "This certainly looks like it," *kaʾannahu huwa*. If Solomon, on the other hand, has kept the throne and has merely sent the Queen an imitation, in making such a reply she has not been entirely deceived but is still only half right. In fact, she bears within herself traces of the old revelations, but so attenuated that she falls partially victim to this first challenge, which is followed by a second (44). The decisive reason for our interpretation, in our opinion, is the symmetry between the second test and the first. The King has the Queen walk across a floor of crystal, which she mistakes for water. She lifts her robe up over her legs in such a way as to evince, *kashafat*, by a sexual suggestion, her surrender to the one who has subjected her to this second ordeal of the enigma. She must then profess Islam.

A Text in Process of Becoming

But it is the whole world which is an enigma, and the discourse of the Koran, which purports to offer a way to its solution, is didactically strewn with ordeals for the believer. Among its verses some are clear-cut, others preserve some ambivalence (*mutashābihāt*). The message of the supreme Invariant, the Koran thus avoids schematism. Rigidity and immobility would be self-contradictory in it.

Just as it "descends" in intermittent fashion, its declaration is continually under construction, in process of completion.[17] It operates by frequent new starts, by accumulation, and sometimes by correcting itself. This may appear contradictory inasmuch as each parcel of the message has definitive value. Hence the difficult theory of the "abrogating," *nāsikh*, and the "abrogated," *mansūkh*. Thus Sura II, verse 106: "Thus what We abrogate or cause to be forgotten among the verses, yea We shall come with another, We shall bring another which will be better than the first." Now the abrogated like the abrogating, the old like the new, are equally part of God's word and have the value of an absolute. But of an absolute that clarifies and amends itself. In this the process of revelation departs from the philosophical stereotype of an immutable truth. Truth is being constructed before our eyes and sometimes remains in suspense.

For his part, its transmitter, the Prophet, intensifies this process in all his human weakness. Thus, it is not uncommon for him, the "best of creatures," to subject himself to what we would call self-criticism. As in Sura LXXX, ʿAbusa, "He frowned": The Messenger was present in a gathering of people from the city's wealthy classes when a blind man or beggar appeared, to whom he paid no attention. He even shoved him aside, preoccupied as he was with catechizing the Quraysh notables. He later reproached himself for this first impulse. A revelation was vouchsafed him, administering the deserved reprimands.

Hence the paradoxical fact that the Koran, although definitively fixed first as the Prophet received it, then as written down under the caliphate, although reigning in the memory of millions of the faithful as something unitary, immutable, and even uncreated, sees itself as in motion, even demanding of men that they read, interpret, and place it in operation. Just as its style makes simplicity of the signifier the underpinning of a storied structure of meanings (the latter embracing individual and collective behavior), it subordinates its phonic consistency to the psalmody the faithful make of it. It thus postulates a chorus composed of men. But the role of this chorus is not only that of performer (in the orchestral sense of the word). An adequate reading is not simply restoration, but also interpretation. Thus men, infinitely poverty-stricken by comparison with God, nevertheless see themselves endowed with His language in their Arabic language. What does this mean, if not that they are to perfect, not of course the substance of the unsurpassable Book, but the earthly role expected of it by Him Who revealed it?

Many of the text's characteristics, in fact, testify to an assumption of the human voice, human thought, and ultimately human history. It is not by chance that the last sura, symmetrical with the Fātiḥa, repeats the noun "men" five times in a mere few lines. Anthropology, if I may say so, here forms the counterpart of the prefatory sura's cosmology: a revealing feature that has not been sufficiently noticed.

An Ancient Mediterranean Object

There is an ancient Mediterranean object that has known unusual vicissitudes. It is a piece of marble from Delphi carved to appear like a twisted shaft. Emperor Constantine had it transported from Apollo's city to Byzantium. It still graces an Istanbul garden under the name of the Serpentine Column. Similarly, until our days references to the Koran and to the poetry of the desert are interlaced in Arab culture.

In this culture memory's share is not confined to these abiding beginnings. For over fourteen centuries an immense layer of thought, behavior, and works has overgrown them, modifying them at times and even contradicting them. To analyze all these permanences—how they have been transformed or disguised; discover their location, their social strata, and their psychic horizons; and assess their future prospects—would require writing another book, and that is not my subject here. It remains true, nevertheless, that there are few of these efflorescences which do not refer back, directly or indirectly, to one or the other of these ancestral sources, or cannot be related to them.

But if this relationship is of course not the only constituent of the Arab heritage, no more does it suffice as a definition of a historical entity which modern times are inviting to draw from within itself, and from others, its own renewal. The first part of this book endeavored to describe this debate between invariance and its own variations, as reflected in landscape and act. In the third I shall examine more closely the ways in which it is expressed and the meanings it seeks to find for itself. It will perhaps be useful, in concluding my Part Two, "Culture and Memory," and as a prologue to what follows, to invoke the testimony of a poet, chosen from among the youngest and most militant. As will be seen, the testimony is both of rupture and of fidelity.

BIRTH

For centuries, O father, you traded incense and beads.
For centuries, you foraged till you returned with treasure.
You protected the water for my sake, you protected the water
And grew date palms in your green oases.
You knew the cave of Ḥarā, you worshipped God.
You destroyed the idols at Mecca.
You wandered over the earth, making the desert bloom.
You came back to me from Shiraz
With silks and perfumes and bread.

Short was my history—and with it, my glory,
While you labored, my father, and brought back the treasure.
You labored for centuries, my father, until you collapsed with weariness
And your burdens sank into the barren sands of catastrophe,
And when the newborn called me,
There was no water . . . no trees,
No more conquerors, no more wandering, no more life.

Don't be angry, my father,
And don't scold me,
If I close my doors in the face of yesterday,
If I change my clothes and abandon the ancient spacious palaces.

And if I say farewell to my flowers
And kiss the tomb of the past goodbye,
Kiss it for the last time, the tomb of the past.

O my father, none of our books crushed under the heel of Hulagu Khan,
Nor our green Eden that was a paradise for the people,
Not the horses of the Crusades,
Nor the memories of Saladin,
Nor the unknown soldier of Ḥiṭṭin
Will keep me in the ruined place of exile.

For from my love for my children
I will build great factories.
I will patch my worn coat
And build a fine house, create a green garden,
And from my love for my grandchildren
I will befriend the noblest people,
And learn in their schools the human sciences, the secrets of the atom.

I will raise my free flag
And around it gather my loved ones.

Don't be angry, my father.
Don't scold me
If I kiss the tomb of the past goodbye,
If I kiss the tomb of the past for the last time in my life.

Goodbye, my beloved father, goodbye, my friend of yesterday.
For my new friends are pounding on the door,
And the sounds of the glorious machines are calling us.
Let us start the journey of the new generations
Before the sunrise! [18]

PART THREE

Expression and Meaning

Submerged in a universe in which the West's dominating objects are ubiquitous, the Arabs are beginning to acquire an infrastructure thanks to the resources of their fields and deserts. One large portion of themselves now belongs to the industrial age, in which petroleum already constitutes for them a means of bargaining, and in which the magnitude of their energy resources ensures them a powerful base for the future. Although the age of scientific and technical revolution is also one of relentless conflicts, they are entering upon it with confidence, assuring themselves that thereby they are guaranteeing their survival and perhaps future victories.

However, their effort to authenticate gains and metamorphoses, the assertion of their identity, the reactions of their language, the up-dating of their heritage—all this is being brought to bear upon them in an ambiguity laden with menace as well as promise. The danger is that, between their ineluctable advance along the technological line which transmits the power of our time and the movement that affects the other dimensions of man and group, there may be not merely a lag but an actual rupture: material accelerations on one side and substituting intensities on the other.

Culture: Regulation/Deregulation

". . . What! Since our equipment is mainly borrowed, when we have made it our own this very appropriation we are seeking will remain equivocal? Our values will be mere compensations, our meanings only myths? Must we waver indefinitely between the risks of borrowing and those of sickness? Very well, then: I will make of the sick and the borrowed, whether they fight each other or ally themselves within us, my hope, a vertigo, and a bugaboo for others! Out of our rush into the future and our obsession with the old, out of the exasperation, that is, of my disharmony, I shall draw power to subvert others and myself. And in this demonic possession I will find my inspiration for the new times!"

Thus might speak, long after our Maldoror, *Mihyār le Damascène*.[1] Am I not, indeed, simply copying him here? Many Arabs, particularly of the young generation, might speak, have spoken, or are speaking as he did. They thus reflect the revolutionary implication of symbols that are in precession over the movement of the social totality, or of languages which anticipate in the cultural mode a collective creativity temporarily paralyzed by the lack of overall regulating mechanisms. Culture thus precedes praxis to the extent that the latter reflects, in stagnation or retrogression, the fact that interchange has been interrupted among technology, organization, belief, and so on, and each of these dimensions operates on its own, separately from the others. Similarly, culture will precede politics, since the latter, at best, strives to restore the connections among sectors so as to re-establish the global movement: but can it succeed in this without ideals and revolutionary images, that is, without a specifically cultural preparation?

One cannot, nevertheless, deny that the many writers and artists wedded to group feeling, majority rule, or power ideologies have some significance. They are still there, these exponents of consensus, for example the classicists and the religious. Can we deny that they have a role as cultural agents? No rupture is to be expected from them, but rather a confirmation, an enchantment with accepted attitudes. They sometimes perform this function with something far beyond mere virtuosity. Let us resign ourselves to it: neither conformity nor nonconformity guarantees aesthetic value, nor does either exclude it.

In the heated polemic in Egypt that greeted Ṭaha Ḥusain's thesis on pre-Islamic poetry, his toughest adversary was certainly Rāfiʿī, and it was he who mobilized the strongest correspondences with Muslim tradition and with Egyptian society of his time.[2] While Ṭaha Ḥusain must be credited with a boldness that made him a precursor of historical reason in his country, Rāfiʿī's commitment to religious invariance represented an apparently victorious response to his adversary's Westernism. On the latter side, a static attachment to received and sufficient values. On the former, deregulation, but a deregulation that in fact was simply regulation in abeyance.

Consider also the controversies that have raged for twenty years over free verse and traditional poetry: Arab continuity inclines decidedly toward the latter, and its great poet is still Shawqī. No one, of course, expected of Shawqī infraction of the rules or even innovation, and yet the public puts him on a level with the greatest classics. It is true that he is accused of leading a pleasure-loving life, and of timidity in his rebellions. The Prince of Poets, as he was solemnly proclaimed in 1927, was also a poet of princes. Now other poets still living, Jawāhirī for example, demonstrate that it is possible to combine classical craftsmanship with revolutionary passion. Shawqī did not do so. In fact, he did the opposite. Nevertheless, even in our day, and outside Egypt still more than in his own country, he is considered a literary paragon. The Damascus Ba'th itself has in no way condemned him as reactionary, whereas it has not shown the same indulgence toward the great Syrian poet, Badawī al-Jabal. Let us pass on, while affirming once again that values still attach to a poetry in which most Arabs still recognize the chant of their identity.

What is true of poetry is true of the other arts. To what do the voice of Umm Kulthūm and the songs of a composer like 'Abd al-Wahhāb, for example, owe their enduring prestige? Certainly not to audacious anticipations of the collective becoming, but instead to the sufficiency of their art to a certain stage in this becoming. Should we conclude, then, that this art thereby takes advantage of substitute values by which a society defers or avoids the necessary readjustments? Bourgeois values, in a word. . . . How, then, can its success on either side of a revolution be explained? If these two artists are still, and more than ever, sacred cows,[3] is it because their response is still adequate? Or has this adequacy shifted its axis? Indeed, it may be that, having been the avant-garde of the 1930s, they are traveling in today's common direction.

Such questions leap blithely over the frontiers of autonomous but related domains: that of concrete history and that of aesthetic value. We are no longer, to repeat, so naïve as to believe that the latter "flows" from the former or "reflects" it, nor that it must inevitably oppose it. Nevertheless, analysis convinces us of close correlations between the two. Culture—if we are so bold as to reiterate the definition proposed earlier—is nothing other than the movement of the social totality as it seeks for itself an expression and a meaning. But we must at once make a distinction. This search for expression and meaning may either comment on the movement of any given time, urge it to return to its structures, or project it into anticipations of the future. In any of these cases it acts upon the social whole and is acted upon by it.

It follows that what is called a masterpiece is often what coincides with the majority tendency interpreted in depth and over a long term. That might account for the consecration of certain values in Egypt during the interwar period: for example, the rationalistic humanism of a Ṭaha Ḥusain, a Tawfīq al-Ḥakīm, or even an ʿAqqād. The ancient sufficiencies, however, inspired by orthodoxy and sustained by a formidable popular consensus, retain acculturating power even if their inspiration diverges from the contemporary history of these societies, whereas another regulator, which could be called bourgeois, is animating and leading the march of this history toward a modernism of the happy medium in which adaptation to the other and faithfulness to oneself are reconciled insofar as possible. Finally, a deregulated culture emphasizes the failures and weaknesses of the two preceding ones. It denounces the one as reactionary, the other as opportunistic. Itself, it strives to establish the premises of the future.

But these distinctions remain schematic. As a matter of fact, in all cultures there is a necessary counterculture element, inasmuch as the writer and artist each demonstrates a creativity of which he sees his society incapable for the time being. Thus they defy inherited tendencies and prevailing taste. In this type of culture, a reaction against continuity and normality enters into means and ends; should we call such a reaction romantic? From the very defects of social synchronism it brings forth values that, mingling vehemences of different, sometimes opposite, signs, may stamp the work of art with an exemplary intensity. Effractions, changes of level, and asymmetry then set their creative quality against the homologies that should affect the overall movement of a collectivity. Was nineteenth-century Western poetry not born of this kind of ruptures? Why should things go differently in the Arab world? Can one not regard the renaissance of Arab letters at the end of the nineteenth century and the beginning of the twentieth as a response, as yet timid, to the invasion those societies were then undergoing?

The invasion is still going on. Response and resistance are going on as well. This drama is making a deep imprint upon contemporary Arab culture. Like the world's other cultures, it is introducing its own values into a process that can succeed only in the long run in readjusting partial and global dynamics, to the extent that they will ever be readjusted. If this success is by no means certain, if the expected progress proves only a truculent hope or bitter nostalgia, the very uncertainty simply makes the effort more poignant.

XI
A Redeployment of Genres— First Symmetry: Painting and Music

Many Arab intellectuals, when drawing up the balance sheet of their generation's accomplishments by comparison with that of the one before—say, that of the generation between the two world wars—confess to a certain uneasiness regarding the progress made. Do the works produced over the past thirty years come up to the standard of the older ones? Has the broadened availability of education not diluted it? Has Arabization, while effecting the retreat of English and French in broad domains, raised the level of Arabic correspondingly? It is not a question simply of a transitory weakness among the elites. In song, on the cinema screen, on the stage, in all fields involving mass support, the interwar glories, now sacred cows, continue and are not being superseded by new talents. Can one not legitimately ask whether a process of "deculturation" is not in operation rather than the contrary? "Our culture?" cries Nizār Qabbānī. "Nothing but bubbles in washtubs and chamber pots!"[1]

This blasphemy and these doubts bear witness to a ravaged subjectivity. They must be weighed against contrary evidence: schools swarming everywhere, a thirst for learning, a revaluation of both popular lore and arts, the avant-garde's break-through into international exchanges; those studious crowds whose very discontent is a motivation; this faith in education that imbues nearly all the governments and leads them to devote journals and laboratories to pedagogical research and to allocate an enormous share of their budgets to the training of youth that, statistically, the preceding period had permitted to stagnate. More certainly still, the growth of a demanding and questioning spirit, the impulse toward historical reason and critical consciousness, in sum the gaining of that right to have problems without which there is no possible culture in this world now in the making! However, it does happen that problematic *people* are swept aside. Many intellectuals have a choice only among silence, compromise, or exile. Worse still: censorship does not explain everything, and authoritarian government provides neither motive nor excuse for the (relative) impotence of potentially creative individuals: otherwise there would have been no Dostoevski.

A Working Hypothesis

Will social history provide clarification in this discussion bearing on the subjectivity of a group to which I myself do not belong, upon the trend of that subjectivity, and upon formal preferences for which it is impossible to control? I think so, as long as the analysis strives, as we tried to do above, to transcend simplistic objectivism also.

Once more, let us consider culture as a particular dynamic, but one not separate from the movement of the whole. The pessimistic opinion of so many Eastern intellectuals regarding their present culture is due to the very overevaluations that have been made of it. The compensating role assigned to it is, in fact, impossible to fulfill. It can satisfy no one because its mainspring, precisely, is dissatisfaction. Hence these lugubrious and largely unjustified judgments. For after all, as we shall presently see, neither talents nor publics are lacking. It would be more apposite to call attention to the disproportion between these aptitudes and actual literary or artistic performance. The relationship between the two is admittedly less favorable in the current generation than with its predecessor. The true deterrent applies at the level of the work's production. The brake itself consists in the global conditions of these societies' renewal, rather than aesthetic weaknesses.

In aesthetic matters as in everything else, the Arabs suffer both from the valuation they place upon their classicism and from their training on foreign models. They attach value to this training itself, since in most cases they take it as an index of modernity and a criterion of survival! Arab expression is thus caught between the two millstones, one coming from the depths of the ages, the other from outside. Let us give our attention only to the latter. Except in a few domains, such as those of the religious sciences and traditional poetry, Arabs must align themselves according to the dominant types of the age. Thus they have adopted almost entirely a classification of genres quite new to them. Their classicism distributed its genres in its own way, and this manner of distribution still dominates instinct and memory. One part of identity is connected thereto, for it had succeeded in making a complementary arrangement between the Koran's inspiration and that of pre-Islam. Today, in our view, it is from the debate between these two types of organization of genres—the traditional and the borrowed or adopted—that the conditionings of most Arab expression result. This debate becomes more heated day by day as the debate between these peoples and the rest of the world rises in temperature.

The variety of genres, the reconsideration of their relative ranking, the redistribution to which they are subjected from one era to another comprise in fact a phenomenon of great consequence, which the Russian formalist school has rightly stressed.[2] If the classification to which Arab culture conforms today reflects that of the West in large part, this means that a portion of the configuration comes from elsewhere. But form, naturally, can do no more than activate a local creativity already engaged with its own conditionings and its own values. One may readily conceive that between this profound force and its more or less alien modes there can be either dispute or convergence. I shall try to make this clear by examining a few genres of expression whose fortunes show significant contrasts.

First Symmetry: Painting/Music

Arab painting[3] was long either passed over in silence or made the subject of myths. It was said to consist solely of miniatures, or rather illuminations inspired from geometry. Representation of nature, it was said, was congenitally proscribed because of the religious prohibition on portrayal of animate beings. What a naïve view! It assumes that artistic creations proceed from the ethic standard, whereas they are generally achieved in spite of it. There was no more reason for there not to be an Arab figure painting than a bacchic poetry or a literature affronting public morals: the latter two both flourished and blithely overcame the opposition of the devout. Thus if there is the same rupture between modern plastic expression among Arabs and what it was in the past, and the same innovation, as in theatrical expression, the reason must be sought elsewhere than in theology! In any case, why lend credence to the presumption that genres are universal by observing that one or another is present or lacking here or there, when the only thing that is universal is the need to which the genres respond—and very diversely—from age to age and society to society?

What is true of painting is true also of sculpture, which did not await the erection of Mukhtār's allegorical group in a Giza square to embody in three-dimensional figures the plastic needs of the Eastern multitudes. This need had long found other responses. What now purports to be architecture, painting, sculpture, and so on, was formerly accomplished all in one piece through other procedures and within other limits. Professionalism was less prevalent, and linkage with the community was stronger. From epigraphy in plaster to soaring stone structures, from the treatment of light by means of glass windows to the contrast of open and filled space in buildings, from the deceptive severity of walls to the luxuriance of the carpets on the floor, the aspect of the city itself ordering the life of the people, all this artifice of lines, colors, and masses, and more still: a truly collective existence, it had no need to embark on our divisions of labor in order to be art, and sometimes very great art. One cannot disregard either the suggestive power of such a past or the effect of the new classifications through which the creativity of its sons must now be filtered.

One example, one memory: the admirable fragments from the facade of al-Masjid al-Nūrī[4] assembled by the Baghdad Museum. On one panel of a *miḥrāb* a strange collusion of planes and reliefs—abstract writings and leafy branches, straight lines and curves—leaps toward the viewer in a mad undulation, a hyperbolism that has to be recognized as baroque. A bit more and we would take these relics of thirteenth-century Mosul to be a foretaste of the Churrigueresque! From this supremely organized functional madness anything could emerge: the statues of Raḥḥāl, the paintings of Jawād Salīm, the architectural mannerisms of Chatterji, and still more the canny mixtures of forms attempted by Ḍiyā᾿ al-ʿAzzāwī. But genealogies of creativity do not, and need not, follow a straight line. The history and variations of artistic genius presuppose discontinuity, interaction, an unexpected intersection of lineages rather than a simple linear succession. Why look among the *taʿziyas*, popular skits, or magic lantern shows for the ancestors of the contemporary theater if the latter does no more than provide a modern language to life's theatricality that formerly assumed quite different forms? With due respect to those who extol the ancient legacy and who always tend to assert that it embraced all things to come, the current rise of painting among the Arabs cannot in any way be traced back to manuscript illumination nor to calligraphy, even though the ancestry is observable (and deliberately so) with some artists; it simply consists, instead, in drawing upon what is visible by means of an imported technique, at a time when the visible is arousing additional needs among the Arabs.

In its own manner, Iran had already passed that way. In seventeenth-century Persia a change took place, under the influence of European artists invited in by the monarch, that, to say the least, shook the old miniature tradition to its foundations. ʿAbbās the Great had moved his court from Qazwīn to Isfahan. He supervised construction of the magnificent urban complex of Maydān-ī-Shāh. He moreover used the services of a colony of those energetic Armenians who at the time were pushing their commercial ambitions from Asia deep into Europe. The richest of them acquired many pictures one may still admire in their old churches beyond the Zayāndeh. Under ʿAbbās II a Flemish and an Italian artist demonstrated on the spot the lessons of the Renaissance, including that of perspective. They were the founders of a new school. A Persian miniaturist sent to Italy itself was there converted, more or less, and combined in his new name, Paolozamān, the patronship of St. Paul and that of his own "time," in which he had good reason to believe as, returning home after a trip to India, he attracted widespread admiration by illustrating a celebrated collection by Niẓāmī.

We are perhaps too severe today toward this intervention of Western technique in the evolution of Asian painting. We are becoming more and more so with respect to cultural influences. But we may rest assured. Through, and in spite of, mutual interchange and exchange of information, it is the discovery, or rediscovery, of their individuality that cultures seek. It is true that in the West itself it was not without loss (proportionate to the gain?) that these discoveries had acted upon the legacy of the Middle Ages. Fortunately, most of the great painters, including Ucello, who is reputed to be one of the inventors and theoreticians of perspective, were great painters rather in spite of it than thanks to its virtues. Their driving force was of a quite different order from that of geometry. It was the rediscovery of the various sorts of ancient naturalism that swelled them with zest, an almost orgiastic naturalism that reinforced the modern exaltation of individualism. The work of art proceeded from a dialectic between the artist's initiative and the world as western Europe thenceforth saw it, acted upon it, and was beginning to master it.

Today, of course, we are reacting against the costly victories of this man with the "true eye," who is accused of having robbed the real of its welling forces and replaced them with the false grandeurs of the blueprint. It remains to be seen whether that other dialectic that today's painting substitutes for the former one, that is, the one it introduces between the artist's act and the world (but in fact is it not rather society, including museums and picture buyers?)—it remains, as I say, to be seen whether this is a better dialectic than the previous one.[5] In any event it is always against norms, not because of them, that great creative works are made, and according to the most bizarre combinations and bifurcations. Then what about academic training? Should it be discarded, along with the so-called French-artist inspiration that reigned so long in Egypt? Even there, should the contribution of a Maḥmūd Saʿīd or a Nāghī be forgotten? Should we not see in them indocile tastes thwarted rather than served by their apprenticeship to foreign procedures? But what if these procedures were simply the alphabet necessary for any expression? It would be consoling to think that these painters simply acquired, at a distance, a neutral technique which they then enlivened with their own experience and fleshed out with a content of their own people and personality. But not so fast! The matter is not that simple. Form itself has its own meaning and does not disown its progeny so easily. As Malraux demonstrated in *Le Musée Imaginaire,* although somewhat exaggerating a Weberian idea, every style has its own history, related only indirectly to that of the artist and his country.

Application to a Specific Case: Iraq

Let us take the example of Iraq, as I was attracted there by that Mosul porch with its baroque serpentine curves and by a quite recent painting exposition at Basra. Contemporary art history in this country began by political chance. In 1940 several exiled Polish artists, some of whom had studied in Paris, took refuge at Baghdad, and it was they who lit the first spark. From the first, two personalities stood out: Jawād Salīm and Fāʾiq Ḥasan.[6] The former, who died young, is the author of the metal bas-relief with a bucolic motif that one admires in Baghdad's Liberation Square, surely one of the most grandiose ornamental groups in the Arab world. He had studied for a time in England, but he drew his inspiration not only from foreign masters, particularly Picasso, but from local sources also. He stressed graphic values above all: perhaps a designer at heart, whereas Fāʾiq Ḥasan delights in color.

Here we encounter the deliberate, perhaps also the "good student," feature of many of these transformations. Iraq had the good sense to send many students to the West on scholarships and to found several institutes and associations, including the Iraqi Artists Society (1956) and the Academy of Fine Arts (1960). All this development, we see, has thus taken place during the past twenty or twenty-five years. It was furthermore during the 1950s that the group which formed around Jawād Salīm published a manifesto in which we find for the first time some of the premises of any innovation in the Afro-Asian countries.

> The Modern Art Group in Baghdad is composed of painters and sculptors each with his specific style but all of whom begin with the inspiration of the Iraqi environment in order to glorify these styles. What they intend to do is to portray the life of the people in a new form defined by their observation or understanding of a land where so many civilizations flourished, disappeared, and revived. [On one hand, an effervescent humanity that takes up all the challenges of modernism; on the other, the restraining and tutelary presence of several deep layers of the past. The problem arises in approximately the same form in Egypt.] They are aware [second point of the manifesto] of the links in thought and expression that join them to the artistic evolution of today's world. At the same time, however, they seek to create forms which will endow Iraqi art with its own character and a distinctive personality.

From these few lines emerges the syllogism of modern aesthetic work in the non-Western world. The obligatory major premise: reference to oneself. But what "self"? There are at least two, the personal self and the collective self. Where else is the latter to be sought than among the people, the guardians of authenticity? But be careful! Romantic individualism and formal refinement may run counter to the communal spirit. The latter, in turn, may assume the most conflicting aspects: spontaneity with more or less calculated naïveties, or ideological, even didactic, schematism. The manifesto is silent on this point, which is a pity. The syllogism's minor premise also needs elucidation. It proclaims the necessity to join in a world-wide expression, a necessity particularly compelling in the case of the arts involving techniques up-dated by contemporary research. Such is the case with painting, sculpture, and orchestral music. Very well; but what if this technique cannot be dissociated from a "content" and is itself the real creator of the message rather than its tool and vehicle? What if the spectrum of genres, expanding and contracting according to the changing needs of eras, environments, and situations, of itself determines the approach to the beautiful, each genre drawing its strength from within itself through all its multifarious appearances in history, or at least in what we experience and perceive under this term?

In acknowledging this does an artist not place himself outside the national becoming? Exclusion of the anecdotal, the subject, or the motif, and insistence in principle and practice that the art in a picture resides elsewhere, is laid down today as a postulate of artistic creation. But it is harder, and perhaps impossible, for the artist to renounce his dialog with his own country's history. One cannot relegate the artist to his own solitude as long as his people shout within him and all around him, the people who plead that beauty be sought not so much for self-expression as for self-assertion. The wish of Jawād Salīm and so many of his colleagues is evidently to attain universality not despite, but by means of, their specificity. But universality in this field means modern styles of painting. Among these styles a complex auction is taking place, in which most of the pertinent factors are those peculiar to the Western world. Hence in the long run, perhaps, new alienations to be corrected by new revolutions.

Polemics in Tunis and Elsewhere

Between 1940 and 1945 there began, among young North Africans, an exploratory movement in which appeal to the depths of the soul, submergence in the potentials of the ancient legacy, and apprenticeship in international techniques were all mingled. Beginning in 1960 abstraction spread without, however, enlisting all artists: thus the late Sharqāwī (Morocco),[7] while the Algerian Benanteur "painted his country with his memory." Really! To achieve a truly Maghrebi painting, does one have to go by way of Klee, Braque, or Jackson Pollock? It is only too true! In the art market, at least, snobbishness is king. It brings one, in sum, into the establishment.

Conversely, in the name of local truth, should one try to be a sort of color slide of one's country, its scenes, its people, and its problems? Is such sincerity or simplicity not, in fact, hypocritical enslavement to what the other wants you to be, or wants you to think you are? In a word, under pretense of accuracy, would you not become a *harkī* of metropolitan painting? This is one of those insulting but expressive terms with which a group of Tunisian painters smitten with world-wide communication—that is, with expressions emanating from the foreign art market—stigmatized their compatriots who remained faithful to descriptive art. Let us not be too hasty in judging one or the other right. Alienation threatens on one side as well as the other. Only talent separates the sheep from the goats. But tomorrow is the judge of talent. . . .

Moreover, that is not the only polemic raging among Arab painters. This one left the most important thing out of the account. Wherever original creation breaks forth, it does so in spite of programs and affiliations. These controversies and rivalries nevertheless have one good effect: that of broadening the field of enquiry. On all sides people are espousing positions of potential fecundity: declaration of the rights of the imagination, like ʿĀṣim Stétiyé; recourse to mythological symbols coming from the depths of the ages as, in Algeria, with the *ouchem* ("tattooing") group; a hand held out toward folklore resources; a baroque combination, by collage or otherwise, of fragments detached arbitrarily from the present or the past; restoration of arabesque, which is far from having said its final word;[8] stylization in the Chinese manner; or return to the French impressionists—what does the trademark matter as long as the painter thus renders the multivalence of the real?

In any event, through the international "launching" of a few artists, by government subsidy of many more, and in response to a vague collective need (rather, it is true, than the support of the various national publics), the Arab plastic arts are broadening their activity. Already they have a history. Some of the trail breakers pass as classics and have museums dedicated to them. Correlatively, those born in the 1920s, such as Ḥamad Nada, enjoy an ambiguous prestige as elders, almost ancestors. For taste is being rapidly renewed and the role is deepening day by day. Recently a dozen intellectuals polled by *Al-Hilāl* stated that one painting or another had had great importance in their lives. These were Egyptians. We are far from the time when an illustrator for that same magazine had to deceive his parents in order to enter the School of Fine Arts! Today thousands of girls study design, interior decoration, and painting at the people's university in Garden City, and instruction in the plastic arts is an integral part of school curricula in most Arab countries.

Return to Basra

Let us go back to the exposition being held in the city of Basra where we, like Jawād Salīm, may evoke a grandiose past of which almost nothing remains. No, there are very few left of those famous houses along the canals, with the *shanāshīl*, the long, jutting loggias with *mushrabiyas* like that of the Bash Aʿyān family, overlooking a canal. Almost none of this woodwork remains. Most of it has been cut to pieces and sent to the antique shops, just as most family libraries have been dispersed. The new Basra, like all cities today, is expanding, in shanty towns for the newly poor, luxurious villas for the newly rich, and look-alike cottages for the petit bourgeois. There is even some virtuous building, by which we mean new government housing and workers' quarters. But this virtue, which seems promising to the patriot, does not entirely compensate, in the visitor's eyes, for the decadence of an old, melancholy beauty, to take the place of which there is as yet no Future Eve in this urban sprawl. The visitor will ask, furthermore, what has happened to the city's familiarity and intimacy, its *uns*, to use the Arabic word. It would doubtless be too much to hope to find it in those dozens of government employees' clubs to which, late in the afternoon, the boredom and vanity of the new times disperse.

As a reply to all these observations and questions the Iraqi painters published their message. On the line one could admire arabesques by Jamīl Ḥammūdī, "Baghdad symbols" by Nūrī al-Rāwī, two "visions" by Shākir Ḥasan, a naïve "Last Supper" by Fuʾād Jihād. Many names, as it should be, many different and rival tendencies. There were artists influenced by American abstract, some by French surrealism; others had remained, or again become, faithful to calligraphy or the Muslim miniature. In any case, a whole creativity was raising its head and beckoning. Beyond Sindbad's nostalgias it was recasting its mythology. A mythology sinking its pilings deep into a world irremediably transformed but which the artist was calling up by the rediscovery of his values. Yes, we were in a Basra lost and rebuilt, among its thirteen million palms, with its ecological problems, its port dominated by an immense grain elevator, its date-processing plant, and its recently constructed university. This did not prevent one from savoring among these young painters of Iraq what one savors also in its writers: violence and dream, the appeal of a mystery in which are blended the vibration of objects and the persistent presence of the ancestral blood. . . .

Arab Music: From Incantation . . .

How powerful oriental music is, and how faithful to so many traditions! It produces in its listeners the *ṭarab*, that is, disturbance of the senses which moves one nearly to tears, and which the "suites," or *nūbas*, unfold and manipulate according to conventional modes. An emotion so typical of a particular people! To have savored it, from outside of course and as a barbarian but nevertheless to have savored it, is the privilege of few foreigners. Thus it was for me, in a cobblestoned courtyard in old Tunis where a *mālūf* orchestra was playing. By one of those correspondences that lend warmth to history, the efforts of a music society, the Rāshidiya, had restored it to esteem at the beginning of the nationalist movement. Can it be said that the genre owes too much to the music of the Turks, master craftsmen in the field? But go to the far west, and in Morocco you will find an Andalusian music more closely related. Seated against a wall beneath a trellis four performers are playing and singing. Beneath the ocher rampart of Oudaya a bluish late afternoon is filtering down. The background, as is the rule, conspires in the incantation. Mist rises from the Bou Regreg estuary, conferring upon these Maghrebian intensities a tinge of Elsinor's sadness.

Or, again, I attend a concert of Arab classical music in a theater Cairo has built for the purpose. This fine term, "classical," music, was used also by the Algerian Republic for its 1967 festival. From these elaborate urban productions one may seek out popular sources which are still flourishing and are not always analogous with the former, far from it. Systematic investigations, in Egypt and Tunisia particularly, are beginning to reveal the wealth of a folklore which is not to be equated either with tradition or with spontaneity. A Rumanian musicologist employed by the Egyptian Ministry of Culture collected from a mason and a porter near Aswan a *marbū*ʿ that, departing from simple repetition, develops a pentatonic melody by shifts of register and polyphonic passages. Might not the future begin here? Bartok thought so. . . .

However, notwithstanding the efforts of the Rāshidiya in Tunis, which reportedly is attracting more and more young people, and despite the meritorious work of certain composers, is all this not permeated by a reactionary charm? Traditional music long since began to go out of style in the East, nearly two generations ago. *Unshūdat al-Fu*ʾ*ād*, "Song of the heart," now gathering dust in the Egyptian sound-film archives, was shown to enthusiastic audiences in 1934 throughout the Arab world. But it aroused more enthusiasm in Morocco, where I saw it at the picaresque Al ʿAlou Cinema, than in Egypt itself, where the musical portions were found disappointing. The lyrics had nevertheless been written by a poet much appreciated at the time, al-ʿAqqād. But the music remained faithful to the *dawr*, or *da capo*, form at a time when Egyptian taste had forsaken it for other, less cyclic, forms.[9] Whatever al-ʿAqqād, the perennial "Number Two," thought about it, it was ʿAbd al-Wahhāb, the "nightingale" dear to Shawqī, who was then managing the evolution of taste. *Takht* ("stage") or *kashk* ("bandstand") music, associated with receptions in walled gardens and with melancholy delights due to satiety, has certainly survived at the social level. Is it the same in the individual's heart of hearts? That is something else again. Does the ancient fiber not persist deep in some heart ostensibly wedded to Western music? Probably. In a more complex way, the genre established by ʿAbd al-Wahhāb oscillates precariously between the rival snares of narcissistic self-conceit and exoticism, here become reverse cosmopolitanism. But does it not, by its very attenuation, express a truth about the Arabs of yesterday, almost of today?

It was in 1930, in a public auditorium at Homs, that Rafīq Fakhūrī[10] heard him for the first time. The artist "let his tender voice lead him to exhale a spiritual balm that, upon touching the soul, purified it of all stain, filled the listener with the most-exalted rapture, and diffused a genuine *ṭarab* throughout his inner being." Such enthusiasm! Forty years later the singer's voice is virtually gone, but his authority as composer and as *ustādh* survives. What a great day it was when this sacred cow and the other one, the vocalist Umm Kulthūm, collaborated on a song after thirty years of hostile coexistence. "Summit Meeting," "Epoch-Making Encounter," *Al-Muṣawwar* headlined its reports, with a perfectly straight face. The librettist Aḥmad Shafīq Kāmil wept in his box. The poet Aḥmad Rāmī, for the first time in his life, changed his seat to the orchestra, which was as widely noticed,[11] relatively speaking, as the change of time of Emmanuel Kant's walk on the day the news of Valmy reached Koenigsberg!

. . . To Doubt

This festival of sentiment and rediscovery dates from February 1964. Already, the performance and the genre itself were dangerously estranged from the taste of a certain elite. A part of the Arab world regarded with a sort of humiliation, with uneasiness at any rate, an art that did not lead into orchestral music, held to be the harbinger of modernity. That is why several countries are endeavoring, with some success, to gain acceptance of symphonic music on the airwaves and to organize orchestras; Cairo's, a large one, is already some twelve years old. Now these efforts reflect to some extent the down-grading of the oriental style that, indeed, more and more voices are raised to oppose.

In Tawfīq al-Ḥakīm's eyes, "this old music, this so-called oriental music, is only party music, born of social gatherings, drinking bouts, and night-time revels, while Western music is born in a serious, tragic setting." Al-Ḥakīm might have added, more sociologically: in an environment increasingly influenced by the industrial revolution. Did Eastern music, the ancient as well as this more hybrid one that has taken its place, imprison the Arabs in the impasse of self-contemplation? In 1950 a committee of writers and musicians submitted this petition to the Lebanese government: "There is no Arab music. What is called such is simply one of the stages in the development of any music."[12] It was said to be a pretechnical and preconceptual art. That was also the position of the Egyptian humanist and musicologist Ḥusain Fawzī, who did so much to promote symphonic music over the radio while he was at the Ministry of Culture.

It is true that a specificity supported so strongly by mass taste seems difficult to adapt to something that is no part of itself. Besides, the configuration in which it is inscribed, along with other modes of expression, is quite special. In Arabic, the points of contact between the orders of spoken language and sung language are numerous. They range from Koranic psalmody (designated, significantly, by the term "reading," *qirāʾa*) to the ancient poetry, which must have been a sort of recitative, and the song properly speaking, felt simply as the melodic extension of the lyric. Still today in the case of the great Lebanese singer Fayrūz, as with Umm Kulthūm, the union of beauty of expression and beauty of voice is stressed.[13] A union of unimaginable delicacy! In the 1950s a Lebanese composer set some free verse to music. The abandonment of prosody and rhyme had the effect of a musical revolution.[14] It can happen, also, that inconsistency in the words can unleash a purely musical power. Then the "O eyes! O night!" are no longer text, but are pretext. It goes without saying that emotion proceeds from sound and rhythm, more than from some bit of information. Arab music is consequently accused today, at one and the same time, of being merely commentary on language, of not "meaning" anything, and of consisting simply in emotional states folded infinitely back on themselves.

Laborious studies denounce its narcissism that allegedly prevents it from communicating anything but "emotion, submission, complaint, and the cry of distress." Its general ethos is pain, seldom joy, and, more rarely still, "what would arouse enthusiasm and purposeful activity. We have no impulse toward creative thought." However, the author adds, Arab melody could reflect nature more exactly than Western melody. But to base upon it a descriptive and interpretative music adapted to a new spectrum of emotions and ideas is not impossible per se, but would require a veritable revolution in technique.[15]

But, I would reply, is it solely a question of technique? Eastern music, this "paradigmatic music" (Roland Barthes) in which nothing leads one to expect that a passage will ever end, is of a sharply different type from Western kinds of music, of which the unfolding is embedded in temporality and seems always to be pointed toward an end or point of escape: a historical music, one might say, although some contemporary developments tend to revise this excessively summary definition.

Perplexity

While not applauding ʿAbd al-Wahhāb's ambiguous modernism, we do not share the excessive pessimism of some. It is, indeed, necessary to admit for the time being a lack of autonomy in the Arab musical genre, which remains closely bound to the modalities of language. Undoubtedly, it arouses an authentic sensibility. But where does authenticity end and narcissism begin? As for the ravages of commercialism and mercantilism, they are no more rife in the field of so-called oriental music than in that of so-called modern painting in the West.

Can one expect much from Arab musicians with Western training? There are some whose protracted study in Europe or America has enabled them to compose like their teachers. Others carry the quest further. Not content with arranging and orchestrating themes borrowed from their native soil, they aspire, like Tawfīq Sukkār in Lebanon and others in Egypt or elsewhere, to borrow some of the characteristics of Arab music and transform them in modern style: use of quarter tones, for example, or the pentatonic scale. But the Arab ear finds this new musicality hard to accept. It finds the efforts that Munīr Bashīr of Mosul, for example, has put forth, using an altered lute, hard to take, even though they are much more intimately integrated.[16] On the other hand, it is by no means receptive to the introduction of new instruments and the unexpected mixtures of themes with which the Rahbānī brothers have been so successful!

Sensitive souls remain perplexed and dissatisfied. Must one resign oneself to a certain incompatibility between old and new, specific and universal? In any case, some seem to believe that most artists trained abroad return well equipped with knowledge, including knowledge of the orchestra, but without creative talent. They are believed to have lost what is considered the essential thing, the "nativeness" of the Arab musician.[17] So what do they do? Mainly they simply stuff their conservatory exercises with local folklore material and imitate or even plagiarize Westerners, expecting that the transformation will thereby be accomplished somehow. Worse still, since they have to earn a living, they devote themselves to popular songs and succeed in a jazz that is assumed to reconcile cultures in a joint collusion. But also, it is said, they lack creative spirit, and in this connection the shades of Sayyid Darwīsh and other *abāqira* of the preceeding generation are conjured up. . . . We have met such language before. It must not be taken as considered judgment, still less as observed fact, but as a symptom.

Restatement and Revision of the Hypothesis

Whoever compares the stages, so different in orientation and scope, that music and the plastic arts among the Arabs have traversed over the past generation is impressed by the contrast between the two evolutions. Evolutions? The word sins by impropriety in both cases.

In the case of the plastic arts one must speak of innovation instead of renewal. A society seeking to know what sort of face it presents looks at itself for the first time, seeing itself as it does so. It is prompted and enabled to do this by virtue of traditions and pictorial conventions whose only common feature is that they come from elsewhere. From the academicism of "French artists" up to Fautrier, by way of Cézanne, the impressionists, and Picasso, the East will put everything to use. In its rush toward apprehension of its own face, however, it stumbles over obstacles: its ornamental atavism, its modesty especially, its turning inward upon itself (another sense of *kitmān*), a taste for moderating intensities and for attenuating violence. It finds inspiring allies also: the world's general impulse toward the pictorial; the growing importance in the life of the masses and the individual of the camera; the union of the visual and the sexual; the excitement of adventure and death unleashed in the cinema; the blustering, gesticulating daily news on the TV screen. The Oriental, too, is becoming the "seeing man," and among other things that gives him the machine. The unveiling, the stripping bare of persons and things, is now the order of things there as it is among us, while science and art are striving to draw from this onslaught its humanistic corollaries. The plastic arts, including painting, not only offer the Arabs response to a need, which they will satisfy by means of color, line, and mass. They further promise the restoration of the meaning in the visible, the conquest of what gives profound life to images and, eventually, restitution of a secret heart that the world's rush toward its destiny had long ago hidden from view. Self-display, in the first phase, and, in the second, a submergence in new esotericisms: second-degree harems, I would go so far as to say. This sequence corresponds, moreover, to the successive stages of technique in international painting, and that is why the Orient has made it its own.

It was able to do so particularly since it was building on virgin soil in the field of representational art. It was building new structures on new foundations, and its endeavor has largely succeeded. It could not have been the same in the field of music. Here, the traditional flow remains as rich as ever or at least appeals as profoundly to individual and group sensuality. That there is another music, appealing to other states of mind or, worse, forsaking desire and pleasure for abstract knowledge, is something that the East accepts and practices in its own poetry but finds difficult to demand from the flow of its own music. Must one desert the latter, then, and plunge into foreign waters? Thus far only certain intellectuals, few in number, have done so. The immense majority remains faithful to the old taste's current, which is too wedded to its intimacy to attach itself to the West as freely as visual processes can.

Not that Western music is incapable of moving Arabs. Verdi's had its faithful admirers at a very early date. More recently, operetta arias, ballads, and, still more recently, jazz have attracted arrangers and won large audiences. But the core of musical taste remains faithful to its home climate. Acculturation and hybridization are accepted and even enjoyed; nevertheless, the most sensitive deplore both the compromises thus imposed on authenticity and the impotence to achieve a genuine transformation. The dilemma thus remains unresolved: either faithfulness to oneself, comprised moreover by attempts at adaptation, or resolute innovation from which one may hope for an eventual restoration of a new kind of authenticity.

The plastic arts, as we have seen, adopted the latter position, but were perhaps able to do so only because foreign techniques themselves were superseding each other in the process of opening toward an international language. Is the same not true of music? After all, is the symphony orchestra the only path toward modernity? And does not the belief that it is constitute in fact the real obstacle to the development of Afro-Asian music?

The West adopted the tempered scale barely three centuries ago. It is now seeking, in serial, twelve-tone, and other techniques, perspectives that may facilitate its conciliation with other musical cultures. This will, of course, require of the West as well as other cultures a self-reconquest through and in newness. But this, because of stubborn facts, lack of generosity on our part, excessive deference on the part of others, and, more generally, lack of analysis, is still the problem in both East and West.

XII
Second Symmetry: Criticism and Imagination

Although the Koran disdains neither legends nor fairy tales, although the Arabs' most widely circulated contribution to world literature is the book *The Arabian Nights*, although picaresque adventures furnished the most characteristic theme of the old *maqāma*, and although the Arabs themselves often seem to others to be heroes of romance and to have long enjoyed the role—nevertheless, when the novel was established among them at the turn of the twentieth century it came as an imported genre. Having already attained in Europe a vigorous maturity closely related to the vicissitudes of industrial man, it offered a medium adaptable to both dream and representation, through which all levels between description of the world and its remaking could be expressed. In both cases it was the individual's adventures, intersecting with those of others, which supported the procedure. Was the latter illusory or not? Did it conceal a weakness or a dishonesty inherent in the capitalist context of the form? That is what Lukàcs and L. Goldmann were later to ask. As yet, at the end of the nineteenth century, we had got as far as Zola and Tolstoy, continuing the Victor Hugo of *Les Misérables*, and novelistic invention rightly appeared to the anxious sons of the East as a liberating instrument.

Brief Review of Fictional Production

How far we have come! A half-century after *Zaynab*, that bucolic evocation of love affairs between a rich youth and peasant girls, a contest organized by Radio Cairo introduced to the public a young man from the provinces, al-Khuḍarī, who, at twenty-eight, had already written two hundred short stories before he had ever left his Upper Egyptian village!

Nearly all the great writers of the past generation had tried their hand at this major genre of modern times: after Jirjī Zaydān and Haykal, Rīḥānī, Māzinī, Ṭaha Ḥusain, ʿAqqād, Maḥmūd Taymūr,

Nuʿaymé. With the end of World War II, simultaneously with the political mutations then rocking the Near East, other talents emerged, infinitely more numerous in the domain of the short, than of the long, story,[1] and almost all types of the form were already being produced. Iraq stood out for its fiction, then marked more than its poetry by symbolistic inspiration: Fuʾād Tekerlī and ʿAbd al-Malik Nūrī introduced the short story; Dhū al-Nūn Ayyūb, the novel. In Egypt, sentimental anecdote and description, tender or malicious, were preparing the way for the vogue of realism. Lebanon with *Al-Raghīf*[2] and Syria with *Qaws Quzaḥ*[3] struck trial blows that may be considered master strokes. Already works were appearing which were destined to remain classics: Sharqāwī's novel *The Earth* (1953), full of love without self-indulgence and ideology without dogmatism; *Qindīl Umm Hāshim* by Yaḥyā Ḥaqqī, who defined the dispute within this society between progress with its distortions and the authenticity of an outmoded past: an insoluble dilemma as long as it is stated in these terms; the short stories of ʿAbd al-Salām al-ʿUjaylī, laden with psychological truth and novelistic tension. In *Arkhaṣ Layālī* (1954), Yūsuf Idrīs revealed a sense of the tragic in social reality. Najīb Maḥfūẓ was beginning to publish his famous trilogy on Old Cairo.

Abundant production; sustained contact with the environment and its vicissitudes; growth of sustained inspiration and breadth of view; an evolution punctuated every ten years, approximately, by changes in style and taste; progressively greater independence from foreign models: do we not have here, in the novel and short story, one of the most-fertile sectors of this culture?

This was still the jubilant morrow of the Nasser revolution. The world, which no longer saw in these Arab militants heroes out of the *Arabian Nights*, nor T. E. Lawrence's evasive rebels, nor its allies from colonial times, was grateful to their writers for describing them in their new mood of anxiety and effraction. Understanding was facilitated by the fact that several Eastern writers, notably North Africans, used French. *Nedjma*[4] was (mistakenly) regarded as a wink by the Algerian revolution at French culture. Publishers pricked up their ears. As for Arabic writings, translators offered themselves as go-betweens. Some interest, at least, was expressed and immediately exploited. The novel, an Arab borrowing from the West, seemed more accessible than their other messages. So much easier than their poetry, and less disobliging than their essays! The translations were not, of course, as well served by fashion as the French-language productions by Maghrebis and Lebanese, but the novel did emerge from under that heavy cloak of obscurity and indifference which Westerners ordinarily throw over anything produced by the Arabs of today. In London, Paris, Prague, Moscow, Tashkent, and Los Angeles several of these writers were seen as guests of international congresses, better understood and accepted than most of their great elders had been, even the pathetic, blind Ṭaha Ḥusain who, until the day he died, awaited the Nobel Prize in vain.

Academic research, happy to incorporate this contribution into its own narcissism, made of these writers, at least the more accessible of them, subjects of dissertations and theses. The collapse of the colonial sources of knowledge and the increasing difficulty of a direct approach to these peoples by foreigners led to heightened interest in this available phenomenology based on fictional material. During the 1950s and 1960s this literature, aside from the decolonization battles, alone spoke for this world which was apparently cutting itself off from its traditional Western correspondences. As it spoke, on the whole, in a less-menacing tone than the leaders' speeches and actual events, it seemed to provide one step toward tomorrow's sociology, anthropology, and social history. The ambiguity of this role, and of its reception abroad, naturally had its price. Too often the amplitude of a work's echo was proportional to its facility. With very few exceptions Arab writing in Arabic—to which I naturally attach most importance here—was neglected to the benefit of heterophonic writing of which the authors, anxious to thrust themselves into European ideologies as dissidents, or even dissidents from Arab dissidence (which should have been matter for reflection on their part), perhaps were, and are, wrong to express such fine talents in what they themselves call a language of alienation. It may be that, at a certain stage of mediacy in creative activity—can there any longer be creativity which is not mediate?—the choice of language is arbitrary. . . . Regarding this serious problem we shall merely note the limited and disproportionate extent to which the Arab novel, properly speaking, is known internationally, and even then only to certain avant-gardes, notwithstanding the active role it alone is playing, whether we like it or not, in the evolution of these societies.

Always Ṭaha Ḥusain

In this chapter and the next I shall study two kinds of Arabic texts which may be evaluated in two ways: as works of art and as testimony. From both aspects it will be of some use to let them speak for themselves, even at the expense of apparently interrupting the train of discussion. The first one I shall invoke, setting it up as a historical landmark and as a standard of literary value, dates from a quarter-century ago.

Shortly before the Nasser revolution, there appeared by isolated installments that "Mirror of the contemporary mind," *Mirʾat al-Ḍamīr al-Ḥadīth*,[5] which may be considered as one of the most-finished examples of Arab humanism. In the form of letters fictitiously addressed to one or another of his compatriots, Ṭaha Ḥusain embarked upon a corrosive criticism of his times. Just as La Bruyère had modeled his *Caractères* on those of Theophrastus, Ḥusain began his admonition with a pastiche of Jāḥiẓ. With a grain of irony respecting the great classic's prose and, I shall be so bold as to say, his own, he revels in his well-known synonymities. Two sentences for the same idea are not enough for him. The rate of reiteration is most often three, increasing to five and even eight. It is wonderful how he takes over from Jāḥiẓ that mixture of pious hopes and biting allusions, quotations from the *sīra*, and anecdotes that lead off in oblique directions. Later the moralist himself takes more direct charge of the argument, but without breaking the continuity of the grand manner. Throughout the book he hangs opulent garlands of language from which, now and then, the density of a rare word or an obsolescent usage bursts forth like a fruit. The savorous blend of the redundant and the straight-to-the-point and this idiomatic use of calculated archaisms to express modern thought are perhaps the secret of a style whose complete Arabism, so to speak, subtly exploits the latent possibilities of the national legacy. That is how this criticism of manners in Egypt at the turn of the twentieth century takes on the character of an exposition by Jāḥiẓ.

But Anatole France had passed that way. And assiduous reading of Westerners, brought along with the Arabs to a common Mediterranean humanism. The topic is modern, as is the method. Psychologies have become much more complex since Baghdad! "I have a taste for complexity," Ṭaha Ḥusain confesses. He might say for perplexity as well. The Eastern elite he is addressing has all at once outgrown the age of sentiment. Its enthusiasms have perhaps been dampened, also. It is no longer enough to "preach the good and root out evil." Either process is vulnerable to confusion and fraud. Characters have lost their sharp outlines. There are no longer any friends in the Egypt of 1950. Definition of virtues, for lack of something better, has to take place within the individual. The "noble" man in Descartes' sense, which is approximately that of the word karīm, *is now above all "one who, in his dealings with others, avoids anything for which he might blame himself." One can expect no reassurance from others' opinions. On all sides one finds only egotism and pharisaism, tinged with a masochistic taste for unhappiness. The country has been transformed, like Kafka's hero. Why? Because of an accelerating mutation in manners. So many souls for sale! So much luxury and misery side by side! So much envy among the young, compromising their legitimate boldness by the desire for sinecures, social conformity, and politics as usual. The press has nothing to say and feels no desire to say anything, notwithstanding the freedom it enjoyed at the time. A general decline of hope, injustice, and incompetence on the part of the rulers are what this illustrious writer, soon to become a minister, is denouncing. The tone of his collection of short stories,* Al-Muʿadhdhabūn fīl-Arḍ, *"The tormented souls on Earth" written during the 1947 cholera epidemic, is readily recognized here.*

This pessimism, anticipating events shortly to erupt but which were by no means to confirm this testimony, finds its consolation only in a classic style and in a belief in progress rendered the more ardent by its very disappointments. "The world is truly miraculous for the man of generous heart." But this miracle presupposes liberty, else youth would be like the legendary genie sealed in a chest at the bottom of the sea.

Let us close this masterpiece of bourgeois humanism. But let us not forget that the antibourgeois regimes which have followed have not produced a message of this quality.

Imagination Takes the Floor

Now let us give the floor to the imaginary, that is, to a restoration of reality truer than the real itself and furthermore endowed with those multipliers which are the distinctive qualities of the short story and the novel: autonomy of outline; tension along one or more axes; an accent bearing, according to the author's preference, upon philosophical or social debate; romantic adventure; sentimental titillation; stylistic refinement; and so on. This diversity of accent marks the most recent developments in the form. Several of the older writers are still producing, exploring new horizons or new modes of language. This is especially noticeable with Najīb Maḥfūẓ. But other talents have blossomed as well. The Syrian Ḥanna Mīna, who started as a manual laborer, has written the saga of an entire city, Lādhaqiya, in *Al-Shirāʿ wal-ʿAwāṣif*, while the Egyptian Fatḥī Ghānim is exploring the internal world, and the Sudanese Ṭayyib Ṣāliḥ describes a bloody "season of exile in the north."

Louis ʿAwaḍ, finally, published his "Phoenix," written fifteen years ago and still up-to-date. Al-ʿUjaylī's style is becoming still more concentrated and poignant. Suhayl Idrīs, one of the first to describe his generation's *qalaq*,[6] is developing an intimate manner halfway between irony and tenderness. Jabrā Jabrā is recounting adventures in exile in a highly refined language. Still others are exploring the outer borders of event and symbol.

But let them speak for themselves, even if it prolongs the discussion, for this reinvention of the Arabs by themselves may fill out and correct the picture I have tried to give in the preceding pages. While the choice is somewhat arbitrary, it is in no way intended as a classification.

Twelve Short Stories: A Montage

The noble tribe of Ṭāy had reigned from time immemorial over the Jazīrah grazing ranges. Near their shaikh's tent a mysterious supplicant was encamped. One day, wishing to repay one of his magnanimous courtesies, he invited him to a feast. After much urging, the shaikh felt obliged to accept. Great was his surprise to find the stranger serving him an elegant mansif *on an immense copper tray which the servants carried in by the rings at its edge. A princely tray! Who was this refugee? What did his presence in the Ṭāy camp mean? Surely, some danger. No more was required for the shaikh to determine to put him to death. . . .*[7]

We, your honors the judges, cherish our honor and know how to wash it clean in the blood of women. I am innocent. I did not kill my sister-in-law, Farḥa. She committed suicide because she had sullied our honor, taking advantage of the fact that her husband had been arrested by the prefect for a violation of the Agrarian Reform Law (he had not followed my advice). How did she do it? By throwing cartridges into the oven where she was baking bread for lunch. . . . [8]

Two Syrians, childhood friends, meet in a bar on the Champs Élysées, each with a woman on his arm. One is a recently deposed military dictator. He reproaches the other, who had held aloof from him all the time he was in power, with having betrayed him. Their conversation becomes more and more heated and their companions are alarmed. To calm them, they continue the dialog in French. X then jokingly accuses Y of having always been an unscrupulous conqueror, even in love. Do you remember that girl in Damascus with whom I was in love, and whom you seduced? Every time the exchange heats up, they switch to Arabic. . . .[9]

The taxi has four passengers. The young, brilliant judge of the Raqqa court, on the Euphrates, has reserved the two front seats for himself. In the rear is a former truck driver who has become rich, his young, pretty wife, and a Bedouin wrapped in haughty silence. The eyes of the young magistrate and the wife meet in the rearview mirror more often than is proper. The car narrowly misses running over a madwoman. The truckdriver explains that she has been going back and forth for the past twenty-five years between these two villages on the Aleppo road. . . .[10]

The girl is dying in an Aden clinic. Of Yemeni origin, she had spent all her youth at Geneva, living a rather free life. She falls in love for the first time with Faḍl, the Yemeni revolutionary leader she has come to interview for a Swiss magazine. Through him she rediscovers her lost homeland and again puts down roots there. Oh, to become once more a black lily of the desert! But now she is racked by fever. . . .[11]

In an old part of the city, the tavern run by a Greek is named the Black Cat, since its most distinguished character is in fact a formidable tomcat. One night the clientele, pleasantly intoxicated, are singing a beery refrain when a very husky man, dressed in sweater and slacks, takes a seat near the door and begins to drink, muttering, "Damnation! Disaster!". . .[12]

Fatḥiya: "poor little lady" she is called since her husband went to the hospital. Even before he, a man who has never outgrown his adolescence, fell ill, it was she who ran the household. He was the good fellow, the faḥlāwī, *who picked out tunes on the piano. After every quarrel it was she who took the initiative for reconciliation. Her breasts are sagging, it is true: three miscarriages and two births. But her waist is still slim, and her mascaraed eyes still have that insatiable look. . . .*[13]

Man is a talking animal, replied the teacher to the student who had asked him what man is. He did not lie. We journalists talk the most. Thank God, when the war broke out our words played an honorable role, confronted our enemies courageously, shot down their planes, destroyed their tanks, and annihilated their troops. Then why did this happen, why this disaster, when our words had fought so well? . . .[14]

One day the one they called ʿAbdullah killed his father. He was thereupon freed and resumed his real name, Aḥmad Hilāl Shūbāsh, after his lost tribe. In search of it, he started off toward the desert. As guide he had only the ambiguity of things between their external and their hidden meaning. But it was also a challenge to constituted authority. So he was promptly arrested. . . .[15]

It was in the time of the beys, the truck driver told the passengers in the taxi. One day when the Bey of N. was riding along this very road in his black limousine, he picked up a peasant and his daughter and let them ride in the front seat. Jokingly, he asked for the daughter's hand for his chauffeur. Another day the girl was waiting for them on the road and they picked her up. Then one day the Bey and his chauffeur were killed in an accident. For twenty-five years the girl has been looking for them on the road. She was driven mad by this marriage proposal annulled by fate. According to malicious gossip she had spent a night in the company of the two men. Who will ever know? . . .[16]

A smile on the one-eyed general's face. He invites me aboard. The boat comes alongside. I step onto the far shore. Oh, not for anything in particular: just to take a look. A noise in the distance attracts my attention. I had come just to look, not to touch anything. Then an endless procession of women. . . .[17]

. . . Your honors the judges, Aunt Wardiya is lying when she says she spent the whole night with Farḥa. But it is true that I did not tell you the truth at first. We Bedouins cherish honor, but we think in several directions at once. The witness lied in saying that my sister threw cartridges into the baking oven to feign suicide. The medical report lies when it says Farḥa died of a revolver bullet in the head. I know very well what weapon I fired to avenge my honor. She committed suicide because of shame. Your honors the judges, show yourselves honorable as well. . . .[18]

. . . In that Aden clinic, the girl learns, despite her delirium, that the man she loves already has two wives. He proposed that she become the third because "the first," he said, "was for children; the second was for the Party. You will be my real wife." Distracted, she listens to the raven which is pecking at the window. The funereal bird at length pierces the glass. Water flows into the room as if through a fracture in a submarine's hull. The girl herself leaves through the fissure and is diffused into the rediscovered nothingness. . . .[19]

. . . She loves me, I love her, yet she refuses to marry me. Why? She told me, "Because in your family you don't bury dead ancestors." Then I dug a grave. But the phantoms dragged me into it with them. The woman did not weep. She took my saber and is waiting for me in case I lack the courage to make war upon the ancestors and the enemies. . . .[20]

. . . Arabic returns each time the conversational tone rises. This is not very polite to their girl friends! After a few inconsequential remarks in French, X reveals to Y, in Arabic, that shortly before his downfall he had refused to participate in a conspiracy. They separate. Both return home. Shortly Y is killed by an assassin. X receives a letter from his European girl friend. "I have learned of the assassination of your friend. How unfortunate! Of course it must have been a love affair, like the one you told about. Politics has also been mentioned. That is surely wrong. That man could only have died at the hand of a rival in love. How hot-blooded you Arabs are!" . . .[21]

. . . The Agency's director sympathizes with the poor little lady's misfortunes. He might be able to find her a position in the airline company where his father worked. Then she obtains a doctor's certificate stating that her husband must have at least six more months of treatment. So she is put on the payroll. She does wonderfully well, and becomes the Agency's key employee. . . .[22]

. . . The shaikh of the Ṭāy has thus resolved to kill the mysterious refugee. But his favorite wife rebels against such a felony. "If you put him, our guest, to death I, your uncle's daughter, cannot bear the dishonor." She draws from beneath her caftan a vial of deadly poison. The shaikh stifles a cry of horror. . . .[23]

. . . Suddenly the newcomer, whom a client has brushed against on his way to the door, turns toward the back of the tavern. He

appears to become aware of the others' presence for the first time. "Who are you?" he growls. "Why are you spying on me? You want to turn me in, do you?" As the client insists upon leaving, he shoves him toward the back. Everyone is silent. "If anyone is sick of living, let him come forward." No one moves. The customers realize with consternation that they are prisoners and will have a bad night of it. But the cat is having a fine time. . . .[24]

. . . In his prison Aḥmad Hilāl is dreaming, or perhaps remembering. Perilous crossings to the islands, alliance with a woman sealed by exchanging blood, interminable marches through torrid Saharas. Finally they reach the vicinity of the lost tribe, descended from an ancestor who, after fighting in the Battle of Nahrawān, had gone west, to a cave where his sons later swarmed forth. Their reappearance was linked to resumption of the war, as a condition of the rediscovery of values. . . .[25]

. . . On the far shore, where I have gone, the group of women passes before me one by one. One pauses, waits for me, broken; broken, she raises her head, expecting that that vision . . . Women's tragedy perfects their femininity! What could be more feminine than captive women? Mourning arouses not pity but virility! Choose the one you want. . . .[26]

We descend the slippery stairway of Joseph's Well. We pass a couple anxious to have children. Halfway down, I tell her I will go on alone. I had promised myself I would look back when I plunged into the darkness, to see the expression on her face. But as I am afraid she does not love me, I do not look back. At the bottom of the well, my hand touches the cold surface of the water. I think I hear Joseph sobbing quietly in the darkness. . . .[27]

. . . When her husband entered upon convalescence, the lady had just been assigned to a position abroad. She persuades the doctor in charge to keep the patient awhile longer. She leaves for Europe. The Agency director also, on the same plane.[28]

. . . I cross back to the other shore. My slender son, who is awaiting me, draws from his jallabiya *a black metal object. No! No! I didn't do anything, I only went to look! . . . I do not hear the shot.*[29]

. . . And so, for love of his wife, the Ṭāy shaikh decides not to kill the refugee. The latter, who is an exiled Shammar nobleman, re-

turns to his people, far to the southwest. Freed of any obligation, he reveals to them the fine vegetation of the Jazīrah and urges them to conquer it. They are there today, having driven out the former inhabitants.[30]

. . . For twenty-five years the madwoman has gone back and forth on the road between the two villages. The young, brilliant judge goes, as he does every Thursday, to join the woman he has loved since his university days and who is now married to another. Similarly, the Bedouin has been traveling the roads in search of another Bedouin who, a generation ago at the time of the tribal wars, killed his father. The taxi driver plies back and forth to earn his living. The rich ex-truck driver is running the roads to catch his wife, who has run away. At least it was he who told the story of the madwoman who, like them all, tirelessly travels the road. But no one will be grateful to him for having helped all the passengers in the taxi—himself excepted–to glimpse their fate.[31]

. . . When, after wandering long in the desert, the son of Hilāl, who so loved music, rain, and freedom, reached the land of the lost tribe, "he bounded like a tiger toward the fields. He kissed the swelling grain, threw himself on the grass to feel it, buried his face in its luxuriant depths. He took a handful of soil and lifted it in his palm to his temple and cheeks. The wheat, the soil, and the grass exhaled a penetrating perfume of which he could not sate himself. He broke into burning sobs and his tears blended with the earth and plants. He no longer knew whether he was silent or singing."[32]

. . . The man plunged his knife into the ground to the hilt and listened. Strange! The earth was weeping. He listened again and "cried in a voice heavy with joy": she is dead. But when he listened for the third time, he no longer heard anything, except the monotonous tread of military boots.[33]

. . . Then one of the drinkers, an old man wiser than the others, said, "We might as well make the best of it." So they returned to their drinking and singing, paying no more attention to the demonic visitor whom only the cat seemed to recognize. How long did this go on? No one remembers, except that suddenly, early in the morning, a very husky man in sweater and slacks set about cleaning up the bar. He was weeping bitter tears, but no one asked him why, or who he was. As for myself, I wonder: what if it were a fallen god, who had then changed into a cat?[34]

. . . My body floated up from the bottom of the Nile, a handful of mud and algae clutched in its fist. It began to float, all blue, on the surface, with a little grass from the river to accompany it on its great journey. Its face was turned toward the sky, a sky "as ancient and infinite as falsehood." One fine day I was thrown up on the bank, then carried away again by the current. My parents wept over their memories of this body. Then my belly burst open. Then the water began to dissolve me and to transform me into daily bread.[35]

Five Novels: A Panorama

In 1948, just after *Zuqāq al-Midaqq,* Najīb Maḥfūẓ published *Al-Sarāb,* "The mirage." This novel is thus roughly contemporaneous with *Mirʾat al-Ḍamīr al-Ḥadīth,* Ṭaha Ḥusain's essay I commented upon above.

*Kāmil Ruʾba, a young man of high Cairo society, lives alone with a tyrannous mother who transfers onto him her disappointments as an abandoned wife. She holds him in a fictitious world, a "mirage" (*Al-Sarāb *is the work's title). Morbidly timid, Kāmil, devoted to solitary pursuits, eventually feels the need to love. In pages of an exquisite delicacy, Najīb Maḥfūẓ shows him falling in love with a girl he meets at a streetcar stop. The marriage which ensues is not consummated. By dint of alcohol he escapes momentarily from this impotence which his wife, Rubāb, however, enjoys. It seems that the peculiarity of the relations between the son and mother, carried to the very borderline of incest, has entered into the young married couple's relationship. All around this anomalous behavior Egypt's abundant normality bursts forth: sex-exalting rituals (although here they play a castrating role), drunkenness, revelry–imperfectly repressed by conformity, pleasure lurking everywhere. With consummate art the author transcribes in language of a virtually documentary realism the Freudian ideogram the whole story depicts.*

But now Rubāb becomes absent-minded and is more and more often away from the house. The husband becomes jealous. One day as he is spying on her furtively from a sordid Nubian coffee shop, he sees a buxom woman at a window in the building across the street; she smiles at him. The revelation of his own virility follows. Thereafter his life is shared between soul and body: the pure wife and the lusty mistress. The latter is obviously maternal. She is the antitype of the real mother, with her severity and gauntness. This time the hero has discovered sensual woman. This sort of life might have gone on for a long time. But it is suddenly interrupted. Rubāb, to conceal from her husband that she is pregnant, has an abortion performed by her lover, a doctor newly returned from Europe. She dies of it. In a destructive fury, Kāmil blames his mother, who has cardiac trouble, so violently that she dies. Does he know that he is avenging himself? Certainly not. He understands nothing about what has happened to him. As soon as he recovers from his nervous prostration, he tries to decide how to live the rest of his life. Mysticism? Simply another escape mechanism. Suddenly, the beautiful woman who had taught him pleasure visits him in his room. Will he decide for real life? If so, why all these confessions (the book is written in the first person)? So as to liberate himself completely, or so as to run away once more?

Najīb Maḥfūẓ's art succeeds admirably in the drawing of characters, all of whom are real and living, and in a pathos filled with pity for the hero, indirect victim of his debauched father and oppressive mother. The integration of plot, customs, landscape, and psychology of the protagonists transforms from end to end a subject reminiscent of *Madame Bovary*. A double Bovary, since the imperious unrealism of the mother is echoed by the son's repressed sexuality.

•

Beirut is the liberal porch of the Arab world, a booth favorable for any business deal, or any conspiracy. But the vertical countryside which rises on all sides is less a commentary on the city than its antithesis in many respects. This mountain range, whose narrowness is compensated, so to speak, by the ruggedness of its scenery and the bottomless antiquity of its terrain, coalesces in districts, villages, and neighborhoods inhabited by energetic communities. The National Pact which has held them together as a nation since 1943 is aging. The debate within the surrounding Arab world has intensified. The threat of Israel subjects to blackmail a life still clinging to mutual tolerance, taste for culture, and passion for material profit. Symmetrical to the towering mountain, an ancient and sanctioned cosmopolitanism promotes a thriving interchange with the vast outside world, throughout which ingenious Lebanon continually swarms. How long will the worm-eaten Pact, conflicts between honor and compromise, between archaism and modernity, hold up? [36] That is what many young people are asking in various languages both linguistic, so to speak, and political. Their question, muffled as it is by the noises of profit and pleasure, is thereby aggravated and tends to set its own violence against the violence which grinds out profit and pleasure: that of Beirut's grain mills, to which Tawfīq ʿAwwād has devoted his latest novel, *Ṭawāḥīn Bayrūt*.

A Shīʿite girl from the South, Tamīma, wants to live at long last. She intends to go beyond the palliatives of social progress which mislead most of her colleagues and gain satisfaction of deeper needs: not only sexuality, moreover, but refusal, adventure, and experimentation. All around her murmur the book's secondary characters: a procuress who is a curate's daughter; a doctor-politician; a leftist journalist; a dull, pleasure-loving brother; a traditionalist mother; a Maronite student from Mount Lebanon, finally, whom she really loves after giving herself to the journalist. The father is in the distance, a murky figure, merchant and versifier in Guinea, where he is troubled with accusations of currency-exchange violations. Amid all this, a students' strike, the formation of a political party, Israeli attacks. Everywhere gesticulation, talk, suffering, pleasure. The storyteller's art alternates the swirling spectacle of the city with calm village scenes, realistic description with soliloquies in a lyric and perplexed mood.

Thus the author of Raghīf *has renewed his talent. The great success of his book proves that he has observed accurately and that* Ṭawāḥīn*'s heroes, problems, languages, and landscapes are truly those of contemporary Lebanon, which recognizes itself in them. The tragic denouement must therefore be taken seriously. It is also a beginning. Tamīma, whose debauched brother has tried to kill her to "avenge the family honor," and who has lost her lover through her own excessive honesty, goes into the underground. Palestines to be reconquered? Oh! more and less than that: "I shall fight under all skies the laws and customs inherited by societies; I shall strike them with my own fist. For it is in their name, under my own country's sky, that I have been refused the right to live."*

•

The place? Somewhere at sea, on this Greek ship transporting passengers from Beirut to Naples.[37] *The time? What it takes for one crossing. The action? What it takes for Lama, that pretty, young Iraqi woman, to get back into her arms Salmān, the man she has always loved since the time he was studying in England, and from whom she is separated by a vendetta between their families. Lama's husband, Fāliḥ, pays for his conjugal failure by suicide. The classical compactness of the plot gives the author opportunity for psychological analyses, with flashbacks, in which description alternates with ideological dialog, presented in the form of diaries alternately of the protagonist, Salmān, and of another hero, Wadīʿ,*

the Palestinian. All the characters seem to be fleeing from impossible situations of one sort or another: forbidden love for Salmān and Lama, despair turning to cynicism and bitterness in the case of Fāliḥ, the loss of Jerusalem for Wadīʿ. These expatriates who, we are given to understand, are at odds with the revolutions in their respective homelands, are all bourgeois, deeply acculturated to the West, all seemingly survivors of a past era or even a past race, may meet in the book's tragic denouement the climax (and also the vindication) of their social attitudes. That is how some critics have interpreted the novel.

But if it is quite true that the characters' words are not in harmony with the contemporary East, their passions are not the result of historical vicissitude nor of their class origin.[38] *Their suffering stems from thwarted love, which has little to do with capitalism or socialism. Of course, they have all renounced service, for want of something better. Their greatest hurt, however, and this has not been sufficiently emphasized, comes from land. The land Wadīʿ has lost and the land which motivated the family crime which torments Salmān and Lama a generation later. Can they exorcize the mystique of this sacrality of dual aspect? Fāliḥ's expiatory death might have provided the opportunity. At that moment, Wadīʿ is tentatively consoled by a mistress. Perhaps his tragic temperament, which has served constantly to reveal the others' drama, will lead him to seek his future in underground combat. As for the other characters, he urges them to confront all prejudices with their love. "Enough of tribalism," he shouts at them. But he adds that they can be saved only by returning to the service of their homeland.*

This ending is a little disappointing. But how is Jabrā to be reproached for not knowing just what end to give to characters who talk like Aldous Huxley's, which underscores still more tragically their fate as Easterners in the twentieth century?

•

"Mr. Muṣṭafā" was born in the year that Sirdar [H. H.] Kitchener, by a frightful massacre, put an end to the Mahdist State.[39] *His instinctive aptitude for English astonished his first teachers. From Gordon College in Khartoum to Cairo University and thence to Oxford his success continued. During the 1920s he was a member of a Fabian intelligentsia, elegantly anticolonialist, which appreciated in this son of Africa an indirect tribute to the Empire. But his real prestige was his sexuality. It cast its spell over many a young woman. But these liaisons, devoid of love, rested on a sadomasochistic exchange between European depravity and his negritude's*

search for malicious revenge. Many affairs ended in the imprudent girl's suicide; finally one culminated in murder motivated by perversion. Mr. Muṣṭafā escaped the death penalty only by reason of the court's taste for the exotic. Abandoning his high hopes, he buried himself in a village on the Nile, with an attractive peasant girl, and that is where, long after, the narrator finds him.

Around this man whose ambitions were thus shattered and who is now shut in behind a wall of silence, the village bursts with strength and continuity. Everywhere one breathes the scent of soil and young vegetation. The narrator, who followed Mr. Muṣṭafā to England a generation later when the Sudan was progressing from condominium to national independence, listens to the terrible, but incomplete, confessions of the older man. He grasps their key only when the twice-exiled man dies by drowning. He secretly loves the young widow. But, unconvinced of her truthfulness, he allows her to marry an obscene old man, whom she murders; then she kills herself. His own suicide in the Nile aborts. But did he merely dream it? Is his generation still able to die?

In this Season of Exile in the North *(1969), Ṭayyib Ṣāliḥ combines the evocation of a luxuriant Africanness and its pernicious relations with the West which made of Mr. Muṣṭafā a tragic failure and of the narrator an ineffectual diploma holder. Around them the coursing blood of this land animates several silhouettes: the centenary grandfather spared from decrepitude: the old woman with her hot-blooded sexual memories; the bald old suitor whose lubricity is set on fire by the young widow. But does the village, deceptively somnolent under its acacias, object of rivalry between an immemorial wisdom and an always-latent frenzy, ensure the authenticity of its sons? The narrator has no illusions, alas. The artificiality of modern times, which is another name for Western culture, will not relax its hold simply because of this adventure. It would be better to remove the drama from all that. Lie, then? At least, let it be a useful lie. So, is this the final word to be said about this story of lust and murder? No, these furious symbols, colliding in a narrative where tones and time spaces, the real and imaginary, continually intersect one with another, permit one to glimpse a solution: probably, to sink to the lowest depths of this Sudanese soil in which births and deaths are equally hidden.*[40]

Among the many novels Najīb Maḥfūẓ has published during his long career, *Tharthara fawq al-Nīl* (1966) appeared nineteen years after *Al-Zuqāq*, eighteen after *Al-Sarāb*. During this breathless period punctuated by the successive stages of the Nasserist revolution, the art of the novel reached its apogee in the descriptive and realistic genre with the Gamāliya trilogy (1956–1958), then suddenly took a new direction with *Al-Liṣṣ wal-Kilāb*, "The thief and the dogs," ostensibly a detective story but in reality a harsh denunciation of careerism and conformism. *Awlād Ḥāratinā*, in which the author makes of domestic life in an old neighborhood something approaching a human epic, was to be published in Beirut. *Tharthara*, "A chat on the Nile," marks a forward step in observation and contestation.

Upstream from the Jazīrah the banks of the Nile are embellished with pleasure boats fitted out for extended sojourns, called "swimmers," or ʿawwāmas. *There a coterie of intellectuals gathers every evening around a narghile whose mixture is liberally laced with narcotics; they are of various professions and are joined by young women, notably Sammāra the journalist. Each in his own way and to his own degree, these loners are united in their escapism, rejection of action, a disillusioned cynicism with respect to morals and politics.*

The conversation focuses on Sammāra, who believes in elevated sentiments and perhaps in general knowledge, and on Anīs, an unsuccessful bureaucrat, half-mad, half-dead, a poetic and enigmatic personality whose gaze, turned inward, invariably encounters the mediocrity of the times by comparison with Egypt's, and humanity's, past. He thus appeals from politics and everyday events to the cosmic, and his singularity interests the young lady more than she might prefer. This could have gone on indefinitely had these young people not run over a poor man during a nighttime ride on the road to Saqqāra. A moral problem thus arises which they would gladly avoid, but Anīs, the dreamer, obliges the driver to turn himself in. He does this not only because refusal has become for him tantamount to an ethic, whereas for his comrades it is merely perverse, but also because he senses that the guilty driver is his rival vis-à-vis Sammāra. In the final scene he confesses his love to the latter. She doubtless loves him, too. But this will in all likelihood lead to nothing more than Anīs' assertion of the moral of a paradise lost and of an endless journey. "He took a tree branch in one hand, a pebble in the other, and set out cautiously, looking far down that road which has no end."

Imagine the night all around, the earthy odor of the Nile, the rustling of the trees, the shadowed but invincible presence of a nature to which Adam's sons must return, shedding all circumstances and evasion. This page, on which the book ends, will rightly take its place as a great moment in Arab literature.

Return to Essays

If, in comparison with Ṭaha Ḥusain's essay, enhanced rather than limited by its classical bias, we examine the innumerable pieces of writing which take up so much space in Arab periodicals in the form of reports, essays, and debate, we are impressed by the many weaknesses. This critical literature has a combativity which is doubtless justified by the circumstances, but which nevertheless allows too much room for the incidental and even for ill humor. It arrogates to itself a normative function, handing down its verdicts quite arbitrarily but without exhibiting any doctrinal stability. Its borrowings from abroad often border on plagiarism, and, despite appearances, it makes no great effort to reroot itself in classicism. Authors put up with it impatiently, as it does not seem to them to play a constructive role, and its mediocre reputation contrasts with its peremptory self-assurance. Far too many of these topical articles are republished in book form, often through the author's own vanity. In the bulk of these writings the outside observer may find only prolixity.

But this would be an overbold judgment. The shortcomings of this proliferous genre, even its vices, are simply the seamy side of its good qualities.[41] Its popularity and energy reflect a need to evaluate. If this need operates principally on literary expression, it is because a relative freedom of discussion is diverted there from domains where greater restraint is imposed. If it does not resign itself to a nondogmatic approach, that is typical of a stage of thinking which persisted a very long time in Western criticism and has not entirely disappeared even yet. These societies, furthermore, as A. Boudhība has rightly said, are still "seeking lost standards," and literary criticism, which is criticism at one remove since it operates on testimony already spelled out, demonstrates in its own way the need for new qualifications. It constitutes, in the last analysis, a means of restoring the significance of men, things, and situations, thus impressing itself at the heart of the cultural act with a virulence proportional to the intensity of the need. If it is haunted by the normative, and even the pedagogical, its proliferation, contradictions, and polemics reveal uneasiness rather than self-assurance. As a matter of fact, what it expresses is interrogation. And this interrogation is registering, from generation to generation and decade to decade, progress in complexity and relativity.

This category of Arabic output is so prolific that one could cite dozens of names, hundreds of titles. Can such a polyvalency be subjected to classification? Literary criticism, political criticism, historiography, philosophical meditation all vie for reflections among which it would be too naïve to erect a hierarchy.

Limiting ourselves to literary criticism, for example, probably the genre of largest volume, many talents should be mentioned: an Iḥsān ʿAbbās, for example, or Shawqī Ḍayf, or Shukrī ʿAyyād, among the many champions of erudite humanism; Maḥmūd al-ʿĀlim, Marxist epistemologist and doctrinaire analyst of current events; Ḥusain Muruwwé, who combines the same convictions with more-aesthetic serenity; Ghālī Shukrī, lucid observer in constant motion; Louis ʿAwaḍ and Jabrā Ibrāhīm Jabrā of whom we shall speak below. In such a gallery almost all the countries would be represented: Lebanon, where Yūsuf Ghaṣṣūb shone, and where the leading figures include Antoine Karam, the delicate exegete of symbolism, and Suhayl Idrīs, moving spirit of that supreme court which is the magazine *Al-Ādāb*; Syria, with Antoine Maqdisī; Iraq and the North African countries; and so forth. In short, all those milieus where the press, the university, and the life of letters intersect in myriad forms of critical investigation, and where so many names should be called without in any way claiming for any enumeration, inevitably unfair, the status of an honors list.

Three Critics

Muḥammad Mandūr, who died a few years ago, had integrated a thoroughly studied Western culture with a pulpy Egyptianness better than many of his colleagues. In all his country's ideological and political debates he carried commitment to the point of passion. Those who knew him remember a powerfully chiseled face, the warmth emanating from long experience lived to the full, a bold militancy which might have saved the Wafd, and his feeling for beauty, whether of physique, deed, or expression. This complete man had devoted one of his first works to Arab methodological criticism, *Al-Naqd al-Manhajī ʿind al-ʿArab*. While particularly concerned with poetry, he took a global view of society, which led him to revise his opinions toward the end of his life. Leaning at first toward an outpouring of subjectivity and intimacy which he called *al-shiʿr al-mahmūs*, "whispered poetry," he later gravitated toward a much more sharply focused sociological aesthetic. This was demonstrated in a slim volume, *Qaḍāyā Jadīda*, which he wrote upon his return from a trip to the USSR. Theretofore enamored with lyricism of the romantic style, he now alters his old predilections. Thereafter, he was to expect literary value from an existential feeling, *wijdān*, of which the sources would no longer be egotistically individual but collective. He at least tries to make a connection between the personal content in great literary experiences, on one hand, and, on the other, the collective aspect in popular upheavals, in which he proposes to participate as a militant intellectual. At the same time the distinction between substance and form has disappeared, in his view. He states it in quite significant fashion: *ikhtalaṭat al-dhāt wal-mawḍūʿ*, "the subjective and the objective merge."[42] This amounts to turning one's back on art for art's sake as well as a presumably social literature and to demand of both poet and society a creativity in which the internal and external are united.

Mandūr was a Sorbonne graduate. Louis ʿAwaḍ, upon his return from England, wrote a brochure of great historical importance: *al-Plutoland*, or "The land of Pluto," god of wealth.[43] This Copt of obscure origins, newly molded by his comparative research on the Promethean myth, now saw his homeland as showing the traits of a capitalist hell. In this collection, of small size but broad view, we find alternately pastiches; a bitter criticism of traditional lyricism, allegedly dead beyond recall with Shawqī's death in 1933; and finally a profession of faith. The horror of the reality before his eyes, he says, forbids him to write poems. Henceforth, he sees everything in red: even trees, the vegetation of eternal Egypt, are for him afire with this revolutionary color.

But in 1947 the same author wrote a strange novel, "The phoenix," *Al-ʿAnqāʾ*, imbued with sardonic criticism of the same view through red spectacles as was conjured up at the end of *Plutoland*. A curious book, in which are mingled anecdotal realism in the Egyptian taste; ideological criticism at one remove, quick to condemn all political orthodoxy; and a fiction which verges on the fairy tale: a virtually unique grab bag in the history of the Arabic novel. It was published only long afterward, in Beirut. Leaving aside theater pieces, despite the importance of *Al-Rāhīb*, let us consider critical works, since that is our present subject: *Revolution and Literature; Socialism and Socialist Literature*, an extended study in several volumes of Western influences in Arab literature; and quite recently a collection of articles significantly entitled *Al-Ḥurriya wa Naqd al-Ḥurriya*, "Liberty and the criticism of liberty."[44] To tell the truth, we would be completely at ease only if the author had added a third term to his binomial title: "the liberty to criticize"! But this may not yet be possible. In any event, liberty knows its own, since, at the moment I wrote this, Louis ʿAwaḍ was being fired from *Al-Ahrām*.

Reading the reporting, sometimes bold and always captivating, that he had long contributed to that newspaper, and following the heated polemics it aroused from time to time, one becomes aware of a muffled hesitation in this writing and an eccentricity of viewpoint similar to that of Sartre. Louis ʿAwaḍ is the typical incarnation of the intellectual's argument from dubious premises. The uneasiness which defines the latter is pervasive and almost attractive. A generation more bitter than Mandūr's thus distinguishes itself by controversy and doubt. Prone to blame and cast suspicion on itself, it suffers, in all its variety of political outlook, from restrictions on freedom of expression which do not, however, induce solidarity. It deserves our esteem, for it has often paid with liberty, and sometimes with life, for an indomitability that seizes occasional concessions from constituted authority without thereby softening the latter's view of it. In any case, it has broadened its experience by comparison with the preceding generation. But it is encountering from its juniors a challenge more unrelenting than its own to the interwar glories.

Let us note, in any event, the ramified character of the critical genre's evolution in most of these countries, its improvement, and the increasing specialization of manner. On the level of aesthetic analysis, as the creative experience itself cannot be dissociated from the act of thought, I shall mention as among the most lucid the work of a Palestinian living at Baghdad, Jabrā Ibrāhīm Jabrā. He is already familiar to us through one of his novels. His latest collection of critical articles is entitled *Al-Riḥla al-Thāmina*, "The eighth journey."[45] Human history, he thinks, reaches a stage where we must follow up natural creation with a distinctively human creation. We have to re-create what had already been created. Jabrā is one of the four or five Arabs best versed in English literature. From his British training he has preserved a somewhat breathless elegance and a detached reserve. He devotes several of the most suggestive studies in his book to European works: Orwell, for example, surrealism, and so on. The memories he recounts of Jawād Salīm are of great interest.

In the chapters devoted to poetry, we find useful observations on topics discussed later in this book. The ancient poetry, he says, was one of clan, community, or court. It had always been so, if only because, while feigning solitude, it implied dialog: *qifā*, "stop" (in the dual), *nabki*, "let us weep" (plural). There are always several listeners, even if only the poet speaks. By contrast, contemporary poetry is by choice one of solitude. A "labyrinth of solitude," we might say in the manner of Octavio Paz. It is a special awareness, devoted to new paths which it prefers to the old games of delectation and unbosoming of which the old poets were so fond. Finally, it is a poetry of montage, or composite, in the sense that it sometimes juxtaposes themes with no apparent logical link. Thus the long enumerations of a Sayyāb or an ʿAbd al-Ṣabūr. Finally, a poetry of implication, *taḍmīn*, as its hidden or unstated meanings count much more than the explicit ones.

Is Comparison Possible?

In sketching these three intellectual portraits I had no ulterior intent of giving pride of place to the critic or essayist over the short story writer or novelist, especially since Louis ʿAwaḍ and Jabrā Jabrā are themselves writers of fiction. And this chapter devoted too much attention to the Arab imagination, letting it speak for itself, to be accused of partiality.

Nevertheless, let us note, or rather repeat in the very words of those directly concerned: if we try to subject the enormous output of Arab fiction to international criteria, we shall be disappointed. The choicest works, at any rate, will be more disappointing than in the case of other art forms. In taking up the novel, have the Arabs been at once too far removed from the major cultural currents and too close to them? In all that they do—with a few notable exceptions for whom our esteem is high, as we have made clear—we recognize Maupassant, Chekhov, Saroyan. Too often the diction remains naïve; characters are excessively simple or do not stand out enough from the crowd. At the very least a certain lag in phase makes the workmanship of most of these authors outmoded, even if engaging, and avarice on the part of foreign publishers is perhaps not solely responsible for the scarcity of translations.

Would it be unjust to all these young talents to say that their elders' shoes are not being filled? The least that can be said is that they have not yet been able to free themselves from a dangerous situation: both too close and too far away from their classical models, too close to reject them and too far to continue in their path. With respect to Western models: too far away to assimilate their teachings but too close to escape their example. This proves a rule we have seen tested in many cases: the conditions suitable for such and such a genre, and its place in a stylistic configuration in which classical and Western models are rivals, eventually condition its success, positively or negatively.

This very configuration ensures the richness and significance of the Arab essay. An Eastern intelligentsia, still dissatisfied, is succeeding brilliantly in this genre in which it is concentrating, at the very least, the questioning attitude induced by the conflict of cultures: that is, it is placing its own contradictions into active operation. The "too near" and "too far" I discussed above become here the genre's very substance. Besides, the formal continuity with the ancient—striking in the case of Ṭaha Ḥusain, ʿAqqād, and several others—is adaptable to transformations which not only express the movement of global reality but also are integrated in it in order to guide it. That is why the Arab essay, its face turned toward the world but buttressed by a tradition, has arrived more easily than the novel at innovation while still keeping faith.[46]

XIII
What to Do? Whom to Be?

The Search for One's Self

I open the Kuwaiti Encyclopedia *in two volumes (1970–1971). It is brimming with historical, ethnographic, dialectal facts. Proverbs, names of fishes by the hundreds, biographies enlivened by humorous silhouettes. The* nawkhadā *commands the ship, the* nahhām *stands at the bow and sings to attract the fish. Violet Dickson, now a Kuwaiti citizen, is the widow of a former colonel and political agent. The naval battle of Raqqa occurred in 1873 between the people of Kuwait and the Banī Ka'b from the Arabistan coast.* Zafān *is "a sort of dance." Shakespeare was British political agent from 1909 to 1915.* Darwāza*: a gate (this is a Persian word). Eighteen sorts of coiffure, each with its name and a sketch. And this historical pearl: the life of the corsair Raḥma bin Jābir, shaikh of the Jalāhma. Formerly a pearl diver, he turned pirate in 1802 with five vessels and more than a thousand companions. He preferred to attack Baḥraini ships, or those of the English. Drawn at first to Wahhābism, he abandoned it it 1812 and continued to sail the Gulf. In 1822, surrounded by his adversaries, he waited until five ships were alongside before blowing them up with his own.*

Let us close this valuable work by Ḥamad al-Sa'īdān! It was published on the tenth anniversary of Kuwait's independence and it is possible to see a connection between the two dissimilar events.

This curiosity about themselves, which is the converse of uneasiness, has always been observable among the Arabs. The one and the other have continued to develop in modern times under other names and by different methods. Many authors thus engaged have been conscious of following an inherited genre. The geographical *Dictionaries*, Yāqūt's among others, had only to modernize their format to become Master Buṭros' *Dā'ira*, and then the *Encyclopedia* of Fuʾād Ephrem Bustānī. The *Khiṭaṭ* of ʿAlī Pasha Mubārak and Kurd ʿAlī explicitly claimed to be inspired by Maqrīzī's famous ones. Almost everywhere erudites—for example ʿĪsā Iskandar Maʿlūf for Zaḥle, Mukhtār al-Sūsī for the Chleuhs, Muḥammad Diwehjī for Mosul,[1] devoted to their city or region painstaking monographs compiling lives of notables, descriptions of usages and customs, to say nothing of prideful mention of innovative heroes: who first used an automobile, who first used glass in windows, and so on.[2] The historian or sociologist finds here an abundance of material, a personal acquaintance with the data, and at times a charm of writing which make these local sources, too often neglected by academic research, documents of prime importance. Naturally, modern preoccupations are looming ever larger in expository writing. Social history, anthropology, and sociology are taking over from tradition without always realizing the use which could be made of it. Doctoral theses are proliferating in Arabic, English, French, and still other languages, each one making its contribution to this new stage of knowledge. If synthesis is still lacking it is perhaps because changes are coming so rapidly, and because growth of the taste or ability to follow them scientifically, being a part of the acceleration, shrinks from drawing up balance sheets, however tentative.[3]

Nevertheless, the quest for self (country as self, people as self, history as self) constitutes one of the most-prominent sectors of contemporary Arab production. Attainment of awareness and, one might say, of a physiognomy. The enthusiasm to recognize, to retrieve, and to reconstruct endows the quest with an important advantage by comparison with the knowledge of colonial times. I need not take inventory here. From the Atlantic to the Gulf many accomplishments would have to be listed. Among the pieces of research which stand out are those of the Egyptian Abū Zayd on the oases, or the Iraqi Shākir Muṣṭafā Salīm on the Chabaish, a strange folk of the Mesopotamian marshes, as well as the efforts of young Tunisian sociologists. Of course the latter, and many other Arabs, write in a language other than their own. They are beyond the purview of the present study. They are nonetheless there. From Abdallah Laroui to Mustafa Lacheraf, by way of Anwar Abdel Malek, they contribute by the dozens to the Arab world's richness. Many names would have to be cited from which these pages have profited. Moreover, the important thing is not the inventiveness or talent distinguishing one or another work, author, or team. It is, to repeat, the avid curiosity the Arabs bring to their problems and to the faces, landscapes, and circumstances in which they take physical form.

Take form, or form their personality? Give thought to the various derivations of the root *sh-kh-ṣ,* "to arise," "to take shape."[4] Open Belot: *tashkhīṣ* is "diagnosis"; *mushakhkhiṣ* is a stage actor, and so on. Art and science converge, in fact, in this endeavor.

The thing that confers upon descriptive art, sometimes called socialistic realism, its tireless fecundity is that it interests the public in itself. In one sense it legitimates the beings and objects of one's existence. This would not be possible if history had not come to load them with a value which was by no means a matter of course. Traditional expression, in any event, carried discretion to the point of rejecting the concrete. By contrast, description today does not hesitate to wallow in it. It doubtless remains as legitimate for those concerned as those identity-card photos which appear so profusely in the pages of the daily press. But the valuable documentary contribution it thus derives, and which is not ordinarily drawn upon in research, is not being reflected in increased depth of analysis or in formal successes, and that is doubtless what—with some brilliant exceptions—renders banal that broad sector which the novel and short story occupy in Arab literature today. Significant at the life level, and also at that of art considered as document, this swarming mass of faces and events is rarely so at the level of art.

The severe judgment which contemporary Arab literature, like all other literatures, deserves simply postulates that the writer and other artists must go beyond mere exactitude. As we have seen, that is the case with certain painters, novelists, and short story writers, and with a few poets also. It is impossible to exaggerate the extent to which literary value, when it is present, enhances a writing over one which is no more than a study, such as an academic exercise for example. Let us repeat once again that the art of the essay, so prevalent among the Arabs, quite often takes its place in these successes. When a critique, an investigation, or a history is also a work of art it enters that Parnassus of creativity in which writing accumulates instrumental power, documentary interest, and radiating influence. It was thus with Ṭaha Ḥusain's essay discussed above and with several others upon which the present chapter will draw.

Portraits of Two Peoples

This sociologist is the son of an artisan, a jeweler.[5] He grew up in the dusty splendors dominated by the golden dome of Kāẓimayn. A doctorate earned in Texas did not deprive him of his sense for the specific and genuine. One who so loves his people must be able to affront them. That is just what ʿAlī al-Wardī has done in several works in which he castigates all pharisaisms: that of the preachers, even his fellow Shīʿites, and that of poets of high-flown language. Very early he exposed the dissociation which causes discord to reign not only among social classes but also within the Iraqi's individual personality. Today he complements this concept of *izdiwāj*, or "split personality," by another: the "acrimony," *tanāshuz*, which sets a husband and his disobediant wife at odds. He finds this, again, in all sectors of society. In recent years this same author, after drawing this searching portrait of his country's people, has undertaken to write the social history of Iraq, in several volumes of an elegant erudition. It is not without significance that, toward the end of his career, he has come to base analysis of the present upon the reconstitution of the past. This is, furthermore, needless to say, a patriot speaking, who sees the source of many vicissitudes not only in dissociation and aggressiveness—a Bedouin legacy, according to him—but also in the poetic impulse which characterizes the Iraqis among all Arabs.

Throughout the nineteenth century, and even before the renaissance of Arab letters took shape in Lebanon and Egypt, this country saw a considerable flowering of poetry closely linked with the largesse of tribal chiefs. This makes it possible for the present author to denounce once again that category of bards, formerly parasites upon princes and governors, who today attach themselves with the same sycophancy to regimes. Prefabricated enthusiasm, bombast, and panegyric are thus not dead. But if this is true of poetry, it is true of all modes of expression. Not only in Iraq but throughout the world artists must reconcile participation and autonomy. Dr. ʿAlī al-Wardī, champion of unpleasant truths and eternal protest, thus finds himself once more at odds with the dominant ethics: those of the governments ruling today, of the Ottomans in retrospect, and even of the Sunni *ijmāʿ*. In this, he finds an illustrious kindred spirit in the person of that "proletarian" companion of the Prophet, Abū Dharr al-Ghafārī, of whom he has helped to dig up a portrait dear to all who seek to reconcile socialism and Islam.

•

Raised in an old quarter of Cairo, a learned oceanographer, knowing the French language as well as he does the Arabic he handles as an artist, Ḥusain Fawzī felt at an early age his vital continuity with a history that, for its sons, was crushing in so many respects.[6] "How perplexing, when I contemplate that civilization, four thousand years old, which has placed my country's name on all lips from the ancient Greeks to our own times, which has exalted us in the eyes of the civilized world, ancient and less ancient, but which has declined to such a low-water point that the world conceived doubts about us. Yes, the world wondered whether we were worthy of our remote ancestors. It even questioned the legitimacy of our birth, observing that we were the people most ignorant of our ancient glory and, at bottom, most disdainful of it." This is in fact a grave problem: the past was rediscovered by Europeans and deciphered by them. Now what is this "ancestral cave," if not the internal being of those living today? The author was to investigate this idea of geographical, social, and psychic interiority in the chronicles and monuments of the past, naturally, but also in the depths of his people. And when he enjoins his compatriot, the *fellāḥ*, to become once more himself, "Egyptian, burly bumpkin!" one thinks of our Michelet addressing Jacques Bonhomme.

In spite of all its misfortunes, nevertheless, Egypt has always built. Pyramids, fortresses, mosques, princely and bourgeois houses: no break in this regard from the Pharaohs to Alexandria and the Mamelukes' truculent regime. This latter era is generally discarded, as it was in reaction against it that modern Egypt was built, after Bonaparte and Muḥammad ʿAlī. Now Fawzī likes them, those Mamelukes. He takes the utmost pleasure in contemplating their traces in monuments, customs, and himself.

While, according to Fawzī, Egypt found its definitive style in Arab culture, he nonetheless remains a fervent devotee of *miṣriya*, "Egyptianity," that reality and idea-force which has been so severely tested by the political developments of the past quarter-century. A quarter of a century is very little in a nation's history! In 1939 Ṭaha Ḥusain had declared to the Beirut magazine *Makshūf*: "Egyptianity is rooted, *mutaʾaṣṣila*, in the Egyptians' soul; it must remain there and even become more firmly implanted." The antithesis with Arabism, *ʿurūba*, which some claimed to deduce, is as superficial as the one which would oppose France's latinity and its Frenchness. Let the pedants take sides. A people has the right to choose one or another language for its becoming.

From its publication *Sindbād Miṣrī*, this Arab version of Michelet-style history, took its place not only as a work of art and science but also as a manual of the future. According to some private communications, political detainees in Kharga Oasis passed this book, which nourished their hope, avidly from hand to hand.

The Islamic Option

Regardless of the fact that in Arab Islam, as elsewhere in accord with a general tendency, the share of religion in society's evolution is being circumscribed, its retreat as an institution has nevertheless not seriously affected its sway over the psyche and over behavior. Studies concerned with it should thus specify which of these two aspects they are addressed to, but they ordinarily neglect to do so.

On the one hand, indeed, publications are accumulating aimed at defending and glorifying Muslim society rather than at exploring the question of *ghayb*, or "mystery," from a Muslim point of view. At a recent meeting between Eastern Muslim and Christian thinkers, communities (I was about to say "families") were contrasted, rather than measuring, one against the other, two rival interpretations of man's situation in the cosmos and the response his conscience makes thereto.[7] There is another approach, laic or agnostic, which attacks Islam as institution, ideology, or escape, that is, its extrinsic aspects, without bringing a vision of the universe under discussion. Religion and atheism thus often meet in their preoccupations and their omissions. Their mutual ambition is to conquer civil society, repressing everything which lies hidden beneath it or in advance over it, in which metaphysics itself is merely an approach of which the teeth have been carefully drawn. How could this surprise us? It is civil society in the Arab East which has been subjected to the most direct threats for a century and a half. It is civil society which imperialism beseiged. The latter generally took care to handle Islam by ignoring it, or by taking account of it only as guarantor of a collective identity or fomenter of political resistance. On their side, Eastern thinkers, headed by Afghānī and ʿAbduh, were above all aware of the extent to which the East was falling behind history, and it was adaptations of a social order, certainly not of a metaphysical one, that they called upon the faith to make.

Islam at this juncture had to face up to the offensive which religion was sustaining in Europe on the part of positivism, but the threat to Islam was far more dangerous because of the contexts in which it arrived. Now since that time religion in Europe has undergone other offensives. Some, the most grave, have come from within itself. Through new methods of exegesis, rejection of mythology, and the deepening of exegesis, they affect the very definition of the faith. In Islam these challenges, obscured by those same historical risks—dependence, alienation, underdevelopment—have not loomed as large. The shape of the problem has consequently remained at the former level. Its axis is still historical and sociological, even political.

It is not as if zeal, and sometimes talent, were lacking. Statements of a temperate modernism, such as those of Shaikh Shaltūt or Shaikh Ṭāhir bin ʿĀshūr,[8] are tinged in the case of the late ʿAllāl al-Fāsī[9] or the regrettably few statements of ʿAbd al-ʿAzīz Kāmil[10] with great relevance as to time and place. Professor Ṣubḥī Ṣāliḥ's methodology assimilates the contribution of orientalists without straying from his own faith.[11] The copious works of Shaikh Muḥammad al-Mubārak, former dean of the faculty of theology at Damascus and now teaching at Mecca, derive lucidly an Islamic attitude and doctrine from the similarities and differences between Islam and other monotheisms.[12] In all this one can see nothing beyond the continuation and amplification of the canonical reform movement's messages. Legitimate defense of Islam has not become differentiated to the point of facing up to questions raised by an intrinsically religious criticism. Doubtless, and for obvious reasons, it has been more preoccupied with temporal strategy than with spiritual inquiry. That is simply one effect among others of the encirclement which Islamic societies have undergone and are still undergoing. But Muslim thought has run the risk of taking a polemical and obsidional turn exemplified by the wretched pamphlets of a Shaikh al-Bahī or a Shaikh al-Ghazālī, to say nothing of the positions, outlawed but still powerful, of the Muslim Brothers.

The shaikhs' Islam has thus left pending certain of man's disquiets, the same ones as nourished the faith of a Mauriac. It has even ignored or attacked them. Too often it has treated unbelief as perversion, and laicism as if it did not exist. Conversely, Arab uneasiness in modern times has only rarely, as far as we know, taken the paths of spirituality. *Qalaq* has found either an existentialist and irreligious expression as with ʿAbd al-Raḥmān Badawī, revolutionary as with the Marxists and Baʿthists, agonistic as with many poets, or purely subversive. Meanwhile Islam, strong in the adherence of the masses, where it is always in large part confused with collective identity, displays among the educated the entire spectrum which goes from rigor to liberalism and from traditionalism to modernism, without forgetting the indifference and laxity which accompany the growing secularization of societies throughout the world.

It is nevertheless fitting to look for the debate where it is taking place, that is, among thoughtful believers and circles of religious thinking, for example around the old centers of doctrinal teaching. The debate is polarized, as might have been expected, on the dual conflict of old and new, the specific and the global. To the same extent, it enters into the global debate over Arab culture and societies. Generally speaking, Islam does not indulge in the backward-looking simplifications of the Brotherhood, according to which the faith demands that the organization of the Medinan state be transferred to the modern world. Such a goal would in fact contribute to weakening rather than restoring Islam, or any other religion. For it, as for Christianity, defense does not consist in detaching a certain content from its historical context so as to inject it into a modern system in large part imported or newly created (cf. in present-day Libya, beneficiary and dependent of the world petroleum economy, the prohibition of alcoholic beverages and the exclusion of scripts other than the Arabic). It consists in incorporating as many features of modernity as possible in a system, preserving its main lines but freeing itself from purely circumstantial anchors. Stated in different terms, that was Shaikh ʿAbduh's position. Three quarters of a century have not, in our opinion, shaken its validity.

The world's challenges have, of course, intensified for Islam, as for other religions. Metaphysics aside, it must resolve the same dilemma as Arab culture as a whole, and any collective identity in general. Scientific and technical civilization henceforth conditions things and situations in a world changing more and more rapidly. It would be a serious weakness to seek to rehabilitate, so to speak, a transcendent message by arguing that it had "foreseen" one or another attitude or discovery of modern times. For quite understandable reasons of circumstance, this belief in a universal "concordance" is working more ravages in the Islamic domain than it did until recently in Christian apologetics.

Thus there appeared recently in Beirut a work with the attractive title, "The Koran in the Light of Dialectical Materialism."[13] The author extols the value of promoting rational intelligence, with which indeed the book overflows, while apologizing for leaving aisde other content equally "modern": appeals to historicity, antagonisms, aesthetic attraction, of "those lofty values, enlightening of themselves, but which must doubtless be related to the essential causes of our times by underscoring the permanence, *daymūma*, of all thought which springs authentically from man's intuitions." One can scarcely see what dialectical materialism or dialectics in general, whether Platonic, Hegelian, Fichtean, or whatever, has to gain from such extrapolations. We probably have to do here with a tactician anxious to construct a bridge between Marxism and Islam. The converse is encountered frequently. Many shaikhs strain their ingenuity in taxing present-day socialisms as useless, by showing that their premises can be found in the holy book. This is to fall victim to the misunderstanding I mentioned previously, of confusing eras and levels, of trading off immutable values one seeks to defend for a relativity of which the ultimate implications are not appreciated.

If it is true that this belief in a universal "concordance" is a (quite unintended) tribute by the faith to the secular world, and by the East to the West, more-axial investigations will doubtless result from approaches less obsessed with the secular world. They must, of course, like the preceding ones, take the text as their point of departure, comment upon it, and eventually reinterpret it. Activity in this branch of the *ʿulūm dīniya* can thus provide an index in the field. But in respect of *tafṣīr* and *ḥadīth* it is one of the least active!

Koranic exegesis, it is true, has always protected itself from indiscreet aspirants by a halo of reverential fear. In this field, to quote the proverb, "to speak truth is already false, to speak falsehood is criminal." In the Maghreb, particularly, prudence imposed silence with but few exceptions, and we may be glad that the Eastern Sunnis and Shīʿites have not observed the same reserve.[14] We have, as has been seen, drawn upon some of their recent approaches. There is thus nothing surprising about the relative scarcity of works of *tafṣīr*. It is principally a matter of custom and is compensated for by a quality at least pedagogical. The penury of *ḥadīth* works is more disturbing. In this field, where Arab methodology achieved triumphs almost on a level with its accomplishments in rhetoric and, especially, prosody, we have seen no notable work since the *Tarātīb Idāriya* by the erudite Maghrebi Shaikh ʿAbd al-Ḥayy al-Kittānī. As for mysticism, it is suffering a disfavor a few judge undeserved. In any case, it has apparently long failed to enrich the Arab literary inventory. Many of the most interesting contributions to Islamic thought strictly speaking—and this is consecrated by tradition—are made at the level of academic commentary in the theology and philosophy *ummahāt*, where there are some useful confluences with Western erudition. The edition of the *Shifāʾ* by Ibrāhīm Madkūr, the thesis of Ḥasan Hanefī, the works of M. Arkoun, Majīd Fakhrī, Father Anawati, ʿUthmān Yaḥyā[15]—these are a few manifestations of a zeal from which bolder productions may emerge some day. Scriptural science would then join the more properly philosophical work of thinkers, whether religious or atheist, among whom I shall again mention ʿAbd al-Raḥmān Badawī as an explorer of the borders between Islam and Hellenism. Although his works have appeared most frequently in French, let us mention the Muslim personalism of Mohammed Aziz Lahbabi, which it will be useful to place opposite that of another personalistic thinker, this one a Christian Arab, René Habachi.

But the most remarkable indicator of this activity seems to me to be sought in the hermeneutical and spiritual research works, some of which have had great success in the bookstores. I have already spoken of Dr. Muṣṭafā Maḥmūd's book. Dr. Kāmil Ḥusain, by whom I have also cited a work of *tadabbur*, carries this vein to a quite high moral and literary level. After the admirable *Wicked City*, a Muslim meditation on the mystery of Calvary, he has just now given us *Al-Wādī al-Muqaddas.*[16]

This "sacred valley" might be the "celestial land" of the alchemists, that is, by his own definition, "the place, moment, and moral state where you rise above your nature and the nature of things." It nevertheless constitutes a projection of that nature. The entire effort of the author, a noted surgeon,[17] is concentrated on basing an ethic of purification and faith upon the exact sciences. From this perspective faith is simply "a latent force in the balanced soul returning to its own formation." Its essence is unitary, whether it is a question of primitive superstitions or of devotion to scientific truth. In this unitarism and naturalism one recognizes a Muslim attitude of which the author, a scientist like Teilhard de Chardin, boldly draws the consequences, as the latter had done from the "ascensional" element in Christian ontology. In both cases the moralist sought to convince not only a believing minority but also an indifferent or atheist majority. The evolutionist perspective for the one, and for the other a functionalism of the human organism as it embraces various physical and moral levels of life, is to furnish a language in which to communicate with laymen.

Dr. Kāmil Ḥusain utilizes this language in a serene expression of the differences among religions. Fear, love, and hope seem to him to characterize, respectively, Mosaism, Christianity, and Islam. Indeed, while the Azharists, although touched by many of his reflections, repudiate his arguments, his book has aroused keen interest among Christians. The latter, however, cannot accept the idea that there is no original sin, and that ethics is rooted in a purely physical law of our life, that is, *kabḥ*, or "retention," "contraction." Laymen, though interested by a theory of *ḥirmān*, or "deficiency" (either physical, social, or moral deficiency), will reject the idea that the most apparently absurd practices can condition spiritual health, just as the ostrich obtains calcium by swallowing pebbles. On the other hand, they will sympathize with the demand for freedom of thought, declared necessary for all intellectual and spiritual life.

The fact is that here we are very far from a system of edicts and prohibitions. Dr. Kāmil Ḥusain conceives religion as man's passion for God, "the Pole of Goodness." He does not thereby renounce transcendance. Certainly, such a position is easier in Islam than in Christianity. It might nevertheless provide an interesting contribution to the debate today between those who, in religious matters, emphasize the existential aspects of faith and those who stress metaphysical content. To close this brief discussion, let us re-read one of the final pages of the book which, for its beauty, I translate here at length.

> There is, for man, another life than this misty one. A profound and secure life: that of the soul. A radiant life whose features are revealed to plain view without causing trance or prostration. It is the life of the sacred valley. There all things sparkle with the light of faith. In all the diversity of their aspirations, all those who have been purified are gathered there. There, good dissipates evil, for the holy company appreciates the good at its true value, whereas in the misty life evil conceals the good. Doubtless, you will desire to take pride in the good you have done, if only in your own eyes. But you cannot truly accomplish this elsewhere than in the sacred valley.
>
> Here below, men begin their life on a clear, straight, well-lighted road. But they let themselves be carried away by the fruit-laden trees on either side. They see all this through the mist. Then they depart from their road, urged on by the instinct to increase their knowledge of its byways and the advantage they will thus secure. But if they arrive at the byways' end they do not find what they had hoped. Then they will try to return to the straight road, to the sacred valley, when most of them have irretrievably lost it.
>
> They attribute their failure to Adam's mistake, a mistake from which none of his sons can save himself since the creation of the world and its creatures.[18]

The Progressivist Option

A re-examination need not specify its language in order to act upon sentiment and practice. Perhaps it is the more powerful for being silent. Thus public demand, in its nationalist phase, overflowed politics in a wave of nameless hopes and angers, and was thereby effective. But its very effectiveness was made up of disappointments. Obstacles encountered on the way toward economic, social, and cultural liberation merely stimulated that undifferentiated revolt of which Muṭāʿ al-Ṣafadī, in a feverish book a few years ago, pointed out the primarily existential accent.[19] But *thawriya* is not the shortest road to revolution. The latter assumes criticism and organization. If an Arab really intends to remedy the ills of his society, he must rise from effervescence to analysis. The observation of poverty, ignorance, and sickness will lead him to several successive indictments. In the first instance he will incriminate oppression by an individual, a group, or a class. But he will soon go beyond these rather brief imputations. The real culprit in the situation is the one which long proclaimed itself such, because it laid claim to both responsibility and profit: imperialism. But imperialism would not have been possible without certain internal weaknesses or shortcomings, which result from the lag behind history. Many indications of the latter are observable: the obduracy of social hierarchies, weak technology, outmoded customs. The theoretical remedy is equally obvious: modernization. But how is one to pinpoint the latter's priorities and points of impact? This would be impossible without that "intellectual and moral reformation" our Renan preached a century ago in similarly dramatic circumstances. But this reformation, of which the intelligentsia seeks to be the champion but to which it sometimes falls victim, demands a pitiless re-examination of everything that is the most widely shared in these societies. What is that? Human respect, conservatism, the taste for immediate enjoyment, the propensity for illusion and escapism? Yes, all these defects together, and their cause, according to some: the excessive role of the irrational. I am theorizing here. But the sequence in the re-examination I have just traced typifies rather faithfully the sorts, phases, and degrees of the Arab protest: struggle against the Other's misdeeds, self-criticism, and attack upon the irrational features in mores, institutions, and ideas.

Many Arabs, believers among them, see the source of this irrationality in the debasement of popular Islam: pharisaism in ritual, worship of saints, quietist and passivist attitudes. Since Shaikh ʿAbduh, enlightened Islam has fought these deviations with a zeal which sometimes ignores their possibly respectable elements. It is in the nature of such an effort that it must be constantly renewed, and that the purification effort must go to further and further extremes. Twenty years or so ago the works of Khālid Muḥammad Khālid created a scandal by what must be termed their anticlericalism. That was nevertheless not radicalism's final word on the subject, for it is indifference, secularism, and even unbelief which took up, and are continuing, the battle not only against these deviations from institutional Islam but also against belief itself in certain respects.

Radicalism must, however, take account of this belief, if only because it is virtually unanimous and because the masses would not brook a direct attack upon it. The most-virulent attacks are generally conducted by proselytes who have left the community as rebels (this was true, long ago, with respect to Christianity, of Fāris Shidyāq) rather than by responsible revolutionaries.

As an example, let us take a bulky volume which appeared without identification of the publisher, Man's Rebellion Produces Civilizations, *by ʿAbdullah al-Qāsimī.*[20] *This is a furious treatise with excesses worthy of a* Père Duchesne, *insisting over four hundred pages that the spirit of rapine and violence is at the origin of religions, that salvation can come only through sin. Ten chapters begin with extended extracts from a previous work of the same author, who thus proceeds by amplification, without the slightest fact or the most obscure name to support his discussion. An inverted dogmatism which may be explained as a reaction against objective evils only too real. But the plea is inoperative, and I shall mention only its curiously surrealistic accent in certain invective passages.*

As against this interminable screed, re-read the twenty-four brief pages of a lecture by Michel Aflaq, In Memory of the Arab Prophet.[21] *The future founder of the Baʿth demonstrates the mutual implications of Islam and Arabism, the broadly human values of the Prophetic message, and the vicissitudes of an Arab personality enjoined to draw from this living source. Islam is the vital stirring which, in the Arab homeland, enlivens* kāmin al-qiwā, *literally "latent forces": internals, potentialities, to use our terms. Then follows a penetrating critique of acculturation, however progressive, inasmuch as it implies the eventual dissolution of personality. This point was aimed at the Syrian Communists who, under their leader Bagdāsh, were to maintain with the Syrian Baʿth, and later with that of Iraq, a sinuous relationship not devoid of mutual hostility.*[22]

It was over the role of the specific, indeed, that the two ideologies diverged, insofar as doctrinal divergence can explain a struggle for power. The history of the Communist party of Algeria was marked by cruel schisms and expulsions over the same point. A poignant account is found in Amar Ouzegane's book. Tactical adaptation to the situation, naturally, required that Marxism, like any other ideology, tailor its activity, if only to counterbalance the universalism of its message: that was the price of effectiveness. But unlike the Ba'th, it does not set up recourse to the specific as a fundamental principle, and it views the authentic as innately reactionary or gratuitous. A political historian would follow the divergences and convergences in detail through an exceptionally dense body of data. This, as may be surmised, is not my purpose. Since it is the Arabs' hesitation over "what to do?" and "whom to be?" and the practical reconsiderations which ensue that interest us here, one need not be surprised if uniat Marxists rub elbows in this paragraph with representatives of specific, nameless, or pretended socialisms. Thus we shall list at random, with no claim to comprehensiveness, the participants in the progressive Ṭalī'a in Cairo, Luṭfī al-Khūlī and Muḥammad Sīd Aḥmad among others; the vast Ba'th output, from Najīb al-Arsūzī to Dr. Elias Faraḥ; the struggle against confessionalism and reaction led by Kamāl Jumblāṭ, which has a strange drawing power by virtue of this leader's complex personality. The struggle is waged amid a wealth of variations among individuals or cliques, if not always of doctrine, by left-wing intellectuals, among whom Ṣādiq al-'Aẓm stands out.[23] The latter attacks all obscurantisms, of the left no less than of the right and even of the Palestine struggle. This is an unquestionable demonstration of a laudable audacity. Al-'Aẓm carries it so far as to condemn all sentiment of *ghayb* as evasive or diversionary. As a matter of fact he does not attack religion but, he says, religious ideology. This being the case, he can be accused of appearing at once too timid on the philosophical level and too unrealistic on the practical level, insofar as religious sentiment in the East constitutes a fact hard to conjure away.

Ghālī Shukrī, in a recently published book,[24] endeavors to disentangle the ruinous dilemma in these societies which, as many see it, sets a grandiose cultural legacy more or less linked to Islam in opposition to modernization. After observing, correctly, the extent to which recourse to inherited values has proved offensive during the past twenty or so years, he proposes re-examination of both this baneful pendulum effect and the simplistic assimilation of the authentic and the ancient, the modern and the borrowed. He envisages a critical and selective solution of the content of both the former and latter terms, in which he is perfectly right. However, in failing to distinguish between substantive content and system or structure—a distinction, in our opinion, alone capable of resolving the pernicious dilemma—he makes of the present, identified as movement toward the left, the criterion of the choices to be made. Such a criterion would, of course, sweep society clean of all influences of the *ghayb*. But this positivism, which was also that of Ṣādiq al-ʿAẓm, ignores the fundamental problem, which should at least be discussed. Moreover, the formidable power of attitudes related to the *ghayb* in the societies under examination transforms the objective of its condemners into a pious hope, since the liquidations judged desirable have not yet been carried out by European societies themselves (including the Eastern European), however unquestioningly these latter are taken as champions of rationality!

The reader will not be surprised that I have taken the field of religion as the proving ground for the Arabs' re-examination. There are, of course, other fields of confrontation, and these are the ones in which actual efforts are now being made. Besides, in these debates Islam has been in some respects simply an alias for the specific. Now the latter may be subsumed under other forms, and that is what most often produces the conjunction between the demands of Arabism and those of democracy, in a manner incomprehensible for many Westerners. That is furthermore why, from the avant-gardes of liberal thought to the various forms of socialism more or less influenced by the example of the French, Russian, and Chinese revolutions, the demand for historical reason and social rationality brings together great numbers of dissidents with links to the intelligentsia, youth, or labor. The sociologist will be sensitive to this vagueness, perhaps regrettable from the standpoint of ideological precision but revealing a general attitude of doubt and refusal which is furthermore expressed by many poets. The individuality of the different movements is to be sought in the color of their action, and in their choice of alternatives in domestic and foreign policy, more than in doctrine. Their relations with the peasantry (basic democracy) and the working class (trade unionism) constitute another criterion, and also their participation, over at least a generation, in the formation and practice of an intelligentsia. In this field, the contribution of Marxist thought (with or without party militancy) to Arab teaching methods, and even to the creation of a new sort of man, must be stressed for its breadth. Today, one no longer necessarily believes in a cause whose "witnesses," to speak in Pascal's terms, are "willing to get their throats cut," but no friend of Arab culture can forget the names, among others, of the Egyptian Shuhdī ʿAṭiya and the Sudanese Maḥjūb. . . .

The creativity of this intelligentsia unfortunately suffers from the hazards to which freedom of expression is generally exposed in the world, and more particularly in the Third World. It has not demonstrated its full capability, we believe, if we are to judge by its works published in Arabic and within the national framework. It must nevertheless be credited with the birth of archival history, with Muḥammad Anīs in Egypt and others, of which one may hope the small group of practitioners will grow.[25] Literary and aesthetic criticism, with Muḥammad Mandūr a short while ago and now Ḥusain Muruwwé and Maḥmūd al-ʿĀlim,[26] demonstrate the same orientation. The latter of these two critics has spoken unsparingly of the great elder, Ṭaha Ḥusain. From the one to the other, reasoning has changed in manner and in commitment.

Al-ʿAlim published his master's thesis only after seventeen years delay.[27] *He prefaced it with confessions which might apply to all his contemporaries. This young philosopher, while yet a student, was then seeking a foundation for metaphysics and thus for faith. Doubtless he had already been beguiled and troubled by European science, of which certain applications, through the questionable intermediary of imperialism, had so profoundly altered his country. Take care! It was in the name of industrial civilization, and thus in many respects of causal reasoning, that the canal diggers and the dam builders had acted. Resistance, on the other hand, had arisen from the faith, cultural specificity, national instinct, and potential, largely unformulated, forces. Patriotism in the Third World has striven, and still strives, to square the circle by allying one of these powers with the other.*

It is of some interest that, in the course of a seminal book, E. Boutroux' On the Contingency of Natural Laws, *several theoretical assaults, including Einstein's, were seen to shake the foundations of determinism, at least in its established positive form. Al-ʿĀlim embarks on the road, familiar to religious apologetics, which consists of turning the adversary's own statements against him. But then he comes across two books: Engels'* Dialectic of Nature *and Lenin's* Materialism and Empirical Criticism. *The thesis which was being sketched undergoes a radical twist. Contingency, probability, and chance in the data ordered by the most-recent science simply complete (*takmīliya*) the objectivity and necessity which are the basis of any science. The historicity which pervades matter and the dialectic which governs its movements while accounting* *for its disquieting dialog with the experimenter's observation confirm, in the eyes of this young enthusiast, Laplace's postulate and, particularly, the attitudes it dictates with respect to the real and to praxis. The resulting optimism is to this luxurious determinism, so to speak, what Max Weber said the spirit of enterprise among Protestants was to the Lutheran "serf-arbiter." Far from reverting, al-ʿĀlim assures us, to a fundamentalism which would seek in some return to the accidental, the mysterious, or the irrational its recourse against Western domination, insofar as it is founded, or claims to be, upon scientific reason, it is on the contrary through a leap forward, through taking advantage of the latest scientific discoveries, that the struggle must find its inspiration.*

This was a progressivist version of nationalism, if the latter term can properly be applied to a subject so definitely universal. The author, naturally, does not derive such perspectives in an academic work in which he does not reveal all his sources or all his predilections. One can nevertheless read them like a watermark in passages where he proclaims the universality of historicity and the possibility that human liberty can be founded, not on an illusory abrogation of scientific laws governing the real, but on permitting them to take charge.

Much time has passed since the student al-ʿĀlim wrote these pages. The vicissitudes which have subsequently carried him, and many other intellectuals, from concentration camp to positions of responsibility have not modified his vigorous talent. As he smites, in turn, bourgeois art, existentialism, Dr. Zakī Najīb Maḥmūd's neopositivism, Fītūrī's Africanism, and formalism, we shall not reproach him for some gross errors in judging one or another, such as so many others have committed. Much less shall we reproach him for espousing a demanding ethic. But we shall regret that he makes deductive applications of it. Finally, he seems estimable to us above all for his acute sense of social totality and his untiring plea for creativity.

He had defended his thesis just when Nasserism was about to be installed, two or three years before the Bandung Conference. By an ironical coincidence, common in the history of the Arab left, al-ʿĀlim lost his position at the university in 1955. That was when I became acquainted with him, and that was also when I paid my first visit to Ṭaha Ḥusain in his little Zamālik villa. As an introduction to contemporary Arab literature, the dean presented me with Najīb

Maḥfūẓ' *Zuqāq al-Midaqq*. . . . This novel had been published in 1947. In the feverish years before Nasser's revolution, thus, were concentrated a first masterpiece of the Arab novel, a peak of liberal humanism with Ṭaha Ḥusain's *Mir'at al-Ḍamīr*, Maḥmūd al-ʿĀlim's thesis, and also, as we shall see, the appearance of a liberated prosody. A quarter-century later we may usefully ask to what extent this magnificent promise has been kept, or has on the contrary been restrained, spoiled, or even stifled.[28] In our view the reply varies according to the country and the genre.

The Liberal Option

Here we have an "occidentalist" (why reject this word, so much more honest than its counterpart, orientalist?),[29] an intellectual who for many years has been teaching John Dewey, Wittgenstein, and Bertrand Russell, and delights in English literature but now wakens with a sudden start. Should he not strive to integrate into the national entity, such as it has come down from the depths of the ages, the best of what comes from abroad, and should he not urge his many students and readers to do the same? This is an anguishing awakening for him, *ṣaḥwa qaliqa*. With the fervor of his frustration he plunges into the works of the *turāth*. He feels there a sense of exile and of anachronism which overwhelms him. Why, then, have they survived, they or at least the values they illustrate, in his people's modes of behavior? Why must they be so incorporated as to raise inextricable contradictions for one who would like both to derive inspiration from them and to keep abreast of present times?

Such an investigation brings into play observations of shortcomings difficult for a foreigner to challenge, but which seem to me either too harsh, or incomplete. Resort to irrational forces: obscurantism, fixation on the past, verbalism, crushing the liberty of thought do not define a civilization. Islam has no monopoly of the traits the author has amassed here. Zakī Najīb has only mockery for the fiṭra, *notwithstanding the fact that God and nature meet therein, and for certain agonistic and sensual features whereby the depth of Arab life is increased with the very things transcendence had stripped from it. I am well aware that he finds positive inspirations also in the heritage. As a philosopher he is too prone to consider only the interplay of concepts; as epistemologist more than philosopher, he does not give an account of what a specificity might be, even one limited to his own Weltanschauung. It is not surprising that the person thus mutilated seems to him incapable of functioning in a contemporary world which is supposedly a scientific world, dominated by the West's imprint. If culture consisted in "modes of behavior," in "ways of confronting life," no doubt the adaptation which is a condition of any survival would postulate that the Arabs must borrow unstintingly from the West, and conversely liquidate anything in their heritage which conflicts with modernity so conceived. But a culture is an identity.*

Now this epistemologist and scientist also proposes to reinstate a morality, and he in no way contemplates a relationship between it and the sociohistorical process by which, always in haphazard and discordant fashion, modernity is being accomplished. Paradoxically faithful to the dualism in which he sees a distinctive trait of the Arabs, facts seem to him to come from earth, values from heaven. Be it understood that by "heaven" he has in mind the ideal, or idea, not a revelation, to which he makes only a very sober reference.

One must admire the violent tone in which he urges his compatriots to perform upon themselves a liberating sorting out. Change, choice, and adjustment have become the lot of all peoples, and their future depends upon their capacity for reorganization. The Arabs are enjoined, on the one hand, to adopt modern science and technology without reserve and, on the other, to remain faithful to spiritual values. Between the two orders, there are none of those collusions which would bring about the mutual deterioration of both fact and value. But, one might retort, is science excluded from the domain of values? That would carry positivism a little too far! Besides, does value emerge ready-made from the empyrean and remain unrelated to the objective context? It would be risky to defend such a view.

The thing lacking in this fine book is a conception of the collectivity in history, that is, of the identity in all its metamorphoses. For him the Arabs' continuity is objectively similar to the debate their ancestors were involved in—that of conciliating reason (in the event, Hellenic reason) and faith—now transposed into an analogous problem: conciliation between the heritage and the Western contribution. Now the latter cannot be taken as synonymous with modernity, any more than industrial civilization can. It simply offers one particular solution, from which the Arabs certainly should take inspiration, but for the purpose of finding their own. The world's movement, with its heady perspectives, goes well beyond the individual solutions of one culture or another, including the Western. Modernity is no one's monopoly. Effort and hope belong to all.

Constantin Zurayq had already made a name for himself before World War II by an analysis of the national consciousness, *al-wa ʿī al-qawmī*. Then in 1948, under the impact of the Palestine defeat, by a merciless re-examination of certain habits and ideas, *Ma ʿnā al-Nakba*, "The meaning of the disaster." Other works appeared later, of which I shall single out the most significant: *Naḥnu wal-Ta ʾrīkh*, 1959, "We and history," and finally in 1964, *Fī Maʿrakat al-Ḥaḍāra*, "In civilization's battle," over which we should pause a moment.

This is an academic work in which many authors are quoted, eclectically, within a wide-ranging perspective. By a kink common to many Eastern intellectuals of English training, the author is wary of theory, or at least purports to draw upon it only through the filter of common sense. As for analysis proceeding directly from the concrete and factual, we find virtually none from his pen, whether because he is suspicious of hypotheses, or because he is reluctant to speculate on certain weaknesses of the Arab world. These weaknesses do not elude him, nor the necessity to correct them. He even coins a phrase: al-fikr al-maṣīrī, *"thought in becoming," and the becoming of thought. He has an acute sense of the relative speed of the different stages, and even of the possibility of omitting certain of them, but also of the cost of such contractions. Revolution, if by revolution is meant specifically the fact of leaping over certain stages—and this is how the question presents itself in the Third World—involves costs which must be compared with the benefits.*

However, can total confidence be placed in evolution? Is everything in society affected by it? When we speak of progress we speak, of course, of overall progress. Now does this progress operate in fact in all categories of life, or only in some? A grave question indeed! Constantin Zurayq finds the finality and reality of progress in technical changes among his people, or else in the growth of positive knowledge in general, but hesitates to admit such an ascending logic in the arts, literature, manners, or faith. One can understand why the author is troubled by social achievements which seek to be both historical and definitive. Is there not a contradiction in regarding invariances from the viewpoint of an ascending progress? Now the author lives among a people of which the overwhelming majority considers that its essential norms go back to a revelation sealed once and for all. But that is perhaps stating the problem in too simple terms. What should be placed in question is not, if you will, the original perfection of these norms as they were revealed, but the modality of their temporal application. The latter, of course, is related to circumstances. And here, perhaps, Zurayq's deeply informed thought and cosmopolitan academicism are somewhat behind the manner in which Shaikh ʿAbduh, sixty years before him, seems to us to have glimpsed the solution.

One must adopt some position on the specific temporality of each individual instance in social development. For it is not simply the categories susceptible of measurement which are subject to a progression over time, but all the others as well. But they are subject to modalities peculiar to each case. Dr. Zurayq would reject in horror, as would we, the colonization of these categories by technology. Although we should reject an undue transfer of what concerns one category, such as economics for example, to the other categories of social life, and vice versa, we must require all these categories, without exception, to agree, each according to its own mode, to the common time span and objective.

The revolution of rationality, he says, is the surest guarantor of any other revolution and a necessary condition for its success. "Its necessity for us embodies all the other needs of the Arab peoples and the most decisive task they must assume in the difficult battle of civilization in which they are now engaged." And further on: "Anyone who might think that our peoples, by thus adhering to rationality, would lose their revolutionary dynamism may rest assured. On the contrary, rationality itself is the path toward their true revolution. It is for them, before and above all, the way to salvation and to victory in the essential, the primordial battle, the battle of civilization."

To call upon the individual to become history, and to adopt the means and methods of that history as it has progressed and torn itself apart over the nearly two centuries just past; to re-establish himself thereby in a contemporary world too unilaterally dominated by others; and meanwhile to safeguard the individual's values and those of the collective identity: thus might be defined the Arabs' objective and their common fund of hopes and perplexities. It is not by accident that their questionings not only over a "what to do?" which can too easily be interpreted in terms of imitation, but of a "whom to be?" commensurate with their grandiose past, feed a culture of groping and unease in their writings. Syntheses which would encompass a vicissitude so global are no doubt premature; for the time being only a few have attempted them, and that from incomplete perspectives.[30]

Unless, of course, the "concrete universal" in works of art as such anticipates such a synthesis: that is undoubtedly what lends significance to the poems spoken of in the following chapters.

XIV
History and Poetry

Less than a hundred years ago the Arab world had its coppersmiths, weavers, potters, decorators, and calligraphers: trays, carpets, marquetry, and illuminations preserved with considerable charm a tradition laden with splendors. But it knew nothing of painting, sculpture, and even literature in the sense modern times attach to these words. Its poetic inspiration had long been frozen in molds that were deemed definitive. Barūdī, contemporary with our Rimbaud, used a language and meters no different from those of Abbasid times. People waxed enthusiastic over assonated prose in the form, for example, of "sittings," or *maqāmāt*, and over homilies and doctrinal epistles. Exegetic dissertation, fond of erudite quotations and prodigal of glances toward the Eternal, still had its masters and devotees. But it did not occur to anyone to write in simple prose to say something bearing on everyday life, or on that other part of life which is imagination. To this archaism must be added the stifling hierarchy of genres. The latter ordered them all, in principle, with respect to interpretation of the sacred text, and excluded several in the name of ethics or simply of polite manners. Thus the dance, strongly entrenched in the countryside and the popular classes, was banished from *thaqāfa*.

If one compares this spectrum of languages, ill assorted with the direction history was taking, with the one Arab artists display today—cinema, choreography, theater, painting, sculpture, architecture, novel, short story, essay, journalism, and many other genres besides—one realizes how far we have come.

A Hypothesis Restated and Broadened

To repeat, the present genres are by no means the continuation of the old. Most stem from foreign models and classifications. They may well, in their quest for national roots, invoke certain antecedents. The novel, for example, might claim ancestry in the narratives in the *maqāma*; the stanzaed ode, in the Andalusian *muwashshaḥ*; the stage play, in the popular skit or the magic lantern tradition. The *maqāma* again, that sort of Menippiad or verbal carnival, might lend authority to many present-day experiments. But this is going to a greal deal of trouble to make apologies for a perfectly common phenomenon, which is that artistic innovation does not proceed by linear projections but by miscellaneous borrowings, by mutation of effects, and by shifts in the frontiers among artistic forms. If this movement responds in most cases to stimuli from outside and fulfills needs of milieus increasingly influenced by international intercourse, why should we be surprised? This in itself, in harmony with other regulating mechanisms attempted on the scale of the global society, brings about an accompanying valuation of attitudes or forms considered to proceed from the past in a straight line. Here, again, fabricating an authenticity may serve as a counterweight to acculturation.[1] A quarrel, such as the one that sets proponents of free verse against those of "vertical" prosody, *ʿamūdī*, is incomprehensible without reference to these compensating swings of the pendulum.

In the preceding pages we have endeavored to organize a description of contemporary Arab culture along certain axes derived from the problems of a particular situation. The investigation thus far doubtless suffers from its deliberate limitations. The theater, perhaps the most-suggestive novelty of recent years, although it already had its precursors (e.g., Muḥammad Taymūr) and its classics (Tawfīq al-Ḥakīm); urbanism and architecture; choreography, which seeks to impress history and beauty upon a festival of the body at the mass level; the cinema; and still other arts deserve analysis along with the plastic arts, music, the essay, or the novel. I shall not attempt such an inventory.[2] It would lapse into encyclopedism, or a didacticism alien to the purposes of the present work. I shall be content with formulating as a theorem the conclusions that seem to me to follow from a very great number of facts.

The modernization of a culture, regardless of the role of continuities within it, is subject to the ranges of genres and conditions of form which, in the present stage, depend closely upon the world's dominant cultures. This dual appropriation operates according to configurations in which, according to the specific case, convergence or conflict predominates, and this produces aesthetic as well as social consequences.

If this is so, the development of the art forms studied above in some detail, and of those that have merely been listed, may have a common explanation:

1. It is certainly a privilege for the theater to innovate not, of course, its function, but a type of expression not used in the East until a quite recent period. The same is true of painting and sculpture. The unquestionable and early successes in these forms are doubtless attributable to this freedom of movement.

2. But how are the generally opposite effects in the cases of the cinema and romantic fiction to be accounted for? In the former case we have to do with an art form that results from industrial economy and is deeply entrenched in mass communications. Now thus far access to the masses and to large-scale finance has not had, for the Egyptian cinema which dominates the market, innovative counterparts, although in Egypt and elsewhere (Algeria) production of high-quality films is beginning. This is because the Arab cinema has had to make concessions to the average taste of excessively broad publics. Modernity thus operates less as creativity than as acculturation, or as a transaction between the archaic and the imported.[3]

3. Despite some interesting successes, as we have seen, the novel and short story demonstrate the same sort of contradiction. This form was not new enough to free itself from tradition; it was too new to carry a continuity forward.[4]

4. The situation is reversed, however, with respect to the essay. Of the latter, one may say that performance is commensurate with the incertitudes of the society it expresses, since they furthermore constitute its substantive material and condition its style. It participates, besides, in a tradition of which Ṭaha Ḥusain found in Jāḥiẓ a direct-line respondent.[5]

5. As for music, the genuinely popular depth of its roots means that modernity's attraction has been confined to certain instrumental contributions and imitative successes by various impresarios. That is why the compromise satisfies the broad public which rejects the experimentation of the few modern-style composers even though it has embraced new forms of creativity in other genres (essay, novel, and to some extent poetry).

This more or less pronounced duality between mass taste and that of small groups or cliques can provide an additional parameter to our analysis. The presence of a cultural *sunna* (to borrow a theological term) beside and despite an avant-garde and irrelevant culture is a trait certainly not peculiar to the Arabs, but it is accentuated in their case by the fact that normality for them implies reference to the ancient, and that exceptions come directly or indirectly from abroad. It is true that this applies fully to music but is no longer valid with regard to literature. In literature, as in technology, costume, institutions, and housing (but most assuredly not cuisine or, perhaps, love), the exceptional is becoming generalized and is establishing a new conformity for the new times. This conformity, however, is always felt more or less as decadence. Hence the uneasiness, the feeling of inauthenticity and even of guilt that prevails among many Arabs troubled by the necessity of reconciling these two portions of themselves: the inherited and the learned, the permanent and the mutant, the consensual and the anomalous. Culture is at once the witness, the agent, and the stake in these dichotomies. How could it be otherwise? For the most part, media and modes of expression are now leaning toward the borrowed. Let it be said loud and clear: the alternative is no longer between being carried along by an irresistible current or restoring its former, opposite flow, even were this possible: the choice is now between a creative tension and compromises of base alloy.

But what precisely is to be understood, in this field of compromise, by fineness and alloy? Is this not a relapse into pure subjectivity? And which: the investigator's or that of the subject of the investigation? Thus far, I have adduced only evidence or circumstances and trends. The ultimate destination, surely, cannot be dissociated from situation and trend, but it involves still other factors and, particularly, values. Disquiet over the distribution of genres and debate over adoption from outside or preservation of one's own do not necessarily affect the quality of works produced. The finest flowerings (or those considered such)[6] may spring from a purely traditional, even reactionary, context, whereas a modernist outlook may breed only imitation and platitude. The range of tastes introduces many other elements besides the taxonomy of genres and the rivalry between inherited and imported models. In one broad sector of creative activity—for example, that which uses only linguistic means, that is, literature—the reappropriation and, so to speak, the reorigination to which the Arabs instinctively resort in assimilating their borrowings from abroad have a decisive auxiliary in the social vitality and aesthetic power of the language.

Therefore it may be that poetry, "labor within language," reaps the benefit of the linguistic primacy that in many respects characterizes this culture, if not all these societies. It may be that it will succeed, better than other art forms, in putting back into practice, within a virtually total renewal, virtues that have always existed, although the reinvention of a form aligned with the actual world may present it with difficult problems in finding an audience. That, at least, is the new working hypothesis we shall endeavor to test.

At Basra Again

Let us return to that poetry conference at Basra in which I participated in 1971. Several sessions were held on Sindbad's Island, an island as devoid of *Arabian Nights* intoxication as any spot ravaged by an atomic explosion could be of its original reality. Besides, this was not the first time that the cleavage between the present and the Arab world's glorious or legendary buttresses had saddened its people and its guests! However. . . . Continuity was rescued here by virtue of the word's grace. Poetry prepared the way for, and in a sense effected, a junction both despairing and satisfying with the outmoded. When Jawāhirī, in his language of ebony and gold, declaimed the stanzas of *Ayyuhā al-Araq*, of which even the hemistichs echoed one another in rhyme or assonance, and the crowd breathed its delight with audible *ṭayyib*, or *aḥsant*, "well said!" the illusion that we were back in the golden centuries nearly dazzled us. "It's Mutanabbī," murmured the Egyptian critic seated next to me. Now what, in 1971, would a Mutanabbī poem have been? This admiration on the part of Muḥammad Nuwayhī, a fierce modernist,[7] was a two-edged sword. Throughout the congress, moreover, partisans of traditional prosody clashed with those of a liberated poetry. Thus we were torn between the insecurity of invasion and the dupery of repetition. . . .

The congress included a visit, or rather a pilgrimage, to Jikūr, Badr Shākir al-Sayyāb's village, that "trench of nocturnal butterflies" whose coolness he celebrated so often during his brief life, Jikūr where his mother's flanks fused with the earth: "thou my pasture, I thine." In short, a poet who died as a virtual victim of assassination. "A day for sackcloth and ashes," Lāmiʿa ʿAbbās whispered to me, a young Mandean whose face brought a Sumerian beauty out of the depths of time. She was right. There seemed to be an impassable gulf between Sayyāb's village, the imagined one, and the real village where the visitors and his own family were milling about. There was nevertheless something touching: a frail little girl, with an uncanny resemblance to the deceased poet, playing in her modest little house. . . . In Arab poetry Sayyāb represents man's new world, assumed in rhythms and images that agitate the ancient world. His memory threw into relief an opposite stylistic, that of the classicizing Jawāhirī. It makes little difference, indeed, whether the age-old form expresses "new thoughts," or whether a new form liberates an eternal poetry: the only essential thing is that the result be a song for mankind.

During these sessions, in any case, the continuing vitality of Arab poetry was affirmed by the quantity of output presented, by the value of certain poems, and by the emotion they aroused. These are some additional indications: the young people who drew one aside and whispered that the real poets, victims of censorship, were boycotting the meeting; or the professional club—that of the customs officials, I believe—that gave a private reception for a few of us where we heard pieces in no way inferior to those of the poets on the official program; or, again, the anger of Khalīl Ḥāwī who, when the chairman at one session described a younger colleague as a pioneer of free verse, left the hall ostentatiously, calling us all "dogs"! Saʿdī Yūsuf, reading one of his poems from the lectern, had to pause, overcome with emotion; this faltering overwhelmed the audience. This abundance of talent, affectivity, and vanity was the corollary of the presence of a poetic speech capable in itself, by its ardor, of resuscitating a Sindbad after all. . . .

Was this simply the situation, the chance conjunction of people and place, a unique moment? I do not think so. With due recognition of its quarrels, its failures, and its occasional backbiting, poetry owes to its atavistic primacy and its raw material, which contains an Arab continuity if there ever was one, a relative excellence among all the other achievements of this culture, the only one perhaps that combines to such a degree the affirmation of the specific and an opening upon the universal.

The Poet Speaks

Before proceeding, let us ask the poet of Jikūr to let us hear, in translation, one of his most tragic songs, *Unshūdat al-Maṭar,* "Song of the rain."[8]

In the hour before dawn
Your eyes are two groves of palm trees
Or two balconies
Passed over by the moon.

When your eyes smile, vines flower
And lights dance . . . like the reflection of the moon in the river
Disturbed gently by the movement of oars
In the hour before dawn,
As if stars throbbed in their depths.

The stars drown in a mist of sorrow,
The sea opens its arms
In the warmth of winter, the chill of autumn,
Embracing death and birth and darkness and light;
The shiver of a sob wakens in my soul
And a wild ecstasy courses through me, reaching the sky—
The ecstasy of a child who fears the moon.

Smaller clouds are lost in the heavy dark clouds
Which, drop by drop, disperse in rain;
The children's giggling in the grape arbors
Tickles the silence of the sparrows in the trees.
Then comes the song of the rain.
Rain . . .
Rain . . .
Rain . . .

The evening yawns and the clouds continue to gush
And pour, pour their heavy tears down
Like a child weeping in his sleep
For his mother whom, when he woke a year ago,
He did not see.
And when he persisted in asking,
They told him,
"She'll be back the day after tomorrow."
She must come,
Though friends whisper that she's there
At the side of the hill, sleeping the sleep of the dead,
Down in her own earth, drinking the rain
Like a disappointed fisherman gathering his nets,
And cursing the fates and the waters,
Singing his mournful songs when the moon wanes.
Rain . . .
Rain . . .

Do you know what grief the rain brings?
When the gutters resound with the sad music of the falling rain,
And how the lonely feel a sense of loss when it rains

Endlessly . . . like bleeding, like hunger,
Like love, like children, like death
Is the rain.

I see your eyes
Which seem to float with the rain,
And across the waves of the Gulf, lightning
Sweeps the shores of Iraq with flashes of stars and coral,
As though the shores themselves would rise up
Before the night draws over them a cover of blood.
I cry aloud to the Gulf:
"O Gulf,
Giver of pearls and coral and death!"
My words return
In the echo of a sob:
"O Gulf,
Giver of coral and death!"

I can hear Iraq storing thunder,
Storing lightning on mountains and in valleys,
And when she has finished,
She will stamp them as her own.
(The great storm left no trace in the valley
Of the village Thamūd.)

I can hear the palm trees drinking rain.
I can hear the villages moaning, and emigrants
Battling, with oars and rough axes,
The storms of the Gulf and the thunder, singing:
Rain . . .
Rain . . .
Rain . . .

And in Iraq there is hunger.
At the time of the harvest the crop is winnowed
So crows and greedy locusts will be fed.
But the people still stand in the harvested fields,
And the mill grinds them with the gleanings and the stones.
Rain . . .
Rain . . .
Rain . . .

How many tears we shed the night we departed,
Excusing our sorrow by saying, "It's only the rain."

Rain . . .
Rain . . .
Since the days of our childhood, the sky
Was always cloudy and dark in winter,
And the rain beat down.
Rain . . .
Rain . . .
Rain . . .
Each drop glows
Red or yellow, from the petals of flowers,
Each tear of the naked and hungry,
Each drop of blood shed by slaves
Becomes a smile awaiting a new mouth,
Or a nipple pink from the sucking
Of the newborn child
In the world of a new tomorrow, the world that will offer life.
Rain . . .
Rain . . .
Rain . . .
Iraq's fields grow green in the rain . . .

I cry aloud to the Gulf:
"O Gulf,
Giver of pearls and coral and death."
My words return
In the echo of a sob:
"O Gulf,
Giver of coral and death."
The Gulf spreads its gifts on the sands,
A foam of flaming coral
And the bones of the drowned,
One of the emigrants who drank death
In the fathomless depths of the Gulf.
Countless serpents in Iraq drink the nectar
Of the flowers watered by the Euphrates, the innocent dew.

I hear the echo
Ringing across the Gulf.
Rain . . .
Rain . . .
Rain . . .
Each drop glows
Red or yellow, from the petals of flowers,

And each tear of the naked and hungry,
Each drop of blood shed by slaves
Becomes a smile awaiting a new mouth,
Or a nipple pink from the sucking
Of the newborn child . . .
In the world of a new tomorrow, the world that will offer life.

And the rain pours down.

The pieces collected under the title *Unshūdat al-Maṭar* were written between 1952 and 1960. During this period free versification, of which Sayyāb was among the initiators, spread like a tidal wave. But this should not make us forget that the traditional versification, called "vertical," *ʿamūdī*, maintained its rights in the inspiration of some poets still producing: a Saʿīd ʿAql, a Badawī al-Jabal, a Jawāhirī, for example, an ʿUmar Abū Rīsha, the recently deceased Bishāra al-Khūrī, and many others, perhaps overshadowed by fashion but in no wise fallen from grace, continue to preserve into our time a message older than Islam, which inspired one of them to this splendidly arrogant apostrophe:

The world will enfold its oceans,
its lands, its constellations, its heavens, its ages;
Will enfold the intoxication of Paradise,
with its delights, its angels, its houris;
All will vanish, but God alone will remain steadfast in
His glory, with me His only companion;
For us, permanence without end; the one who survives the
other will moan on throughout bitter eternity.[9]

Thus, at this Basra conference I have chosen for backdrop, Jawāhirī set ringing in his timeless rhythms the rhymes, assonances, and iterations of *Ayyuhā al-Araq*, "O sleeplessness," attaining now and then that descriptive, lyrical, and gnostic power that made one believe one was hearing Mutanabbī again:

O my companions
        The stars are constant
                Catching
                        Their last breaths

Floating
        Exhausting their nebulae
                Waiting for the approach of day

Restless
    Like sorrows
        In a heart full of sorrows, bewildered.

Should they go on, traveling the old familiar paths,
Or should they turn and flee, and escape? [10]

It is with good reason that the Syrian poet Sulaymān Āl ʿĪsā imagined the old prosody legislator, Khalīl, listening alternately to pleas by advocates of one and the other mode of production.

Brief History of Contemporary Arab Poetry

In this quarrel, which is far from ended, the major insult is the accusation of borrowing, whether from the classics or from foreigners. But this raises a problem common to all literature. Everywhere inherited influences and imitation of others are a matter of course. The question is, in what measure has creativity gone beyond response to the other, inspiration by the other, revolt against the other, whether the other be ancestor or foreigner. It is, in fact, by drawing on his personal resources, linked to a total collective consciousness, that the Arab poet has a chance to keep faith with his heritage while joining in a world-wide dialog. Rediscovery of Nature and the use of new modes of expression were to play a leading role in this return to the sources, which makes a clean and advantageous break with what simply following the traditional path had theretofore seemed to offer. The emigrants' school, *al-mahjar*, played an appreciable role in this.[11]

Feeling for nature, and its expression, thus acquired a new tone when Faraḥ Anṭūn, for example, devoted an assonanced poem to Niagara Falls. This naturalist breakthrough was complemented by a deluge of internalism. Sentimental effusion, questioning of ideas, and the first investigations of symbolism were met in Jubrān. Names like Rīḥānī, the two Maʿlūfs, and now also Mikhāʾīl Nuʿaymé are inseparable from this progress in language and emotion.

Meanwhile the poet many Arabs considered their greatest in centuries disappeared (1933): Shawqī, of whom Louis ʿAwaḍ wrote at the time that Arab poetry died with him.[12] Poetry of one certain type, of course! Shawqī carried its musical, lexicographical, and circumstantial afflatus to the point of perfection. He had thereby eclipsed all the bards of his time, including the most skillful, like Muṭrān, or the most sincere, such as Ḥāfiẓ Ibrāhīm. For his juniors he remains today a model or a challenge, tyrannical in either case.

At the time Shawqī died a group of Egyptian poets was forming, centered on the magazine *Apollo*,[13] whose delicate romanticism was the distinguishing quality of Abū Shādī and a few others. This vein was carried forward almost to our own day by ʿAlī Maḥmūd Ṭaha. Perhaps its most original exemplar was Shabbī, a poet of the Tunisian Djérid and a heartbreaking singer of civilizations' frontiers.

Variety of environment, indeed, played its part. The Sudanese Tījānī can be considered a parallel to Shabbī. Iraq had embarked upon its distinctive development even before Ruṣāfī's death. In Lebanon, after a long period of groping, emerged a poet of the first rank: Elie Abū Shabaké. This biblical poet discovers the struggle between good and evil around and within himself and endeavors to convert it into words. On this level the writings of Saʿīd ʿAql attain the splendor of a Platonian empyrean.[14]

One thing must also be mentioned that we have thus far barely glimpsed: that is, popular poetry, which still remains lively and of a truthful power which the poetry of the lettered no longer often attained.[15] A learned Tunisian, Ḥasan Ḥusnī ʿAbd al-Wahhāb, said that true inspiration in his country had long since taken refuge in vernacular works. Similarly in Iraq, Syria, Egypt, and also in Lebanon where a refined modernism has succeeded (with Michel Ṭrād, for example) in adopting the dialectical mode without sacrificing quality: charming byways, but the principal current takes the main road, that of the classical idiom. It is true that experiments are proliferating aimed at producing new effects by renouncing the received forms. I shall give the most space to these, because of their correspondences with innovations in all domains.

Arab Prosody's July 14

Rigorous meter had dominated Arab versification from the beginning without notable change. But in 1947 two of the most-respected Iraqi poets went over to free verse, independently of each other.[16] Nāzik al-Malāʾika's poem on the cholera in Egypt and "Was It Love?" by Sayyāb established simultaneously the new poetic scansion, followed closely by Bayātī (1950) who, perhaps more than the first two, joined modernism of subject to that of form. In that same year Sayyāb's new collection, *Asāṭīr*, confirmed the innovation that was to win over most writers during the following decade. Of course, there had been earlier attempts;[17] one may, for example, ask whether Amīn al-Rīḥānī had not already inaugurated the genre a generation before, with *Hātif al-Awdiya*. However, it was after 1947, and torrentially since 1950, that the new form established itself. Now this period also marks decisive junctures in contemporary Arab history: the Egyptian bourgeoisie gained control over the country's affairs and promptly failed; Palestine was partitioned, and a cruel drama began. The assassination of an Egyptian prime minister bore witness to the rise of extremism; the founding of the Ba'th party and the "free officers" conspiracy signaled the summons to new political horizons. Coincidences, to say the least, between a new stage in the Arabs' social history and a transformation of style all the more striking because, traditionally, poetry had been, as it still is, their most significant mode of expression and even of existence.

Should we therefore say that the shift to free versification "reflected" the change in collective attitudes, or "resulted" from it? It is highly unlikely that such simple relationships obtain among categories so diverse, unless one adopts schemas with hierarchical classifications by super- and infrastructures. Even in this case it would remain to be explained why the upheavals experienced by Eastern societies since the last third of the nineteenth century at the latest "led" only to the classicism of a Shawqī, manifestly ratified by both elite and masses.[18] Actually, the correspondences between aesthetic creation and the other modes of collective affirmation, in postulating creativity and dynamism on both sides, assume a history that is not linear but plural, in which each dimension tends, certainly, to follow the general rhythm but according to its own logic. One may furthermore wonder whether renunciation of the ancient prosody constituted the only possible path for the development of Arab poetry. It has not been even for Western poetry since, after all, Mallarmé is Rimbaud's contemporary and long after Walt Whitman![19] But it afforded one path, accredited moreover by the accelerated development of poetic form during the past fifty years in Europe and America. And when this transformation in craftsmanship coincides with the renewal of inspiration, manners, and materials, how can we fail to see a decisive trait of modernity?

In the East, during the second third of the twentieth century, all the rhythms of traditional man, formerly bound up with religious belief, collapsed and made way for the unknown. Even the old dominances, foreign or indigenous, classical imperialism or feudalism, against which one had strained so long, collapsed also, leaving one face to face with exhausting responsibilities. A paradoxical challenge! At the very time when the Arab peoples, their poets in their midst, began to gain their freedom, or at least a relatively free approach to their history, the East was revealed as a world in ashes, pulverized, like that wasteland T. S. Eliot had described forty years after Nietzsche had proclaimed that "God was dead."

T. S. Eliot made his appearance in the East at the same time as Frazer, in whom the Arabs sought particularly the story of Tammūz. Eliot's *Waste Land*, of which Jabrā, Tawfīq Ṣāʾigh, and others had already published fragments, was for the first time translated in its entirety and published in 1960 by Adonis and Yūsuf al-Khāl.[20] The translation of Frazer's Volume IV, done between 1945 and 1946 by Jabrā but refused publication by Cairo and Baghdad officials as offensive to public morals, circulated in manuscript until Buland al-Ḥaydarī published the essential passages in the sole issue of his magazine *Al-Fuṣūl al-Arbāʿa* (1954); that is when Sayyāb read it for the first time. A complete edition, with cover illustration by Jawād Salīm, appeared in Beirut in 1957 and was very widely distributed.

As we see, God's death and his springtime resurrection became accessible to Arab readers at the same time as the revolution in poetic meters. On the latter, Nāzik al-Malāʾika published a well-informed book, but one in which she apparently sought, if not to reverse that revolution, at least to circumscribe it.[21] Her cholera ode, for which the inspiration came to her one fine day in 1947, broke with rhyme and with the combination among different meters characteristic of the old masters, but not with prosody. In fact, she used a uniform foot, recurring in sequences of unequal length throughout the text.[22] Her book was the most severe toward those, at Beirut particularly, who transgressed these bounds and seemed to her to introduce something unacceptable both in rhythm and in word combinations. Political choice, cleavages already noticeable between nationalism and progressivism, and a reaction against mythological inspiration among many of these poets all contributed to such reticences.

Free verse became a fashion in Egypt also, linked to modernist and progressive attitudes, although the established prosody still had aggressive partisans among conservatives. Thus, in 1964 an Egyptian association protested against the allegedly allogenous character of the new rhythms and the themes of inspiration. This declaration, which does no honor to its authors, forgot that even a classicism may be politically uncomfortable: witness the opposition poetry of Khamīsī. But it correctly underscored the cleavage that a change of style renders respectable within a continuity.

Thematic Values I

The theme of Eliot's poem was that of history and the mechanism of time, in which was mingled, according to an English critic, "the desire for cosmic and personal salvation. Never has a poem demonstrated a more profound sense of the past's pressure on the present, and its existence in the present."[23] These young Arab poets similarly confronted past, present, and future, now freed from their lockstep succession and rivals for possession of individual and society. *Al-zamān al-saḥīq*, "scrambled time," says Khalīl Ḥāwī; *al-zamān al-maṣlūb*, "crucified time," says ʿAfīfī Maṭar; *al-zamān al-maksūr*, "shattered time," says Adonis, and also "little," *ṣaghīr*, time; *al-zamān al-kasīḥ*, "emaciated, extenuated time," says Michel Hayek; *al-zamān al-mahjūr*, "abandoned time," says Fītūrī; *al-zamān al-jarīḥ*, "wounded time," says ʿAbd al-Ṣabūr. Many other formulae could be cited marking a sort of "detemporality" which, paradoxically, seized Arab poets at the moment their peoples thought they were regaining possession of history. But this may be only seemingly a paradox. What is history, if not such a challenge of precedents, an unveiling of possibilities, and this recourse to the seedbeds of human action: those, precisely, evoked by the Tammūz myth?

During the 1950s, indeed, several of these poets transposed into their own modes the disillusioned observation that "God was dead" and that the universe was in process of losing its meaning.[24] But the *Shiʿr* magazine group in Beirut did not stop at the death of their gods. The latter is merely seasonal, and spring will become verdant again like the body of Osiris or Tammūz. In *Al-Farāgh*, "The void" (1954), Adonis gave the first poetic formulation of this myth. Meanwhile, Khalīl Ḥāwī spoke of the desperate wandering of a sailor "in whose eyes the lighthouses along the way had died." A very different sailor from the gallant Ulysses whom ʿAlī Maḥmūd Ṭaha was still evoking only a few years before! However, Ḥāwī's sailor, after unsuccessfully consulting the dervish of the Ganges and despairing of the East as of the West, is not frozen forever in the ice. After the freeze, *ma baʿd al-jalīd*, there will still be new germinations. They will go deep for, as Yūsuf al-Khāl says, "the secret holds its wake in the roots." And Adonis' *Mihyār le Damascène* (1961), which speaks also of the dead God, ends by entrusting to words "the sob of an age to come." Similarly, Sayyāb's Christ will be reborn among Jikūr's verdures: "My heart is water. My heart is the awn of grain. It dies to be reborn, it relives in whosoever bites into the loaves round as life's breasts." Hope, therefore, but implying a preliminary death. It is easy to understand why the proponents of the triumphalism exhibited at the time by certain Arab regimes judged these poets harshly and accused them at best of being politically lukewarm.

At the same time, among some of them there was a committed optimism that echoed the combative energies evinced at the time by Arabism. Since then, the 1967 disaster and the ensuing perplexities have lent to current statements an accent at once more bitter and more energetic (Maḥmūd Darwīsh, Qāsim Ḥaddād, Amal Dunqul, Samīḥ al-Qāsim, etc.), while formal experiments, no less than excursions of inspiration, continue to express a closer and closer dialog with the rest of the world. Largely inspired from abroad, this poetry seeks no longer to address fellow tribesmen, but the foreigner, and is furthermore beginning to be translated. It thus enters into an intercultural discussion typical of our time. Like technical accomplishment and social struggle, it is one way for the Arabs to discover the world within themselves and affirm themselves before the world. This critical access to historicity does not, of course, exclude themes that have always existed: the beauty of creatures and landscapes, desire, love; few are the poets who do not share in these enthusiasms. Some have renewed the genre. Nizār Qabbānī is teaching his immense public new languages of tenderness and sensuality. In restoring the feminine person he counts for more than the many female poets, among them quite estimable ones, such as Nāzik and Lamīʿa already mentioned, Fadwa Ṭūqān, and others. Nizār's heroine is like a Van Dongen nude: laden with symbols of the good society. Other visions, sensualities, and questionings seek in the loved one's body synonymities with the occupied homeland (Manāṣira), or the approach of an absolute form analogous to that of the Word (Adonis). Or else, by an opposite process, in conformity with an ancient poetic tradition, terrestrial beauty is called upon to furnish signs to evoke the divine. The lofty idealism of certain talents, few in number but highly influential (Michel Hayek, Kamāl Jumblāṭ), thus serves as counterpart to the historicizing immanentism claiming kinship with mystics like Niffari (Adonis), Ḥallāj (ʿAbd al-Ṣabūr), Ibn ʿArabi (Bayātī), the "wandering dervish" (Fītūrī). After myths were destroyed, myths are being created anew.

Among inspiring themes there are naturally those that Arab poetry has always drawn from its own identity, stubbornly returning to its initial discourse. Fītūrī says that his first aesthetic enthusiasms were aroused by ʿAntar's *Muʿallaqa*. Manāṣira imitates that of Imrū᾽ al-Qays. A poem by Tawfīq al-Ṣā᾽igh begins like that of Shanfara. Sayyāb so admired Dhū al-Rumma that he gave his own son the first name of Ghaylān. Adonis published an anthology of classical poems, the appearance of which was rightly regarded as a literary event and, strictly speaking, a repatriation.[25] Many authors are taking up in their own writings the evocation of an abandoned camp, *aṭlāl*. Jawāhirī: "O comrade! is life but imaginary, or a fabric begun over again on the loom? / Sixty have passed by, weighty, stooped like camels / too heavily laden / or else dissolved in images as in a saga / the heroes . . . / O comrade! The vestiges rise up, for we are but absence and evanescence!"[26] ʿAbd al-Ṣabūr: "Vestiges, vestiges, oblivion walks over all, a shroud in his hand as the sole sepulchral memory, and among these sepulchers my own. . . . Vestiges, vestiges, end of all hopes. I walk toward the sun, and the sun is at my back."[27] Nāzik devotes to these proud vestiges a poem in the *ḥamāsa* tradition,[28] while in a more bitter vein Qāsim Ḥaddād, in a parody of the great *Muʿallaqa*, rejects the exhortation to halt and weep: "Halt? Nay! Friend, therein is no success, and to stop would kill us, the tear would put us to death. Arise, let us laugh!"[29] Even one of Adonis' latest poems, *Qabr li-ajli New York*, "Tomb for New York," seeks the same commemoration in highly elaborate fashion: "On the mossiest side of the universal rock I remember a slope I call life or a country, or death in a country, this wind hardened like a sail, that countenance murderous of play, those eyes that banish light."[30] This "hardened wind," by the way, is the same as the "flapping of a tattered sail" evoked fifteen centuries ago by Imrū᾽ al-Qays. So true it is that the persistence in poetry of a theme is simply poetic invariance, itself closely related to a certain image or association of words.

Thematic Values II

But references to contemporary reality can be made more direct and concrete. Thematic analysis of the works of Adonis, Ḥāwī, or ʿAbd al-Ṣabūr, among others, would point out things that scientific investigation of these societies discovers only rarely with equal relevance, and never so tensely concentrated: the break with traditional man, disintegration of the former groupings, accelerated but nostalgic urbanization, "quest for roots,"[31] insistance upon identity, bitterness tempered by adherence to new credos, and so on. Politics, history, and society are in fact revealed in this poetry precisely because of what goes beyond them. *Realia*, beyond any doubt, but on condition that they be transfigured.

Historical analysis would thus result in reduction if it separated out from this poetry all that does not refer to specific time or place but is a dynamic linkage with a reality in which the poet participates and upon which he acts. Similarly straying beyond the documentary is that contrast between village and city which several sing of: Bayātī, Saʿdī Yūsuf, ʿAbd al-Ṣabūr, Sayyāb, nostalgic friends of the village and those, usually the same ones, who express their emotion at what sociologists now describe under the name of urbanization. Thus Bayātī: "The city's abysses / spew the dead onto the dusty sidewalks, still warm / in the arms of night / consumptive night / . . . Like a black she-cat / the city's abysses / suckle the living at a maternal breast . . ."[32] And Sayyāb: "The city's streets surround me / with cords of clay that gnaw my heart / and change its embers to clay / with cords of flame whipping the miserable, naked fields / burning Jikūr deep in my heart sowing ashes of hate."[33] It is the same with al-ʿAdwānī, a great, if unpublished, Kuwaiti poet, who sings the nomad's sorrow at the city which now occupies his open spaces of yesterday, *maʿkūsa al-ṣuwar*, "with inverted images."

It is no accident that expression of unease—for which Asʿad Razzūq has found among *al-Shiʿr*'s contributors some fifty synonyms and paronyms[34]—pervaded the output of the 1950s. Refusal in the face of poverty, injustice, pain, and atony (to borrow Baudelaire's term) marks a choice not only aesthetic but also existential, even political. *Lan*, "Not . . ": such was the title of a collection by Unsī al-Ḥājj. The Syrian Khālid al-Barādiʿī: "Wine, blood, smoke. Eyes seeking their pasture. Here there is nothing, nothing yonder." And the Iraqi Buland al-Ḥaydarī, under the meaningful title "Journey of Zero Figures," expresses his suffocation: ". . . I feel / that I shall choke / as if I had swallowed our entire earth: its airs / its seas / and that in its veins there remain only my own / to be burned."[35] One may well be surprised that the critic Maḥmūd al-ʿĀlim, just released from prison, reproached his compatriot ʿAbd al-Ṣabūr for writing melancholy poems in a socialist state! But the reproach was based on a misunderstanding: that of the objectivity and commitment demanded of the artist, justly, as long as he expresses them in his own way, according to his own creative logic.

Even if they reject their era, in fact, the poets live it profoundly. They lavish their commitment, while not always providing it a content limited as to regime or party. In their view, history takes shape only beyond those anthropological foothills where language confronts event and fate in the struggle between one power and another. The important thing is that most of these poets react, if not always against allegiances per se, against parasitism upon princes, to which their immediate predecessors still resigned themselves, and are generally found on the side of those struggling for freedom.

The thrill of Tawfīq Ziyyād's ode to the Paris Commune will be appreciated.[36] One may be shaken by the wild energy of Qāsim Ḥaddād singing the emigration of the revolutionary movement from the "treasonous cities." Or we may share the ashen nostalgia of Rabīʿa bin al-Mukaddam, whom Sulaymān Āl Aḥmad depicts marching toward his final battle: "All 'round the knight, like troops of pilgrims, the legends prowled . . ." Adonis' "Book of Metamorphoses" (1965) was commented upon as a "return" to the past. Its first part was devoted to extolling the Umayyad ʿAbd al-Raḥmān al-Dakhīl, the "Falcon of Quraysh."[37] Pursued by his intended murderers, the hero throws himself into the Euphrates and crosses it as if undergoing an expiatory trial, then goes far to the west, toward Andalusian Hesperides. History, we see, has changed into myth by the same alchemy that makes a rose emerge from misery, new life from dead ashes, a poem from silence. Thus might be achieved the reconciliation of historical time, quest for the absolute, and verbal creation.

The same ambitions stand out, with more or less breadth and success, and with more or fewer of those correspondences I dare to call intersectory, in all the poetry inspired by the resistance. Thus, for example, Salāḥ Kherfī and Mufdī Zakaria, and still more among the Palestinians. In the case of the latter, from rather naïve beginnings,[38] through the unfolding of the 1960s with Maḥmūd Darwīsh or Samīḥ al-Qāsim among others, the genre's evolution has registered significant intersections among historical context, ideological debate, the verbal message, and its social effects. But within this perpetual renewal the echo of the old invariances never ceases to resound. One of these poets rewrites the "Song of Songs." Two others exchange variations on the thousand-year-old *qifā nabki*: "Halt, let us weep over the traces of those who have departed. The house weeps for its builder, who has gone. . . . Say not: would we were a river, that we might reach it! Nor say: we are in the homeland's flesh, for it is within ourselves. . . ."[39]

These invariances have nevertheless emerged from the shroud of simple continuation. The thing that sets them apart from the old *ḥamāsa*, in which they were mired only fifteen years ago and which bears the same relation to today's Palestinian poetry as Rostand to Eluard, is the will to restore to the word, too long tamed, its power to destroy and also to rebuild.

So! . . .
My country is a pair of golden earrings
Swinging from earth's orb.
Yes, O woman, you whose thighs
Were opened by the western winds,
You, you are the oars of the boat,
The prodigal child.
Will you return and cast off our miseries,
Will you arise and relieve me of my burdens,
Will you become, like others, a true nation? [40]

XV
Poem, Language, and Society

Analysis of poetry cannot stop short at its "content," no matter how completely the latter may be dissociated from its words. Current research is hunting in other directions for the characteristics of this type of language: integration of "form-meaning," emphasis upon "paradigmatic" aspects, recurrences or at least internal regularities in signifiers, and so on. It would be tempting to explore Arab poetry from this viewpoint, as it has been excluded from this sort of inquiry by the Orientalists' customary methods.

Three Poets Speak

Let us first, however, read three poems, chosen from among the most significant in the past decade's output.

The first, by a politically committed young Egyptian, Amal Dunqul, is nevertheless entitled:

EMIGRATION TO THE INTERIOR

I leave everything in its place:
The book, the time bomb,
The hot cup of coffee,
The medicine chest,
And the record still singing its song,
The open-mouthed door,
. . . the door, and the emerald eyes of the cat.

I leave everything in its place.
And I cross the crowded streets,
Leave behind the crowded market,
          The red fountain,
          The great monument of stone.
I go off to the desert!

I turn into a dog, my paws bleeding
As I scrabble and scrabble until I find the corpse,
        Until I bite into the death that sullies the earth.
I press my avid, fevered face into the dark hole,
And the hole tightens, like a silent trumpet, around my
  downward-pressing mouth.
Deep in the womb of earth I scream . . .
        I cry: O magic carpet of the defeated city
Do not slip from beneath my feet
        Or all things will fall
From their quiet shelves in the cupboard of history.
        Great names, great events will fall.
I cry . . . but no sound carries.
No answer comes except the sweat of the earth,
        Except death and silence.
A violent humming surrounds my head,
        A humming which violently rocks the air,
And, upright, I fall down,
        Afraid
That the echo may carry my calls
        To the air above the rooftops,
That the sounds will betray my exalted voice,
        My suppressed voice!

I weep until my tears flood the dark hole,
I weep until my fury is calmed.
I weep until my words are fixed in the memory of this earth.
Then I return, but I am lost.
        I follow the barbed wire, the accumulated blood,
        The recently shed blood,
Searching for the city I left behind,
        But I cannot see it.
I search for my city!

Ah, Iram of great pillars,
Ah, Iram,
O you nation of villains and noble men,
Give me back the page of the book,
And the cup of coffee and my moment of peace.

My voice echoes
        Like a worn record.
Ah, Iram of great pillars,

Ah, Iram,
Give him back the reins of his horse
And the books of dawn
 And some bread
 For his knapsack.
For his heart, split in two,
Lies within the lotus flower, in exile,
 Looking toward his destiny,
Waiting until the cup boils
 In his hand,
Wrapping his body in a turncoat garment
Amid the beating of hearts.

The year below zero, that year arrived empty-handed
While we lay asleep in the consciousness of the past.
That year knocked at the door, and called to us shyly.
We turned over in our warm beds,
 Adjusted the covers,
And left our chance outside, in the cold blowing wind.

I was in the coffee shop
When the parrot broadcast the news
 To the rats in the wheat fields.[1]

History's ill fortune does not always leave the poet alone with the city and his desert. The Palestinian Maḥmūd Darwīsh experiences it within a couple's love, itself evocative of the entire universe.

THE BEAUTIFUL WOMAN OF SODOM

On your body
Death
Takes the form of forgiveness.
I wish I could die
In this ecstasy, O my apple!
My broken-hearted woman,
I wish I could die
Outside the world . . . in a tempest beneath the earth.

(For the one I love has two faces,
A face outside this being
And a face inside ancient Sodom.

And I am between them,
Searching for the face of truth.)

In your eyes
The silence
Brings me to the edge of intoxication.
I'm in the prime of my youth,
But I've seen that silence,
            And the skull that drinks coffee.
I know the disease and the end,
            But . . . you are so beautiful!

I am spread upon your body
Like grains of wheat,
Like the reasons for my staying and departing,
I, who know the earth is my mother,
And that on your body my lust will soon be slaked.
But I know, too, that love is one thing,
And what joins us tonight is something else.
Neither of us believes in the impossible;
We each desire another, far-away lover,
And, behind the façade, would destroy each other.

(The one I desire
Is as beautiful as the meeting of dream and reality,
The sun that meets the sea
In flaming garments of orange.
The one my body desires
Is as beautiful
As the meeting of today and yesterday,
The sun that meets the sea
Behind a veil of mist.)

We never spoke of this love
That is dying.
We did not speak of that.
Yet we are dying now.
Now. Music and silence.
Why? We are withering
Like memories.
Neither of us asked: Who are you?
Where did you come from?
We were both at Ḥiṭṭīn
When the days grew bored with seeing the living
Dead.

Where are my flowers?
I want to fill my house with lilies.
Where are my poems?
I want to hear the murderous music of knives
Give birth to a lover.
And I want to forget you
So death will leave me a little.
Beware! Beware of the death
Unlike the death
That surprised my mother.

(For the one I love has two faces,
A face outside this being
And a face inside ancient Sodom.
And I am between them,
Searching for the face of truth.)[2]

For Sargon Boulos, an Iraqi from Mosul, whose mother tongue is Syriac,[3] poetic expression is, properly speaking, a second language. In the following poem, published in *Al-Shiʿr* magazine, he takes up the biblical theme of Abishag, the girl who was placed in the aging David's bed but was unable to revive his passion: pessimistic symbol of the world's decrepitude and the loss of meanings.

FEAST OF ICE

The sunshine in the shrines is a feast for ice.
Isfahan is dying on the roads without end.
In the streets the harlots wear gowns of snow
Under their heavy fur coats.
King David's mustache trembles with cold,
The elders and priests around him
In the chamber, with its sacks of withered roses.
King David is dying, drowning in the ice!
They have brought him a virgin with warm breasts,
Lithe and beautiful, summer in her limbs,
But the King is cold.

She raises her arms like two boughs of spring
Above the arc of her vibrant body,
But the King is cold.
His eyes are blank, two glass beads,
Two pieces of stone.

Wrapped in rugs, the King huddles in his bed.
On the second day, the hands of the clock cracked.
The specter of death unsheathed his dagger,
And Adonijah came to the King his father.
"I shall inherit the kingdom," he cried to the priests,
To the horsemen waiting on iron crackling with frost.
The King dying in the chill of the ice,
Though the virgin with warm breasts stands before him.
On the second day Adonijah destroys the King's empty tower,
Adonijah, younger brother of Absalom.
His horsemen watch the palace and wait,
Sustained by the laughing fires of youth,
Fires which destroyed the prophecies.

O David, King, what your hands once gathered they now scatter.
They degrade the holy prayers, the sacred idols of gold.
They do not recognize the nobility of death's presence.
King David's mustache trembles with cold
And Isfahan is dying on the roads without end.
In our lands, the people, too, scatter as the ice descends.
They see the specter of death before them
And hurl themselves helplessly into the cold.
Is there no virgin, noble, lithe limbed,
The sunlight of innocence and childhood in her eyes,
Who can free us from this sin?

For the harlots in the streets are wearing gowns of snow
Under their heavy fur coats.
And the sunshine in the shrines is a feast for ice.
Passing through the window panes, it is exhausted, extinguished
And dies on the road without end.[4]

Poetic Configuration, Old and New

Now that we have read—heard?—these three poems, or at least what translation can render of them, let us try to analyze wherein they depart from traditional craftsmanship. The gap appears so wide that, for both poet and audience, it produces the effect of a revolution, some would say of a denial.

Certain contemporary studies apply themselves with a growing and at times tedious technicality to defining that text *par excellence* that is a poem.[5] They throw into relief the role played by repetition

Level	Traditional	New poetry
Sociological	Poet is herald or censor of his group; tone of dialog, or discussion, interspersed with individual outpouring of sentiment	Poet isolated or in minority status, irrelevant to his society and to society in general, negativity, at least as a preliminary
Morphological	An indefinite series of monostichs of which each one is assumed sufficient unto itself	Poem tends toward "organic unity" and presents itself as a whole, as event or object
Signifier	Observance of pre-established meters, rhyme obligatory	Freed from meter and rhyme, the poem stresses other regularities
Signified	Information content plays a deliberate, essential role in the effect	Information obliterated for the benefit of other effects of a semiotic order

of sounds and meanings, syntactical arrangements, a multiplicity of planes endlessly intersecting or disjoined, the axial displacement which turns a becoming with objective referents (cf. any "natural" prose) into a model with unlimited suggestive capability: hence the role assumed by invariances. When the poet of the past invoked the muse or his own inspiration (*layta shiʿrī*, "oh, that my poem . . ."), or in our day when he implies the presence of an on-looker, whether the ideal, fate, God, or it might also be history or nature, he is simply relating his utterance to paradigms from which it derives some of their virtue as models. In any event a paradigm of a quite different nature is necessarily involved: the language system, which the poem therefore illustrates with murderous vigor.

If that is where the distinctive quality of poetic utterance lies, resort to approved meters then appears simply as one possible form of regularities of the signifier. Other forms may be equally efficacious, or more so. Another consequence is that the poem, of which the intimate complexity is thus exhibited for the first time in intelligible fashion, is governed more by semiotics than semantics. Or, rather, it makes meaningful the most diverse arrangements—phonic, distributive, grammatical, and so forth—without the intermediary of an information content. One might say that everything in it becomes meaning, did the use of this term not itself risk confusion. One thing is certain: the prolonged effect it produces. To call it "mysterious" or "inexplicable" is to evade the problem. Reducing it to coincidence between meaning and form, a dualistic and ultimately Platonian concept, although bearing Saussure's authority, no longer holds up under the rigorous analyses it is now possible to make of what H. Meschonnic calls "form-meaning." But is it even a question of meaning? Let us note simply that the poem exerts a thrust. It acts upon the most concrete element of the collective psyche. Now is that not where it draws its inspiration? But to act upon this internal becoming it must cut itself off from the flow that has nourished it. Its condensation and crystallization thus reflect the distance that separates it from types of utterance which merely represent the world and history, whereas the poem signifies them, "modelizes"[6] them. Beyond doubt, it acts because of the very rigor of its compulsion.

Important consequences may ensue from these views in the field of Arab poetry. Curiously, as they aspire to reduce the poetic effect to certain traits amenable to analysis, they narrow the gap between the traditional and the new form. As between Shawqī and Sayyāb there may well be but a single poetry, even if procedures have changed radically from one to the other. Abandonment of traditional meters and rhyme, the subject of the controversy, may in fact have been compensated for by other linguistic regularities sharing no less than they in the poetic vocation. There remains the outrage constituted by deserting a millenary canon. This takes its place among many other ruptures experienced by Arab man over less than a generation. From this point of view there has indeed been an effraction, and a serious one.

A Procedural Change

In this way stylistic innovation manifests both its autonomy and its homology with respect to social history. Whether this dual aspect is perceived explicitly or only inchoately, its emergence, characteristic of our times, has brought about both the elimination of the old "occasional" verse, or *munāsabāt*, and the development of a poetry intended to be not only history's interpreter but its agent as well.[7]

The procedural change under which I subsume a large share of the innovation, while implying no substitution of kind in poetry, has nevertheless had decisive consequences for its components. It is hardly surprising that the attention of both public and writers has been polarized on this aspect, and attributes the phenomenon to a change not of procedure but of kind. For example, one striking feature of any Arabic writing is its lexicographic tenor. Now as between traditional and new poetry a variation of degree and function has occurred in this field. The accusation of obscurity so often directed against contemporary poetry is generally met by pointing to the limited range of its vocabulary. If obscurity exists, it therefore results from the brusque succession of sentences, associations, and word combinations, or from a deliberate ambiguity, but not from the difficulty of words, and this is symmetrically inverse to the old poetry.

Listen to this description of the traditional process by a Sudanese critic, himself a classicizing poet: "When the poet composes, he cannot help feeling in his breast a rumbling which he either represses or allows to rise and resound upon his lips, or else perhaps a groan or a warble. In either outpouring or retention, as soon as he begins to place words in order, he cannot help putting one of these words in relief at the beginning or the end of the hemistich, thereby endowing it with a special resonance."[8] *To versify is thus to impose upon this "rumbling"—doubtless related to the group subconscious—constraint and order. Both place in operation a traditional rhythmic code offering a sure guarantee of collective effects, rather than proceeding from the author's own choices.*

Even today the informed amateur, and even more so popular audiences, attach to each one of the various meters its own suggestion.[9] *The* madīd, *for example, implies violence, wildness of some sort. It preserves an echo of the beat of war drums. On the contrary,* khafīf *breathes finesse, subtlety, dare I say transcendence? In any case it is the meter of Būṣīrī's celebrated* Ḥamziya. *Although it has become outmoded, the mystic genre still uses it today. The "lustful" meters,* shahwāniya, *arouse the emotions powerfully at drinking or gambling sessions. The* ramal *evokes melancholy. The* kāmil, *which resounds so magnificently in Shawqī's poems, is an extroverted meter, one might say, that of the grammatical* shawāhid, *of bravura pieces, and of any sort of vehemence. These notations, which I am again borrowing from ʿAbdullah al-Ṭayyib, of course represent only a part of the differentiated scale of collective emotions to which the fifteen or sixteen traditional meters correspond with an almost unimaginable exactitude.*

This code is extremely complex and difficult. One could not explain the possibility of a classical versification without a mutual appropriation of this code and the language, both in the individual's psyche and the tribe's. Hence the communal nature of a craftsmanship that places in operation actively or passively orderings atavistically bound to correspondences between the language and collective behavior: how can we be surprised that part of Khalīl's terminology is anthropomorphic?

This operation, unbelievably complex, implies that the poet, as he builds sequences, hemistichs, and lines, performs a sort of scanning of all the synonymic possibilities the language makes available to him so as to select the one that fits exactly into the chosen grid. Where he resorts to dialectal, rare, or anomalous terms (*gharīb*) it is not mere adornment: it is a practical corollary of applying the code. That is why the critic just cited looks askance at the abandonment of classical meters and the impoverishment of lexicographical knowledge among today's poets. At the same time he notes discerningly that liberation with respect to prosody often leads the poet into other complexities.[10] What he does not say is that this trend to opaqueness is functional. Poetry must always, in some way, keep its distance from prosaic information. The old did so through metrical complexity and wealth of vocabulary. Otherwise the language, whose structure is virtually mathematical, would sink into banality and redundancy: which, indeed, it does not always avoid. The new poetry endeavors to avoid this danger by a tighter adjustment of the internal elements of creativity, and by the violence of word combination. The same effect achieved by other means!

There seems thus to have been in this field, as in other domains of life in these societies, destruction followed by reconstruction, and substitution of features compensating for those eliminated in the operation of a given collective function. A process analogous, as we see, to that of Arab societies taken as a whole.

Demand for "Organic Unity"

What advantage do the poets who have embraced free verse since 1950 claim to find in it? First, enhanced communicative ability, at a time when socialism and existentialism, paradoxically conjoined, were arousing the intelligentsia and demanding that Arabic render so many "new thoughts." Increasingly free techniques furthermore lent themselves better to conveying the meanderings of inspiration than did the repetitive isomorphy from line to line that the old prosody favored. Thus we saw emerging the long phrasing, à la Fadwa Ṭūqān or Sayyāb, the vehemences hacked to bits to the point of oxymoron as in Samīḥ al-Qāsim and many others, stanzas producing many-leveled but subtly cumulative effects in Adonis, and so on. But the essential progress consisted in achieving the poem's *waḥda ʿuḍwiya*, or organic unity.[11]

Although traditional poetry had long been expressed in the form of texts, it rarely subjected them to a unitary logic. Most frequently it offered more or less extensive fragments of what I would call less a poetry than an uninterrupted poetic utterance remaining close to its sources and to its collective destination.[12] This situation exhibited both strengths and weaknesses. These latter seem less tolerable since confrontation with the foreigner and the exigencies of access to the industrial world have introduced a more exacting awareness of the text as a unit. What is more, the effect the traditional style was calculated to produce through observance of an atavistically socialized code could henceforth be expected only from a denser construction. Now such internal arrangements presuppose the presence of a contour. Conversely, the more-detailed regulation of recurrences of sound and meaning imposes an undulatory structure on the new poem favorable to its creation as a unit.

Outlines for Textual Analysis

Insistence upon internal symmetries and on the overall contour in fact characterizes most of the new works. The *qaṣīda* (but should it still be called by that name?) closes sometimes by folding back on itself and repeating the opening formula, sometimes by projecting a sort of tangent: such as a verb evoking, purely and simply, uncompleted action—for example, *yaẓall*, "he remains there . . ." This is what Nāzik calls, a little maliciously, *uslūb yaẓall*, "*yaẓall* technique."[13] Thus Sayyāb in his "Grave Digger." But in this case, conclusion on the unfinished simply reinforces the escape from the present moment and the appeal to the paradigm, as other features in the body of the poem had done. Abandonment of meter necessitated this device, or others of a similar sort, as its replacement.

Nāzik quite rightly underscores the development of iteration, *takrār*, that has occurred in the new poetry.[14] She distinguishes three kinds, according to whether it is intended to serve a rhetorical end, *bayānī*, a distributive one, *taqsīm*, or even a "subconscious" one, *lā shu'ūrī*. Whatever one may think of this distinction, she at least points out how frequently the device is used, sometimes felicitously, sometimes lapsing into artificiality. Thus the *lā shay'* repeated ten times or so in one piece in 'Abd al-Ṣabūr's "Night thoughts," *Ta'ammulāt Layliya*. Thus the somewhat bathetic "forget me not" that recurs obsessively in the poem Sayyāb wrote in his hospital bed. Let us not, however, subscribe to the intellectualist criterion some would like to impose on iteration, according to which it would be permissible if intended to evoke monotony, but otherwise illegitimate. This would be falling back into the dualism of form and content from which poetics was so long in freeing itself.

Iteration is not the only feature of this reassembly of poetic speech which, in the end, free verse constitutes. The internal divisions within the text also contribute to it. As there is no question of having to obey a logic of narrative or thought, they revert to their appropriate role, dimly perceived by the old rhetoric under the name of "accumulation." Thus, in Bayātī's "Old Market Place," a simple enumeration of objects, among them an old pair of military boots, takes on poetic value. These parataxes—to call them by their right name, whether or not they use the coordinating conjunction *wa*, which always retains at least something of its old exclamatory value—admit of ascending, descending, or alternating movements. The incoherence of these sequences may be real. But it can also be merely apparent. In the latter case it indicates, within the syntagmic progression, that vertical plurality, so to speak, of planes that constitutes poetic speech. Here and there an image or a sound serves as a "trigger," or as a shifter (to talk like American linguists), that is, in practice, as a sudden link between one plane and another. Today the poet uses such effects without the inhibition formerly imposed by tradition, an ideal of information, or simply human respect. There is nothing new in the procedure itself. It has simply become more widespread.

As we have seen, there is liberated versification when the text substitutes, for the traditional meter's automatisms, more-demanding requirements coming to closer grips with what might be called poeticizing the language. This poeticization is no longer simply equivalent to adopting a metrical canon and adding on ornaments[15] —two conditions, it had long been supposed, that produced poetry *ex opere operato* when applied to common language. Whether instinctively or deliberately, moreover, the new technique, far from repudiating these two conditions, follows them in their deepest exaction. The requirement of meter and rhyme is, after all, merely that of phonic regularity. The new speech, as we have seen, also imposes such regularities on itself and has even multiplied them. As for "ornament," *zakhrafa*, this is a very compromising term to apply to the figurative or metaphorical aspect of poetic language, with which the new poem, far from freeing itself therefrom, tends to identify itself.

This is the more true since recourse to iteration and accumulation, coinciding with breaks in rhythm, imposes also a reduction of the number of images. To the breathless haste of typographically isolated syntagms corresponds a predilection for *suwar*, "forms, images," or also "silhouettes."

This word serves as the subtitle of one of Khālid al-Barādiʿī's collections.[16] *Hear, for example, the hero Durayd express himself in miscellaneous syntagms: "My saber is a pomegranate flower, why should I permit life to become base, as long as a caravan song assuages exile's burning, the horses' slenderness is silhouetted against the light, and heroes' histories flow from pillars with branching plinths." And Nāzik al-Malāʾika, in her "Ode to the Moon," sees in that heavenly body by turn a glass of iced milk, a rill bearing seashells along in its current, a white shadow on night's cheek, a box filled with colored perfumes, a fragrant lily, a flower's kisses . . . "O hiding place for beauty, lips for the light that descends and caresses the faces of tender bowers, O lovers' barque through heroes in dreams and in idleness, O springs, O fingers, O isles . . ."*[17]*—and that goes on for pages and pages. Ḥasab al-Shaikh Jaʿfar, in describing a love scene in a garden, uses intersecting planes and the most unexpected word combinations. "Her breasts pant like tired horses drawing the carriage's traces. . . . I drew the veil from her brow, and when I had embraced her I closed my arms again around dust. O prophetess of a stony eternity, O time's spider, you have lifted from my sight the smoky veils. . . . Are you the dusty one beneath my fingers? Are you a broken glass, a blue glass, I was for centuries in the depth of this night of clay, searching still in the years' dust. O debris of shattered glass, return as once you were."*[18]

By another of those compensations inherent in the history of an art form, intensification of metaphor in today's Arab poetry balances the loss of rhyme and meter. The image—in which I include onomatopoeia—is after all only a sensorial and sensual involvement with the external world. As denotation or connotation it had always characterized poetic language which, moreover, thereby simply intensifies and systematizes procedures of everyday language, such as the tropes that Dumarsais gathered from the speech of porters in Port-aux-Foins.[19] Whether the trope acts on the signifier or the signified, whether it appears as parabola, metaphor, comparison, catachresis, anacoluthon, paranomasis, or under some other barbarous name, its use now typifies poetic language so completely as to strip it even of differentiated procedures. In many respects we might see in the poem one giant trope of which each constituent element—words, concepts, locutions, sounds, sequences of all sorts—should be the subject of microanalysis, like the *phèmes* and *sèmes* that A. J. Greimas has so helpfully identified at the level of simpler semiotic units.[20] Yes, that is it: the poem has now become a giant trope and has asserted its autonomy. In so doing, it detaches itself from the collective subjectivity upon which the ancient poetry was supposed to act, and is tending to integrate itself objectively into a history, in the very proportion to which it rejects the binary naïveties of representation.[21]

Risk or Stake

Doubtless, supercharged figures of speech may lead toward a questionable excess, an affected incoherence, a new conformity. But what should be the criterion of such abuses? Why, for example, reproach ʿAfīfī Maṭar for writing "I see you 'neath the roasted storm cloud" or "I saw her through summer's fissures," as some critics have done? Quite some time ago André Breton, writing from a viewpoint still based on representation and analogy, expressed his preference for the greatest possible gap between two associated terms. But it is still necessary that there be a metaphor and not accidental discord or, worse, laborious illogic and inverted redundancy. Let us confess that it is sometimes risky to decide between hallucinating eccentricity and pure prattle, between art and self-complacency, facility or imposture. When poetry no longer clings to the guardrail of pseudodiscourse as the traditional versification of both West and East had previously done, it is exposed to refusal and doubt and assumes the risk of being considered (or even of being) mere glossolalia: and that, precisely, is the price of its new powers.

These powers and their price of absurdity are intensified at each phase in the renewal of an art. They cannot expect judgment to be reserved. More seriously, the art may inflict a contradiction upon itself, for example by pursuing at the same time the unitary delimitation of the work and its internal discontinuity. An ultimate homogeneity should coalesce these discordant series, harmonize these kyrielles. Does this always happen? The assertion would be overbold. Several of the greatest of these poets. Sayyāb for example, do not seem to have mastered their disparate series. Thus in the ode to Lorca: "In your heart shines / a fire that nourished the hungry / a water wells up from thy hell . . ."; the "liquid" image is followed up with "deluge," "rain," "spring," "river," "waves," but "knives budding the voluptuousness of fruits," "Christopher Columbus' sail," and "boats of a child who has torn up a book" restore no unity.[22] It is often this way with Sayyāb. An unfinished quality for which Adonis criticizes him.[23] In both life and text, Sayyāb is the interrupted poet. Of course, but what of Adonis himself? Listen to Ḥusain Muruwwé defining the style of Adonis' *Taḥawwulāt*: "Its language transmutes familiar meanings and lexical context, even the aesthetic effects expected in poetry and literature. It becomes dense symbols, suggestions in which the hidden is divorced from the ostensible. The modes of expression proceed from the kernel of the existential burden involved in this strange adventure. They find their coherence only in this kernel, internally, and from there they extend in both musical qualities and evocative forms." In aesthetizing terms one could not be more exact. But this admiring judgment cannot obscure the extent to which this manipulation of planes, parataxes, disparates, sudden junctions and disjunctions, this density and instability of enigma, disconcerts a public of which the majority remains faithful to the ancient taste. Once again, the revolutionary act has remained a minority one!

Social History and Poetics

It seems indispensable here to give a precise definition of some terms thus far employed somewhat indistinctly. In the process, the position of the "poem" in society may become clear, as well as the legitimacy of seeing a historical parameter in some aspects of its recent development. I shall be so bold as to reproach the investigations into poetical semiotics upon which, as has been seen, I have drawn for not being sufficiently sociological, in that they do not take adequately into account the poet's participation in the collective moment in which he is swept up and upon which he acts. A justified reaction against the historicism that dealt with the poem only as testimony has perhaps been followed by some exaggeration in dealing with it as a combinatory, however "objectal." For such an object cannot dispense with acting upon the listener.[24] What does this mean? That it produces an immediate or delayed effect upon the group. The poem's "significatum" is in our terms, as will be recalled, the thrust it produces, or will produce, in symmetry with the thrust from which it proceeds. Thus history and society converge, so to speak, both upstream and downstream from it, without in any way diminishing its specificity.

But what is this "it"? At this point in the discussion we should distinguish among several aspects that are too generally confused.

1. Poetry as a collective role arising from a certain relationship between human society and life, nature, and cosmos. This is what Hölderlin had in mind when he said that "man lives on earth poetically." Now language, particularly when it is a very ancient language like Arabic, records and systematizes this sort of relationships, furnishing a virtually unlimited keyboard for their expression.

2. Poetry as tradition, or the cumulative legacy of all that, within a given group, which has been felt as poem.[25] Here again, the notion of legacy, or *turāth*, so powerful in these societies, will reinforce an aspect of which our three centuries and a half of French poetry can give us only a rather vague idea.

3. Poetry as event. Active event, not a circumstance undergone! This is where modern poetry has introduced the greatest change. Not that it withdraws from the happening; quite the contrary, it impresses itself upon it. It seeks to make the poem an object entering into the march of things, just as, moreover, was the case with certain odes in the past. But those odes, in which the poet, with great verbal virtuosity, multiplied one by another effects drawn respectively from a specific poetics, the language system, and his own social role applied here and now, nevertheless neglected to integrate all that into an object which was to poetry as, according to Saussure, the word is to the language.

The contemporary Arab poet, on the contrary, is determined to break with (2), that is, with the traditional accumulation, the current practitioners of which he accuses, with some plausibility, of formalistic degeneracy and of neglecting (1), that is, the world's poetic quality. He himself proposes to endow the poem with a unity which will make of its message a thing among other things. Less "social," doubtless but more sociological.

Everything thus occurs at the level of the poem's creation, a dynamic junction between an upstream and a downstream, two infinities, in short, with regard to which the poem will be a point, respectively, of concentration and of radiation. That the poem is such a bifunctional prism is simply a metaphor, but it explains the process of this linguistic transformation. By contrast with prose, the master function of poetic discourse is neither to express nor to represent, which would assume a dualism and relative equivalence between signifier and signified. It is meaningful to the extent that it condenses, that is, eliminates. This negative role, which Julia Kristeva[26] saw especially at the inspiration level, is still more obvious at that of composition, and so demandingly that poetic expression seems at each moment like the throw of the dice that realizes a single possibility while destroying all others. Add the various linguistic reductions that draw the maximum effect from a minimum of material and, at the extreme, all from nothing. While all external data, in which society is to be found, act upon the poet only by way of an individual imagination, he thus causes them to converge, and transmutes them, bringing them to a density approaching exhaustion (Mallarmé's "purest meaning"). For the poem, this is an extension of one role of language: to construct rarity.[27] This process is integrated with the combinatory that—through unexpected combinations of signifier and signified, iteration, arrangement of sections, and so on—tends to make the poem a unitary and synchronous object: here again, "crystallization." However long it may be, indeed, a poem revolves in a recurring simultaneity, rather than unfolding over time. Furthermore, it is not told: it is retold, is memory. This is what the ancient Arab poetry illustrates by the name *dhikrā*. The oldest theme in Arab literature, that of *aṭlāl* (elegy on the vestiges of the abandoned camp), raises its own process to the level of inspiration by creating the poetic object out of the void. Whether the void results from a tribal emigration or from a poetic convention of rarefaction, the result will be the same: to make this vacuum the source of subsequent intensities.

Many of these intensities are not merely aesthetic and psychic, but social. Arab poets often play an effective role in the course of events. In this capacity they enjoy power taken quite seriously by political leaders. To some extent this poetic power might be defined as a plus-value produced by the poem as a transformer of collective energies. We may state that the effect it produces is of greater potential than those it undergoes from the environment. Should we go so far as to say that the agent of this plus-value, the poet, is the wage slave of his own word? One would think so, considering the price he pays: disappointment, misfortunes of a personal or public nature, prison, persecution, exile. Of this I could at this moment cite the most precise examples.

But here we face a contradiction because of the fact that this new poetry, like many other categories of the Arabs' collective activity, has not been drawn from within themselves but introduced on Western models. Even if it achieves success in some cases, even if its new combinations exploit the language more fully than the classics had, even if it translates more-complex experiences and may in the end reconstitute a secondary authenticity, the only one still possible in our time,[28] the historical conditions in which it is operating create for it an additional risk.

Its major risk is not the break with poetry in the sense of (1) and (2), above. It does not dissociate itself either in fact or by right from the upstream and downstream of collective emotion. The expansion, however hermetic, of this poetry is there to prove it, and also the "commitment" of all these poets which, although not always as simplistic as "social realism" would like and thus regarded with suspicion, is nonetheless generally active. Failure, for the Arab poet, would be to break with the language since, in his culture, that is what carries imperiously along, if it does not actually constitute, poetry in all the three senses distinguished above. He would lose the capability not so much to transmit information (this function being in this instance ancillary although, I believe, inevitable) as to exert his "thrust" in the short or long run. His poetry would no longer be "poetry for . . . ," but an utterance addressed to himself, which in the case of the Arabs would be unadulterated absurdity.

Poetry in Evolution of Language

Quite recently an avant-garde review in Baghdad,[29] proponent of the prose-poem, rejected in horror the imputation that it was tolerant of colloquial language. This position is understandable. Popular literature certainly constitutes a treasure, but of artisanship rather than art. Deliberate attempts at dialectal poetry are sometimes touching and charming, but could hardly go further. I think the reason is simple. If any poetry illustrates the language's system, one cannot weigh the system of such a great, inaugural, language as classical Arabic with that of such social derivatives as dialects. Contemporary Arab poetry must face up to other dangers than the vernacular's claim: first of all, that of going against the current not only of everyday language but also of written prose. Two divergent evolutions must in fact be distinguished on one and the other side.

Arabic prose constitutes the remarkable success of a median language, *al-ʿarabiya al-wusṭā*, which in a hundred years or so has demonstrated assimilative and transmissive capabilities on all levels of modernity. But this modernization has relaxed, rather than tightened up, linguistic structures. It has paraphrased rather than concentrated. While it has created many neologisms it has narrowed, not expanded, the lexical spectrum, and particularly it is by amplification and conformity, not by semantic progress, that it has attained its objectives, at the risk of multiplying stock phrases and clichés. Now poetry has followed an opposite path over the last two decades or so, at the price of a concentration and ambiguity that many object to. We have already come across that accusation. It is in large part tautological. Any message of which the axis is an aspect other than information is deemed obscure. But modern poetry will continue to be obscure, or rather opaque, not only because of its access to "new thoughts" but also because of its increased density and its unusual associations. If it explodes the "couplings," or *tarākīb*, that increasingly flood our day's favored communications—radio broadcast, newspaper article, political speech among others—that is additional proof of its subversive nature. It is also the foreshadow of a dangerous tension between itself and society's other modes of expression, including literary ones.

In any case, questions arise on all sides. Here is one of the boldest and best informed. It comes from a Syrian professor and poet, Sulaymān Āl Aḥmad.[30] *In the magazine published by the Syrian Writers Union he published "Prolegomenas on an Arabic Language," which deserves comment for purposes of our discussion. It is an article significant, if only because of its disorder, of the multiplicity of preoccupations that beset an Arab writer today. He observes that poetic language today still claims to be identical with that heard in the sixth and seventh centuries of the Christian era. This conventional immutability stems from a mythology that has positive, preserving, effects, but some negative ones as well. We must remember that this is a socialist speaking. Was this language of Shanfara and others, he asks, not already separated from the people? We can easily believe it: it was simply a poetic* koïnè, *separate by definition from everyday speech. But should one therefore demand that poetry speak colloquial language, simply on condition of subjecting it to rhythm and rhyme and ornamenting it with tropes? This definition by the old critics no longer holds up. As we now know, poetry is a separate language, even a separate linguistics. In any case, its social radiation among Arabs is such as to raise disquieting problems for partisans of communicability extending to the "people."*

Thereupon the author, in order to show how seriously the ancient legacy is already compromised by mythological excess, tries to show that the ancient language itself, that of the poets for example, teemed with inaccuracies. He judiciously points out a long series of grammatical and syntactical "errors" in some of the great authors: errors from which literary historians modestly avert their eyes. Whose responsibility? That of the philologists who, in Abbasid times, inventoried all the forms of the language as they found them, without the slightest critical selectivity. That is why today, as an amusing example, the comb used daily by a hundred million Arabs can be named in any of the following classical ways: mushṭ, mashṭ, mishṭ, mashiṭ, mashuṭ, mushuṭ, mushaṭṭa. *And let us not even mention the plural! Its range of possibilities is even more picturesque. Many words that display an equally extended scale could be cited. The classical language in this way becomes something both immutable and incoherent. A contradiction that must be exploded. But how?*

As always happens in this sort of essay, the positive part is weaker and also shorter than the criticism. Sulaymān Āl Aḥmad favors a simplification of the language, at least on the lexical and syntactical plane. But once the simplifications are made, how are they to be put into effect? By simple agreement among educated persons? Or academies? Or teachers? Would this not be a relapse into the same sort of mandarinate he objects to in the ancient language, and this time without the sanction of masterpieces and usage which are, after all, worthy of respect?

We shall leave the responsibility of arguing for this critique to its author, himself a poet and among the most viable ones. He is no doubt wrong in hoping for the establishment of a single linguistic and social common ground as between poetry and daily life. But he is right in condemning mythologies and false modesties. When elucidated, transformations become clandestine and incoherent. His somewhat blasphemous conclusion is to be taken seriously: "I fear," he says, "that in poetic language a series of these transformations is now taking place, as it is in physics, imperceptible, quantitative transformations that suddenly explode in a qualitative leap. I am afraid that one fine day we shall find that Arab poetry is being expressed in a language other than Arabic."

The Temptation of "Nonlanguage"

This may already have begun. The danger of a break with life is real. Certain poets believe they can avoid it by simplifying their discourse as much as possible. Nizār Qabbānī addresses himself to the average listener. Others aspire to being understood directly by the peasant and the laborer. But can one reject the classical structures without replacing them with others, more truly demanding?

As a matter of fact, the decadence of the "labor within language," which poetry is in many respects, stands out wherever the new product results not from a rearrangement of linguistic values but from facile workmanship. Vocabulary simplification may then no longer produce a compensatory tension in the signifier, but indicate impoverishment, pure and simple. That is, moreover, a general phenomenon revealing the spread of cosmopolitanism, and such languages as English, French, Castilian, and Italian are in no way exempt from it. But the phenomenon becomes particularly obnoxious in so-called literary Arabic, and still more in poetry, when it debases the vocabulary as well as diminishing it. Of the *Lisān*'s 120,000 words, which embrace only one-hundreth of the resources afforded by the full deployment of the roots, *ishtiqāq,* we would wager that contemporary expression does not enlist one-tenth. The monotony of vocabulary is further accentuated by the tiresome reiteration of certain words expressive of existential anxiety, or rather the knee-jerk reactions that are its symptom. As cross-check, resort to triviality does not rescue it from banality, and the effect of surprise is not always as great as the impropriety. Sayyāb himself may be quite right in using so many womb images, but wrong to impute a uterus, laden with an embryo, to himself, and to use *raḥim* in the masculine gender! Among other young poets the strength of the poem owes nothing to "my homeland raises her thighs," to the fact that dung, urine, and excrement occur so often, or that one asks the way to the restroom and finds the toilet bowls "stopped up by harlots' sanitary napkins."

These gross vulgarities constitute a poor excuse for an approach to what a "people's" language might be. That they are resorted to indicates much less a lusty realism than a systematic search for incongruity, and still more a reaction against the language's increasing banality. Banality, loss of meaning! The ravages of this sort of process, bound up with the evolution of industrial societies, are not limited to the Arab world. But there it gives rise to crueler contrasts with a phase, still recent, in which the language was lived fully as the "abode of the person." Today, Walīd Sayf must look for poetry "beyond the word's coffin." "Children are born who have no names," says ʿAbd al-Razzāq ʿAbd al-Wāḥid. Amal Dunqul sees "names come tumbling down, and what they name." For Ḥijāzī, "words whirl about, hide in the breast, then reappear on the lips frail, lying. They whirl around fear, their unending fear . . ."[31] Nāzik, it is true, refuses to "fear words," which are sometimes "a door through which we may enter our ambiguous tomorrow." But ʿAbd al-Ṣabūr lacks this brave confidence. "Color in words has destroyed us. Leave them nebulous, *sadīm*, for form in words has destroyed us. Leave them fashioned of clay, let not the soul's throbbing abide in words."[32] Refusal of a dualistic distinction between signifier and signified, rejection of the picturesque and flashy, resort to a language that—and here a magnificent expression of Khālida Esber, speaking of Adonis—"shall be *lugha hāyuliya*, language of primal matter . . ."[33]

Face to face with this banalization of the word, typical of the time, which the Arab poet encounters every day as he reads his paper or listens to his radio, if not in his own works, what can be done? Restore the lost power by recharging the language with its evocations. As we have seen, that is what many of these poets are attempting to do through their quest for the "purest meaning." Or the exact opposite: carry still further the profanation of the dethroned word. "The age of solecism is upon us," says ʿAbd al-Razzāq ʿAbd al-Wāḥid. "Who dares apply a genitive to universal suffering? . . . our existence: subject. Our disintegration: subject. Its overcoming: subject. But all subjects seek an object . . . I act, you act, he acts, but there is no action, *fiʿl*, and let Sibawayh tear his guts."[34]

Still others go beyond these exercises in grammatical poetry, which would charm Jakobson. They resort resolutely to "nonlanguage," *lā-lugha*. The expression was applied by Khālida Saʿīd to Unsī al-Ḥājj, *Māḍī al-Ayyām al-Ātiya*, "The past of the days to come." His latest collection, "What Have You Done with the Rose," may mark some relaxation in this bitter pessimism.[35] But he still evinces that negative bias that turns the poet against his own language and against poetry itself, which is thus (as our Denis Roche writes) "out of the question"![36]

One must recognize the class correlations, so to speak, that obtain at a given time in a language's history between its organization and that of society. That is precisely wherein certain poetical experiments are revolutionary. But it would be a great blow to the Arabs if the uncreated word itself were attacked by parody. The self-destruction of Arabic would culminate in ridicule of the Koran, or the writing of an anti-Koran (Mourad Bourboune). That is what has been attempted (although he denies it) by the Tunisian Bel Madanī in his "Zero Man" monologues, a character searching for his own shadow, and in his psalmodies in which the flexional endings turn into blasphemous comedy. Another grammatical poetry, if you will, but deriving its effect from contemporary man's evanescence.[37]

Poetry and Creativity

In Arab, as in other, poetry, the line separating true experiment—even unconscious or playful—from self-satisfied aberration is the one which separates the true poet from the word merchant. There is but one criterion: creativity.

Like all of us, the Arab world is more than ever in need of creativity. Although the need has a different incidence in the atomic age from that of pre-Islam, it makes demands of our contemporary, the Arab poet, as it did of Imrūʾ al-Qays. If the elegy on the abandoned camp coincided with the handling of verbal symbol, showing in theme and material that something could be developed from nothing, some great poems of today carry still further the tricks of a negativity that is the necessary condition for the present and future fulfillment of man in a universe in danger of losing its meaning.

It will furthermore not be without importance if these poems prove to be more truly poems than the *qaṣīdas* of their great forebears in that they propose to bolster their contours with objects. Industrial achievements, man-made environments, consolidation of ideologies, organization of group life: henceforth it is surrounded by such figures that the poet produces his compositions; the latter are eminently revelatory of a contemporary culture, since in the best instances they identify themselves with that same experiment by which the collective formations of a contour and a meaning are found. In the final analysis, what lends value to certain great Arab poems of our time is that, addressing a world that has been dislocated, they refashion one portion of reality.

PART FOUR

Why the Arabs?

XVI
Algorism and Life

For the Arabs, *wijdān* is a particularly rich and dynamic relationship between essence and existence, and vice versa.[1] The recent phases of their history have given it expression in mass movements, emotional violence, and ardor to transform life. Is this not simply one aspect, one effect among others, or the content, of revolution? Is "transforming life" viable in itself, or is it only a symptom or corollary of more-hidden movements which may be distinguished and analyzed?

What Is Collective Life?

Etymologically, the Arabs' *thawra* means their effervescence.[2] Thus it only partly covers what we mean by revolution, but also goes beyond it. We are in the habit of defining revolutions in terms of class relationships. We perceive in them the operation of a hidden logic which, in the final analysis, determines shifts among the factors of production. At least that is what the Marxist gospel maintained before recent exegeses undertook to refine or expand it. But this is not the place to inject ourselves into the debate over genesis and structure, structure and superstructure, dominant factor and its consequences or reflections, or over the "superdetermination" which is simply the accidental in sly people's parlance. It was seen in Part One of this book that in our opinion the idea of a binary dialectic, in which economics governs and conditions all else, should give way to a plural dialectic in which technology is simply one dimension among others. Let us not return to that subject. What I wish to point out here, as a theoretical projection of the Arab *wijdān*, is the importance in actual history of individual and collective lived experience, and its importance for our analyses, since one must pass that way to attain any significant depth.

Life in these terms is not reducible to "daily life." The sociologist to whom definition of the latter is credited considered it primarily the counterpart of the historicism and economism then in vogue.[3]

But his useful discovery of both depths and spontaneities irreducible to history may have left aside one property of history which, precisely, is manifested only in and through daily life.

After all, how was the depression which shook the world after 1929, and can today be reduced so masterfully to curves and graphs, really lived through? Depression is a laborer losing his job and his wife, embittered by having to economize, picking quarrels with him. Imperialism, the "last stage . . . etc.," is a French zouave pissing against a mosque wall in Constantine, or an Indian adolescent being accused of rape by an English spinster, as in Forster's novel. What right do we have to say that such things are merely indicators, that the reality to which they refer and which "conditions" or even "produces" them rests elsewhere, and that by acting upon this "elsewhere" one can act on all the rest? What is the "rest"? What right have we to say that what counts for science lies hidden elsewhere than in Pareto's "residual," the eventual, and the superstructure instead of in yourself? "There is no knowledge except of what is hidden," Gaston Bachelard used to say. But he, who lived life to the full and had no lessons to learn on the subject from anyone, would not have taken it amiss if I had suggested that he extend the sentence as follows: "except of what is hidden," agreed, but "on condition that relationships be established between the hidden and the manifest." Relationships which are shown to operate in more than a single direction.

Let us admit that what we call history walks "pigeon-toed." It reveals itself by dissimulating, so that to grasp what it really is one must start by deciphering what it shows or pretends. A deciphering which, like any reading, interprets, interpolates, extrapolates, altering under my very eyes the presumably fixed outlines of a picture of which I am a part, actor/acted upon, reader/author, and so on. In short, you labor endlessly to discover who is running the game, the secret motives, the algorism, finally, of this enigmatic tumult, now gay, now somber, often meaningless but always in quest of meaning, which is collective life, in which I myself am submerged and which, in many respects, I am. But when you have broken my code, are you then really sure you have deciphered me? I fear that your passage to and fro between the disclosed and the hidden, and vice versa, may be scientific in one direction and not in the other. I fear that, in assuming that you have reconstituted life on the basis of its algorism, you are exhibiting the naïveté of which you accuse empiricism.

Someone reproached Oscar Wilde for judging people by their appearance. "How else can I judge them," he replied wittily. But if it is hard to judge persons and if, when all is said and done, one can do so only on the most untrustworthy of evidence, how much more difficult it is to judge societies! We nevertheless have, for the purpose, two converging methods. Squeezing dry, so to speak, the phenomenon in which they manifest themselves, and the analytical penetration of their internal movement should, by their mutual intersection, lead to an adequate approximation of what they are. What they are, I mean, at various levels, from which I have no right to exclude the level of manifestation. For this alliance of methods, an ideal of the human sciences, must take account of an awkward fact. Between life and its internal code, whatever it may be, discontinuity is no less certain than correlation. To account for the felt depths within a society it is in no way sufficient to boil them down to vertical linkages which would "reduce" them to their underpinnings, whatever these might be. Qualitative jumps must be taken into account which, through and despite this framework of relationships, make reality as we live it.

Similarly, it is illusory to suppose that physical beauty can be reduced to its bases in anatomy, physiology, or why not biology and chemistry? Its aesthetic effect, distinct from sexual attraction, stems from a special harmony (or disharmony) into which enter centrifugal elements—of consciousness, notably—and combinations with the external: a facial expression, for example, largely related to the social context. When they depict it, our painters are no longer so naïve as to assume that it consists of putting flesh on sets of bones and tendons, as was so often done in fine arts academies. Not only do they liberate it from its supposed buttresses; they also cut it off from its social collusions; aesthetic convention, or associations of custom, pleasure, or anecdote. This latter exclusion, which by the way is leading contemporary painting into placing contradictory bets, does not interest us here. Let us note only the former, which restores autonomy to the corporal screen, recomposed with other pictures on the world's palpitating surface. This is how Picasso recomposed his *Picnic*, in which the seated nude becomes a variation of the foliage surrounding her, and vice versa.

Social analysis and practice should do as the painter does. They must restore the rightful autonomy of collective living.

The French Revolution can doubtless be reduced to the conquest of political power by a bourgeoisie already ripe for industrial enterprise. But this reduction is only the final analysis. It experienced itself, inasmuch as it was a revolt against injustice, as a choice for happiness.[4] Even these were simply more or less intense rationalizations experienced by the people of the time, which lent their deeds, their adventures, their faces, and even their landscapes an accent of which we still feel the vibration. How can we not admit the right of this dimension to be taken into account with all the others, provided that they all be placed in proper relation with each other?

That should be the task of any historical sociology and even, we believe, of a scientific socialism.

Reversal of Perspective?

This is carrying research and programmatic ambition to horizons that were until recently beyond their range of vision. These perspectives must be reconciled with certain contemporary trends that I will enumerate in no particular order.

Existentialism opposes its phenomenology, and its taste for the immediate and spontaneous, to approaches based on causality, essence, or origin. The multidimensional concept challenges that of linear history and of "unidimensional man," whether that man be the supposed *Homo economicus*, feeling man, or whatever. The pressing of private against public interests demonstrates that it is not true that life can always be reconstructed as a function of centripetal data, but that it is subject as well and more to a growing thrust of autonomies: here again I refer to Henri Lefebvre's analyses. Michel Foucault interposes between subject and object, beyond the historical moment and even beyond language, the positive quality of discursive formations. Not only does the new semiology lead Jean Duvignaud and others to a better reading of certain obscure social features, but it also promises to free society from the narrow confines of an "Italian stage." Immediacy, spontaneity, indigenousness, chance happening—all defy the various sorts of long-range determinism and the lessons deduced from them. An appeal for joy, bitter and convulsive, all the stronger for all the denials it is subjected to, pleads for restoration of the agonistic in the world.

These notions all conflict more or less with those on which so many analyses, practices, and ideologies of the distant and recent past were based. Recourse to spontaneity challenges the organizing perspective so favorable, as we know only too well, to bureaucracy. Sexuality is acknowledged, or rather exhibited, or even feigned. A revolutionary romanticism, which had never surrendered but was simply hunching its shoulders against the storm, is pressing demands long repressed by the fetichism of relative power. Utopia is buffeting moralities that were only programs, promises that were intended to be only analyses projected into the future. Is this reversal not going too far? Does its proper reaction against the abuses of regimentation take into account imperatives of any creation, at a time when creativity extends world-wide? Does its desperate vitalism not reserve to itself, a little selfishly, a counterbalance in the form of a sort of purgatory of structures and codes? Serious questions which I need not discuss here.[5] Let it suffice to have shown, by this random enumeration, that the idea of collective life is new to the world.

Dissymmetries

Manipulaton of societies is advancing no less surely. Also advancing is their elucidation, both practical and theoretical, which for its purpose is increasingly adopting formal languages. Abstract reduction furnishes the breviary for any practical application, and the criterion for all "scientific" activity. A large proportion of knowledge has as its goal, if not to deobjectivize observation, at least to mediatize it. In the Marxist view, or what the *Annals* school retains of it, technical invention and the appearance on the market of Indian or African gold, their effect on prices, changes in land tenure, and so forth, all affecting the terms of production and class conflicts, provide the bases of history. Another step and all these variables are combined in a figurative (or generative?) curve of the world's movement.[6] One more step and the recording of climatic cycles, their effects on land productivity, and their correlation with demographic data to calculate changes in caloric quotients provide an "explanation." Yet another step and exegesis is carried to the point of seeking the basis for explanation in quantifiable variables of probability and certainty and, at last, in fluctuations of ribonucleic acid. But Jacques Monod, who in this way liquidated Marxist dialectic and religious moralities, had a little difficulty in deriving a morality, or even a sociology, from ribonucleic acid.

It is true that exegeses of a different type address the lights and shadows of subjectivity. They follow individual and mass motivations to their abysmal roots. They bring to light the layered, concealed impulses underlying behavior. By means in no way formal or quantifiable they manage to construct all sorts of matrices for the conduct they claim is governed by them. In this, as in the former, case the specialist, with a perfectly serious face, teaches us to discount as superficial, empirical, and unscientific everything we see, do, and feel, for the benefit of an innately hidden reality which comes to light through an infinitely devious approach. This has become a commonplace. Personality complexes and secret motivations are adduced today in court proceedings and in columns of advice to the lovelorn.

But even if the raw materials market, as Marx said more than a century ago and as demonstrated in the Arabs' recent increase in the price of their oil, is "the modern form of destiny,"[7] this does not undermine the values of justice and desire which alone are able to stir the individual and the mass to action. We see these values as virtually immutable since prehistory, by their mode of expression if not by their nature.

While the expansion of the scientific and technological revolution has been reflected in world power relationships as imperialism, and then decolonization, ensuring to certain peoples not only hegemony but also, according to some, the "absolute superiority" of their ways of thinking, this in no way alters the universal drive that leads groups, from the largest to the tiniest, to demand the right to survive and assert themselves—and to achieve this progressively, notwithstanding their relative power.

Whether memories of early infancy precondition all affectivity, whether the death wish lies hidden behind desire, whether abstinence explains Robespierre or a hunchedback Gramsci, whether morality is merely disguised superego, by snatching off these masks I have not gone far toward grasping individual and collective life on its own terms, which may in fact be carnival terms.

What if life were exotic with respect to what is used to analyze, condition, or stimulate it? When I have pressed analysis down to its subterranean pilings I have at best only exposed the pillars which rest on them. Doubt should begin when one seeks to traverse these laboriously constructed levels in the opposite direction, to rise from the pilings to Babylon's hanging gardens where throbs the grandiose and fragile existence of men . . .

> Oh, for those charming workmen
> Subjects of a king of Babylon,
> Venus! Leave for awhile these lovers
> Whose soul is as a crown . . .[8]

. . . That is it: I shall go up from the basements toward the gardens. A very arduous undertaking! For the ascent, of course, I am equipped with the determinist's ladder that makes economics the foundation and the rest its consequences or reflections. On the other hand, I have the ladder of psychoanalysis which, from threshold to threshold, from guilt to disguise, provides me, in addition to causal explanation, with a hermeneutics of signs. The combined use of both ladders, and some others, will lead me to valuable results, but not ultimately viable ones. As far as we know, it cannot make it possible to locate, within the scientific and technical revolution which is the dawn of our planet's maturity, the thrill of the masses, the rise of three continents' cultures, and my own pursuit of happiness.

Must we resign ourselves to dealing with each order on its own? Must we, as is usually done, subordinate one order to another: the experienced, that is, to the reduced, the conceptualized, the manageable? Take care, for this latter option is that of the technocrat. Long ago it was the magician's. It could lead to latter-day esotericism. We can avoid this only by allotting their mutual roles to the various orders, including collective life, that third estate which in one sense is everything, and is seeking to become something.

This does not mean, at least in theory, that there is no democratic leadership capable of placing itself at the level of opinion in a continually unified field between concern at the bottom and decisions at the summit. But even if this came about generally—and we are far from there—the dichotomy would still not be eliminated between lived history and history as it is thought and managed: thought by abstract methods of growing complexity, and managed by instrumentalities increasingly hidden. The best proof of this disturbing disjunction comes from an obvious fact. The motivations imputed to the citizen and acting upon him have not changed between the language of Roman history and that of an electoral campaign today. Analysis would turn up the same words, the same notions, at any rate, in confrontation: pleasure/austerity, tradition/innovation, treason/loyalty, authority/liberty—more broadly, happiness and misery, good and evil. If this is a question of "human nature" we must admit that it has been very little affected by two thousand years of history which meanwhile subverted the definition and the tasks of group life. We are no longer in the times of the Gracci, and Aristotelian rhetoric ought by now to have been up-dated.

But one suspicion comes to mind: this distressing continuity may not be that of lived experience but that of strings which leaderships in any era pull in order to manipulate it. Such constancy has a rather frightening quality. It furthermore confronts us with an enigma. For, after all, these phrases do not correspond either to the lived reality of the masses or, so to speak, to their analytical reality.[9] How is their lasting efficacity to be explained? Raising this question should be preliminary to any political sociology.

An operation would then have to be undertaken that can only be called dialectical: the determination, first, of where an increasingly abstract scientific endeavor is located with respect to an expressivity and creativity that touch the heart, are recognized instinctively, and are realized in spontaneity; and, second, determining how the interaction between the former and the latter is organized.

We are far from there! For even if we see that the reductive analysis of persons and things alone can enable one to get on top of them, even if we note that the specialist has made some progress in investigating agencies covered from view,[10] we do not see the reciprocal procedure applied, nor that anyone is practicing dereduction after reduction, nor how, and by what analogies, mastery of the foundations will be transposed into broadly lived experience.

Supplement to Fabricius' Prosopopoeia

As we alluded above to the concions of Roman history, let us imagine a character, Citizen or Comrade, haranguing the consuls as follows:

"You wish to institute a scientific policy, and I think that does you credit. You are asking me for ardent and honorable support, and that is fine. But how can you reconcile these two things? You cannot at one and the same time assume that men's actions will be governed by a truth which has become as remote as that of the Kabbala and also expect of it the immemorial innocences of virtue. A virtue which you sometimes use as an excuse to make fundamental changes! What right do you have to assume that the subterranean complexities of history enter into individual and group existence with such prompt simplicity? I do not blame you, mark my words, for appealing to the heart's testimony. This concern does you honor, as it is a concession you are making to good people. But I am embarrassed for you when you propose to make these projections of the oldest idealism serve an affectively neutral abstraction, completely foreign to any classification as good or bad. You must admit that that is one of our era's problems. It is up to you to solve it, and then we shall speak more seriously of socialism. We may even attach the future of political virtue to the burgeoning phantasmagoria of technology. But you cannot go on combining mechanisms worthy of the growing achievements of technology with conditioned-reflex motivations worthy of the *Veillée des Chaumières*."

Let our new Fabricius go on talking while we pass to various other observations.

If the conscripts of the year II rose up to save the Revolution, it was not because it was bourgeois and promised the emergence of manufacturing capital or because it provided their papas with national goods. They saved it because it set them afire. If the anticolonial underground defied the industrial powers' bombers, it was not because the flow of technology, long the privilege of the center, was now reaching the periphery (we hasten to disavow this concentric metaphor) and they were getting ready to recover from the colonist the plus-value so long confiscated; it was because they fought better than the adversary, in the name of dignity, liberty, identity, values which neither the adversary's experience, his edge in equipment, nor his recourse to games theory was able to disarm: is this not what we saw in Vietnam? If these are "idealistic" motivations, it is simply too bad for me if I do not realize in time that they determine the issue, and to the extent I subsume them under supposedly objective laws I am unwittingly guilty of reductionism as well as falsehood.

Would you go so far as to say that you are mobilizing the modern counterpart within us of the age of belief, in the service of the technical and scientific era's *unum necessarium*? But then are you sure you have proceeded far enough into its re-use? Others can succeed better than you in accomplishing such a diversion, and may turn it against you. May? They have already done so, and will again. Thus far only Nietzschean amorality has proved consistent: it took contemporary analysis seriously in separating the empirical and the inherited. Neither Marx nor Freud was so bold. If Nietzsche is wrong, as we would like to believe, why sweep the problem under the rug, pretend that the dichotomy does not exist, and, in the era of chance and probability, indulge in prosopopoeias of the good soul? Are these, truly speaking, not simply demagoguery?

Granted, it would not suffice to restore to life its creative autonomy: this would merely trade one dissymmetry for another. In this case one would derive one's reasons from living experience and organize them as a collective norm. Who has proposed this so far? Existentialism, local autonomy movements, cultural revolutions? Their justified criticism of deductive procedures has not led them, apparently, to any theoretical or practical way of putting back together the liberty thus derived or of responding to the unlimited challenge of technological growth, or to a sustained approach to the ultimate of persons and things. Another contradiction follows the first, or rather both act to reinforce each other. For, after all, master and slave may both deceive one another.

Aggravation in the Third World

Let us leave the problem pending. Only an Earth-wide system, we believe, can resolve these contradictions. The revival of the oppressed cultures points the way toward such a system. This will be their recompense for protracted historical disgrace and their present extra tasks. Let us take a look at these. Many nations of the three continents are trying to lay the bases for a heavy industry, a competitive economy, and at the same time promote a socialism resting on neither coercion nor persuasion but descending to the level of the individual and group motivation, or rather rising from it. In a way, they are seeking to moralize and culturalize their development. What could be more legitimate, or more necessary? They are thus demonstrating to us the opportunities we have let slip by, the future we have missed.

They are measured, however, by the fatal differences in level of which I have just spoken. How is a meeting to be produced between scientifically based programs and desire? At best, leaders assume that, the truth of the era or of societies having been discovered, a certain set of attitudes will flow from it which will impose itself by logic, practical success, and international recognition. This putative reconciliation between Rousseau's natural man and social regimentation pushed to its outermost limits is today one of democracy's postulates. In accepting it we must nevertheless note the difference of phase between the order of collective life and that of the secret controls—others would say the real ones—everywhere in the Third World. We must face the fact that the two are out of phase if we wish to synchronize them some day.

It is still more painful in the case of the oriental peoples, still attached to the memory of the age of faith, when ontology was enthroned within actuality. Then, by virtue of the cyclical nature of life and of the rites and models which organized institutions and even the outward features of city and persons, an intimate interchange prevailed between the two orders. Human society wanted to imitate prophets and sages, and believed it was doing so. Most of its signs, in fact, not only referred to principle but also were analogous with it, seeking thus to reproduce its languages and physiognomies. All social semiotics was, so to speak, iconic.[11]

It is not enough to say this system has collapsed. It has condemned itself to death! When conservatism and traditionalism strive, amid the universal embrace of the Other's system, to preserve some fragment of the former life by inflating its value, this means that the old system is renouncing its claim as a system. Thus we have these self-denying, wounded, rudderless societies which must nevertheless put forth the effort to modernize! It will not be easy, obviously, for them to summon up the effort involved. Thus the best of them subject themselves to an austerity which defers to some later time enjoyment of the goods secured or to come, including the exercise of liberties. Contact with developed societies, which many of their citizens know at first hand as students or laborers, demoralizes them by the contrast in standards of living and opportunity for competition. If the bourgeois Revolution, strong in its technology and wealth, was able, with Saint-Just, to envisage happiness as a new idea, political virtue appears to many of the three continents' societies as a justified form of unhappiness.

The industrial nations' example has furthermore lent prestige to training and planning. The changes introduced in the environment, in the rural and urban landscapes, are supposed eventually to modify men's behavior in the desired direction. Once it becomes possible to act upon material conditions, plants, and processes, it is assumed that progress in well-being, and at least the external manifestation of the collective will, will indirectly shape the citizens' attitudes. Finally, direct psychological conditioning through the mass media is counted upon. On the best hypothesis, this is based on an ingenuous conviction, namely that information of itself will bring about change in behavior and win man over to his true interest. It would be easy to poke fun at this way of bringing everything to the level of dogma, at a time when scientific discovery is excavating truth so dizzyingly.[12] But let us proceed. It is certain that scientific progress has impact at all levels. Is it not incarnated in life through the education of youth and adults? Modernity places more and more instruments for this purpose into the hands of officials: radio, press, television, satellites, and so on, which is also to say, propaganda facilities. Add to these the various insidious or acknowledged processes of social control, pressure by classes or by ruling cliques, the exemplary status ascribed to certain individuals. All these are means of acting upon life. How can we pass over demagogy and despotism in silence? We see them at work in many Third World countries from whose achievement of independence something better might have been hoped for.

These abuses stem not so much from the rulers' perversity as from their generic unsuitability. Moreover, conditions, people, and things resist them more than one might think. Despite all the means with which the modern era endows regimes to transform collective life, the latter, for better or worse, refuses to follow. The acceleration and, sometimes, the anachronism of established goals limit their meaning. Now change is not propagated in the absence of meaning. Recent history has fragmented Third World societies into internal discontinuities. The traditionalism of some and the progressivism of others interrupt mutual communication while obstructing the expansion of power, whether good or bad. But the most-effective limitations stem from the difficulty the Third World societies have in joining the values of collective life with the increasing abstraction demanded by mastery over things. A mastery which thus far, in most cases, bears foreign names and places foreign concepts in operation.

If so much effort expended, rightly or wrongly, upon transformation were to fail, even in the short run, this would be serious anywhere. It is more so in societies which seek, while remaining themselves, to become participating partners in the new industrial world. Their seeming submission to the authoritarian State in most cases simply widens the cleavages they suffer. Their naïve enthusiasms—rallying around a great leader, slogans, the craze for acculturation, ego-flattering triumphs—do not long deceive them. So are further upheavals to be anticipated? That often happens. Often, also, setbacks inflicted upon group life, exposure of deceit, realization of failure will produce a blocking, stalling, demobilizing effect. Thus most of the legendary moralities with which the leaders had armed themselves to inspire the masses end by falling flat and make cold societies of these societies which had been fully fired up by history. Worse still: hedonistic as well as cold. That is where neocolonialism is awaiting them.

Third World Promises

Fortunately that is not the inevitable outcome. These societies, which we call and which call themselves underdeveloped, victims of ignorance, sickness, and poverty, are in many respects in better shape than our own.

Decolonization is not, as is sometimes implied, the contrary of imperialism and its reversal. To repeat, it is not a question for decolonization of taking the opposing position and doing the exact contrary of imperialism. It is a question of liberating a superabundance of persons and things. All problems are then revealed as broader, more boldly outlined, and of a loftier quality than in the preceding period.

To speak of decolonization is to speak of an existential unfolding, an experience of the previously unfelt, a housecleaning both material and anthropological—all shattering the constraints of the preceding phase. People must be fed, where no one had bothered about supply; the masses must be educated, which had previously concerned no one; a meaning must be given to the course of events by which one can orient himself. Certainly, one may feel even unhappier than before, since the man as individual and as group now emerging has only just acceded to his problems and the discovery costs dear. The general magnification aggravates the distortions born of the necessity to adapt the handling of realities to collective life: an adaptation that, of course, goes well beyond the requisitions of state capitalism! In the final analysis, the example these societies offer us is not, needless to say, that of tranquility and happiness, but of a groping in which all possibilities are touched. That is also why they teach us to reject the compartments of social analysis, all the real or so-called divisions of labor, while positing that a problem cannot be solved or even defined before it is traced to its roots.

What roots? (*a*) Ecological roots, to begin with. Any problem must be traced to the level of junction between societies and Nature, on one hand, and, on the other, those world perspectives imposed by the observable evolution of all peoples toward planet-wide unity. (*b*) Second, and this observation follows from the first, the enterprise must grasp man and group at the base, that is, radically. Liberated society cannot be content with mere reorganization; it must determine to be a society in the nascent state, with all the false starts and vehemences this implies: and that is called revolution. (*c*) And then this society, obliged to transpose into modern-day terms an identity coming from the depths of the ages, will subject its identity to a sort of systematic vibration. To set it in a tight mold would destroy it. It must shatter the narrow frameworks in which we enclose our problems or, better, expand them all to the anthropological, since after all its own effort tends to reject society as form in order to remake it as the unlimited activity of collective man. The virtues of such an enterprise are not only patience and study, but also adventure and game. (*d*) Finally, declaration of the right to differ, to escape the configurations and perhaps even the laws of the industrial world. This entails freeing oneself from terrible deferences, more costly than servitudes.

Digression in the Form of a Dialog

"Then what about class struggle?"

"We give it its genuine scope, which is not merely social but also anthropological."

"You take away its . . ."

"Schematics? Monopoly? No, that is not the only struggle in the world. No need to be sorry about that. And if the broader objective went beyond the recovery of confiscated plus-values, and it were defined as *conferring* value, would it be less attractive?"

"Take care, or you will confuse the issue, or avoid it."

"Take care, or you will lapse into reductionism or self-congratulation."

"You seem to be saying that the real proletariat . . ."

"The greatest proletariat in the industrial age is nature, the element of nature in us. That is why capitalism denatures society, and eventually man and even nature."

"You would agree with the bucolic antipollution bullies!"

"On the contrary, I remain faithful to technological optimism, which you once had but are pretty coy about these days. However . . ."

"However what?"

"If society is plural and unfolds in multiple dimensions, including technology, the latter will exert its drawing power on all the others, and all the others must advance . . ."

"You say 'advance'?"

"I mean to say, advance with its rhythm, but each according to its individual logic."

"Go over that again, please."

"Belief in the temporality of human progress in all its modes, belief in the quickening tempo industrial enterprise impresses upon it, is one postulate of socialism and present-day democracy, and probably the best founded. But . . ."

"But?"

"It would be destroyed and corrupted if, among homologous and interacting, but autonomous, dimensions, the rhythm and determinants of a single one were imposed on all. You may call that Marxism, but I call it positivism, and of the crudest kind."

"Please, let's get back to pollution."

"Those of us who feel guilty over our growth make of it a bugaboo to liquidate all claims in a panic flight from the industrial age."

"You yourself say that deterioration goes much further than its impact on class relationships, that it proletarianizes nature, even denatures it. Isn't this ignoring other problems?"

"And so we see that the Third World refuses to take so tragically that pollution, brandished by developed societies as a bugbear to relegate all other wounds into the shadows. But neither the Third World nor socialism seems willing to respond to the realities the trick is meant to distort and cover up."

"What response could there be?"

"Broaden the social revolution to the ecological level."

"What do you mean by that?"

"Redistribute the Nature/culture relationship, broken and repressed by the preponderance of many other forms than exploitation of the working class. Renaturalize culture, reculturalize nature: that is the real meaning of decolonization, and of all revolutions."

"Go ahead. But why the Arabs?"

"Justification for these propositions and hopes could, beyond doubt, be provided by other regions of the planet, and other human histories. But theirs does so through specificities which for me (and for them) are full of savor."

"Savor? I thought you were a sociologist!"

The Arabs' Contribution

That among so many Afro-Asian and Latin American societies that of the Arabs illustrates, on both the negative and positive sides, the features I have just distinguished is all the more evident to me since these hypotheses are derived directly from their present experience. I even find them repeated by their essayists and especially their poets, phrased and presented in their own way.

But I must return here to a notion which sums them all up. The Arab *wijdān* relates the immediacies of life to the presence of a fundamental. It thus resolves the cleavages and contradictions emphasized above into a certain type of attitudes. It is true that in this case the fundamental is habitually transcendental, and that contemporary history interprets return to basics in a different way. It nevertheless remains true that this presence of basics (whether defined theologically or naturalistically) and their emergence in personal and collective life characterize the Arabs' behavior in persistent fashion. They endow it, at the very time the Arabs are entering the industrial world, with an enviable ability to draw upon resources and even to begin from scratch.

The instrumentalities of modern times, because they arise from more and more specialized approaches, in large part formal, indeed seem to exclude these primordial presences. That most of these instrumentalities come from abroad further aggravates their mediacy and consequently the social and moral dislocations whose ravages I have emphasized. The mingling of different levels in which I see the cause of many Arab failures might then appear to be the disastrous counterpart of a beneficial impulse toward the unitary and toward recapitulation. If we suffer from the sterilizing inertia brought on by the compartmentalization of life, the Arabs, who suffer from it less, have a dangerous tendency to confuse levels, to mix action and dream, calculation and gamble. Salvation can come only through critical reconsideration of the mediate and compartmented for us, of the immediate and the undivided for the Arabs.

But it is not inconsequential that their *wijdān* itself implies a crossing from level to level, a feeling that lived experience is implied in the principle and vice versa. Nor is it inconsequential that the density of life, the depths of the fundamental, and the rigors of abstraction are felt by the Arabs—the first two terms reciprocally with one another, and both with respect to the third—as less adverse than by us. This might, in the end, be their surest weapon in their struggle for progress, and their most precious contribution to a world civilization.

XVII
The Wandering Gaze

In a world of artificial frontiers and population transfers, the Arabs' obstinate claim to their Palestinian territory is a subject of astonishment to many foreigners. To the latter this appears as a refusal of history, whereas for the Arabs it is the refusal to accept that history be refused them. At a time when dependent peoples were being emancipated in a chain reaction, in Palestine a blockage occurred in what seemed to be a universal series. By hundreds of thousands the country's sons endured occupation, eviction, exile. Dispersed abroad or gathered into camps, their claim crystallized. It became resistance, conspiracy, and, more recently, terrorism. Above all it became testimony. In its view, this was an appeal from unhappy history to something higher than history: God, unwritten laws, a world-wide justice to come.

The energy flowing from such a recourse is doubtless only moral. At the hands of its own architects it has suffered the most stinging of disillusionments. Some have used it for their own ends, others have distorted it. Hence its setbacks. Hence the misunderstanding it encounters. One cannot, however, lightly disregard the manner in which it raises protest to the level of an absolute. Why an absolute? There have been plenty of precedents for the misfortune of this torn land: those of Poland, Alsace-Lorraine, Armenia, Korea, Kurdistan, and so on. Alas, yes. But we must note the fact that none of these cases, although in each special values were at stake, created the same sort of drama. They were painful, scandalous. That of Palestine involved the world's tragedy. That had been the case, not so long ago, of the millions of Jewish victims of Nazism. A frightening coincidence! But the great voices of Louis Massignon and Martin Buber are no longer there to extract its meaning . . .

Let us confine ourselves to observing, quite lamely, that peoples do not all feel, nor practice to the same degree, that reference to the things from which their historical entity, language, happy and unhappy experiences draw significance for themselves and for others. To confine ourselves to the Palestinian case, this reference is properly subsumed under tragedy in Aristotle's terms:[1] that is, under the fact that the drama unfolds under a gaze other than that of the actors and spectators.

History and the Sacral

Many of these attitudes distinguish a personality that long defined itself by reference to the transcendental. For centuries Muslim man, and particularly the Arab, felt himself summoned and favored by God. He believed that the Absolute's attention presented him with a binding alternative. It was not so important to belong to the "best of nations," which however entailed the assumption of certain duties. But Islam reconciled him with himself. It is a religion of *yusr*, a term that might be translated as "free will." The divine promise saves man's nature without imposing upon it restrictions other than obedience to the Law. Because of it, human nature and nature in general will flow with more intensity once they have come to terms with certain quite-moderate prohibitions. The revelation has not condemned these two natures but cultivated and, so to speak, brought them to completion. In the Koranic conception of the integral man, *basharan sawiyyan*,[2] there is a summons to harmony, to wholeness. Not only does sexuality here carry no original sin, its most impetuous exercise is among the individual's most normal and, one might say, normative attributes.

At the same time, the other side of the divine gift must be taken into account: arduous trials, temptations, and eschatological threat. Thanks to the Prophet, human nature emerged from the self-satisfied soliloquy in which the pre-Islamic poets had confined it. It is henceforth incorporated in a responsible relationship with the Unknowable, *al-Ghayb*. God is presence/absence, sublimity beyond reach, and meticulous retribution by punishment or delightful reward. He is the "King of judgment day."[3] So to testify is to enter into a pact. The watchword of the ritual, "testimony" or, better, "attestation," *shahāda*, in fact evokes a bilateral act (like *tawba*,[4] or *ṣalāṭ*[5]). The Arabs have preserved both its sacred power and its lay extrapolations until our day. Just as any testimony presupposes a witness, any behavior refers to what gives it meaning. Until a short time ago the Muslim's every act began with the *bismillah*.[6] The soldier's death in holy war was testimony *par excellence*. But the believer's existence was no less so. Rites reinforced its communal warmth. But it was enough to be a believer to be never alone. This sort of posture endowed these men's conduct with a unique majesty;

at the same time, it exposed them to the risk of not being understood. They were long portrayed as metaphysical champions, acting on behalf of the Absolute, which they probably never were, even in the time of the orthodox caliphs! This minimized their earthly nature, which was manifested, thick and stubborn, in the least of their actions. Witnesses, certainly, witnesses to a single view, but agitated by a carnal violence: the Arabs are all of that at one and the same time, and that is how they so often lead their adversaries, and their friends, into error.

Here we would express a reservation concerning the theological interpretation of these attitudes which Louis Massignon set forth in somberly incendiary pages. For the latter to have seemed adequate to us, they would have had to cover the subsequent developments, more and more secular, more and more revolutionary, which are the principal concern of this book. But they did not. I shall go further. While Islam as religion accounts for many Arab traits, it does not account for all of them. Many go back to pre-Islam. These, as well as several others, have nothing to do with the sacred. What of the new developments now flooding in! More and more, the Arabs are interpreting their vicissitudes as a function of political and social justice. The motivations, circumstances, and viewpoints in the Palestine problem are obviously historical. At any rate they are becoming so. To confirm this one need only compare the claim fulminated by the Mufti of Jerusalem with the one now advanced to elicit international action, and with the period in between when Arabism was the moving spirit. The Mufti argued in apocalyptic terms, the leaders who followed him in nationalistic terms. Those of the current resistance claim the rights of all dispossessed peoples. Through them Palestinian militancy joins a tricontinental coalition seeking the revocation of the traditional East no less than of Israel.

But this growing secularization, it would seem, does not still a clamor inseparable from the sort of echo it appears to expect from elsewhere than history. When it borrows the language of terrorism it reverts to its tragic essence which needs no heavenly or earthly sanction to derive the values of trial by fire. Indeed, the Arabs' evolution that the astonished world has observed since they were first dispossessed of Palestine arises from neither religious hatred, nor ethnic messianism, nor ideology. All these aspects, and yet others, share in a semantic configuration that might account for the Arab personality and for something much more general: the role of the tragic in these collective behaviors. Thus the Palestine problem has been alluded to only for the sake of what the analysis one can make of it as a particular case may reveal concerning the role of the tragic, that is, still in our own view, the respective position of events and invariances in history.

History and Paradigm

In linguists' usage the terms *paradigm* and *paradigmatic* contrast with *syntagm* and *syntagmatic*. Their heuristic power, greater than their operative value, contributes to an extended use which we cannot be sure, even with the most meticulous specialists, does not fall sometimes into metaphor. The connotations of this rather new notion have by no means been strictly fixed.[7] The safest thing for the social science researcher, if he wishes to avoid too risky a projection, is to begin with the strict linguistic usage. I will therefore be excused if, in the next paragraph, I sum up a few notions now current.

An utterance extends over time in syntagms. But it would not be an utterance if it did not place in action, while helping to create, a system going beyond any succession of events: language. Now the latter offers simultaneously to the speaker various possibilities of which he chooses a single one. The possibilities and the choice would be without meaningful result if, in addition to the actualization of the word and the expression *hic et nunc,* he did not bring into operation structures of a lexical and syntactical nature. In doing so he uses not only a sound sequence and what it "means," but also the presence/absence of a *paradigm* that combines that sequence with other elements into a linguistic system. For only a system held in common by the participants makes encoding and decoding, and thus dialog, possible.

Will this brief reminder now permit us to make an analogical transfer? I would risk this only as a working hypothesis. History, like discourse, is made by selection from ranges of possibilities. Any individual or collective act occurs at the intersection of a temporal series and of regularities transcending it.

In the case of the Arabs, for example, there are several striking regularities: (*a*) references, obviously, to God as established in the Koran and as the postulate of much of their conduct. But if, through methodological scruple, one looks for nontranscendental invariances, one would find them (*b*) in historical constants owing their survival to linkages between the group and its ecology, or (*c*) reflecting continuities of attitudes or a world-view without appreciable change over the centuries. This multiplicity of regularities may seem incongruous. We nevertheless find it in the facts wherever we seek to define one collective identity or another. We then notice that (*d*) stable patterns structure the synchronic unity of an aggregation and its persistence over time: the unit then survives, despite variation, even total variation, in its content because it is a system, and maintains among its variable terms a relationship that does not vary, or varies only over a much longer term. This is the price of all historical continuity.[8]

It follows that in any observable series the occurrence of facts and the choice of conduct leave a great number of other possibilities open. If these possibilities had become actuality, determinist explanation, as we know only too well, would not have failed to attribute to them retrospectively, whatever their nature, an explanatory cause-and-effect chain, and that is one of historicism's delusions. Just as vainly, moreover, others would have seen the demonstration of an abstract human freedom, and that is where the theologians and idealistic philosophers go wrong. But what counts for us at the moment is not that one possibility among others has been actualized, but the exclusion it has perpetrated on its equals: the latter are then, with respect to it, in the same paradigm situation as that of linguistic structure with respect to a linguistic event.

History's possibilities are such only because of the multiplicity of suggestions typical of a system.[9] Rejected, they persist in their stubborn latency. It may happen that they emerge to be actualized in their turn. Some sort of historical ricochet may one day reactivate one or another of these dormancies. Their exclusion may have been only provisional. And rightly so when we consider that, contrary to the assumption of a short-sighted determinism, most historical renewals come about by a break with the past and by bringing to light potentials long repressed. Revolutions, then, erupt from the waiting wealth of possibilities. They are revolutions to the extent that they break with proximate determinants to draw upon energies previously not involved. In so doing they take recourse from history in action to potential history, which is to say that they put the system back into operation, and this is not done without substantial semantical effusions.

A revolution is not tragic, in the strict sense of the word, merely because it causes bloodshed. It is tragic in that it increases the group's awareness of its own presence, that is, directs its gaze toward itself. It concentrates this gaze as a magnifying glass does the sun's rays.[10] Then the masses catch fire from a "new idea" and freely offer their lives for it, since "the gods are athirst." But perhaps they were simply tired of being warmed only by their own continuity. Like a winter sun, the glow of the ideal had forsaken them. It might, instead of inflaming them, have become diffused and remained above them as a sort of presence/absence propitious for a succession of indecisive phases, for historical hibernation. At least three kinds of collective behavior, each defined by a certain relationship between its temporal course and its models. Should we say, between its syntagm and its paradigm? That would doubtless be forcing the linguistic analogy.

One thing is certain at any rate: that there are societies in this world and at this time dedicated single-mindedly to advancement, to skipping over stages and eliminating possibilities, which have even raised it to the dignity of myth under the name of progress. Might we say that they have made progress a myth because myth had abandoned them, and made history a god because in them God had died? That could be argued. Absorbed in the process of practical choice, and its peculiar field of production and consumption, they escape stultification and an exhausting banality only by their revolutions, that is, by stirring up possibilities and setting the system afire: an operation on the historical plane analogous to that of poetry on the plane of language.

Other societies, in their "sleeping time, floating time" (Lucien Febvre), in fact live simultaneity. By this we mean that they keep all their possibilities intact; in their own language this amounts to invoking the cyclical or the eternal. For the foreigner, swept along by the univocal accelerations of what he calls progress, they appear stagnant but also imbued with human wholeness, or perhaps as messengers of spirituality. Caretakers of absence, they are societies which bear witness. Might we call them "paradigmatic"?

Recapitulation of the Arab Case

The Traditional Stage

This was doubtless the case of the Arab societies before upheavals, which however have not spread everywhere nor always gone deep, tended to align them with the former type with its due bill of revolution.

There has been no need to strain the term *paradigm* in applying it to this context, inasmuch as the Islamic revolution called itself *al-*

imām al-mubīn, and this two-element name may be translated as "the explicit paradigm."[11] Before these societies were disrupted by importations and effractions from the West, moreover, they were governed by models of which some drew their power from the Revelation, others from the agonistic heritage of pre-Islam.[12] How could such disparate referents have been combined? In our view, this was the work of the second century of the Hegira. The Arab expansion, face to face with all the civilizations of the ancient world, stirred up a veritable whirlwind of ideas and things and made possible a multitude of experiences. But it imposed a systematization that in practice stood the test of the facts. That is why a sort of concordat came into being between the ethical and the agonistic, although not without some encroachment one upon the other. This is how the great taxonomies are to be understood which then ordered theology, law, grammar, and versification, all of which were oriented toward the virtue of models.

For many centuries thereafter the framework of all social life placed in effect schemas drawn from the chronicles of the Prophet and his companions. "Antecedentism," *salafiya*, never lost its force. The blessed model set forth was to be imitated indefinitely: *qudwa, uswa, mithāl*.[13] Success consisted in conforming to it, at some risk of falling into "conformism," *taqlīd*, but with the hope of attaining the religious state of "harmony," *tawfīq*. The very richness of vocabulary in this field is persuasive on this point. As time passed, of course, the increasing complexity of conditions demanded more resort to reasoning. But then one would apply an "analogical syllogism," *qiyās*; that is, one would draw from the same schemas applications at one or more removes. The role played by poetry continued to enliven this prosody of existence by throwing its fantastic values into relief; it maintained for the delectation of the lettered, who remained moved, and publics never sated by the models an inexhaustible application of the original norms. Poetry was furthermore held to be the supreme exaltation and, therefore, the language system laid bare, and thus obeyed immutable canons almost to our own days. In addition to which, the language was organized according to a trilateral paradigm from which even today the most modernistic neologisms strive to derive strange treasures.

The ideal of such a society was not, as has been alleged, either immobility or imitation in the sense that Christians apply to imitation, but unlimited resort to its own structures, these latter coinciding with the originals to the same extent as the free play they allowed. Suffice it to characterize these modes of conduct, in whatever field, (*a*) by the strength of the relationship they maintain with what we have, very approximately, called paradigms, models, and invariances, and (*b*) by the palpable, even sensual, richness of this relationship: qualities for which the entire Arab tradition is indebted to the origins and feels as immediacy.

Change

Let us now imagine the way in which these traditional traits gain access to the new horizons that open up to the Arabs the type of humanity suited to industrial societies, a type which the Arabs have for a century and a half been borrowing from the West in circumstances that turn many of modernity's teachings into alienation and degeneration.[14]

Only half a century ago in the East most names were theophoric. ʿAbdullah, ʿAbd al-Kabīr, ʿAbd al-Qādir, ʿAbd al-Nāṣir—"Slave of God, of the Great, the Mighty, the Protector"—all formulae referring the individual to the divinity. This reference was clearly more insistent than the naming of individuals in the West after a saint on the calendar about a thousand years ago, before patronymics came into general use. Now during the generation just past, the kind of names has changed, although the patronymic remains foreign to Egypt and certain other countries. Shedding reference to God's service, they drew first upon knightly evocations of the Arab past,[15] somewhat as our Jacobins took their names from Roman history. Even this secular referent seems today to be tending toward a zero qualification, just as European given names have. One sign among others of an evolution that is transporting the individual from the "forest of symbols / whose eyes follow you with an intimate gaze" toward the precincts of statistical neutrality in which he will be designated simply by a serial number: the imminent arrival of Lefebvre's Cybernanthropus!

We have not come that far in the East, far from it. Beirut's streets are numbered, but that is in order to spare the municipality involvement in quarrels over eponyms! Eastern cities call most buildings by their owners' name or some other distinguishing feature. For individuals, the custom of *kunya*, by which you are called by your eldest son's name, persists in its charming intimacy and, tragically—and not by accident—furnishes fighting names to Palestinian commandos.

Traditional man has nonetheless suffered a shattering from which, no more among the Arabs than among us, no acceptable synthesis has so far emerged. The discord, certainly, is not of the same sort in one and the other case. Among them, despite the changes that have occurred, the mass remains faithful to religious observance, to respect for ancestors, and so strongly to the ancient taste that it even fiercely resists abandonment of classical prosody in favor of free verse. The accusation of unbelief, by which I mean inauthenticity, is always fatal to a political leader or movement. The same mass nevertheless participates more and better than some think in collective activities in step with the surrounding world: attachment to technology, aspiration toward democracy and socialism, progress toward a consumer society. It does so, naturally, as a function of itself and its own continuities. Under the stimulus of leaders who know how to mobilize it, or of elites trained in Western style, it is rushing toward history. But take care: it fits this motion into its own framework. It demands that leaders express a sort of *ijmāʿ*, "canonical unity." Its *ḥishma*[16] condemns any deviation or marginality, even though it changes its orthodoxy rather frequently. Read the edifying literature in the Egyptian press arising from the account, repeated a hundred times over, of entry into the modern age: a new kind of sermon of which land reform and industrialization have become the litany. The Orient has entered history and must make of history, modernity, socialism, and so on new paradigms intersecting with the old.

Of course, other segments of society, part of the working class among others, and the intelligentsia, whether bourgeois or Marxist but particularly the Marxist, have undergone and are propagating a more-radical mutation. If they have not made history of all the absolutes they have at least circumscribed them and given them relativity. On their side, national leaders know they are caught up in a becoming that they can take control of only by temporal means. Even if they did not believe it, pressure from abroad; the necessity for mapping out programs, instituting projects, and balancing budgets; and the influence or competition of ideologies would force them to adjust their methods. They consequently offer themselves as mediators between age-old attitudes and the march of time and the surrounding world. This is called demagogy on their part. For all mediation is compromise, and compromise is never innocent. Real failures and alleged abuses or treason will confirm its negative aspects, or simply the erosion to which all power is subject. But power will have had its moments of triumph, if not its "singing morrows." For a time it will have known how to speak the language of becoming. Eloquence, of course, will have been the vehicle of these promises.[17] Hence the luxuriant growth of that art form. Its effects on the collective psyche are considerable. What does it matter if these effects are based on misunderstanding if the latter casts a spell over things as they are, and occasionally transforms them. . . .

Alteration/Compensation

Change, in any event, will have intensified and accelerated. Nowhere has the diachronic been entirely substituted for the paradigmatic: how could it be otherwise? Such a substitution has occurred in no country in the world. The respective dosage does vary with local conditions. Both, however, agitate Arab societies more tragically than elsewhere, and conflict can lead to a split in both individual and group personality.

Most often, where modernity emphasizes technical activity, their identity is sought by a compensating increase in the value of other orders of life, and for that reason in sectors the least vulnerable to alienation. Alas, they are even more vulnerable to falsification! A single example: the support many seek from the great classical past. Not only do they adopt foreign methods in establishing facts and texts, but they also believe they can balance this borrowing by a vengeful nostalgia for the great "legacy," or *turāth*. Thus they invoke invariance in certain domains to compensate for others' variations they have failed to master. Belief, language, family status, sexuality, and other spheres will thus be affected by distorting values. Thus a "traditional sector" will be set up in opposition to the "modern sector" of the individual, group, and landscape. Cosmopolitanism on one side, self-obsession on the other.

In the end, even these dissymmetries are no longer enough to ensure even a faulty regulation. Everywhere bursts forth the cleavage between the old and the new typology, the former finding in the latter its unhappy consciousness, or its distorting mirror. Already, in their bumpy journey onto the international scene, the Arab peoples have long felt that sort of compulsion that assumes another must see you in order for you to become a face. For a century or more the "eyes of the West" have exerted upon them a deforming hypnosis. In vain do they revolt, rail, and confiscate. Protest becomes more destructive day by day, without at all diminishing the "mirror" element in ideas, conduct, or accomplishment. To present oneself such as others refuse to see you, to refuse to be as others see you, and nevertheless to require for your own self-reaffirmation the reassurance of those whose manner of viewing you you repudiate—this way of being has weighed, and still weighs more than is generally believed, upon Arab attitudes. It creates between you and the other, whom you claim to deny but who is necessary to you as a witness, an ambiguous relationship as productive of hatred as of dialog. Hence the frequent political ups and downs, the abrupt shifts in relations with the United States, the Soviet Union, France, Federal Germany. . . .

The time has of course long passed when the Arabs went to the other's school unquestioningly as docile pupils. This naïveté, moreover, was never without its reverse side, no matter what self-congratulatory colonial history or anticolonialist vituperation may say. Tradition, nationality, and honor, at the height of dependency, had always limited adherence and submission. To the Western gaze, alienating and transforming, the East opposed, as it still does, a gaze, coming from an infinitely more-remote and deeper source: that of Islam. God's gaze thus served as counterweight to that of alienated history to rescue the face that millions of men were determined to bring into the future's shining light.[18] This gaze had been focused on one's life for fourteen centuries, which meant virtually since eternity began. Palpable at the best-preserved levels of the population, penetrating the collective subconscious to depths no other testimony had reached, or doubtless will ever reach, it ensured that the Arab was never alone and lent him a triumphal attribute equal to all his misfortunes.

In practical life Occidentalism, *tafarnuj*, nonetheless appeared as the only route to follow. The most consecutive series of Arab experiences in contemporary history, that of Egyptian history, demonstrates this in striking fashion. There, as elsewhere, bitterness and rejection prevailed, in the adaptation to others, as self-assertion increased. It seems as if the more and more tenuous differential to which identity clings becomes exasperated in proportion to the collapse of the dams of differentiation. Besides, this is only one feature among others of a general movement transferring the values of macrosociology to microsociology. One example: like other religions, Islam is losing all or some of its morphological powers; it is transferring to lay agencies more and more of its collective constructive and managerial functions, and no one can say whether this growing internalization decreases its inspiriting force or disturbs its appeal in the depths of men's hearts.

Toward the World in the Making

If at precisely the same time linguistics and information techniques are developing and ethnology is being founded anew on the basis of differences, sometimes pursued to the infinitesimal, it is because the evolution of analytical methods is responding, in its own domain, to that of concrete history. While the world, in its advance, its consumption patterns, and its dissemination of information, is becoming one, yet the distinctive qualities of groups are intensifying and, far from deterring their participation in the global system, demand it.

That is a statement which will shock scorners of the specific! According to them, collective identity is a booby trap. If we were to believe them, there is personality only in situations, not in national or cultural continuities. It will also shock adherents of the sort of essentialism for which certain qualities—a genius, destiny, or substance—define a system once and for all. I will not pause to refute objections proceeding more from a priori ideas than from case studies. At the same time I should warn the reader against a possible misinterpretation. Not only does the state of transition, division, and ambivalence which seems to me to characterize the Arabs at this stage in their history not imply a pejorative judgment, any more than an admiring one, but also it explains the potentialities thus open to them in their approach to the present and the future.

The sort of sparkling agility that permits them to change their hypotheses or their language without affecting their feeling of personality and legacy constitutes an effective weapon for them in their struggle for modernity. The configuration remaining untouched, it will be enough for them to change paradigms. Just as a Ṭaḥṭāwī or an ʿAlī Mubārak in the last century, or a Ṭaha Ḥusain closer to us, sought to reform the Arab East on the Greco-Roman model, now many call for referents upon a proletarian classicism borrowed from Eastern countries. Fixing their attention on such new models will in no way interrupt the continuity of things and people, any more than imitation of bourgeois Europe did over a period of two or three generations. Moreover, is Marxism not the supreme agent of Westernism in these countries? One might be tempted to think so, were it not that in the past several years the Chinese referent and tricontinental solidarity have offered a virulent alternative.

But if I say solidarity, not simply referent, it is because something has changed! Independence, which has terminated the sort of two-party soliloquy, so to speak, in which the colonist confined the colonized, permits either the bursting forth or the dilution of alterity. When Syria calls upon ten or so nations reaching from China to England to undertake technical projects; when Egypt introduces the teaching of Russian and Czech and tries (without much success, to be sure) to arouse popular enthusiasm for learning these languages; when Algeria reorganizes its university in three departments, one of them for foreign languages among which French, ironically, is included—the effort to break up a tyrannical dyad is justified. Certainly, there has been a decline in the familiarity with British, and particularly French, culture which might have gone as far as assimilation, but even that was voluntary. This is part of the times' demystification which may be paid for dearly; but no price seems too high for a people to free itself of former servitudes.

Decolonization, of course, utilizes concurrently for its goals national, international, and newly naturalized models, and in many cases this leads to dispersion and confusion. What does this matter if at first it can lean upon them to realize its objectives? In this respect the old quarrel between ancient and modern, between *qadīm* and *jadīd*, raised a false dilemma. As all the Third World's recent history teaches, only revolution can save the authentic, which alone in turn can ensure and sustain it. Now the authentic resides in the people. That is not simply a populist profession of faith (which of itself would not be democratic). It is a reasoned, observed fact. Among collective roles those of the peasant and the laborer are the ones in which exchanges between society and its natural substratum operate the most directly. These classes constitute, literally, the foundation in all meanings of the term, not only ecological but also psychic and psychoanalytical.[19]

Now the distinguishing feature of Arab Islam is not, as is too often said, the ubiquity of the sacred, but the enduing of the social totality with *uṣūl*. *Uṣūl* are both its structure and its origin. For Arab Islam, fundamental becomes synonymous with radical. If the totality is repossessed by the foundation, which is also the principle and the origin, this means that this unity is manifested at the level of lived experience. As we have seen, that is a trait of the Arab *wijdān*. It involves the ambiguous consequence that fundamentalism can take opposite directions according to whether it is referred to nature or to transcendence. Conversely, the horizon of totality, traditionally dominated by Islam, may reveal itself in the most apparently adverse directions—those of historical materialism, for example—without really modifying the implications for collective life. That may be disconcerting for our political classifications and the ideologies which echo them among the Arabs. But look at the facts. Over a score of years bourgeois nationalism, discredited by its compromises, gave way in the post-Suez period to Nasserist, Algerian, and Baʿthist socialisms in the name of the same return to fundamentals that had inspired the Muslim Brothers movement in the opposite direction! A dangerous ambivalence, admittedly, and an ever-present risk of a change in sign. But what historical dynamism is without its bifurcations? [20]

Like others, the Arabs will thus have used everything that has come to hand in solving their difficult problems. In their case, mirror tricks, demystification of the foreign, and strategic self-variation have been used successively and simultaneously as means. A priceless variety! Drawing on their own resources preserves what can be preserved, while opening up innovative vistas whose fertility is far from exhausted by the experiences of which we are aware; meanwhile, the most tumultuous espousal of this or that hypothesis arouses specific counterparts in the form of available alternatives, or even of irony. The well-known Egyptian *nukta* [21] is in many cases liberty's night watchman or, better still, that of collective creativity. . . .

Facing New Contradictions

If the role of invariance in many types of Arab conduct has been insisted upon, this has, to repeat, been a working hypothesis and in no way a value judgment. Such a judgment, which Eastern and Western thinkers often believe they can formulate, would be the more dubious to us since, to resume an analogy already examined above, history and model, genesis and structure, endow any collective movement with a double dimension. We might, if you will, compare them to an airplane whose motor pushes it forward and whose wing sustains it in the air: how could it do without either one or the other?

This is so true that the present world, whose avant-garde excursions have liquidated a large part of the "old song"—by which we mean many of its traditional invariances—sees new paradigms soaring over triumphant history, and is thus far unable to harmonize history and paradigms: hence its anguish.

In an expanding universe, when Darwinism appears to be confirmed at the molecular level, when the effort of the African, Asian, and Latin American masses is revitalizing praxis, the idea of synchronism is invading the human sciences, and linguistics is replacing history as the ideal of the other disciplines. The stunning ubiquity of communications is visibly rendering people and things uniform, the whole planet is becoming "simultaneous," and yet discord and incompatibility are intensifying. Many are proclaiming the victory of structure over origin, at a time when a common becoming is proceeding headlong. This growing primacy of the formal ought at least to reshape the world and give it a face in which one could recognize oneself! Instead of which the world is losing its shape, and its meaning, under our very eyes. At the outset the new uniformities accede, of course, to power to which the theocracies of the past could not hope to aspire. But they are aggravated by the fact that they are now accepted as fruits of prosperity, and creativity is deserting them. In our institutions, and almost in our thoughts, sign is taking the place of cause, but without an accompanying quest for meaning. Biologists and chemists recognize in information that which moves mass and resists entropy: but they neglect to tell us what information is, where it comes from, and where it is headed. Literary criticism apportions a text's effect among numerous codes. Ethnology does the same. But whence come these codes, and why retain of the real only its regularities? Whose conventions, and concerning what? Have we come to the point where the world is so finite that I cannot hold dissenting views, or rebel, except as a maniacal fragment detached from the pre-established system?

Dissidence, while emitting revolutionary signals more than ever, no longer aspires to act upon the totality, nor to use it as underpinning, but merely to subject it to an ironical demolition. The philosophers themselves discard the idea of totality as old-fashioned bric-a-brac. And this at a moment when, for the first time in history, the power of communications has made man's unity no longer simply a metaphysical plea but an observable fact, and almost a last resort. Rebellion insists more upon the violence of its manifestations, or the manifestation of violence, than upon giving birth to something—in which it converges with the immense tide of words overflowing the world. A species of man tangential to things, prone to make of his life and that of others a perpetual "happening," is thus proliferating in these upstart societies as a sardonic insult both to the old abuses and to the old virtues. History has not been the gainer! Many are retrying its case, and are promising it the same death as Nietzsche proclaimed of God nearly a century ago.

But these discouraging, and as if dangling, views doubtless apply only to tired-out cultures and societies defeated by overdevelopment. Even within their own domains they find themselves contradicted and challenged by ever-reawakening angers which are able to find sap under "civilization's petrified cements" (Ch. Fourier). The peoples of the Third World, free of any doubt as to their unhappiness or their aspiration, are in this respect solidary with all the young, still verdant forces throughout the five continents.

Let us share in their hope. Man's existence would be reduced to impotent banality, though sustained by a triumphant production and consumption, if it were not a presence for itself: if, that is, no gaze were directed upon it. That is the gaze which makes a destiny of an act. Rilke said it along ago:

> What is called destiny is this: to be face to face,
> Nothing other than that, and always to be face to face.

For to be "face to face" with something is also to face up to it.

Appendix A

"Muʿallaqa" by Imrūʾ al-Qays
French Translation by Jacques Berque

J'ai essayé, comme on voit, de distinguer typographiquement les différents *tons* du poème: (*a*) un ou plusieurs récits; (*b*) des propos rapportés (en italiques); (*c*) des élans lyriques (dont le rythme se rompt dans la traduction en courtes sentences, correspondant à une image ou à une émotion); (*d*) des rappels de scènes, rendus ici sous forme de périodes continues. La coupure originelle des vers arabes a été marquée par le signe /, puisqu'elle ne coïncide pas forcément avec le rythme de ma traduction.

Qu'il me soit permis de dire ici ma gratitude à celui qui m'accompagna dans ces deux tournées, le cheikh ʿAlī ʿAbdel Monʿim, et à ceux avec qui j'ai discuté de la scansion ou de l'interprétation de l'un ou de l'autre de ces poèmes: lui encore, Régis Blachère, Toufic Touma, Zafer Kassimy, Diane Tomiche, sans oublier des poètes français, tels Henri Michaux, Michel Deguy, Jean Grosjean, à qui j'ai soumis, interrogativement, cette poésis du désert. Je resterai naturellement seul responsable des erreurs ou des faiblesses de ma traduction.—J.B.

LA MUʿALLAQA

«Halte! Pleurons au rappel d'une aimée»
et du campement au défaut de la dune
entre al-Dakhkhûl et Ḥawmal / et Tûḍîḥ et l-Miqrât.
L'empreinte n'en demeure que par le tissage du vent
qui du nord et du sud / afflue mollement sur ses faces
la brise d'est l'habille d'un raclement de voile effrangé /
on ne voit plus sur ses aires et ses places
que des crottes de troupeaux sauvages serrées comme graines de piment. /
Au matin de l'exil, tandis qu'eux rechargeaient
moi près des épineux du camp, briseur d'écales amères /
en elle je demeurais.
Me dirent mes amis du haut de leurs montures
«Ne meurs pas de chagrin supporte bellement /

laisse aller de toi chose passée sa route
affronte plutôt l'épreuve du jour». /
Et moi je demeurais en elle attendant que vacille
une folie de deuil confiante en sa fureur /
quand ma seule guérison eût été une larme
si seulement j'en avais pu verser
«Qu'attendre d'une empreinte évanouie?
ainsi avais-tu fait pour Umm al-Ḥuwayrith avant elle
et pour sa voisine Umm al-Rabbâb à Ma'sal» /
. . . quand elles se levaient du musc s'exhalait d'elles
brise du matin porteuse d'une odeur de girofle . . . /
Enfin coulèrent les larmes de ma soif
sur mon col jusqu'à mouiller mon baudrier /
«Avec elles aussi que de beaux jours goûtés!»

Oui, ce jour-là surtout dans le cirque de Djuljul / et cet autre jour quand pour les jeunes filles j'égorgeai ma monture, oh merveille d'un harnachement endossé / et merveille quand elles le déposèrent, et merveille de moi prodigue dépeceur! /
De la viande pour elles à s'en jeter, de la graisse comme les houppes d'un damas frangé / le suif de la bosse circulant dans nos écuelles, à nous le tendre avec du grain pilé! /

Et le jour où j'entrai dans la logette, le palanquin de ʿUnayza, elle me dit: *«Malheur, tu me fais piétonne!»* / ainsi disait-elle car nous faisions à deux le bâti pencher. *«Tu vas tuer mon chameau, Imrû'l-Qays, descends!»* / mais je lui dis: *«Va, lâche-lui la rêne, ne me bannis de ta cueillette humide / ni ne plains le gaillard de notre doublement, va laisse-moi goûter ta cueillette de girofle»* /

o bouche rayonnante comme la marguerite
aux contours nets et purs et bien rangée . . . /

Et toi l'enceinte l'allaitante je te visitai je t'ai distraite de l'Un-an pourvu d'amulettes / si derrière toi il pleurait, du buste vers lui te détournais, mais le reste de ton corps sous moi me dérobais / . . .

Un autre jour sur le dos de la dune elle se refusait, jurant d'un serment sans échappatoire / *«O Fâṭima, de grâce, trêve aux coquetteries. Si tu as seulement décrété que je parte sois plus clémente, / mais si quelque chose de ma nature t'est contraire, alors démêle du tien mon habit, soyons quitte* /

ce qui de moi t'égare. c'est qu'à mourir je t'aime, qu'à tes ordres obéisse mon coeur, que tu aies divisé mon foie, une moitié tuée l'autre entravée de fer / *et que tes yeux ne se mouillent que pour planter leurs flèches dans les tronçons d'un coeur humilié»* /

Et l'oeuf de préservation, l'inaccessible au désir dans sa cache, j'ai joui d'elle à ma fantaisie, sans me presser /

vers elle j'avais passé les gardes, une coterie guettant pour m'occire en secret / quand au ciel obliquèrent les Pléiades comme obliquent les torsades d'un sautoir articulé /

lors je vins, elle avait pour dormir ôté ses robes, derrière le rideau sauf l'ultime vêture / elle me dit: *«Par Dieu! Contre toi point d'astuce, et non plus que je voie ta folie te quitter!»* /

Nous sortîmes, elle menant derrière elle sur nos traces les traînes de sa mante à figures / nous passâmes les abords du camp, et quand à nous s'offrit un creux sûr entre des bosses de sable grumeleux / je l'attirai par les deux tempes

elle se laisse aller sur moi, maigre de taille
plantureuse à ses bracelets de cheville /
vers moi quand elle se tourne elle exhale son parfum
brise d'est porteuse d'une odeur de girofle /
quand je lui dis laisse-toi prendre
sur moi se laisse aller
maigre de taille, plantureuse aux bracelets /
svelte blanche irrépandue polie comme un miroir /
elle dérobe et révèle une joue tendre aux aguets
et le regard de la sauvageonne suitée de Wajra /
encolure de gazelle, blanche
si gracieuse la dresse sans que rien l'encombre /
chevelure parant le dos charbonneuse touffue
comme le régime impétueux du dattier /
chignonnée vers le haut
noyant les aiguilles dans ses noeuds et ses ondes /
et la taille grêle comme une rêne tressée
et les jambes pareilles aux tiges de l'irrigué rampant /
elle s'éveille, épandeuse de musc sur la couche de la méridienne
sans avoir à ceindre le peu qu'elle a gardé /
ô toucher délicat comme les vers de Daby

ou la mâchure de l'*ishil* /
ô pareille à l'oeuf vierge de l'autruche
blancheur ocrée nourrie du plus pur d'une eau défendue /
ô lumineuse dans les ténèbres du soir
comme la lampe nocturne de l'ermite solitaire /
telle te scrute la patience de ma soif
quand tu bouges vêtue entre la femme et l'adolescente. /
Car la furie des hommes se dissipe avec leur jeunesse
mais point mon coeur sa passion d'elle n'a dépouillée. . . /
n'en ai-je pas repoussé
de réprimandes contre toi insistantes
malgré leur acharnement à blâmer! . . . /

•

O nuit vagues de la mer répandant sur moi tes volutes
varieuses de peines m'éprouvant /
je t'ai dit
lorsque étirant le dos tu ramassais
ta croupe vers un poitrail s'éloignant /
«N'est-ce pas nuit longue qu'il n'y aura plus pour moi de matin
de matin qui mieux vaille!» /
triste nuit aux étoiles fixées par des tresses de lin
à la surdité de la roche. . . /

De bon matin, les oiseaux encore aux nids, j'enfourche mon ras-
crinière
jeteur d'entraves aux bêtes sauvages, galbé /
il assaille il se dérobe il charge et tout ensemble volte
comme roche compacte dévale le torrent /
bai-brun de son échine il secoue le tapis de selle
comme glisse une pierre de l'escarpement /
du talon tu l'émeus il geint quand s'émeut sa brûlure
comme gronde un chaudron sur pieds /
déverseur, ô nageuses de ma fatigue
soulevant la poussière sur l'esplanade par les sabots durcie /
il rejette de son dos l'adolescent allégé
ôte à qui veut le forcer vêtures même pesantes /
inlassable comme le jouet actionné par l'enfant
et qui tourne à deux palets sur la ficelle jointive /
de gazelle a les flancs et d'autruche les jambes
la course du loup la détente du renardeau /
fort des côtes le vois-tu par derrière son entre-deux il cache
d'une queue balayant la terre de haut et bien d'aplomb /

son garrot quand il dort debout près de ma tente
est comme la pierre où broyer le parfum de l'épouse
ou l'amertume. . . /

Et puis nous découvrîmes un troupeau de vaches sauvages pareilles à une ronde de vierges sous leur voile à traîne / elles se rabattirent, alternantes comme la parure sur un col doté d'oncles paternels et maternels / nous joignîmes aux guideuses les traînardes, dans un tumulte indivisible / lui passait du taureau à la vache d'une seule foulée, sans même de sueur qu'on aurait à rincer / les cuisiniers du clan s'activeraient à dépêcher la grillade et forcer le bouilli / quand au soir nous reviendrions

et revient le regard impuissant à le saisir,
quand l'oeil sur lui monte il doit redescendre /
le sang des guideuses sur son poitrail
comme broyure de henné sur virile blancheur /
avec la selle et les rênes sur lui
debout il dort sous mes yeux sans s'étendre /

•

«Ami l'orage
viens en voir l'éclair»
deux mains illuminant la brume opaque /
tel son scintillement
ou comme la lampe de l'ermite quand il force l'huile sur la mèche
tressée: /
avec des amis l'avons attendu
entre Ḍârij et ʿUdhayb éloignements de mon souci /
sur Qaṭân nous guettions la dextre de la pluie
sa gauche sur al-Satâr et Yadhbul /
et voici que l'eau giclant à pleine mamelle
reploya sur sa touffe la cime du gommier /
comme si les merles de Jiwāʾ dès l'aurore
avaient bu la primeur d'un moût poivré /
il atteignit Qunnân de son mascaret
débusquant le mouflon de toutes les falaises /
à Taymâʾ ne laissa ni stipe de palmier
ni château qui ne fût bâti sur le rocher /
pareil le mont Abân sous les sortes de l'averse
au grand d'entre les hommes
quand il se drape dans son manteau rayé /
pareille sera demain matin

la cime du Mujaymar dans la crue les épaves
à la rotation d'un fuseau /
et pareils les lions noyés hier soir dans ses aires lointaines
à des bulbes d'oignons sauvages /
seront comme le yéménite sa pacotille déballe
projetés au désert de Ghabîṭ.

Appendix B

Sources for Poems Translated from Arabic into English

Boulos, Sargon. "Al-Mawāʾid al-Bāridah," *Shiʿr*, nos. 29–30, Winter 1964 (Beirut).

Darwīsh, Maḥmūd. "Imraʾah jamīlah fi Sadūm," in *Maṭrūn Naʿim fī Kharīfin baʿid.* Nasrah: Matbaʿat al-Hakīm, 1971.

Dunqul, Amal. "Al-Hujra ilā al-dākhil," in *Taʿlīq ʿalā mā Ḥadath.* 1971.

Imrūʾ al-Qays. "Muʿallaqa." Text from two sources: *Dīwān Imrūʾ al-Qays*, edited by Muḥammad Abū al-Faḍl Ibrāhīm, 3d ed. Cairo: Dār al-Maʿārif bi-Miṣr, 1969; *Imrūʾ al-Qays amīr shuʿarāʾ al-Jāhilīyah*, edited by Ṭāhir Aḥmad Makkī. Cairo: Dār al-Maʿārif bi-Miṣr, 1968.

Al-Jawāhirī. Lines from *Ayyuhā al-ʿAraq.* Beirut, 1971.

Labīd. "Ode" and "Muʿallaqa," in *Sharh al-Muʿallaqāt al-Sabʿ*, edited by Muḥammad Muḥyī al-Dīn ʿAbd al-Ḥamīd. Cairo: Maktabat Muḥammad ʿAlī Ṣabiḥ wa-Awlādahu, 1966.

Al-Qāsim, Samīḥ. "Al-Mīlād," in *Dami ʿalā Kaffī.* Nazareth: Hakim Publishing Co., 1967.

Shākir al-Sayyāb, Badr. "Unshūdat al-Maṭar," in *Dīwān.* Beirut: Dār al-ʿAwdah, 1971.

Notes

Introduction: Why the Arabs?

1. Saying attributed to the Prophet.

I. The City Speaks

1. The term and meaning are absent from the Koran and are not listed in the *Lisān*. It is frequently used by Ibn Khaldūn, on the other hand, and on that basis is noted by Dozy. V. Monteil counts two dozen occurrences in the *Prolegomena* alone.
2. Jirjī Zaydān (1861–1914), *Ta'rīkh al-Tamaddun al-Islāmī* (1902–1906).
3. Ṭaha Ḥusain, *Mustaqbal al-Thaqāfa fī Miṣr* (1938, 1944). Cf. our *Egypt: Imperialism and Revolution* (London: Faber, 1972).
4. Such as Maḥmūd Amīn al-'Ālim, *Al-Thaqāfa wal-Thawra* (1970), and Ghālī Shukrī, *Mudhakkirāt Thaqāfa Taḥtaḍir* (1970).
5. In Egypt, Nasser's disappearance raised many questions over the right path to be followed and—something eminently propitious for the progress of historical reason—conflicting evaluations of his contribution.
6. Friday "sermon" at the mosque.
7. Newspaper circulation, however, falls short of the burgeoning increase of the population. The press is concerned about this and, rightly, blames illiteracy and poverty.
8. The social columns.
9. This is an important dimension of Eastern sociability. Cf. Aḥmad Bahjat, "How Damascus Thinks" [street, clique, coffee shop], *Ṣabāḥ al-Khayr*, May 1, 1958; Anwar al-Jundī, "Some Historical Circles," *Al-'Arabī*, June 1970; and the ironical description of the "gay dog," *al-faḥlāwī*, great conversationalist and backgammon player, in Ḥāmid 'Ammār, *Fī Binā' al-Bashr*, with commentary by Aḥmad Bahā' al-Dīn, *Al-Muṣawwar*, February 12, 1965. On Ramadan nights as cultural vehicle, cf. *Ākhir Sā'a*, December 20, 1967.
10. The escape valve for a repressed antagonism, the joke through which the people's zest operates.
11. Used here are analytical schemes I have set forth more systematically in "Logiques plurales du progrès," *Diogène*, No. 79 (July–September 1972), pp. 3–26.
12. An enormous effort has been accomplished in this direction. Cf. Louis 'Awaḍ, "Al-Ta'līf wal-Tarjama wal-Nashr," *Ahrām*, May 7, 1965. But what books do the Arabs read? Cf. Bahīj 'Uthmān, *Al-'Arabī*, February 1961; Salīm al-Jisr, *Al-Jarida*, August 2, 1964; Hiyām Mallāṭ, *L'Orient*, no. 78 (February 1965). And the disillusioned observations of the Jordanian writer 'Īsā al-Na'ūrī, *Al-Adīb*, no. 4 (April 1972). An unheard-of phenomenon: a poet founds his own publishing house, and it prospers (cf. *Nahār*, December 18, 1966). But this was Nizār Qabbānī.
13. Besides, the history of the Arabic press has been the subject of documented studies too well known to cite here.

14. M. Aḥmad Ṭālib Ibrāhīmī has recently collected several of these texts in a book: *De la décolonization à la révolution culturelle* (Algiers, 1973).
15. S. Kherfī, *Al-Thaqāfa*, May–July 1972, p. 77 ff.
16. Note also the articles by M. Zniber in the Moroccan magazine *Aqlām*, 1972–1973, and more recently Mawlūd Qāsim n-ayt Belqāsem, *Aniya wa Aṣāla* (1975).
17. Cf. the instructive diversity of approach in the symposia *Al-Qur'ān* and *Muḥammad* (Beirut, 1973).
18. "Spirit" and "matter."
19. "Community consensus" (ancient canonical category).
20. These views will be expanded upon below, p. 193 ff.

II. Trajectory of a Language

1. Article of 1933–1934, reprinted in *Questions de poétique* (Paris: Seuil, 1973), p. 122.
2. Mu'allim Buṭros al-Bustānī (1819–1883), in *Rawā'i'* (1950 ed.) p. 35 ff.
3. Assonant prose.
4. See, particularly, Ch. Pellat, "'Arabiya," in *Encyclopedia of Islam*, new ed. (Leiden: E. J. Brill, 1960), 1:561–603; Vincent Monteil, *L'arabe moderne* (1960); Ibrāhīm al-Samarrā'ī, *Al-Jadīd fil-Lugha wal-Mu'jam al-'Arabī al-Ḥadīth* (Baghdad, 1966); A. F. L. Beeson, *The Arabic Language Today* (London: Hutchinson, 1970); Fück, *'Arabiya* (1950), trans. Cl. Denizeau (1955); H. Wehr, *Arabisches Wörterbuch für die Schriftsprache der Gegenwart* (Leipzig, 1952–1956). And quite recently I. Samarrā'ī, *Tanmiyat al-Lugha al-'Arabiya fīl-'Aṣr al-Ḥadīth* (1973), which is essential to our subject; O. Petit, "Langage, culture et participation dans le monde arabe contemporain," *Ibla*, 1971–1972, p. 259 ff. A good example of regional monography: Nash'at Ẓabiyān, *Ḥarakat al-Iḥyā' al-Lughawī fī Bilād al-Shām* (Damascus, 1976).
5. The classical Arabic language.
6. This despair was noted by the Duc d'Harcourt, Charles Francois Marie, duc d'Harcourt, *L'Egypte et les Egyptiens* (Paris: Plon, 1893).
7. Among other collections of *maqāmāt*, we may cite Aḥmad Fāris al-Shidyāq (1804?–1887); Nāṣīf al-Yāzijī (1800–1871); Ibrāhīm al-Aḥdab (1826–1891). Cf., more recently, 'Abd al-Fattāḥ Ghabū, "The Hero in Bayram's *Maqāmāt*," *Ākhir Sā'a*, January 4, 1967.
8. An unexpected feature, which Rīḥānī did not fail to remark upon in his account, *Mulūk al-'Arab* (1924, 5th ed., 1972).
9. "Nationalistic assertion of specificity."
10. In *Egypt: Imperialism and Revolution* we traced this evolution in detail, listing the bibliography of the various genres.
11. "Canonical science" and "knowledge," the latter tending toward esotericism.
12. The late Georges Henein saw this clearly, in the preface to *Anthologie de la littérature arabe*, vol. *Poésie* (1967), pp. 5–6.
13. See Muṣṭafā Āl-Shak'a, *Muṣṭafā Ṣādiq al-Rāfi'ī* (1970).
14. *Rakāka/jazāla*: that which characterizes style as thin and pallid or as rich and substantial.
15. Rāfi'ī, *Taḥt Rāyat al-Qur'ān*, 4th ed. (1952), p. 32 ff.
16. See below, pp. 69 ff., 216 ff.
17. The word dates from 1934.
18. *Al-Ahrām*, April 6, 1936.
19. The expression is Tawfīq al-Ḥakīm's.
20. At the Sirs al-Layyān Center in Egypt.
21. Modern Arabic would thus no longer desire to be an extension of the classical, but rather a linguistic prospect into the future.
22. See below, Chapters XIV and XV.
23. Which, nevertheless, he did not himself renounce.

III. Unitary and Plural

1. Enclosed, private gardens.
2. Since I wrote these lines this friend, too, has died.
3. The question does not arise, of course, with regard to the Arab world only. With respect to the Latin American world, Efraín Hurtado's talented magazine recently began systematic examination of the same question (*Uno y Multiple* [Caracas], Summer 1975).
4. Witness, in America, the very active Association of Arab Graduates of American Universities, which includes personnel not only from the universities but also from the liberal professions, commerce, and even industry. Note also the success of Arabs in Latin America.
5. The only notable exception, to my knowledge, being the Damascus University, proudly and totally Arabized from its foundation, at the price of some damage.
6. In the long run the partner who is the most deeply acquainted with the other's language and psychology will have the advantage. The Third World, from this point of view, would appear to have the advantage over today's world leaders, who are quite retrograde in this respect.
7. *Al-Nahār*, January 12, 13, 25, 1971.
8. One of the studies in which the problem seems to us to have been best treated is that of Abdullah Mazouni, *Culture et enseignement en Algérie et au Maghreb* (Paris: Maspéro, 1968).
9. In the fine translation by Sarwat Okasha.
10. Cf. on all these points the judicious remarks of A. Memmi, *Anthologie des écrivains français du Maghreb* (Paris, 1969); J. Dejeux, *La Littérature maghrébine d'expression française*, 3 vols. (1970).
11. Cf. in this connection the relevant analysis of the concept of "minor literature" by G. Deleuze and G. Guatari, *Kafka* (1975), p. 29 ff.
12. Of such distinguished quality when compared with another synthesis of genius: that of Ibn Khaldūn.
13. "Cultivated people" and "doctors."
14. On this point I take the liberty of referring to my essays "Qu'est-ce que la base?" in *L'Orient second*, 1970, p. 74 ff., and "Pluriels," in *Esprit*, August 1972.
15. To borrow the fine, very programmatic, expression of Jean Duvignaud in his book of that title, 1973.
16. The "small group of elect," or "cenacle," as distinct from the "masses," *ʿāmma* or, rather, *jamāhīr*.
17. A notion recently made into an exergue. See our account of "Différence" in Duvignaud, *La Sociologie* (1972), and especially H. Lefebvre, *Le Manifeste différentialiste* (1970).

IV. Apprenticeships, but to What?

1. For the late master's life I refer of course to his autobiographical work and to the volume of essays, with a preface by ʿAbd al-Raḥmān Badawī, which we dedicated to him on his seventieth birthday, *Ṭaha Ḥusain* (Cairo: Dār al-Maʿārif, 1962). Some vivid details have come to my attention through interviews and press reports, notably those collected in a special issue of *Al-Hilāl*, February 1, 1966. See also *Al-Muṣawwar*, April 12, 1963, December 3, 1965, December 2, 1966; *Al-Ahram*, December 19, 1965; *Ākhir Sāʿa*, January 13, 1965, and November 25, 1970; *Al-Ahrām* and *Ākhir Sāʿa*, February 12, 1965; *Al-Shaʿb* (Beirut), February 8, 1964. For a dissenting opinion see the iconoclastic article by Fatḥī Raḍwān, *Al-Muṣawwar*, January 19, 1968. For a more-balanced appraisal see Rajāʾ Naqqāsh, *Al-Musawwar*, December 1, 1967.
2. *Al-Hilāl*, February 1, 1966, p. 62.

3. *Mudhakkirāt* (1967).
4. Cf. J. Berque, "Une affaire Dreyfus de la philologie arabe," in J. Berque and J.-P. Charnay, *Normes et valeurs de l'islam contemporain* (1966), p. 267 ff.
5. *Anthologie de la littérature arabe contemporaine*, vol. 1, *Essais* (1965), p. 407.
6. *Al-Hilāl*, February 1966, p. 116 ff.
7. *Mudhakkirāt Thaqāfa Taḥtaḍir* (1970), p. 369 ff. Cf. also *Thaqāfatunā bayna Na'm wa Lā* (1972).
8. An analysis of this book may be found in my *Egypt: Imperialism and Revolution*, pp. 637–641.
9. Jamāl Ḥamdān, *Shakhṣiyat Miṣr*, 2d ed. (1970).
10. *Mustaqbal al-Tarbiya fīl-Sharq al-'Arabī* (1962).
11. Ibid., p. 62 ff.
12. *Al-Qāmūs al-Falsafī*, 2 vols. (1973).
13. 'Abdullah 'Abd al-Dā'im, *Al-Takhṭīṭ al-Tarbawī* (1966).
14. For more recent documentation see the volume in which are assembled the *Proceedings* of the meeting at Marrakesh among ministers of education of the various Arab states, organized by UNESCO (1970).

V. New Fields of Meaning

1. This will be the subject of our Part Three, which will undertake a searching analysis of the linkages between history and expression.
2. Zakī Najīb Maḥmūd devotes a large part of his book *Tajdīd al-Fikr al-'Arabī* (1971) to advocating the transformation of a civilization of words into one of facts. This reflects a Western trait in him.
3. This was the subject of a UNESCO colloquium in September 1971. See *La Science et la diversité des cultures* (1974), p. 133 ff.
4. Which would imply the "withering away" of states, following that of the big companies. We are still far from that. . . .
5. A "Ransom," outrageously copied from a model lent by Émile Biarnay.
6. On this labor progress, see an interesting report in *Ākhir Sā'a*, April 15, 1964. But this article deals only with progress in training. Innovation in manual skills and technical invention in the workshop have unfortunately not been the subject of studies which, together with the analysis of patents, alone would make it possible to evaluate actual technological progress.
7. According to the International Monetary Fund, the combined reserves of Algeria, Iran, Iraq, Kuwait, Libya, Oman, and Saudi Arabia rose by some twenty billion dollars in 1974 alone!
8. *Al-Ahrām al-Iqtiṣādī*, no. 1 (1972).
9. Ibid., July 1973.
10. This is how I translate the title *Humūm al-Shabāb*.
11. This had been correctly noted at the time by Clovis Maqṣūd, *Azmat al-Yasār al-'Arabī* (1960).
12. Is this because the new "isms" broke faith with themselves or because they were thwarted by reactionary forces? Both, undoubtedly; hence the necessity for objective analyses.
13. General Muḥammad 'Amrān, *Tajribatī fīl-Thawra* (n.d.), p. 72 ff.
14. The evolution which has followed, mainly on Egyptian initiative, has only accentuated the divergences, while Lebanon is tearing itself to pieces.
15. "Charisma" inherent in a person or a style of action.
16. The underground cellars of old Mesopotamian houses.
17. In the early stages of independence this fact led to controversies into which, of course, I shall not enter here.

VI. In Search of Imrū' al-Qays

1. Koran, LIV, 27 ff., and passim.
2. The name is accented on the final vowel. Cf. Doughty, *Travels in Arabia Deserta*, chap. IV (on Madā'in), p. 181 ff.
3. The "rock people" also left traces, and even inscriptions, not far from the Wādī al-Dawāsir area that will be spoken of later; these are the ruins of Fao. See A. al-Anṣārī, "Inscriptions at Fao," *Majallat Kulliyat al-Adab* (Riyad, 1974), p. 27 ff.
4. Shaikh Muḥammad bin Bulayhad, *Ṣaḥīh al-Akhbār 'ammā fī Bilād al-'Arab min al-Āthār* (1951), part I, p. 16 ff.
5. In the English translation of the *Mu'allaqa*, the rhymes have not been reproduced; thus, we have tried to set off differences in tone by arranging the poem in stanzas. See Appendix A for Professor Berque's French translation of this poem.—Trans.
6. This is the name applied to what is not classical (in speaking of poems) or, in speaking of peoples, refers to an origin or way of life earlier than the Revelation and external to it. See 'Abdullah Wayḥān, *Rawā'i' al-Shi'r al-Nabaṭi*, 2 vols., and especially 'Abdullah bin Khamīs, *Al-Adab al-Sha'bī fī Jazīrat al-'Arab* (1958). Re the Euphrates and Shāmiya areas, cf. Shafīq al-Kamālī, *Al-Shi'r 'ind al-Badū* (1964); on Bedouin chivalry cf. Muḥammad al-Sudayrī, *Abṭāl al-Ṣaḥrā'* (Riyad, 1968). Muḥammad bin Sa'd bin Ḥusain, *Al-Adab al Ḥadīth fī Najd* (Cairo, n.d.), mentions an illustrious poet among the Dawāsir: Muḥammad bin 'Athimīn, b. 1853/4 (p. 33).
7. Meaning "coffee" here.
8. An enormous ostrich was shot by hunters in 1938 on the Iraq-Arabia border. But the Qatar ostriches, which I saw after writing these lines, were imported from Sudan.

VII. Grandeur and Weaknesses of Agonistic Man

1. To such an extent that it inspired a collection by one poet present, the Syrian Sulaymān Āl 'Isā, *Jazīrat Sindibād* (1971).
2. Favored by Ḥusain Fawzī.
3. Koran, XXVI, 226.
4. Who found himself accused, with some verisimilitude, of incorporating in one of his poems an entire sequence from a Jordanian poet.
5. Essentially Margoliouth and Ṭaha Ḥusain, followed on this point since 1925 by the late R. Blachère. It must be admitted that the emergence in the sixth century of an Arabic poetry resembling nothing else in neighboring literatures—Byzantine, Syriac, Sasanid, Abyssinian—raises a formidable problem. But giving its emergence a later date, by ascribing precisely the same originality to eighth-century philologists, in no way solves the problem.
6. Shafīq al-Kamālī, *Al-Shi'r 'ind al-Badū*, p. 301. The same phenomenon is noted by Muḥammad al-Marzūqī for southern Tunisia.
7. To borrow Julia Kristeva's expression. In our time, one of Jawāhirī's most-celebrated poems was thus improvised, in a moment of intense collective emotion, at the funeral of his murdered brother.
8. I have followed the text of Dhū al-Rumma established by Macartney, 1919, and the remarkable commentary by 'Abdullah al-Ṭayyib, *Sharḥ Arba'a Qaṣā'id li-Dhī al-Rumma* (1958).
9. Cf. pp. 145–146, our attempt at translation.
10. Reprinted in L. Massignon, "Les méthodes de réalisation artistiques de l'Islam,"

Opera minora (1963), p. 9 ff. There is thus both "rise" and "descent" in Arabic metaphor, and this vertical movement is in itself revealing.

11. The term *dumyā*, probably borrowed from Aramaic, David Cohen tells me, evokes an image or simulacrum in that language, which notably enriches Nābigha's expression.
12. The violent impulse resulting from hunger (onager), combativeness (wild bull), parental love (ostrich). The procedure is called *tashbīh*. See the edition of al-Aṣnāʿī by Aḥmad Shākir and ʿAbd al-Salām Hārūn, 1964, for a useful index of comparisons.
13. Whereas in detail it is the comparison that operates; hence the role of the conjunction *kaʾanna*, which recurs with tiresome frequency.
14. For some, a multiplicity of themes may have constituted an aesthetic criterion of the earliest *inshād*. On the question of origins, see the perspicacious remarks on pre-Islamic poetry by F. E. Bustānī in his section of *Al-Rawāʾiʿ*, 5th ed. (1963), p. 10 ff.
15. This river-of-diction may have had as its habitual rhythm the *rajaz*, which is traditionally conceded to have evolved earlier than the other meters.
16. "Anthroponym referring to descent" or, if you will, "gentilitial name."
17. See below, p. 286 ff.
18. Gotthold Weil, "ʿArūḍ," *Encyclopedia of Islam* (1960), 1:692.
19. Muḥammad Ṭāriq al-Kātib, *Mawāzin al-Shiʿr al-ʿArabī bi-Istiʿmāl al-Arqām al-Thanāʾiya* (Basra, 1971).
20. Other scansions are possible permitting one to identify the meter without the help of the foot count and also ignoring the divisions into feet. See the innovative study by Kamāl Abū Dīb, *Mawāqif*, no. 22 (1972).
21. Is it an accident that an exception is Ruʾba bin ʿAjjāj, who is famous for the length of his pieces, veritable continuities in *rajaz*, and his archaizing tribalism?
22. Arab poetry would thus have arrived, so to speak, perfectly formed, like Athena from the head of Zeus, which would raise a rather considerable question. See Shawqī Ḍayf, *Al-ʿAṣr al-Jāhilī*, 4th ed., p. 194 ff.
23. And two contrasting types of behavior with respect to the group they came from.
24. Cf. Ṭaha Ḥusain's witty ironies on the subject of Yemeni poets supposedly contemporary with Ishmael: *Fī al-Adab al-Jāhilī* (1927), p. 194 ff.
25. R. Blachère, *Histoire de la littérature arabe* (1964), 1:96–97.
26. The agonistic character of these ancient commercial exchanges emerges clearly from the detailed condemnations they are subjected to in the *ḥadīth*, which treats the matter at length: a significant reaction.

VIII. Dirge for Pre-Islam

1. Throughout this chapter, I draw upon Iḥsān ʿAbbās' edition, *Sharḥ Dīwān Labīd* (Kuwait, 1962).
2. The monarch is mentioned no less than fifteen times in the *Dīwān*.
3. R. Blachère, *Histoire de la littérature arabe*, 2:345 ff.
4. In this description of Medina I have used, in addition to oral evidence and Brother Buhl's article in the *Encyclopedia of Islam*, several Arabic works of which the most important are cited below. More generally, I have profited by consulting Amīn al-Rīḥānī, *Taʾrīkh Najd al-Ḥadīth* (1952 ed.), and Sayyid Muḥammad Ibrāhīm, *Taʾrīkh al-Mamlaka al-ʿArabiya* (Riyad, 1973), cf. on Medina, p. 38 ff.
5. Ibrāhīm Āl ʿAbd al-Muḥsin, *Tadhkira ūlāʾ al-Nahy wal-ʿIrfān* (Riyad, n.d.), 1:13 ff.
6. ʿAlī Ḥāfiẓ, *Fuṣūl min Taʾrīkh al-Madīna al-Munawwara* (Jidda, n.d.), p. 35 ff.
7. Ibid., p. 4 ff.
8. ʿAbd al-Ḥamīd al-ʿAbbāsī, *ʿUmdat al-Akhbār fī Madīnat al-Mukhtār*, preface by Shakīb Arslān (n.d.), pp. 235–443.
9. Cf. ʿAlī al-Būlāqī, "Taʿqībat," in *Majallat al-Azhar*, February 1976, p. 195 ff.

10. "Innateness," a characteristic attributed to the Arabian Bedouin as repository of ancient revelations.
11. Signs of collapse: the invasion of manual occupations by Yemenis, among others; migration from the rural areas; the inequality of opportunity in reclaiming land by pump irrigation (decree dated September 28, 1968); the rush toward capitalism. It is true that the "Guidelines" of the latest plan appear to take some of these dangers judiciously into account.
12. *Dīwān*, esp. p. 158 ff., 163 ff.
13. XIII, 10.
14. This is how I translate *ṣubābāt al-karā*, XXVI, 28.
15. IV, 23–24.
16. II, 8; XI, 2; XVI, 6.
17. XXIV, 1. The line became current as a proverb, as did several others of Labīd.
18. XXVI, 25.
19. XIII, 19. Cf. some useful discussions on this root in M. Bravmann, *The Spiritual Background of Early Islam* (1972), p. 227 ff.
20. XXXV, 5.
21. XV, 15.
22. XVIII, 5.
23. XIV, 20.
24. XIV, 18.
25. XXV, 92.
26. XV, 50; XXXIX, 23.
27. II, 30.
28. XXVI, 68.
29. XIII, selection translated here *in extenso*.
30. Bisha is still the name of a river in southwestern Arabia and of a town which has a small airport!
31. II, 8.
32. XVI, 6.
33. XI, 2.
34. I, 1.
35. XXXV, 36–37.
36. IV, 1.
37. X, 1.
38. XLVIII, 55.
39. XI, 10.
40. Unless this term should be understood in its ancient meaning of physician-deviner.
41. XLVIII, 72.
42. XXVII, 30.
43. I, 45.
44. VIII, 38. Note the curiously Pindaric accent.
45. XXIV, 1.
46. V, 3.
47. XXXVI, 8.
48. According to Shawqī Ḍayf, Labīd became a Koran reader at Kūfa in his old age.
49. XXVI, 142; cf. also VII, 1.
50. XXVI, 13.
51. XVI, 7.
52. VII, 6. *Mudāris*, "one who studies the book" or "one guilty of a crime"; but cf. also *daras*, "scars left by scabies," "residue of something that used to be."
53. XIV, 9–10.
54. XXXIX, 1.
55. XXXIX, 2 ff. I have translated as "masses" *khawāliqahā*, or "densities."
56. XXXIX, 5 ff.

57. Or rather, of course, Heraclius, the Byzantine Emperor who also figures in the *ḥadīth*.

IX. Paradigm and Arab Rhetoric

1. Koran, II, 143.
2. I have set forth these ideas previously in the preface to Jean Grosjean's translation of the Koran (Paris: Club du livre, 1972).
3. Koran, LXIX, 42.
4. R. Blachère, *Histoire de la littérature arabe*, 2:194. Drawing upon an observation, previously quoted, by F. E. Bustānī on the subject of *inshād*, which is said to be the undifferentiated matrix both of the classical poetry and of *saj*ʿ, dare I say that the Book's "descent" served as an agent of revelation (no pun intended) which contributed to a retrospective discrimination between the two genres, and to their subsequent divergence?
5. Koran, XVII, 88.
6. Which has, for the purpose, developed one of its most-advanced methodological tools, as is shown by the well-known studies of I. Goldziher and J. Schacht.
7. ʿAlī Ḥāfiẓ, *Fuṣūl min Taʾrīkh al-Madīna al-Munawwara*, p. 79 ff.
8. On *musāqāt* and *muzāraʿa*, see Shaikh ʿAbbās Mutwallī Ḥamāda, "Mashrūʿiya al-Muzāraʿa fīl-Fiqh al-Muqāran," in *Majallat al-Qānūn wal-Iqtiṣād* (Cairo, 1967).
9. ʿAlī Ḥāfiẓ, *Fuṣūl min Taʾrīkh al-Madīna al-Munawwara*, p. 261 ff.
10. The French businessman who carried out this pumping project, and who has settled at Riyad, told me he could never have completed it except for the confidence King Saud showed in him.
11. For a good discussion see Ṣubḥī Ṣāliḥ, *Mabāḥith fī ʿUlūm al-Qurʾān* (1958).
12. P. Guiraud, quoted by J. Dubois et al. (Mu Group), *Rhétorique générale* (1970), p. 8.
13. Treatise translated and commented upon by G. von Grunebaum.
14. *Rhétorique générale*, p. 33 ff.
15. *Al-Itqān* (1967 ed.), 1:184 ff.
16. An unfinished commentary, which the Algerian Shaikh Ben Badis subsequently undertook to complete in the same spirit.
17. *Maḥāsin al-Taʾwīl*, in several vols. (1914).
18. *Tafsīr al-Marāghī*, 3d ed. (1962).
19. *Tafsīr al-Taḥrīr wal-Tanwīr* (Tunis, 1971).
20. Muṣṭafā Āl Shakʿa, *Al-Rāfiʿī* (1970), p. 204 ff.
21. Ibid., p. 56 ff.
22. Labīb Saʿīd, *Al-Muṣḥaf al-Murattal* (n.d.), p. 106 ff.
23. *Tafsīr al-Taḥrīr wal-Tanwīr* (Tunis, 1964), 1:90–116.
24. From the book's introduction. Cf. especially the monumental commentary, at once preaching and impressionistic, *Fī Ẓilāl al-Qurʾān*, 5th ed., 8 vols. (1967).
25. Bashīr bin Salāma, *Al-Lugha al-ʿArabiya wa Mashākil al-Kitāba* (1971), p. 38 ff.
26. This comment is, however, no longer strictly true for modern Arabic.
27. The author seems to echo the recent concept of grammatology.
28. Muṣṭafā Maḥmūd, *Al-Qurʾān Muḥāwala li-Fahm ʿAṣrī*, 3d ed. (1973).
29. Ibid., p. 10: "And the night, when it is stilly."
30. Dr. Kāmil Ḥusain, *Al-Dhikr al-Hakīm* (1971), cf. esp. p. 55.

X. Reading the Koran

1. Koran, XXXVI, 12.
2. Unless one adopts a view vulnerable to the accusation of "Sociologism," by which language consists of the aggregate of words exchanged, within a specific ter-

ritorial area, among its speakers at a particular moment in time. Its "structure" would then consist of the regularities observed in these data.

3. As a consequence of this very contraction, cf. p. 125 ff. But is this reduction not a characteristic of vocabulary formation as such? Cf. Aḥmad ʿAbd al-Ghaffār ʿAṭṭār, *Muqaddima lil-Ṣiḥāḥ*, preface by ʿAqqād (1962). Khalīl, on the basis of the number of roots, assumed the existence of twelve million words; barely one percent appear in the *Lisān*! This is still far from the 45,000 words in the *Oxford Dictionary*.
4. ʿAlī Ḥāfiẓ, *Fuṣūl min Taʾrīkh al-Madīna al-Munawwara*, p. 233.
5. On this personage see Michael Field, *A Hundred Million Dollars a Day* (London: Sidgwick and Jackson, 1975), pp. 186–187.
6. See, however, P. Jomier, "La place du Coran dans la vie quotidienne en Egypte," *Ibla*, no. 58 (1952), pp. 131–166. Less directly pertinent to our subject is W. S. Cuperus, *Al-Fātiḥa dans la pratique musulmane au Maroc* (Utrecht, 1973). Van Nieuwenhuijze, "The Koran as a Factor in the Islamic Way of Life," *Der Islam*, 1963. A virgin subject, certainly!
7. Suyūṭī, *Itqān*, 3:323 ff.
8. XCXII, 4. This is how I translate *saʿyākum la-shatta*.
9. As in the sura The Thunder.
10. The witty self-criticism by one who has been engaged in this work (J. C. Gardin, *Les analyses de discours* [1974], p. 14 ff.) compels me to make clear that I exaggerated my thought here somewhat.
11. Dr. ʿAlī Ḥilmī Mūsā, *Dirāsa Iḥṣāʾiya li-Judhūr Mafradāt al-Lugha al-ʿArabiya* (University of Kuwait, 1971).
12. As H. Meschonnic has done for the Song of Songs, *Les cinq rouleaux* (Paris: Gallimard, 1970).
13. Abū al-ʿAbbās al-Tījānī, "Jawāhir," manuscript, Algiers, 1711. See Collège de France, *Annuaire* for 1973, p. 467 ff.
14. As Dr. Muṣṭafā Maḥmūd does, *Al-Qurʾān Muḥāwala li-Fahm ʿAṣrī*, p. 52.
15. Aristotle makes a significant distinction between the two directions poetic language may follow: that of rare works or that of enigma (*Poetics*, trans. G. M. A. Grube [New York: Liberal Arts Press, 1958], p. 44 ff.).
16. Shawqī Ḍayf, *Surat al-Raḥmān wa Surat Qiṣār* (1971).
17. Ṭaha Ḥusain seems to have anticipated our point of view on this point; cf. *Al-Fitna al-Kubrā: ʿUthmān* (Cairo: Dār al-Maʿārif, 1970), p. 24, line 14 ff.
18. Samīḥ al-Qāsim, "Al-Mīlād," in *Damī ʿalā Kaffī*, 2d ed. (1970).

Part Three: Introduction

1. The admirable collection of Adonis (1960).
2. And even the opinion represented by the Wafd, which in this connection failed to support an innovating tendency that it was itself demonstrating in the political field. Out of phase. . . .
3. Umm Kulthūm's death was the occasion for a nearly unanimous chorus of veneration in the Arab press. Cf. Muṣṭafā Amīn, "The Fate of U.K.," *Akhir Sāʿa*, November 12, 1975, also contributions by Ahmad Rāmī, Anīs Mansūr, etc. All daily, weekly, and monthly publications contributed to the obituary.

XI. A Redeployment of Genres—First Symmetry: Painting and Music

1. "Yawmiyāt Marʾa lā Mubāliya," in *Dīwān* (1968), p. 634.
2. Ideas disseminated in France in recent years by the studies of Julia Kristeva and T. Todorov, and other articles in the magazine *Tel Quel*.
3. Although it is concerned with ancient art, we shall cite the monumental thesis of

A. Papadopoulos, "Esthétique de l'art musulman: La peinture," 6 vols., mimeographed (Lille, 1972), which points out usefully the "improbability principle" whereby this art seems to have defended the imagination's rights against all "faithful copy" tendencies.

4. Saʿīd al-Diwahjī, *Jawāmiʿ Mawṣil fī Mukhtalab al-ʿUṣūr* (Baghdad, 1966), pp. 17–54.
5. In December 1975 a resounding article by Roger Caillois in *Le Monde* set off a re-evaluation of Picasso.
6. Jabrā Ibrāhīm Jabrā, *La peinture contemporaine en Iraq* (Baghdad, 1970), and especially *Jawād Salīm wa Naṣb al-Ḥurriya* (1974).
7. See the album of Sijelmassi, *La peinture marocaine* (1972).
8. Shākir Ḥasan Āl Saʿīd, *Al-Buʿd al-Wāḥid: Al-Fann Yastalhimu al-Ḥarf* (Baghdad, 1971).
9. See a very suggestive history of Egyptian music by Fatḥī Ghānim, *Sabāh al-Khayr*, October 3, 10, 17, 29, 31, 1957. For Iraq, a sociology of musical instrumentation has been compiled by Miss Shahrazade Ḥasan, unpublished thesis, 1975.
10. Rafīq Fākhūrī, *Shabaka*, July 5, 1956.
11. *Akhir Sāʿa*, February 12, 1964.
12. Cf. Aḥmad Rajab, "Min Bāb al-Inṣāf," *Al-Muṣawwar*, June 7, 1963; Salīm al-Ḥulū, *Al-Maʿārif*, March 1961; Walīd Ghulmiya, *Nahār*, September 25, 1966. Umm Kulthūm herself must step aside to make way for new forms stemming from the symphony (*Rose al-Yūsuf*, June 3, 1963).
13. For Umm Kulthūm's opinion, see *Al-Muṣawwar*, May 3, 1963. On the relation between classical meters and music, see M. Wayardī, *Al-Maʿrifa*, August 1962. Commenting on the Second Conference on Arab Music in Cairo (1969), Ṣāliḥ Jawdat accused the organizers of having misunderstood the essential role of lyrics in music (*Al-Muṣawwar*, January 16, 1970). Less old-fashioned, Kamāl al-Najmī expressed concern at the impoverishment of verbal sounds in the poetry then appearing (*Al-Muṣawwar*, July 19, 1968).
14. *Al-Jarīda* (Beirut), September 14, 1960.
15. See two remarkable articles by Mikhāʾīl Allah Wayardī, *Al-Maʿrifa*, October and November, 1962.
16. See the unpublished thesis by Dr. Chabrier, 1976.
17. Article by Aḥmad Rajab cited above, n.12. See also Ṣubḥī al-Wādī, *Al-Maʿrifa*, September 1964.

XII. Second Symmetry: Criticism and Imagination

1. The precocity of Najīb Maḥfūẓ in this field also must be noted, however.
2. By Tawfīq ʿAwwād (1939).
3. By Shakīb al-Jābirī (1943).
4. By Kateb Yāsīn (1956).
5. Fifth ed. (Beirut, 1967).
6. Short story with that title, *Al-Ādāb*, July 1956.
7. ʿAbd al-Salām al-ʿUjaylī, *Aḥādīth al-Aʿshiyā* (1965).
8. Fuʾād Tekerlī, "Al-Tannūr" [The oven], special issue of *Al-Ādāb*, April 1973, p. 93 ff. We shall draw on this special issue, quite representative of current trends in the Arabic short story, which was complemented, instructively, by a later issue devoted to criticism of these texts.
9. Al-ʿUjaylī, "Ḥadīth bi-Lughatayn" [Story in two languages], ibid., p. 137 ff.
10. Al-ʿUjaylī, "Hikāya Majānīn" [A tale of madmen], ibid., p. 100 ff.
11. Ghāda al-Sammān, "Al-Sāʿatān wal-Ghurāb" [Two clocks and a raven], ibid., p. 13 ff.
12. Najīb Maḥfūẓ, *Khammārat al-Qiṭṭ al-Aswad* ["The black cat tavern"] (1969). The

great novelist and short story writer has since continued his productive quest, culminating in *Ḥikāyāt Ḥāratinā* (1975), a collection of short stories of an incisive simplicity.
13. Yaḥyā Ḥaqqī, "Imra'a Maskīna" [Poor lady], *Al-Ādāb*, April 1973, p. 154 ff.
14. Zakariya Tāmir, "Al-A'dā'" [The enemies], ibid., p. 146 ff.
15. Ḥaydar Ḥaydar, "Al-Fayaḍān" [The flood], ibid., p. 113 ff. A coincidence with the invention of Kateb Yacine is observable in this superb short story.
16. Al-'Ujaylī, "Hikāya Majānīn."
17. Yūsuf Idrīs, "Al-Barā'a" [Innocence], *Al-Ādāb*, April 1973, p. 158 ff. The author is also one of the creators of the modern Arab theater; see his *Naḥwa Masraḥ 'Arabī* (1974).
18. Tekerli, "Al-Tannūr."
19. Al-Sammān, "Al-Sā'atān wal-Ghurāb."
20. Tāmir, "Al-A'dā'."
21. Al-'Ujaylī, "Ḥadīth bi-Lughatayn."
22. Ḥaqqī, "Imra'a Maskīna."
23. Al-'Ujaylī, *Aḥādīth al-A'shiyā'*.
24. Maḥfūz, *Khammārat al-Qiṭṭ al-Aswad.*
25. Ḥaydar, "Al-Fayaḍān."
26. Idrīs, "Al-Barā'a."
27. Muḥammad al-Mansī Qandīl, "Laḥẓa Yamtali' al-Jarḥ bil-Ramād" [In a moment the wound is filled with ashes], *Al-Ṭalī'a*, July 1973. Given here as an example of the rise of "metarealism" (Khālida Esber), which lately appears to be renewing the genre in Egypt, echoing the recent revival of poetic writing in that country. A new feature, in our opinion, of post-Nasserism (cf. Chapter I, note 5).
28. Ḥaqqī, "Imra'a Maskīna."
29. Idrīs, "Al-Barā'a."
30. Al-'Ujaylī, *Aḥādīth al-A'shiyā'*.
31. Al-'Ujaylī, "Hikāya Majānīn."
32. Ḥaydar, "Al-Fayaḍān."
33. Tāmir, "Al-A'dā'."
34. Maḥfūz, *Khammārat al-Qiṭṭ al-Aswad.*
35. Qandīl, "Laḥẓa Yamtali' al-Jarḥ bil-Ramād."
36. Hence the saddening confrontations of the past few years which are apparently undergoing a murderous crescendo.
37. Jabrā Ibrāhīm Jabrā, *Al-Safīna* (1970).
38. Notwithstanding what Bāsim Ḥammūdī writes in "Riḥlat al-Tīh al-Burjawāzī fī Safīnat Jabrā," *Al-Adab al-Mu'āṣir* (Baghdad), no. 4 (1973).
39. Al-Ṭayyib al-Ṣāliḥ, *Mawsim al-Hijra ilā al-Shimāl* (Cairo, n.d. [1967?]), French translation by Fady Noun in the Sindbad collection, 1972.
40. In fact Ṭayyib al-Ṣāliḥ's latest writings reflect a still more insistent desire for assimilation into the homeland.
41. See, for example, a gallery of rather malevolent portraits of Egyptian critics in Tharwat Abāẓa, *Shu'ā' min Ṭaha Ḥusain* (1974), p. 60 ff. Rare are the isles. . . .
42. *Qaḍāyā*, p. 8.
43. 1947.
44. The book contains valuable chapters on the role of Ṭaha Ḥusain when he was minister of education.
45. Baghdad, 1967.
46. This observation, made at a certain point in time, may now give way to more-optimistic evaluations if we take account of promising attempts which are now being made to renovate the novel, notably in Egypt (cf. Jamāl al-Ghītānī, among others) and elsewhere (cf. Hānī al-Rāhib, *Sharkh fī Ta'rīkh Ṭawīl*, etc.). Arabic style seems to us, in this connection, to be taking a new step forward.

XIII. What to Do? Whom to Be?

1. Also worthy of mention are ʿAbbās al-ʿAzzāwī for Mesopotamia, ʿAlī al-Miṣūrātī for Tripolitania, ʿUthmān Kaʿʿak for Tunisia, and the meaty magazine *Ṣawt al-Furāt* directed by ʿAbd al-Qādir ʿAyyāsh. A *Mawsūʿa* of Basra by a scholar of the Bash Aʿyān family exists in manuscript. The *Encyclopedias* properly speaking should not be forgotten, such as the ones by Fuʾād E. Bustānī (Islamological), ʿAbdullah al-ʿAlāʾilī (philological), Edward Ghalīl (natural sciences). A full inventory would be excessively long.
2. Cf. for example the monograph on Bikfāya by Shaikh Bulaybal.
3. On the subject of this chapter one may usefully consult ʿAbd al-Raḥmān Badawī, "Sciences humaines et culture dans le monde arabe," *Cahiers d'histoire mondiale* 14, no. 4 (1972): 771 ff.
4. Thus Ṭaha Ḥusain, *Ḥadīth al-Arbaʿāʾ*, 9th ed., 1:296: "Do you seek to personify (*tushakhkhiṣ*) life in the time of the early Abbasids? You will find no personification (*tashkhīṣan*) as strong, clear, and true to life as in Abū Nuwās."
5. ʿAlī al-Wardī, *Shakhṣiyat al-Fard al-ʿIrāqī* (1961); *Wuʿāẓ al-Salāṭīn* (1954); *Lamaḥāt Ijtimāʿiya min Taʾrīkh al-ʿIrāq al-Ḥadīth* (1969–), 4 vols. published thus far.
6. Ḥusain Fawzī, *Sindbad Miṣrī* (1961), preceded by several other "Sindbads" demonstrating both this great humanist's erudition and his broad first-hand experience.
7. Y. Moubarac, *Les Musulmans . . .* (1972).
8. Shaikh Maḥmūd Shaltūt, *Al-Islām ʿAqīda wa Sharīʿa*; Shaikh Ṭāhir bin ʿĀshūr, *Tafsīr al-Taḥrīr wal-Tanwīr* (1971).
9. ʿAllāl al-Fāsī, *Maqāṣid al-Sharīʿa* (1963).
10. ʿAbd al-ʿAzīz Kāmil, *Al-Islām wal-ʿUnṣuriya* (UNESCO, 1970); "Al-Islām wal-Idāra," lecture at Cairo Cultural Season, January 1, 1972.
11. Ṣubḥī Ṣāliḥ, *Mabāḥith fī ʿUlūm al-Qurʾān* (1958).
12. Shaikh Muḥammad al-Mubārak, *Dhātiyat al-Islām* (1962); *Naḥwa Waʿyin Islāmī Jadīd* (1963); *Al-Fikr al-Islāmī al-Jadīd fī Muwājahat al-Afkār al-Gharbiya* (1968).
13. Muḥammad ʿItānī, *Al-Qurʾān fī Ḍaw al-Fikr al-Māddī al-Jadalī*.
14. At the end of the last century a *fatwa* of Shaikh "Bel Khayyāṭ" of Fez (lithographed) confirmed this quasi prohibition, while endorsing the litanies of the religious brotherhoods!
15. See the important Preface to his translation of *Theologiespoliticus* by Spinoza, *Risāla fil-Allāhāt wal-Siyāsa* (1971).
16. Cairo, 1968.
17. Whom ʿAqqād, long ago, jokingly reproached for philosophizing, as he was not a philosopher by training. A strange reproach from the mouth of a self-taught man!
18. Ḥusain, *Al-Wādī al-Muqaddas*, p. 205 ff.
19. *Al-Thawra wal-ʿArabī al-Thawrī* (1961). *Thawriya*: revolutionism.
20. *Al-Insān Yaʿṣī, li-hadhā Yaṣna ʿal-Ḥaḍārāt* (1972). Cf. the lucid review of a previous work by this author by Ḥusain Muruwwé, *Dirāsāt Naqdiya* (1965), p. 143 ff.
21. *Dhikrā al-Rasūl al-ʿArabī* (1943). Spirituality outside the framework of majoritarian orthodoxy and even outside Islam itself, with thinkers such as Kamāl Jumblāṭ and Mikhāʾīl Nuʿaymé (cf. his *Last Day* [1963]), should be the object of special attention.
22. Cf. Elias Faraḥ, *Taṭawwur al-Fikr al-Marksī, ʿArḍ wa Naqd*, 2d ed. (1971).
23. See especially Ṣādiq al-ʿAẓm, *Al-Naqd al-Dhātī baʿd al-Hazīma* (1971); *Dirāsat Yasāriya ḥawl al-Qaḍiya al-Falasṭīniya* (1970).
24. *Al-Turāth wal-Thawra* (1973). This work should be compared with the one cited

in the following note and with the rather brief study, older but penetrating, by Ḥāfiẓ al-Jamālī, *Al-Wafā' lil-Turāth* (Damascus, 1960).

25. We should cite, notably, professors Khālidī in Lebanon, Faiṣal al-Sāmir in Iraq, and in Egypt the remarkable essay of Ṣalāḥ 'Īsā, *Al-Thawra al-'Urābiya* (1969).
26. See particularly his collection of articles, *Al-Thaqāfa wal-Thawra* (1969).
27. *Al-Muṣādafa* (1970).
28. In this connection see the lucid observations by al-'Ālim, *Markyūz* (1972), p. 5 ff.
29. Zakī Najīb Maḥmūd, *Tajdīd al-Fikr al-'Arabī* (1971). We should cite also this author's important work *Al-Ma'qūl al-lā Ma'qūl fī Turāthinā al-Fikrī*, published later (n.d.).
30. Notably Hishām Sharābiya, of whom I shall cite here an important article of very critical tone, "Mujtama'unā," supplement to *Al-Nahār*, December 1, 1974, and especially *Muqaddimāt li-Dirāsat al-Mujtama' al-'Arabī* (1975).

XIV. History and Poetry

1. See above, p. 28 ff.
2. To confine ourselves to literature, let it suffice to refer to the remarkable *Introducción a la literatura árabe moderna* by Pedro Martínez Montávez (Madrid, 1974).
3. After an Algerian film was awarded a gold medal at the Cannes Festival in the spring of 1975, a review in *Al-Mujāhid*, significantly, accused its author of having compromised with the bourgeois West.
4. Hence the interest of recent experiments (especially in the short story) that break with Western models and endeavor to form links with the Arab imagination. The ancestor in this field, still unequaled, is Ṭaha Ḥusain's continuation of the *Arabian Nights, Aḥlām Shahrazād* (1943). We should also cite—as of a different orientation—Tawfīq al-Ḥakīm's play *Yā Ṭāli'an Shajara*, which touched off the quarrel over the irrational, or *lā ma'qūl*, raising immediate questions regarding Western inspiration (Ionesco, Beckett) and even political viewpoints, thus muddying the problem anew.
5. See above, p. 216 ff.
6. Such as Shawqī, Rāfi'ī, and many others.
7. *Qaḍiyat al-Shi'r al-Jadīd* (1964). According to this critic, many traditionalist productions are simply "echoes of echoes."
8. Badr Shākir al-Sayyāb, *Unshūdat al-Maṭar* (Beirut, 1960), p. 160 ff.
9. Badawī al-Jabal, poem recited in 1950 at Faisal II's coronation.
10. Al-Jawāhirī, *Ayyuhā al-Araq* (Beirut, 1971), p. 43.
11. Dāwud [Anas], *Al-Ṭabī'a fī Shi'r al-Mahjar* (Cairo, [1967?]). 'Umar al-Daqqāq, *Al-Naqd al-Ijtimā'ī fī Shi'r al-Mahjar*, Muḥāḍarāt al-Mawsim al-Thaqāfī, 1967–1971, no. 9, Damascus.
12. Louis 'Awaḍ, *Al-Plutoland* (1947).
13. On this school, see the excellent thesis of 'Abd al-'Azīz al-Dasūqī, *Jamā'at Apollo* (1960).
14. Especially *Cadmus* (1956), *Rindala* (1959).
15. 'Aqqād said of the Sudanese Ḥardallo that he would have equaled Ibn al-Rūmī had he not written in dialect.
16. Nāzik al-Malā'ika has recounted at length the circumstances that led her, almost unconsciously, to this innovation.
17. By Nasīb 'Arīḍa, for example, and others. See S. Moreh, *Modern Arabic Poetry, 1800–1972* (London: Brill, 1976).
18. It still is. During his lifetime, and immediately after, it would be hard to find dissenters: 'Aqqād, doubtless (but he acted on personal motives); the philologist Buṭros al-Bustānī in Lebanon; and, more revealingly, in Syria, the

inaugurator of surrealism, Urkhān al-Muyassar. It goes without saying that his reign, like that of all the greats of the old generation, is being breached today under the challenge of youth.

19. What are we to think of the return to regular prosody by a poet like Aragon? Or, again, the role of the Alexandrine in *Éluard*?
20. I am indebted for these details to a personal communication from Jabrā Ibrāhīm Jabrā. See also ʿAbd al-Wāḥid Luʾluʾa, *Al-Baḥth ʿan Maʿnin* (1973), p. 167 ff.
21. *Qaḍāyā al-Shiʿr al-Muʿāṣir* (1962).
22. This was, and is, true of much of this free versification—to the point where Kamāl Abū Dīb, who pointed out astonishing metric regularities in Adonis, proposed the term "unitary," *aḥadiya*, for what we call free verse. Observations of this nature by ʿAbd al-Ṣabūr, *Dīwān* (1972), p. 343 ff.; Sulaymān Āl Aḥmad, "Al-Taqlīd wal-Tajdīd fī al-Shiʿr," *Al-Muʿallim al-ʿArabī* (Damascus), August 1971. Discriminating notes on the subject by Fāʾiz Khaddūr, Preface to his collection *Amṭār fī Ḥarīq al-Madīna* (1970), pp. 8–9.
23. H. L. Gardner, in *T. S. Eliot, poésie* (Paris: Seuil, 1969), p. 91.
24. Cf. J. Berque, "Neuf Poétes arabes et la mort de Dieu," *Nouvelle revue française*, August 1973.
25. The work, significantly, aroused voluminous comment in the press, and something like a sigh of relief among partisans of Arabism.
26. *Ayyuhā al-Araq*, p. 50.
27. ʿAbd al-Ṣabūr, *Dīwān*, p. 50 ff.
28. "Song of the Arab Atlal," *Shajarat al-Qamar* (1968), p. 64 ff.
29. *Khurūj Raʾs al-Ḥussain min al-Mudun al-Khāʾina* (1972), p. 13 ff.
30. Adonis, *Dīwān*, 2:650.
31. Khālida Saʿīd, *Al-Baḥth ʿan al-Judhūr* (1960).
32. *Abārīq Muhashshama* (1954), p. 84.
33. Sayyāb, *Unshūdat al-Maṭar*, p. 103.
34. Asʿad Razzūq, *Al-Usṭūra fīl-Shiʿr al-Muʿāṣir* (1957).
35. Buland al-Ḥaydarī, *Riḥlat al-Ḥurūf al-Ṣifr*, p. 101.
36. Tawfīq Ziyyād, *Dīwān*, p. 563 ff.
37. *Dīwān*, 2:25 ff. See the review by Ḥusain Muruwwé, *Dirāsāt Naqdiya* (1965), p. 265 ff.
38. Nāṣir al-Dīn al-Asad, *Al-Shiʿr al-Ḥadīth fī Falasṭīn wal-Urdun* (1961).
39. Darwīsh, "Yawmiyāt Jarḥ Falasṭīnī," *Dīwān*, p. 383.
40. Samīḥ al-Qāsim, opening piece in *Suqūṭ al-Aqniʿa*.

XV. Poem, Language, and Society

1. Amal Dunqul, *Taʿlīq ʿalā mā Ḥadath* (1971), p. 59 ff.
2. Maḥmūd Darwīsh, *Dīwān*, p. 636 ff.
3. A case analogous to that of another avant-garde poet, Ṣalīm Barakāt, who is a Kurd.
4. Sargon Boulos, *Al-Shiʿr*, nos. 29–30 (Winter 1964). The same theme inspired Rilke.
5. We shall cite here only Roman Jakobson, *Questions de poétique* (Paris: Seuil, 1973), pp. 15–16; and Youri Lotman, *La structure du texte artistique* (Paris: Gallimard, 1973).
6. An expression repeated insistently by Youri Lotman.
7. A view defended by Adonis on a number of occasions. Hence his useful insistence on the notion of "creativity," *ibdāʾ*.
8. ʿAbdullah al-Ṭayyib al-Majdhūb, *Al-Murshid* 1 (1955): 153.
9. Ibid., p. 74 ff.
10. "Muḍāʿafat al-Quyūd al-Lafẓiya," ibid., p. 9.
11. See Muḥammad al-Nuwayhī, *Qaḍiyat al-Shiʿr al-Jadīd* (1964), p. 109 ff. He calls it *waḥda ḥayawiya*.

12. Cf. above, p. 135 ff.
13. Nāzik al-Malā'ika, *Qaḍāyā al-Shi'r al-Mu'āṣir*, p. 228.
14. Ibid., p. 228 ff.
15. Iḥsān 'Abbās, *Ta'rīkh al-Naqd al-Adabī* (1971), p. 64 ff. and passim.
16. Barādi'ī, *Ṣuwar 'alā Ḥā'iṭ al-Manfī* (1970).
17. Nāzik al-Malā'ika, *Shajarat al-Qamar* (1968), p. 77 ff.
18. *Al-Tā'ir al-Khashabī* (n.d.), p. 93 ff.
19. Reprint of Dumarsais' book *Traité des tropes*, in *Le Nouveau Commerce*, nos. 15–16 (1970).
20. *Sémantique structurale* (1966), pp. 20, 30.
21. Cf. Henri Meschonnic, *Le signe et le poème* (1975).
22. Sayyāb, "Ode to Lorca," *Unshūdat al-Maṭar* (1969), p. 23.
23. Adonis, preface to his Sayyāb anthology.
24. Cf., for example, the objection referred to by R. Jakobson in *Questions de poétique*, p. 500 ff.
25. Dare we say "positive poetry," as we say "positive law"?
26. "Poésie et négativité," in *Seméiotikè* (Paris: Seuil, 1969), p. 246 ff.
27. Thus, in Arabic, the roots actually found cover barely one-fifth of the possible combinations. The "emptiness" effect Michel F. Foucault rightly saw as conditioning "discursive formation" (*Archéologie du savoir* [1969], p. 156) conditions lexical production itself. And thanks to the trilateral feature of Arabic, this can be demonstrated arithmetically.
28. This is the thesis of our *Orient second* (1970).
29. *Al-Kalima*, 1973.
30. "Prolegomenas on an Arabic Language," *Al-Mawqif al-Adabī* (Damascus), July 1971.
31. *Lam Yabqa illa al-I'tirāf* (1965).
32. 'Abd Al-Ṣabūr, *Dīwān*, p. 120 ff.
33. Khālida Sa'īd (Esber), *Mawāqif*, nos. 17–18, p. 137.
34. 'Abd al-Razzāq 'Abd al-Wāḥid, *Khaymat 'alā Mashārif al-Arba'īn* (1972), p. 39 ff.
35. Khālida Sa'īd, *Mawāqif*, nos. 17–18, p. 131 ff.
36. Because it would itself be a kind of *establishment*!
37. "Al-Insān al-Ṣifr," *Al-Fikr*, December 1968.

XVI. Algorism and Life

1. Cf. 'Ādil 'Awwā, *Al-Wijdān* (Damascus), 1961.
2. The *Lisān* makes this root a synonym of *hāj*. In the concrete it is said of an erupting volcano, or hair raised on the head by anger (of which an example occurs in the *ḥadīth*). *Al-thawr*: "redness on the horizon" (ibid.).
3. Henri Lefebvre, *Critique de la quotidienneté: La vie quotidienne dans le monde moderne* (1968).
4. As well as certain more-intimate phenomena, such as the loss of sexual innocence, pointed out by E. LeRoy Ladurie, *Le Territoire de l'historien* (1973), p. 316 ff.
5. They simply place in opposition to the sociohistorical level (i.e., a level at once existential and constructed, ideological and concrete) the problem of what Whitehead called "Bifurcation," which he himself, Russell, and Wittgenstein approached from the point of view of the relationships between mathematical logic and physics. See J. Vuillemain, *La logique et le monde sensible* (1972).
6. There has recently, however, been an observable reaction in social history toward the study of "mentalities."
7. But a "destiny" different from that of Antigone, without attaining tragic quality. Would this then be simply an objective trend?
8. A. Rimbaud, *Illuminations*.

9. Might the persistence of these instrumentalities without appreciable change over the centuries be the objective of the various processes by which power is instituted and exercised? In any case, note that their efficacity contrasts paradoxically with their dual inadequacy!
10. Noteworthy also is the justified rejection of empiricism and ideology where they represent the protrusion of opinion. But the empirical is not lived experience, any more than opinion is truth!
11. In the sense C. S. Pierce gives the word, and frequently borrowed by Youri Lotman. But should this whole "iconic" theory not be situated within the Heideggerian perspectives of "unveiling" or, in the same spirit, of the eidetic? See J. Beaufret, *Dialogue avec Heidegger*, vol. 2 (1973).
12. Opinion/truth. Suppose a government continually adjusted its action according to public opinion polls; would it therefore be democratic? We dedicate this aporia to Rousseau.

XVII. The Wandering Gaze

1. *Poetiqué*, ed. Budé, 1452, section "q," pp. 43–44.
2. Koran, XIX, 17.
3. Koran, I, 3.
4. Repentance.
5. "Prayer" or, far better, "consecrating formula" (by man to God, and the reciprocal on God's part).
6. "In the name of God," propitiatory or inaugural formula.
7. Cf., for example, the entry "paradigme" in Tz. Todorov and O. Ducrot, *Dictionnaire encyclopédique des sciences du langage* (Paris: Seuil, 1972).
8. This, at least, is the hypothesis advanced here, and the one put into practice, unwittingly, by all progressive policies in our era.
9. In a different domain, narrower and more precise, analysis of the *actant* level, in narrative discourse, has led A. L. Greimas to observe the same multivalencies. "Les actants, les acteurs et les figures," in Cl. Chabrol, ed., *Sémiotiques narrative et textuelle* (1973), p. 170.
10. It seems to us that here resides the difference between "coup d'état," "subversion" (called *inqilāb* by the Arabs), and "revolution," *thawra*, strictly construed. The strict sense, naturally, suffers the widest possible improprieties. . . .
11. Cf. above Chapter IX and p. 171.
12. Cf. Adonis, *Al-Thābit wal-Mutaḥawwil* (1974).
13. These three words, with different literal meanings, all evoke the idea of "model."
14. Cf. our *The Arabs: Their History and Future* (New York: Praeger, 1965).
15. Which furthermore had the advantage of not distinguishing between Christians and Muslims.
16. "Human respect" would be our translation were it not for the theological referent.
17. The role of political speech and action in unifying the "strings" spoken of above (p. 311) should be defined here as a matter of operational research.
18. Here I am leaving aside the other "paradigm," that of the pre-Islamic past.
19. Cf. J. Berque, "Pluriels," *Esprit*, August 1972.
20. Many misfortunes of the Arab left can be explained by the neglect (or rejection) of this trait. Such a rejection, on the one hand, forces the left to fall back on imitative tactics; on the other hand, when it quite naturally seeks foundations for itself, it is placed in unequal competition with Islam. The whole situation is disrupted.
21. "Sarcastic joke."

Index